Final Aug 11

ECONOMIC ANALYSIS OF
CAPITAL INVESTMENTS
FOR MANAGERS AND ENGINEERS

ECONOMIC ANALYSIS OF CAPITAL INVESTMENTS
FOR MANAGERS AND ENGINEERS

G. T. Stevens, Jr.
University of Texas at Arlington

RESTON PUBLISHING COMPANY, INC.
A Prentice-Hall Company
Reston, Virginia

Library of Congress Cataloging in Publication Data

Stevens, G. T. (Gladstone Taylor), 1930-
  Economic analysis of capital investments for
managers and engineers.

  Includes index.
  1. Capital investments—Evaluation. I. Title.
HG4028.C4S7149   1983   658.1′52   83-4406
ISBN 0-8359-1582-4

*Editorial/production supervision and
interior design by Camelia Townsend*

CONTENTS

APPENDIXES   295

INDEX   345

PREFACE

This book is intended for use as a beginning text in economic analysis. It is primarily concerned with the techniques for evaluating and comparing capital investments. There are many books that consider these techniques, and from this standpoint this book is not unique. However, it does have some features that are not usually included in a book of this type. These are (1) explicit definitions of equity and total cash flows; and (2) a detailed discussion of minimum annual revenue requirements and their use in the evaluation of single projects, cost comparisons, and replacement analysis. This book also includes an extensive treatment of certain tax regulations that are related to capital investments. Although some of these tax regulations are not directly related to the topics considered in this book, it is highly likely that they will be encountered, sometime, by persons who are continually involved in the economic analysis of capital investments. Also, consideration of these additional tax aspects provides and introduction to the vocabulary used in tax regulations. Methods for including inflationary effects are detailed in the discussions of cash flow models and minimum annual revenue requirements.

This book is intended for students of accounting, economics, engineering, and finance. From a mathematical standpoint, a proficiency in the use of algebra is required. Some basic calculus is desirable for the topic of nonlinear break-even analysis. Included in the appendices are interest tables, a computer program for determining the internal rate of return, and a computer program for determining minimum annual revenue requirements. In recent times, there has been some discussions about the desirability of including interest tables in a text of this type. There are some who contend that with the capabilities of the hand-calculator, interest tables are not required. This book takes a middle-of-the-road approach in this regard. Some problems and examples allow the use of the interest tables; other problems and examples require the numerical evaluation of the interest factors.

I would like to take this opportunity to thank my wife Jane and our children Bob and Bartlett for their patience and encouragement during this venture. I would also like to thank Ann von der Heide for her understanding and diligence during the typing of the final manuscript. Finally, special acknowledgment is due Dr. Leighton L. Smith for his many helpful suggestions regarding the topics and format of this book.

G. T. STEVENS, JR.
University of Texas at Arlington

ECONOMIC ANALYSIS OF CAPITAL INVESTMENTS
FOR MANAGERS AND ENGINEERS

1

INTRODUCTION

Today, most business and engineering college curriculums require courses that involve a study of the techniques used to evaluate capital investments. These courses are taught under such names as managerial economics, finance, and engineering economy. Whatever the name, it is generally recognized that the study of capital investment analysis is an important part in the education of a business or engineering student. At some point in their careers, business and engineering graduates will be faced with the responsibility of evaluating capital investments.

THE NATURE AND SCOPE OF CAPITAL INVESTMENT ANALYSIS

Private companies produce products and provide services for one basic reason. This reason is the expectation of some economic gain. Companies do not engage in scientific or engineering activities simply to achieve some scientific breakthrough or demonstrate their engineering capabilities. They engage in these and other activities in the belief that they will realize, at some point in time, an economic advantage. Also, companies do not employ people simply to provide them with an income. Companies employ people as a needed resource for the attainment of the company's economic goals. Basically, a company requires and expects that the economic value of the output resulting from their activities to be larger than the economic value of their inputs. Stated another way, a company requires their economic efficiency (output divided by input) to be greater than 100%. The techniques used to measure this economic efficiency are the primary concern of this book; more specifically, the techniques used to measure (evaluate) the economic desirability of capital investments (expenditures). Capital investment decisions are concerned with answering such questions as the following:

1. Should a company produce a new product?
2. Should a company replace some of its existing equipment?
3. Should a company increase its manufacturing capabilities?
4. What are the investment alternatives and which ones should be chosen?

Capital investments are a critical business decision. Errors in the evaluation of capital investments can result in high costs because evaluation errors are largely irredeemable once the capital is committed. The cost of correcting a capital investment error is greater than the cost of simply "putting up" with the error. Consequently, it is important that economically sound techniques be used to evaluate capital investments. It is the purpose of this book to present some of the accepted techniques for evaluating capital investments. However, it must be understood that regardless of the technique used there is always some degree of risk in the evaluation of a *proposed* capital investment. The evaluation of proposed capital investments involves the estimation of many variables over long periods of time. Consequently, an incorrect evaluation should not discredit an economically sound evaluation technique. More often an incorrect evaluation is a result of incorrect estimates or omitted considerations. Also, a given evaluation technique, in itself, does not make the decision to undertake an investment. There is always the need for a decision-maker. The evaluation of a capital investment only provides an indicator of possible economic worth of an investment, and the evaluation is only as good as the input data (estimates). The decision-maker must always weigh the evaluation of a particular capital investment against other considerations. A capital investment decision is not an independent decision. The investment of capital is related to financing (debt-equity ratios) decisions and dividend decisions. The decision-maker must also consider any intangible (qualitative) factors—factors that cannot be expressed in monetary terms.

In the future, capital investments will continue to be a critical business decision due to the increasing complexity of technology and demands for greater productivity. Large commitments of capital will be required over long periods of time before expected returns will be realized. Consequently, it is most important that capital investments continue to be evaluated using the best techniques available.

THE OBJECTIVES OF A COMPANY

This book takes the point of view that the basic objectives of a company are (1) survival and (2) the maximization of the stockholder's wealth. The first objective is understandable. The second objective, from the stand-point of evaluating a capital investment, is equivalent to the maximization of the net present value (an evaluation technique discussed in Chapter 5). It is sometimes true that short-term considerations such as liquidity requirements and/or governmental restrictions override the objective of maximizing the stockholder's wealth. However, within these and possibly other constraints, the objective of maximizing the stock-holder's wealth is a sound basis on which to evaluate capital investments.

AN OVERVIEW OF THE BOOK

The chapters in this book have been sequenced such that the topics in one chapter serve as a foundation for the discussion of the topics in the following chapter. Chapter 2 is a fundamental chapter that discusses the concepts of *time value of money, interest, interest rates,* and *equiva-lence.* These concepts are used throughout this text.

Depreciation and depreciation models are discussed early in this book, Chapter 3, because of their relationship to the topic of federal income taxes discussed in Chapter 4 and the concept of capital recovery used in Chapters 6, 8, 9, and 10. Federal income taxes and the other tax regulations discussed in Chapter 4 serve as a foundation for the discussion of after-tax cash flows in Chapter 5. These after-tax cash flows (total and equity) are a basic requirement for discussing, in Chapter 5, the techniques (internal rate of return, net present value, payback period, and benefit-cost ratio) used to evaluate capital investments.

Chapter 6 discusses minimum annual revenue requirements as a technique for the economic evaluation of a single capital investment. This discussion serves as a foundation for the use of revenue require-ments in cost comparisons (Chapter 9) and replacement analysis (Chapter 10).

Chapter 7 discusses capital budgeting and uses as a foundation the internal rate of return and net present value techniques presented in Chapter 5. Chapter 8 discusses break-even models and the relationship of profit and net cash flow. The topics discussed in Chapter 5 serve as a foundation for the topics in Chapter 8.

Chapters 9 and 10 are the final two chapters in this book. They discuss cost comparisons and replacement analysis and use largely the discussions in Chapters 5 and 6.

2

INTEREST AND INTEREST FACTORS

Most people realize, intuitively at least, that a dollar today is more desirable than a dollar five years from now and this is true even if inflation is disregarded. This implies that the value of money is related to time. Or stated more succinctly, there exists *a time value of money.* This time value of money is a result of earnings (returns) that might be realized over time if money is available today. Consequently, it is directly related to the concepts of interest and interest rates. Interest is a payment for the use of money and as such can be considered in two ways. To the lender, interest is a return but to the borrower, interest is a cost. Corporations and institutions are also borrowers and lenders of money (usually referred to as capital in this context). They, in effect, loan money whenever they build a new plant, expand production facilities, buy a new piece of equipment, etc. In addition, corporations borrow money through the sale of stocks and bonds as well as from banks and insurance companies. In all of these transactions, the interest (sometimes given a different name) received or paid is an important economic consideration. Consequently, a discussion of interest, interest rates, and interest factors is fundamental in any text concerned with economic analysis.

SIMPLE INTEREST

Simple interest (sometimes referred to as add-on interest) occurs when interest is paid (or received) only on the principal. It is calculated using the equation

$$I = Pni \qquad (2\text{-}1)$$

where

I = simple interest

P = the principal (amount borrowed or lent)

n = number of interest periods

i = simple interest rate expressed as a decimal

The final amount, F, due (or received) on a simple interest transaction is

$$F = P + I = P + Pni \qquad (2\text{-}2)$$

Example 2-1

What is the interest and amount due at the end of five years if $4,000 is borrowed at 8% per year simple interest?
Using Eqs. (2-1) and (2-2), the interest is

$$I = (4{,}000)(5)(0.08) = \$1{,}600$$

and the total amount due is

$$F = 4{,}000 + 1{,}600 = \$5{,}600$$

COMPOUND INTEREST

Compound interest occurs when interest is paid (or received) on accumulated interest and principal. For example, if the interest rate in Example 2-1 is compounded annually, the situation shown in Table 2-1 is the result.

The results in Table 2-1 can be put in the general form shown in Table 2-2. This table indicates that the amount due, F, at the end of a particular year, n, is given by the relationship

$$F = P(1 + i)^n \qquad (2\text{-}3)$$

For example, using the values in Table 2-1 and Eq. (2-3) gives

$$F = 4{,}000(1 + 0.08)^5 = \$5{,}877.32$$

TABLE 2-1

Compound Interest Calculations

End of Year	Amount Borrowed	Interest		Amount Due	
0	$4,000	—		—	
1		4,000 (0.08)	= $320.00	4,000 + 320	= $4,320.00
2		4,320 (0.08)	= $345.60	4,320 + 345.60	= $4,665.60
3		4,665.60 (0.08)	= $373.25	4,665.60 + 373.25	= $5,038.85
4		5,038.85 (0.08)	= $403.11	5,038.85 + 403.11	= $5,441.96
5		5,441.96 (0.08)	= $435.36	5,441.96 + 435.36	= $5,877.32

for the amount due at the end of the fifth year, and

$$F = 4,000 (1 + 0.08)^3 = \$5,038.85$$

for the amount due at the end of the third year. These are the same values given in Table 2-1.

The term $(1 + i)^n$ in Eq. (2-3) is referred to as an *interest factor*. Consequently, a general discussion of interest factors at this point is required. Initially this discussion of interest factors is limited to discrete interest rates compounded annually and time periods measured in years. Other compounding periods (semiannually, quarterly, etc.) and time periods (months, weeks, etc.) are discussed later in this chapter. Also initially, this discussion is largely approached on the basis of borrowing (or lending) money because this provides a familiar setting that facilitates an understanding of interest factors. The nomenclature used in this discussion is

i = interest rate compounded per interest period (initially, the interest period is a year)

n = number of interest periods (initially, the number of years)

P = an amount at the present time (often called the initial amount or principal)

F = an amount at the end of n interest periods (a future amount)

A = a series of equal amounts occurring at the end of each interest period

Single Payment Compound Amount Factor   This interest factor is the term mentioned earlier; namely, $(1 + i)^n$. It is designated as

$$(F/P \; i,n) = (1 + i)^n \tag{2-4}$$

TABLE 2-2

General Form for Table 2-1

End of Year	Amount Borrowed	Interest	Amount Due	
0	P	—	—	
1		$P(i)$	$P + P(i)$	$= P(1+i)$
2		$P(1+i)(i)$	$P(1+i) + P(1+i)(i)$	$= P(1+i)^2$
3		$P(1+i)^2(i)$	$P(1+i)^2 + P(1+i)^2(i) = P(1+i)^3$	
.		.	.	
.		.	.	
.		.	.	
n		$P(1+i)^{n-1}(i)$	$P(1+i)^n$	

and is used in the formulation

$$F = P(F/P \ i,n) \tag{2-5}$$

Eq. (2-5) determines the amount of principal and interest (F) that accumulates over n years at an annual compound interest rate (i) if an initial amount (P) is deposited. The relationship between F, P, n, and i is shown in Figure 2-1.

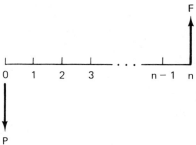

FIGURE 2-1   The Time Relationship Between *F* and *P*

Values for the F/P factor are obtained from the tables given in Appendix A. For example, the F/P factor for an interest rate of 8% and 5 years is

$$(F/P \ 8,5) = 1.469$$

Example 2-2

If $5,000 is borrowed at an interest rate of 10% compounded annually, determine the amount due at the end of six years and the amount of interest paid.

Using Eq. (2-5), the amount due is

$$F = 5,000 \ (F/P \ 10,6)$$
$$= 5,000 \ (1.772)$$
$$= \$8,860$$

and the amount of interest paid is

$$I = F - P \qquad (2-6)$$
$$= 8,860 - 5,000$$
$$= \$3,860$$

Single Payment Present Worth Factor The reciprocal of the single payment compound amount factor is the single payment present worth factor. Mathematically, it is

$$(P/F \ i,n) = \frac{1}{(1+i)^n} \qquad (2-7)$$

and is used in the formulation

$$P = F(P/F \ i,n) \qquad (2-8)$$

In financial circles (and in this text) the P/F factor is often referred to as the *discount factor* and has wide application to topics considered later in this text.

Example 2-3 _____

How much money must be deposited in a savings account that earns 6% compounded annually in order to have $10,000 after seven years?
  Using Eq. (2-8), the deposit amount is

$$P = 10,000 \ (P/F \ 6,7)$$
$$= 10,000 \ (0.6651)$$
$$= \$6,651$$

where the value 0.6651 is obtained from the interest tables in Appendix A.

Uniform Series Compound Amount (Future Worth) Factor
If an equal amount is deposited at the end of successive years as shown in Figure 2-2, the future amount can be determined in the following manner.

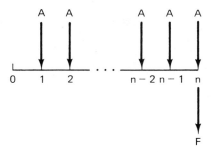

FIGURE 2-2   Uniform Series Amounts

$$F = A(1 + i)^{n-1} + A(1 + i)^{n-2} + \ldots + A(1 + i) + A(1 + i)^0 \qquad (2\text{-}9)$$

or in terms of the F/P factor

$$F = A(F/P\ i,(n - 1)) + A(F/P\ i,(n - 2))$$
$$+ \ldots + A(F/P\ i,1) + A(F/P\ i,0) \qquad (2\text{-}10)$$

Such an approach can be tedious. Consequently, another interest factor can be defined which simplifies the determination of the future amount (F).

Multiplying Eq. (2-9) by the term $(1 + i)$ gives

$$F(1 + i) = A(1 + i)^n + A(1 + i)^{n-1} + \ldots + A(1 + i) \qquad (2\text{-}11)$$

and subtracting Eq. (2-9) from this result gives

$$F(1 + i) - F = A(1 + i)^n - A \qquad (2\text{-}12)$$

Rearranging Eq. (2-12) gives

$$F = A\left(\frac{(1 + i)^n - 1}{i}\right) \qquad (2\text{-}13)$$

The term in the parentheses in Eq. (2-13) is called the uniform series compound amount (future worth) factor. It is designated as

$$(F/A\ i,n) = \frac{(1 + i)^n - 1}{i} \qquad (2\text{-}14)$$

and used in the formulation

$$F = A(F/A\ i,n) \qquad (2\text{-}15)$$

Example 2-4 _____

Determine the accumulated amount of money in an account and the interest earned at the end of ten years if equal deposits of $2,000 are made each year, assuming the account pays 8% compounded annually and the first deposit occurs one year from now.

Using Eq. (2-15), the accumulated amount is

$$F = 2,000 \ (F/A \ 8,10)$$

$$= 2,000 \ (14.487)$$

$$= \$28,974$$

and the interest earned is

$$I = 28,974 - 2,000 \ (10)$$

$$= \$8,974$$

A Comment   The scheme of deposits shown in Figure 2-2 may seem impractical. That is, why not start the deposits now? Also, why make a deposit in the last year since it earns no interest? The answer to these questions is that some convention must be used when establishing uniform series factors. The usual convention is the one shown in Figure 2-2. This convention choice, however, does not result in any limitations. Beginning-of-the-year deposit problems can be solved with a slight extension as shown in Example 2-5.

Example 2-5 _____

Rework Example 2-4 on the basis that the first of the ten deposits is made now.

This example implies the deposits shown in Figure 2-3 and can be solved in the following manner.

$$F = 2,000 \ (F/A \ 8,10) \ (F/P \ 8,1)$$

$$= 2,000 \ (14.487) \ (1.08)$$

$$= \$31,291.92$$

The interest earned is

$$I = 31,291.92 - 2,000 \ (10)$$

$$= \$11,291.92$$

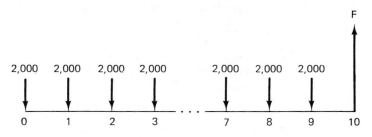

FIGURE 2-3 Deposits for Example 2-4

Uniform Series Sinking Fund Factor   This factor, often abbreviated to sinking fund factor, is the reciprocal of the uniform series compound amount (future worth) factor

$$(A/F \ i,n) = \frac{i}{(1+i)^n - 1} \tag{2-16}$$

It is used in the formulation

$$A = F(A/F \ i,n) \tag{2-17}$$

Example 2-6

A woman is setting up a retirement fund and believes she must have $100,000 available ten years from now. If she finds a fund that pays 8% compounded annually, what is her equal annual deposit for ten years assuming the first deposit is made one year from now?

Using Eq. (2-17), the annual amount is

$$A = 100,000 \, (A/F \ 8,10)$$

$$= 100,000 \, (0.0690)$$

$$= \$6,900$$

It should be noted that this result assumes the first deposit is made one year hence. If it is decided to make the first deposit now, but still only ten deposits, then each deposit required is

$$A' = A(P/F \ i,n)$$

$$A' = 6,900 \, (P/F \ 8,1)$$

$$= 6,900 \, (0.9259)$$

$$= \$6,388.71$$

in order to have the $100,000 at the end of ten years.

Uniform Series Present Worth Factor This interest factor allows the determination of the present amount required for a uniform series of withdrawals. This situation is depicted in Figure 2-4.

P can be determined by finding the future amount at the end of year n and then discounting this amount back to the present. Expressed mathematically,

$$P = A\,(F/A\ i,n)\,(P/F\ i,n) \tag{2-18}$$

By considering the two interest factors in Eq. (2-18), the uniform series present worth factor is defined; namely,

$$(P/A\ i,n) = (F/A\ i,n)\,(P/F\ i,n) \tag{2-19}$$

$$= \frac{(1+i)^n - 1}{i\,(1+i)^n}$$

It is used in the formulation

$$P = A\,(P/A\ i,n) \tag{2-20}$$

Example 2-7 _____

A person has a certain debt obligation where $1,000 a year is required over the next five years. How much must be deposited into an account that pays 6% compounded annually in order to just meet these debt obligations?

Using Eq. (2-20), the deposit is

$$P = 1,000\,(P/A\ 6,5)$$

$$= 1,000\,(4.2124)$$

$$= \$4,212.40$$

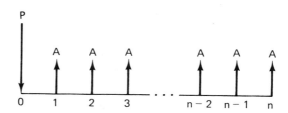

FIGURE 2-4   Present Worth of a Uniform Series

Uniform Series Capital Recovery Factor This factor is the reciprocal of the uniform series present worth factor

$$(A/P\ i,n) = \frac{i(1+i)^n}{(1+i)^n - 1} \qquad (2\text{-}21)$$

and is used in the formulation

$$A = P(A/P\ i,n) \qquad (2\text{-}22)$$

Example 2-8 _____

If $8,000 is deposited into an account that pays 8% compounded, what equal annual withdrawal can be made over the next six years?

Using Eq. (2-22), the withdrawal is

$$A = 8,000(A/P\ 8,6)$$

$$= 8,000(0.2163)$$

$$= \$1,730.40$$

Gradient Conversion Factor Situations often occur where the withdrawals (or payments) increase or decrease by a constant amount. Such a situation is shown in Figure 2-5. If it is desired to find the present amount that makes possible the series of withdrawals shown in Figure 2-5, one method ($i = 10\%$) is

$$P = 100(P/F\ 10,1) + 150(P/F\ 10,2) + 200(P/F\ 10,3)$$

$$+ 250(P/F\ 10,4) + 300(P/F\ 10,5)$$

$$= \$722.17$$

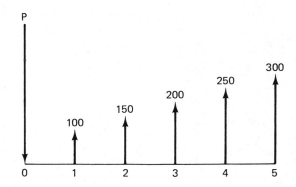

FIGURE 2-5 A Constantly Increasing Series of Withdrawals

This solution is not difficult but could be tedious for a long series of constantly increasing withdrawals. Consequently, another interest factor is defined that simplifies calculations involving a uniformly increasing series.

If the series of withdrawals shown in Figure 2-5 is considered, it can be seen that there are two parts: a constant amount (A_1) and a uniformly increasing amount (A_2). For example in Figure 2-5,

$$A_1 = \$100$$

$$A_2 = (n - 1)(50)$$

where n is the year number. In general, the yearly withdrawal, A_n is

$$A_n = 100 + (n - 1)(50)$$

or in more general form

$$A_n = A_1 + (n - 1)(G) \qquad (2\text{-}23)$$

where G is the annual gradient.

The second part of Eq. (2-23), called A_x, is shown in Table 2-3. Each item in column A_x in Table 2-3 is a constant amount. Therefore the future amount of all of these items is

$$F = G(F/A \ i,(n - 1) + F/A \ i,(n - 2) + \ldots + F/A \ i,1) \qquad (2\text{-}24)$$

or

$$F = G\left(\frac{(1+i)^{n-1}-1}{i} + \frac{(1+i)^{n-2}-1}{i} + \ldots + \frac{(1+i)-1}{i}\right)$$

TABLE 2-3

An Increasing Gradient

End of Year	Amount (A_x)	Expanded Amount
0	—	—
1	0	0
2	G	G
3	$2G$	$G + G$
4	$3G$	$G + G + G$
.	.	.
.	.	.
.	.	.
$n - 1$	$(n - 2)(G)$	$G + G + \ldots + G + G$
n	$(n - 1)(G)$	$G + G + \ldots + G + G + G$

$$= \frac{G}{i} \left((1+i)^{n-1} - 1 + (1+i)^{n-2} - 1 + \ldots + (1+i) - 1 \right)$$

$$= \frac{G}{i} \left((1+i)^{n-1} + (1+i)^{n-2} + \ldots + (1+i) - (n-1) \right)$$

$$= \frac{G}{i} \left((1+i)^{n-1} + (1+i)^{n-2} + \ldots (1+i) + 1 \right) - \frac{nG}{i} \tag{2-25}$$

Now in Eq. (2-25) the terms in the parentheses define the F/A factor. Consequently, Eq. (2-25) can be written as

$$F = \frac{G}{i} \left(\frac{(1+i)^n - 1}{i} \right) - \frac{nG}{i} \tag{2-26}$$

Eq. (2-26) can be converted to an annual amount by multiplying it by an A/F factor, which gives

$$A_x = \left\{ \frac{G}{i} \left(\frac{(1+i)^n - 1}{i} \right) - \frac{nG}{i} \right\} \left(\frac{i}{(1+i)^n - 1} \right)$$

$$= G \left(\frac{1}{i} - \frac{n}{i} (A/F \ i,n) \right) \tag{2-27}$$

The expression in the parentheses in Eq. (2-27) is the gradient conversion factor and is designated as

$$(A/G \ i,n) = \left(\frac{1}{i} - \frac{n}{i} (A/F \ i,n) \right) \tag{2-28}$$

and is used in the formulation

$$A = A_1 \pm G (A/G \ i,n) \tag{2-29}$$

In Eq. (2-29) the plus sign is used for an increasing series and the negative sign for a decreasing series.

Example 2-9

In this example the present amount is determined for the withdrawals given in Figure 2-5 using the gradient conversion factor.

$$P = (100 + 50\,(A/G\ 10,5))\,(P/A\ 10,5)$$
$$= (100 + 50\,(1.8101))\,(3.7908)$$
$$= \$722.17$$

A Comment   In all of the examples presented up to this point, values for F, P, and A are determined with given values for i and n. This is not always the case. There are many situations where either i or n is required. For example, if F, A, and n are given, i can be determined. In fact in later discussions the determination of i is a prime consideration.

Example 2-10

If \$2,000 a year is deposited into an account and there is \$12,706 in the account at the end of five years, what rate of interest did the account pay?

   Since an annual and future amount are involved, this implies an F/A (or A/F) factor; namely,

$$F = A\,(F/A\ i,n)$$
$$12{,}706 = 2{,}000\,(F/A\ i,5)$$
$$(F/A\ i,5) = 6.353$$

With the value 6.353, the interest tables are searched for an F/A factor with the same value at $n = 5$. The same value is found in the 12% interest table. Consequently, the answer is 12% compounded annually.

LINEAR INTERPOLATION

In Example 2-10, the exact value 6.353 is in the interest tables. This is not always the case. Consequently, it is sometimes necessary to use interpolation. *Linear* interpolation, in these cases, is considered sufficient as long as the increments between values are small. Also, it is applicable to continuous interest factors (discussed later) as well as discrete interest factors.

Example 2-11

Suppose in Example 2-10 the amount in the account after five years is \$14,000; what is the rate of interest paid?

   The solution to this problem takes the same form as that given in Example 2-10, only now

$$(F/A\ i,5) = 7.000$$

In searching the interest tables there is no interest rate for an F/A factor of 7.000. Consequently, interpolation is necessary. The interest tables indicate that the interest rate is somewhere between 20% and 15% since the corresponding interest factors are 7.442 and 6.742. This information is shown in Table 2-4 and is the basis for the following calculations.

$$X = 15 + \frac{7.000 - 6.742}{7.442 - 6.742}(20 - 15)$$

$$= 15 + (0.369)(5)$$

$$= 15 + 1.85$$

$$= 16.85\% \text{ compounded yearly}$$

NOMINAL AND EFFECTIVE INTEREST

The prior discussion of interest factors and rates has been limited to an annual compounding period. However, interest rates are often specified with compounding periods other than one year. An interest rate is completely defined if *two time periods* are specified (or at least understood). For example, 8% per year compounded per year is a completely defined interest rate. However, it is common to specify this rate as 8% compounded per year. The first *per year* phrase is understood. As another example, an interest rate might be specified as 12% compounded semiannually. This interest rate implies 12% per year compounded semiannually. Again, the per year phrase is understood. It is not unusual to see an interest rate specified as 1% per month. This usually means 12% per year compounded monthly. As a result of these considerations it is important at this point to define effective *annual* interest rate, effective interest rate, and nominal interest rate.

Effective Annual Interest Rate   When both time periods are expressed on an *annual* basis, this is an effective annual rate. For example, 8% per year compounded per year is an effective annual interest rate. As mentioned previously, this is often abbreviated to 8% compounded annually.

TABLE 2-4

Interpolation Values for Example 2-11

Interest Rate	F/A Value
20%	7.442
X	7.000
15%	6.742

Effective Interest Rate   When both time periods are the same, this is an effective interest rate. For example 3% per month compounded per month is an effective interest rate. It should be noted that with this definition an effective *annual* interest rate is always an effective interest rate. However, the reverse is not true.

Nominal Interest Rate   When the time units are not the same but the first time period is per year, this defines a nominal interest rate. For example, 12% per year compounded semiannually is a nominal interest rate and is usually abbreviated to 12% compounded semiannually. The phrase *per year* is understood. With this definition the conversion of effective rates to nominal rates can be accomplished by the relationship

$$\text{effective rate} = \frac{\text{nominal rate}}{c} \tag{2-30}$$

where c is the number of compounding periods per year. For example, 8% compounded semiannually (remember the per year phrase is understood) is equivalent to an effective interest rate of 4% semiannually compounded semiannually ($c = 2$). An effective interest rate of 1% per month compounded monthly is equivalent to a nominal rate of 12% compounded monthly ($c = 12$).

Converting a nominal rate to an effective annual rate is accomplished by using the relationship

$$\left(\begin{array}{c} \text{effective annual} \\ \text{interest rate} \end{array} \right) = \left(1 + \frac{r}{c} \right)^c - 1 \tag{2-31}$$

where r is the nominal rate and c is the number of compounding periods per year. For example, 12% compounded monthly is an effective annual rate of

$$\left(1 + \frac{.12}{12} \right)^{12} - 1 = 0.1268$$

$$= 12.68\%$$

In this text the convention is to omit the first per year phrase when specifying effective annual and nominal interest rates. Also when an interest rate is simply specified as 8%, this implies, in this text, an interest rate of 8% compounded annually.

In conjunction with the previous discussion of effective annual, effective, and nominal interest rates, the relation between the compounding period and the timing of the payments (receipts, withdrawals, etc.) must be considered. The basic approach in these situations is to convert the interest rate to an effective rate with time units that agree with the timing of the payments and to convert the number of years (n) to the number of interest periods. When only single amounts (F or P) are involved, these conversions are relatively simple.

Example 2-12

If a person deposits \$5,000 into an account that pays 8% compounded quarterly, how much money is in the account after five years?

The solution to this problem is

$$F = P\,(F/P\ i,n)$$

$$= 5,000\,(F/P\ \frac{8}{4},\ 4\,(5))$$

$$= 5,000\,(F/P\ 2,20)$$

$$= 5,000\,(1.486)$$

$$= \$7,430$$

It should be noted that in the solution to Example 2-12 the interest rate is converted to an effective rate in accordance with Eq. (2-30) and the number of years is converted to the number of interest periods (20).

When equal amounts (A) are involved in a problem, the necessary conversions may be slightly more involved.

Example 2-13

A person makes an equal quarterly deposit of \$4,000 in an account for a period of five years. Determine the amount in the account after five years if:

a. The interest rate is 12% compounded quarterly.

b. The interest rate is 12% compounded semiannually.

The solution for Part a is

$$F = 4,000\,(F/A\ \frac{12}{4},\ 4\,(5))$$

$$= 4,000\,(F/A\ 3,20)$$

$$= 4,000\,(26.870)$$

$$= \$107,480$$

It should be noted that all the time units agree. That is, the deposits are quarterly, the interest rate (3%) is per quarter compounded quarterly, and there are 20 quarters in the five-year period.

There might be a tendency to solve this part of the problem in the following manner:

$$F = 4{,}000\,(4)\,(F/A\ 12{,}5)$$

$$= 16{,}000\,(6.353)$$

$$= \$101{,}648$$

This solution is *incorrect* because it does not fully take into account the time value of money. That is, interest is being earned each *quarter* on the quarterly amounts being deposited.

The solution to Part b is a little more involved since the compound period (semiannually) for the given interest rate does not agree with the timing of the deposits. The procedure in this case is to first convert the interest rate to an effective annual rate. Using Eq. (2-31), this is

$$\left(1 + \frac{.12}{2}\right)^2 - 1 = 0.1236 = 12.36\% \text{ compounded annually}$$

Next, this result is converted to a nominal rate with a compounding period that agrees with the deposit (quarterly, $c = 4$). This is also accomplished using Eq. (2-31):

$$.1236 = \left(1 + \frac{r}{4}\right)^4 - 1$$

$$\frac{r}{4} = (1.1236)^{0.25} - 1$$

$$= 0.0296$$

$$r = 4\,(0.0296)$$

$$= 0.1184$$

$$= 11.84\% \text{ compounded quarterly}$$

With this result, the solution to Part b is

$$F = 4{,}000 \left(F/A\ \frac{11.84}{4},\ 4\,(5)\right)$$

$$= 4{,}000\,(F/A\ 2.96,\ 20)$$

$$= 4{,}000\,(26.761)$$

$$= \$107{,}044$$

The value for the F/A factor in this solution can be obtained either by interpolation or by direct evaluation of the mathematical expression for the F/A factor. This is the approach in the example; namely,

$$F/A \ 2.96,20 = \frac{(1 + 0.0296)^{20} - 1}{0.0296}$$

$$= 26.761$$

CONTINUOUS INTEREST FACTORS

Interest rates are sometimes specified on the basis of continuous compounding. An interest rate with continuous compounding is a *nominal* rate. For example, 10% compounded continuously implies 10% *per year* compounded continuously. Continuous interest also requires different interest factors than those previously given.

Single Payment Compound Amount Factor   For discrete interest rates, the formulation involving the F/P factor is

$$F = P(F/P \ i,n) \tag{2-32}$$

and writing this in terms of a nominal rate gives

$$F = P\left(F/P \ \frac{r}{c}, cn\right) \tag{2-33}$$

Substituting the mathematical term for the F/P factor in Eq. (2-33) gives

$$F = P\left(1 + \frac{r}{c}\right)^{cn} \tag{2-34}$$

which can be written as

$$F = P\left[\left(1 + \frac{r}{c}\right)^{c/r}\right]^{rn} \tag{2-35}$$

Taking the limit of Eq. (2-35) as c approaches infinity gives

$$F = Pe^{rn} \tag{2-36}$$

With continuous compounding, the single payment compound amount factor is the expression e^{rn} in Eq. (2-36) and is designated $[F/P \ r,n]$. It is used in the formulation

$$F = P[F/P \ r,n] \tag{2-37}$$

It should be noted that continuous interest factors use brackets in order to distinguish them from discrete interest factors which use parentheses.

Example 2-14

If $2,000 is deposited into an account that pays 8% compounded continuously, the final amount in the account at the end of five years is

$$F = 2,000\,[F/P\ 8,5]$$

$$= 2,000\,[1.492]$$

$$= \$2,984$$

The value 1.492 is obtained from the continuous interest tables given in Appendix C.

Single Payment Present Worth Factor This factor is the reciprocal of the F/P factor and consequently is designated as a P/F factor.

$$[P/F\ r,n\,] = \frac{1}{e^{rn}} \tag{2-38}$$

It is used in the formulation

$$P = F\,[P/F\ r,n\,] \tag{2-39}$$

Uniform Series Compound Amount (Future Worth) Factor
If the series of uniform deposits in Figure 2-2 is considered, the future amount with *continuous* interest is

$$F = A\,[F/P\ r,(n - 1) + F/P\ r,(n - 2) + \ldots$$

$$+ F/P\ r,2 + F/P\ r,1 + F/P\ r,0\,] \tag{2-40}$$

Substituting the mathematical expressions for the F/P factors in Eq. (2-40) gives

$$F = A\,[e^{r(n-1)} + e^{r(n-2)} + \ldots e^{2r} + e^{r} + 1\,] \tag{2-41}$$

The terms in the brackets in Eq. (2-41) form a geometric series with a common ratio of e^{r}. Therefore, the sum of n terms is

$$\frac{e^{rn} - 1}{e^{r} - 1} \tag{2-42}$$

This expression is designated as $[F/A\ r,n\,]$ and is the uniform series compound amount (future worth) factor for continuous compounding. It is used in the formulation

$$F = A \, [F/A \; r,n \,] \qquad\qquad (2\text{-}43)$$

Example 2-15

An account pays 8% compounded continuously. Determine the amount in the account after three years if:

   a. $1,000 is deposited every year.
   b. $1,000 is deposited semiannually.

The solution to Part a is obtained using Eq. (2-43)

$$F = 1,000 \, [F/A \; 8,3]$$
$$= 1,000 \, [3.257]$$
$$= \$3,257$$

The solution to Part b is also obtained using Eq. (2-43). However certain modifications must be made because the deposits are semiannual. The solution is

$$F = 1,000 \left[F/A \; \frac{8}{2}, \, 2\,(3) \right]$$

$$= 1,000 \, [F/A \; 4,6]$$
$$= 1,000 \, [6.647]$$
$$= \$6,647$$

This solution converts the yearly continuous compounding rate to a semiannual continuous compounding rate.

Uniform Series Sinking Fund Factor   This factor is the reciprocal of the F/A factor; namely,

$$[A/F \; r,n \,] = \frac{e^{\,r} - 1}{e^{\,rn} - 1} \qquad\qquad (2\text{-}44)$$

It is used in the formulation

$$A = F \, [A/F \; r,n \,]$$

Uniform Series Present Worth Factor   This factor is a combination of the previously defined F/A and P/F factors. Mathematically, it is

$$[P/A \ r,n] = [F/A \ r,n][P/F \ r,n]$$

$$= \left[\frac{e^{rn} - 1}{e^r - 1}\right]\left[\frac{1}{e^{rn}}\right]$$

$$= \frac{1 - e^{-rn}}{e^r - 1} \tag{2-45}$$

and is used in the formulation

$$P = A[P/A \ r,n] \tag{2-46}$$

Example 2-16 _____

What minimum initial amount must be put into an account that pays 8% compounded continuously if it is desired to withdraw from this same account

    a. $1,000 per year for five years?
    b. $1,000 quarterly for five years?

The solution to Part a is

$$P = 1,000 [P/A \ 8,5]$$

$$= 1,000 [3.9584]$$

$$= \$3,958.40$$

and the solution to Part b is

$$P = 1,000 \left[P/A \ \frac{8}{4}, 4(5)\right]$$

$$= 1,000 [P/A \ 2,20]$$

$$= 1,000 [16.3197]$$

$$= \$16,319.70$$

Uniform Series Capital Recovery Factor   This factor is the inverse of the P/A factor. Consequently, it is defined as

$$[A/P \ r,n] = \frac{e^r - 1}{1 - e^{-rn}} \tag{2-47}$$

and is used in the formulation

$$A = P[A/P \; r,n]$$ (2-48)

Example 2-17

A person deposits \$6,000 into an account that pays 12% compounded continuously. What is the maximum equal monthly withdrawal that can be made for two years?

The solution to this problem is obtained using Eq. (2-48)

$$A = 6,000 \left[A/P \; \frac{12}{12}, \; 12(2)\right]$$

$$= 6,000 \, [A/P \; 1,24]$$

$$= 6,000 \, [0.0471]$$

$$= \$282.60$$

A CONTINUOUS RATE TO AN ANNUAL RATE

A continuous interest rate can be converted to an effective annual rate using the equation

$$\text{effective annual rate} = e^r - 1$$ (2-49)

For example, the effective annual rate for 8% compounded continuously is 8.33%.

FUNDS-FLOW FACTOR AND CONTINUOUS CASH TRANSACTIONS

In previous discussions, the cash transactions are assumed to be discrete. That is, the cash transactions occur at particular points in time. Another approach is to consider that the cash transactions flow at a uniform rate during the time period.

One approach that is often taken in discussions of continuous cash transactions is to define another set of interest factors and tables. Another approach is to convert the continuous cash flow to a discrete amount, then use the continuous interest factors and tables. This latter approach is the one used in this text.

A uniform continuous cash transaction, $\bar{A}$, in a year may be considered as a series of X equal amounts spaced at the end of equal time periods as shown in Figure 2-6. Now, the future sum, F', of these equal amounts at the end of one year using a continuous interest rate, r, is

$$F' = X \left[\frac{\left(1 + \dfrac{r}{c}\right)^c - 1}{\dfrac{r}{c}} \right] \qquad (2\text{-}50)$$

Since $X = \dfrac{\bar{A}}{c}$, Eq. (2-50) can be written as

$$F' = \frac{\bar{A}}{c} \left[\frac{\left(1 + \dfrac{r}{c}\right)^c - 1}{\dfrac{r}{c}} \right]$$

$$F' = \frac{\bar{A}}{r} \left(1 + \frac{r}{c}\right)^c - \frac{\bar{A}}{r}$$

Substituting $k = \dfrac{c}{r}$ gives

$$F' = \frac{\bar{A}}{r} \left[\left(1 + \frac{1}{k}\right)^k \right]^r - \frac{\bar{A}}{r} \qquad (2\text{-}51)$$

If c approaches infinity, then k approaches infinity and the limit of the term in the brackets is e. Consequently, Eq. (2-50) can be written as

$$F' = \frac{\bar{A}}{r} e^r - \frac{\bar{A}}{r}$$

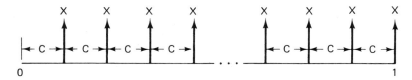

FIGURE 2-6 Continuous Cash Transactions in One Year

$$F' = \bar{A} \left[\frac{e^r - 1}{r} \right] \tag{2-52}$$

Eq. (2-52), in effect, converts the yearly continuous transaction to a discrete amount at the end of the year. Consequently, if there are n years of a uniform continuous cash transaction, the term in the brackets can convert these continuous transactions to a series of equal annual *discrete* amounts that occur at the end of each year. Therefore at the end of n years, the future amount is

$$F = F' \, [F/A \; r,n]$$

$$F = \bar{A} \left[\frac{e^r - 1}{r} \right] \left[F/A \; r,n \right] \tag{2-53}$$

The first bracketed term in Eq. (2-53) is called the funds-flow conversion factor and is designated as

$$[A/\bar{A} \; r] = \frac{e^r - 1}{r} \tag{2-54}$$

Values for this factor are available in Appendix D. Substituting Eq. (2-54) into Eq. (2-53) gives

$$F = \bar{A} \, [A/\bar{A} \; r][F/A \; r,n] \tag{2-55}$$

If the continuous transaction, $\bar{A}$, is desired, Eq. (2-55) can be modified to

$$\bar{A} = F \, \frac{[A/F \; r,n]}{[A/\bar{A} \; r]} \tag{2-56}$$

The present amount of a uniform continuous transaction can be obtained by

$$P = \bar{A} \, [A/\bar{A} \; r][P/A \; r,n] \tag{2-57}$$

or if P is given, $\bar{A}$ can be obtained by

$$\bar{A} = P \, \frac{[A/P \; r,n]}{[A/\bar{A} \; r]} \tag{2-58}$$

As mentioned earlier in this section, some texts algebraically combine the two interest factors in Eqs. (2-55) through (2-58) and define a new set of interest factors. For example, Eq. (2-55) could be written as

$$F = \bar{A} \left[\frac{e^r - 1}{r} \right] \left[\frac{e^{rn} - 1}{e^r - 1} \right]$$

$$F = \bar{A} \left[\frac{e^{rn} - 1}{r} \right] \tag{2-59}$$

The term in the brackets is designated as

$$[F/\bar{A}\ r,n\,] = \frac{e^{rn} - 1}{r} \tag{2-60}$$

and used in the formulation

$$F = \bar{A}\ [F/\bar{A}\ r,n\,] \tag{2-61}$$

Similiar factors can be defined for Eqs. (2-56), (2-57), and (2-58). This approach is not taken in this text.

Example 2-18

If the interest rate is 8% compounded continuously, what is the final amount after five years of:

a. A continuous cash transaction of $1,000 a year?

b. A continuous cash transaction of $1,000 per quarter?

The solution to Part a is obtained using Eq. (2-55)

$$F = 1,000\ [A/\bar{A}\ 8]\,[F/A\ 8,5]$$
$$= 1,000\ [1.041088]\,[5.905]$$
$$= \$6,147.62$$

In the case of Part b two solution methods are possible. The first is

$$F = 1,000\,(4)\ [A/\bar{A}\ 8]\,[F/A\ 8,5]$$
$$= 4,000\ [1.041088]\,[5.905]$$
$$= \$24,590.50$$

and the second is

$$F = 1,000\ \left[A/\bar{A}\ \frac{8}{4}\right]\ \left[F/A\ \frac{8}{4},\,4\,(5)\right]$$

$$= 1,000 \, [A/\bar{A} \; 2] \, [F/A \; 2,20]$$

$$= 1,000 \, [1.010065] \, [24.346]$$

$$= \$24,591.04$$

The difference in these two answers is due to rounding off. Theoretically, these two methods are the same and would give the same results if the two F/A factors were carried out to more significant figures.

The two solution methods used in Part b of Example 2-18 require a word of caution. The first solution in Part b converts the quarterly flow to a yearly flow by multiplying by the number of quarters in a year, then the factors are evaluated on the basis of an annual rate with continuous compounding. This approach is *only* valid in case of continuous transactions. It is *not valid* in the discrete case. The reason it is possible in the continuous flow case is due to the relationship between the funds-flow and continuous interest factors. For example, in Part b the interest factors in the second solution method can be written as

$$\left[A/\bar{A} \; \frac{8}{4} \right] \left[F/A \; \frac{8}{4}, \, 4\,(5) \right] = \left[\frac{e^{\frac{.08}{4}} - 1}{\frac{.08}{4}} \right] \left[\frac{e^{\frac{.08}{4}\,(4)\,(5)} - 1}{e^{\frac{.08}{4}} - 1} \right]$$

$$= 4 \left[\frac{e^{.08\,(5)} - 1}{.08} \right]$$

which is exactly the same as the combined effect of the interest factors in the first solution method; namely,

$$4\,[A/\bar{A} \; 8]\,[F/A \; 8,5] = 4 \left[\frac{e^{.08} - 1}{.08} \right] \left[\frac{e^{.08\,(5)} - 1}{e^{.08} - 1} \right]$$

$$= 4 \left[\frac{e^{.08\,(5)} - 1}{.08} \right]$$

EQUIVALENCE

Many comparisons of economic alternatives require the comparisons of receipts and disbursements of money occurring at different times. In these situations, the receipts and disbursements must be placed on an *equivalent basis* in order to make a valid comparison. In order to put receipts and disbursements on an equivalent basis, the magnitude, interest rate, and timing of the receipts and disbursements must be considered. As a result, equivalence calculations involve an application of the interest factors in order to obtain either an equivalent present amount, an equivalent future amount, or an equivalent annual amount. The meaning of *equivalence* should be clearly understood. An equivalent amount does not imply an actual cash transaction. It is an amount that has the same monetary effect, taking into account interest and timing, as the actual cash transaction. For example, $1,000 today is equivalent to $1,539 five years from now at an interest rate of 9% compounded annually. Theoretically, a decision-maker is indifferent between these two amounts assuming, of course, that the decision-maker believes 9% is an accurate representation of the time value of money.

Example 2-19 _____

Given the series of disbursements shown in Table 2-5 and an interest rate of 8% compounded annually, determine:

   a. An equivalent present amount.
   b. An equivalent future amount.
   c. An equivalent annual amount.

    The solution to Part a is obtained by discounting all of the disbursements back to year zero. This could be accomplished by multiplying each disbursement by an appropriate P/F factor. However, this would involve

TABLE 2-5

Data for Example 2-19

End of Year	Disbursement
0	—
1	200
2	200
3	200
4	200
5	200
6	200
7	400
8	400
9	400
10	400

ten factors. A more direct solution is to employ the P/A in the following manner.

$$P = 200(P/A\ 8,6) + 400(P/A\ 8,4)\ (P/F\ 8,6)$$
$$= 200(4.6229) + 400(3.3121)\ (0.6302)$$
$$= \$1,759.49$$

The solution to Part b can be obtained by carrying the answer to Part a forward ten years.

$$F = 1,759.49\ (F/P\ 8,10)$$
$$= 1,759.49\ (2.159)$$
$$= \$3,798.74$$

If the answer to Part a is not available and only the future amount is required, a direct solution is

$$F = 200(F/A\ 8,6)\ (F/P\ 8,4) + 400(F/A\ 8,4)$$
$$= 200(7.336)\ (1.360) + 400(4.506)$$
$$= \$3,797.79$$

The difference in these two answers (\$0.95) is due to rounding off the interest factor values. Using the previous results, the equivalent annual amount is

$$A = P(A/P\ i,n)$$
$$= 1,759.49\ (A/P\ 8,10)$$
$$= 1,759.49\ (0.1490)$$
$$= \$262.16$$

or if the future amount is used

$$A = F(A/F\ i,n)$$
$$= 3,798.74\ (A/F\ 8,10)$$
$$= 3,798.74\ (0.0690)$$
$$= \$262.11$$

Again, the difference is due to rounding off the interest factor values.

In general, it is usually necessary to first determine either an equivalent present or future amount before an equivalent annual amount can be determined.

SOME SPECIAL CONSIDERATIONS

At this point, some special topics are considered. These topics are (1) automobile loans, (2) house mortgages, (3) bonds, and (4) inflation. These topics are considered because there usually is wide interest in them. Also, they provide additional examples of applications of the concepts presented earlier in this chapter.

Automobile Loans   Quite often the interest rates that are quoted on automobile loans are simple (add-on) interest rates. The monthly car payment is calculated by dividing the future amount, based on simple interest, by the number of monthly payments. This procedure results in a considerably larger annual compound rate than the simple interest rate. The specifics of this procedure are shown in the next example.

Example 2-20 _____

A person borrows $6,000 for an automobile loan that is to be paid back over 30 months. The loan agency quotes a simple (often, not specifically stated) interest rate of 8%. What is the effective annual compound rate paid on this automobile loan?

The monthly payment is calculated in the following manner.

$$\text{monthly payment} = \frac{P + P\,(n)\,(i)}{\text{number of months}} \qquad (2\text{-}62)$$

$$= \frac{6{,}000 + 6{,}000\,(2.5)\,(.08)}{30}$$

$$= \$240$$

The following formulation is used to calculate the effective rate

$$P = A\,(P/A\ i,n)$$

$$6{,}000 = 240\,(P/A\ i,30)$$

$$(P/A\ i,30) = 25$$

$$i = 1.23\% \text{ per month compounded per month}$$

Therefore, the nominal rate is

$$r = 1.23\,(12) = 14.76\% \text{ compounded monthly}$$

and the effective annual rate is

$$i = \left(1 + \frac{.1476}{12}\right)^{12} - 1$$

$$= 0.158 = 15.8\% \text{ compounded yearly}$$

House Mortgages The manner in which house payments work is best explained with a numerical example.

Example 2-21

A person borrows \$60,000 for a house loan (mortgage) that is to be paid back in monthly payments over a period of 24 years. The interest rate quoted on this loan is 12%. Answer the following questions:

  a. What is the monthly payment?
  b. How much of the monthly payment determined in Part a is interest and how much is principal?

First, it is usual for the interest rate quoted on house loans to be a nominal rate. Therefore, the 12% in this example is compounded monthly, and the answer to Part a is

$$A = P \ (A/P \ i,n)$$

$$= 60,000 \left(A/P \ \frac{12}{12}, \ 12\,(24)\right)$$

$$= 60,000 \ (A/P \ 1,288)$$

$$= 60,000 \ (0.0106)$$

$$= \$636$$

The value for the interest factor (0.0106) is not available in the interest tables and is determined in the following manner.

$$(A/P \ 1,288) = \frac{(0.01)\,(1 + 0.01)^{288}}{(1 + 0.01)^{288} - 1} = 0.0106$$

The answers and calculations for Part b are shown in Table 2-6 for the first ten months. As an extension to Example 2-21, the unpaid

TABLE 2-6

Interest and Principal Payments for Example 2-21

End of Month	Payment	Interest Paid	Principal Paid	Unpaid Principal
0	—	—	—	60,000
1	636	$60,000(.01) = 600.00$	$636 - 600.00 = 36.00$	$60,000 - 36.00 = 59,964.00$
2	636	$59,964(.01) = 599.64$	$636 - 599.64 = 36.36$	$59,964 - 36.36 = 59,927.64$
3	636	$59,927.64(.01) = 599.28$	$636 - 599.28 = 36.72$	$59,927.64 - 36.72 = 59,890.92$
4	636	$59,890.92(.01) = 598.91$	$636 - 598.91 = 37.09$	$59,890.92 - 37.09 = 59,853.83$
5	636	$59,853.83(.01) = 598.54$	$636 - 598.54 = 37.46$	$59,853.83 - 37.46 = 59,816.37$
6	636	$59,816.37(.01) = 598.16$	$636 - 598.16 = 37.84$	$59,816.37 - 37.84 = 59,778.53$
7	636	$59,778.53(.01) = 597.79$	$636 - 597.79 = 38.21$	$59,778.53 - 38.21 = 59,740.32$
8	636	$59,740.32(.01) = 597.40$	$636 - 597.40 = 38.60$	$59,740.32 - 38.60 = 59,701.72$
9	636	$59,701.72(.01) = 597.02$	$636 - 597.02 = 38.98$	$59,701.72 - 38.98 = 59,662.74$
10	636	$59,662.74(.01) = 596.63$	$636 - 596.63 = 39.37$	$59,662.74 - 39.37 = 59,623.37$
Σ	6,360	5,983.37	376.63	—

principal at the end of the k payments, B_k, can be calculated using the relationship

$$B_k = P\,(F/P\ i,k) - A\,(F/A\ i,k) \qquad (2\text{-}63)$$

For example, the unpaid principal at the end of the tenth payment is

$$B_{10} = 60,000\,(F/P\ 1,10) - 636\,(F/A\ 1,10)$$

$$= 60,000\,(1.104622) - 636\,(10.4622)$$

$$= \$59,623.36$$

The interest factors used in this calculation have been calculated using their respective formulas in order that rounding off errors will not be significant.

The principal paid at the end of k payments, C_k, can be calculated using

$$C_k = P - B_k \qquad (2\text{-}64)$$

For this example, the total principal paid at the end of the payments is

$$C_{10} = 60,000 - 59,623.36$$

$$= \$376.64$$

The total interest paid at the end of k payments, I_k, is given by

$$I_k = A\,(k) - C_k \qquad (2\text{-}65)$$

and for this example is

$$I_{10} = 636\,(10) - 376.64$$
$$= \$5,983.36$$

The slight differences in these answers and the values in Table 2-6 are due to rounding off various values.

Bonds Bonds are financial instruments issued by private corporations, nonprofit organizations, and governmental organizations to obtain funds. From the standpoint of an issuing institution, a bond is a debt. From the standpoint of purchaser, a bond is an investment. Bonds are issued on the basis of a face (par or stated) value which is to be paid at the bond's maturity date (a specified number of years). In addition, certain amounts of money are paid between the time the bond is issued and its maturity date. This amount of money is usually paid either annually, semiannually, or quarterly and is a function of a contractual (bond) rate and the face value. The cash transactions resulting from the purchase of a bond are shown in Table 2-7. The negative signs in Table 2-7 indicate a

TABLE 2-7

Cash Transactions Resulting From the Purchase of a Bond

End of Period	Cash Transaction
0	$-P$
1	$+\dfrac{kV}{C}$
2	$+\dfrac{kV}{C}$
3	$+\dfrac{kV}{C}$
.	.
.	.
.	.
n	$+\dfrac{kV}{C}+V$

cash disbursement and the positive signs indicate cash receipts. The nomenclature used in Table 2-7 is

P = the purchase price of the bond

V = the face value of the bond

k = bond contractual rate

$\dfrac{kV}{c}$ = amount (interest) received (paid) per period

c = number of periods per year

n = number of years to maturity

If the equivalent present amount of the cash receipts is set equal to the purchase price the result is

$$P = \frac{kV}{c}\left(P/A\,\frac{r}{c},\,cn\right) + V\left(P/F\,\frac{r}{c},\,cn\right) \qquad (2\text{-}66)$$

where r is the earned nominal rate with c compounding periods.

Example 2-22

A $1,000, ten-year, 12% semiannual bond is purchased. Determine the rate of interest earned if the bond is purchased for (a) $1,000 and (b) $900.

For Part a the data is substituted into Eq. (2-26) which gives

$$1{,}000 = \frac{(0.12)(1{,}000)}{2}\left(P/A\,\frac{r}{2},\,2(10)\right) + 1{,}000\left(P/F\,\frac{r}{2},\,2(10)\right)$$

$$1{,}000 = 60\left(P/A\,\frac{r}{2},\,20\right) + 1{,}000\left(P/F\,\frac{r}{2},\,20\right) \qquad (2\text{-}67)$$

In order to determine r, a trial-and-error solution is required. If r is estimated to be 12% compounded semiannually, Eq. (2-67) gives

$$1{,}000 = 60\,(P/A\ 6{,}20) + 1{,}000\,(P/F\ 6{,}20)$$

$$= 60\,(11.4699) + 1{,}000\,(0.3118)$$

$$= 1{,}000$$

This result indicates that the estimated interest rate is correct and consequently the rate of interest earned is 12% compounded semiannually (or 12.36% compounded annually). At this point, a generalization can be made. That is, if the purchase price is equal to the face value, the contractual rate (k) and the rate earned (r) are equal.

For Part b, the formulation, using Eq. (2-66), is

$$900 = \frac{(0.12)(1,000)}{2}\left(P/A\ \frac{r}{2},\ 2(10)\right) + 1,000\left(P/F\ \frac{r}{2},\ 20\right)$$

$$900 = 60\left(P/A\ \frac{r}{2},\ 20\right) + 1,000\left(P/F\ \frac{r}{2},\ 20\right)$$

The approach in a trial-and-error solution is to bracket the value on the left-hand side of the equality sign with values of the right-hand side at different interest rates. In the solution to Part a it is shown that at 12% compounded semiannually the value of the right-hand side is $1,000. If 14% compounded semiannually is used, the right-hand side has a value of $894.04. Consequently, using linear interpolation, the rate earned is

$$X = 12 + \frac{1,000 - 900.00}{1,000 - 894.04}\ (2)$$

$$= 13.88\% \text{ compounded semiannually}$$

or 14.36% compounded annually. Two more generalizations can be made: (1) if $P < V$, then $r > k$ and (2) if $P > V$, then $r < k$. These generalizations provide guidelines in making initial estimates of the earned rate.

In Example 2-22 reference is made to the rate earned by the purchase of the bond. This same rate can also be interpreted as a cost to the seller of the bond. That is, in this example the seller is paying 12% compounded semiannually if the bond is sold for $1,000 or paying 13.88% compounded semiannually if the bond is sold for $900.

Inflation   As a result of economic trends in past years, the inclusion of the effects of inflation in economic analyses has received considerable attention in the literature. There are two basic methods used to include inflation in economic analyses. These methods depend on the basis upon which future dollars are estimated. They can be estimated either on the basis of (1) *actual* or (2) *real* dollars. Actual dollars, sometimes referred to as *then-current* dollars, are the actual currency (paper) transactions that are estimated to occur at some point in time. In this case, the inclusion of inflationary effects is accomplished through the use of a combined inflation and interest rate. Real dollars, sometimes referred to as *constant-worth* dollars, are dollars with the same purchasing (or payment) value as the dollars at some reference point in time which, in economic analysis, is the present time. In this case, inflation has implicitly been included. Consequently, the interest rate without adjustment for inflation is used. These definitions of actual and real dollars imply the following relationship between the two types of dollars

$$A_t = R_t (1 + e)^t \tag{2-68}$$

where

$$A_t = \text{actual dollars at the end of } t \text{ periods}$$

$$R_t = \text{real dollars at the end of } t \text{ periods}$$

$$e = \text{inflation rate}$$

It should be noted that Eq. (2-68) assumes that the inflation rate, e, is a constant rate over t periods. With this assumption and Eq. (2-68), an equivalent present amount for a series of cash transactions based on actual dollars is

$$P = \sum_{t=0}^{n} A_t (1 + e)^{-t} (1 + i)^{-t} \tag{2-69}$$

$$= \sum_{t=0}^{n} A_t (1 + e + i + ei)^{-t}$$

$$= \sum_{t=0}^{n} A_t (1 + f)^{-t} \tag{2-70}$$

where

$$f = e + i + ei \tag{2-71}$$

and is the combined inflation and interest rate. If real dollars are used, the equivalent present amount is

$$P = \sum_{t=0}^{n} R_t (1 + i)^{-t} \tag{2-72}$$

Example 2-23

In order to illustrate the previous discussion of inflation, the following examples are worked. Suppose the cash transaction shown in Table 2-8 are in terms of actual dollars and it is desired to calculate an equivalent

TABLE 2-8

Cash Transactions for Example 2-23

End of Year	Cash Transaction in Actual Dollars
0	−8,000
1	3,000
2	3,500
3	4,000
4	5,000

present amount using an inflation rate of 8% and an interest (discount) rate of 15%.

Using Eq. (2-71) the combined interest and inflation rate is

$$f = 0.08 + 0.15 + (0.08)(0.15)$$

$$= 0.242$$

$$= 24.2\%$$

and using Eq. (2-70) the present worth is

$$P = -8,000 + 3,000(1 + 0.242)^{-1} + 3,500(1 + 0.242)^{-2}$$
$$+ 4,000(1 + 0.242)^{-3} + 5,000(1 + 0.242)^{-4}$$

$$= \$873$$

If the actual cash transactions given in Table 2-8 are converted to real cash transactions as shown in Table 2-9, the present worth using Eq. (2-72) is

$$P = -8,000 + 2,778(1 + 0.15)^{-1} + 3,001(1 + 0.15)^{-2}$$
$$+ 3,175(1 + 0.15)^{-3} + 3,675(1 + 0.15)^{-4}$$

$$= \$873$$

which shows that both methods give the same results.

If the inflation is not considered and the actual cash transactions are used, the equivalent present worth is

$$P = -8,000 + 3,000(1 + 0.15)^{-1} + 3,500(1 + 0.15)^{-2}$$
$$+ 4,000(1 + 0.15)^{-3} + 5,000(1 + 0.15)^{-4}$$

$$= \$2,745$$

This value of P is considerably larger than the previously obtained values and points out that in some situations the exclusion of inflationary effects could lead to incorrect decisions.

TABLE 2-9
Conversion of Actual to Real Cash Transactions

End of Year	*Actual Cash Transaction*	*Inflation Factor* $(1 + e)^{-t}$	*Real Cash Transaction*
0	−8,000	1.0000	−8,000
1	3,000	0.9259	2,778
2	3,500	0.8573	3,001
3	4,000	0.7938	3,175
4	5,000	0.7350	3,675

From a calculation standpoint, neither actual nor real dollars offer strong advantage at this point (later considerations may change this point of view) when including inflationary effects in economic analyses. However, whichever method is used it must be clearly understood whether estimates are in terms of actual or real dollars. The previous discussions in this chapter did not specifically mention inflation. This was done in order to facilitate the presentation of the topics considered. It can be assumed, therefore, that either the cash transactions were in the form of actual dollars and the associated interest rate included an inflation component or the cash transactions were real dollars and the associated interest rate was not adjusted for inflation.

In the previous discussion of inflation, it was assumed that the inflation and interest (discount) rate were both constant rates. Of course, these rates can change from one period to the next. If this is the case, the present value, in terms of actual dollars, is given by

$$P = \sum_{t=0}^{n} A_t \prod_{x=0}^{t} (1 + e_x)^{-1} (1 + i_x)^{-1} \qquad (2\text{-}73)$$

Although the use of Eq. (2-73) is not difficult, it can be tedious. It also requires an estimation of the inflation and interest rates for each period. The use of Eq. (2-73) is shown in the next example.

Example 2-24

Given the data in Table 2-10, determine the present value of the actual dollar transactions.

TABLE 2-10
Data for Example 2-24

End of Year	Actual Dollar Transaction	Inflation Rate, %	Interest Rate, %
0	—	—	—
1	1,000	5	10
2	2,000	6	12
3	2,500	7	15

Using Eq. (2-73) gives

$$P = 1{,}000 \, (1 + 0.05)^{-1} \, (1 + 0.10)^{-1}$$
$$+ \, 2{,}000 \, (1 + 0.06)^{-1} \, (1 + 0.12)^{-1} \, (1 + 0.05)^{-1} \, (1 + 0.10)^{-1}$$
$$+ \, 2{,}500 \, (1 + 0.07)^{-1} \, (1 + 0.15)^{-1} \, (1 + 0.06)^{-1} \, (1 + 0.12)^{-1}$$
$$(1 + 0.05)^{-1} \, (1 + 0.10)^{-1}$$

$$= \$3{,}806$$

which shows that calculations involving Eq. (2-73) can be tedious.

Explicitly including inflation in economic analyses is a debatable issue. Some argue that differences in economic alternatives are the same with or without inflation. Or, they argue that estimates of cash transactions and the discount rate implicitly include inflationary effects. Consequently, inflationary effects can explicitly be ignored. These arguments do have merit. However, care should be taken before inflationary effects are dismissed in economic analyses.

Some additional points are required in this discussion of inflation. First, different components in an economic analysis may have different inflation rates. For example, labor costs may have a different escalation rate than, say, fuel costs. Second, there are some components that are unresponsive to inflation; namely, depreciation, lease fees, and interest charges resulting from loan agreements. Such unresponsive components are an important consideration in after-tax economic analysis. These components and other considerations involving inflationary effects are discussed later in this book.

PROBLEMS

2-1. If a person borrows $4,000 at a simple interest rate of 8% per year, how much will be owed at the end of three years? How much of this amount is interest?

2-2. A person is informed that if he borrows $8,000 now, $10,000 will be due after four years. What simple interest rate is implied?

2-3. If a person borrows $2,000 at a simple interest rate of 10% per year, how much will be owed at the end of six months? How much of this amount is interest?

2-4. A person desires to have $50,000 in an account at the end of eight years. If the account pays 7% compounded annually, how much money must be deposited now?

2-5. If a person places $1,000 into an account that pays 6% compounded annually, how much money will be in the account after five years?

2-6. In how many years will a deposit in an account that pays 6% compounded, double in value?

2-7. If a person puts $1,000 in an account and has $1,500 in the account after five years, what compound rate of interest was earned?

2-8. What is the final accumulated amount resulting from a series of equal annual deposits of $3,000 for eight years if the interest rate is 10% compounded per year? Assume the first deposit is made one year from now.

2-9. Repeat Problem 2-8 assuming the first deposit is made now. Note, there are still only eight deposits.

2-10. If a person wishes to have available at the end of ten years $10,000, what equal annual deposit must be made, for ten years, into an account that pays 5% compounded annually? Assume the first deposit is made one year from now.

2-11. Repeat Problem 2-10 but assume that the first deposit is made now. Note, there are still only ten deposits.

2-12. How much money should be deposited in an account that pays 8% compounded annually in order to make six equal annual withdrawals of $2,000 with the last withdrawal exhausting the account?

2-13. A deposit of $6,000 is made into an account that pays 6% compounded annually. What equal annual withdrawal for five years can be made with the last withdrawal exhausting the account?

2-14. Four years ago a person borrowed $10,000 at an interest rate of 8% compounded annually and agreed to pay it back in equal payments over a ten-year period. This same person now wants to pay off the remaining amount of the loan. How much should this person pay? Assume he has just made the fourth payment.

2-15. A person is considering depositing some money in a savings account. Several local banks pay different interest rates on savings accounts. If the interest rates are those given below, which bank should be chosen?
(a) 5.5% compounded per year.
(b) 5.0% compounded continuously.
(c) 5.2% compounded quarterly.
(d) 5.3% compounded semiannually.

2-16. A local department store charges 1½% per month on credit accounts. What effective annual rate is being charged?

2-17. A person deposits $10,000 into an account that pays 8% compounded quarterly. How much money will be in the account after five years?

2-18. Repeat Problem 2-17 assuming that the interest rate is:
(a) 8% compounded semiannually.
(b) 8% compounded continuously.

2-19. A person wishes to have $5,000 in an account after six years. How much money must be deposited in the account now in order to have this amount if the account pays:
(a) 10% compounded quarterly.
(b) 10% compounded weekly.

2-20. If a person borrows $2,000 and agrees to pay it back in 24 monthly installments of $105.74, determine:
(a) The nominal interest rate paid.
(b) The effective annual interest rate paid.
(c) The amount of interest paid.

2-21. What is the accumulated amount resulting from a series of equal quarterly deposits of $1,000 for five years if the interest rate is 8% compounded quarterly? Assume the first deposit is made three months from now.

2-22. As a result of a certain debt obligation, a company must pay $10,000 a year for the next eight years. The next payment is due one year from now. The company now wants to cancel this debt over the next three years. If the interest rate is 12% compounded annually, what is the payment for the next three years?

2-23. What is an equivalent present amount for a series of equal annual amounts of $1,000 for five years if the interest rate is:
(a) 6% compounded semiannually?
(b) 6% compounded continuously?

2-24. If an equal quarterly deposit of $400 is made into an account for five years with the first deposit made three months from now, determine the amount in the account if:
(a) The interest rate is 12% compounded per quarter.
(b) The interest rate is 12% compounded continuously.

2-25. If a deposit of $4,000 is made into an account, determine the amount in the account after five years if the interest rate is:
(a) 10% compounded semiannually.
(b) 10% compounded continuously.

2-26. Determine an equivalent annual amount for the series of payments shown below using an interest rate of 9% compounded annually.

End of Year	Payment
0	1,000
1	1,000
2	1,000
3	1,000
4	2,000
5	3,000
6	4,000
7	4,000
8	4,000
9	500
10	500
11	500
12	500

2-27. Determine the equivalent present amount of a series of equal quarterly amounts of $10,000 for five years if the interest rate is 12% compounded semiannually.

2-28. If a person deposits $1,000 into an account that pays 8% compounded annually one year from now and then increases his deposits by $200 each for the next ten years, determine the amount of money that will be in the account at the end of the ten years.

2-29. What is the equivalent present amount of an eight-year series of decreasing amounts if the interest rate is 10% compounded annually, the first year amount is $20,000, and the rate of decrease is $800 per year?

2-30. Find an equivalent present amount for the series of cash disbursements shown below using an interest rate of 12% compounded annually.

End of Year	Cash Disbursement
0	—
1	3,000
2	3,000
3	3,000
4	4,000
5	5,000
6	5,000
7	5,000
8	5,000

2-31. Find an equivalent present amount for the series of cash disbursements shown using the following:
(a) An interest rate of 10% compounded annually.
(b) An interest rate of 10% compounded continuously.
(c) An interest rate of 10% compounded semiannually.

End of Year	Cash Disbursement
0	—
1	5,000
2	5,000
3	5,000
4	5,000
5	8,000
6	8,000
7	8,000

2-32. Convert the series shown below to an equivalent five-year equal amount series using an interest rate of 10% compounded annually with the first amount occurring one year from now.

End of Year	Amount
0	1,000
1	1,000
2	1,000
3	1,000
4	5,000
5	6,000
6	6,000
7	6,000
8	6,000
9	3,000
10	4,000

2-33. A company borrows $10 million and agrees to pay it back in 20 equal yearly installments at an interest rate of 10% compounded annually. Determine the amount of interest and principal paid in each year for the first four payments.

2-34. What is the equivalent quarterly funds-flow series for a present amount of $60,000 over ten years if the interest rate is 12% compounded continuously.

2-35. Determine the future amount for the following funds-flow series using an interest rate of 10% compounded continuously.
(a) $2,000 per year for six years.
(b) $2,000 semiannually for five years.

2-36. A person borrows $12,000 in order to buy an expensive automobile. If the bank makes the loan at a simple (add-on) rate of 8% for 30 equal monthly payments, determine:
(a) The monthly payment.
(b) The effective annual interest rate.

2-37. A person pays $1,600 for a $2,000, 10% bond that matures in ten years. If the bond pays interest annually, what rate of interest does the person receive?

2-38. A $3,000 bond matures in ten years. The bond rate of interest is 12% paid quarterly. If a person buys the bond for $2,300, what effective annual rate of interest will the person receive?

2-39. A $1,000 bond that pays 8% semiannually and matures in 15 years is for sale. What is the maximum amount that should be paid for the bond if:
(a) 12% compounded semiannually is required on bond investments?
(b) 15% compounded annually is required on bond investments?

2-40. Given the cash transactions shown below, an inflation rate of 8% per year, and an interest rate of 10%, determine an equivalent present amount if:
(a) The cash transactions are in terms of real dollars.
(b) The cash transactions are in terms of actual dollars.

End of Year	Cash Transactions
0	1,000
1	1,000
2	1,000
3	1,000
4	2,000
5	2,000
6	2,000

3

DEPRECIATION

In this chapter depreciation and depreciation models are discussed. Depreciation is introduced at this point because of its relationship to taxes (discussed in the next chapter) and other future topics.

Depreciation may be considered as the reduction in value of an asset as a result of wear, deterioration, or obsolescence. Depreciation can also be considered as a procedure for the systematic recovery of capital invested in an asset (a viewpoint usually taken by the accountant). In either case, depreciation must be taken into account in economic analyses.

The estimation of *yearly* depreciation amounts either for tax or capital recovery purposes is accomplished through the use of *depreciation models*. These models are discussed in this chapter using the following nomenclature:

P = capital investment (first cost, initial investment, or capital expenditure)

n = depreciation life (usually in years); this is sometimes called the estimated life, useful life, or depreciation period

L = salvage value; this occurs at the end of the depreciation life; it is sometimes called the final value, terminal value, or final worth

D_j = depreciation amount (charge) for the year j; it can also be considered as an estimate of the capital recovered during the year j

B_j = book value (unrecovered capital or undepreciated balance) at the end of year j

STRAIGHT-LINE DEPRECIATION

The straight-line depreciation model gives a constant yearly depreciation amount, and as a result, the book value decreases at a constant rate. The depreciation amount in any year, D_j, is

$$D_j = \frac{P - L}{n} \tag{3-1}$$

and the book value at the end of year j is

$$B_j = P - \frac{j}{n}(P - L) \tag{3-2}$$

Example 3-1

Using a straight-line depreciation model determine the depreciation schedule (yearly depreciation amounts and book values) for a capital asset that costs $100,000 and has a salvage value of $10,000 and a depreciation life of eight years.

Using Eq. (3-1), the yearly depreciation amounts are

$$D_j = \frac{100,000 - 10,000}{8}$$

$$= \$11,250$$

The book values are determined using Eq. (3-2) and for the first two years are

$$B_1 = 100,000 - \frac{1}{8}(100,000 - 10,000)$$

$$= \$88,750$$

$$B_2 = 100,000 - \frac{2}{8}(100,000 - 10,000)$$

$$= \$77,500$$

The entire depreciation schedule is given in Table 3-1.

TABLE 3-1

Straight-Line Depreciation Schedule for Example 3-1

End of Year	Depreciation Amount	Book Value
0	—	$100,000
1	$11,250	88,750
2	11,250	77,500
3	11,250	66,250
4	11,250	55,000
5	11,250	43,750
6	11,250	32,500
7	11,250	21,250
8	11,250	10,000

At this point two useful expressions are introduced that relate depreciation amounts and book values; namely,

$$D_j = B_{j-1} - B_j \qquad (3\text{-}3)$$

$$B_j = P - \sum_{x=1}^{j} D_x \qquad (3\text{-}4)$$

These two equations are applicable regardless of the depreciation model and can be helpful when generating an entire depreciation schedule.

The term $\sum_{x=1}^{j} D_x$ in Eq. (3-4) represents the total accumulated depreciation through the end of the year j.

SUM-OF-THE-YEARS-DIGITS DEPRECIATION

The sum-of-the-years-digits (SYD) depreciation model provides an *accelerated* depreciation schedule. That is, yearly depreciation amounts decrease with time. The depreciation amount for the year j is given by the expression

$$D_j = \frac{(n-j+1)(P-L)}{\dfrac{n(n+1)}{2}} \qquad (3\text{-}5)$$

and the book value is given by

$$B_j = (P-L)\left(\frac{n-j}{n}\right)\left(\frac{n-j+1}{n+1}\right) + L \qquad (3\text{-}6)$$

The denominator in Eq. (3-5) provides the basis of the name sum-of-the-years-digits. For, the sum of the digits $1 + 2 + 3 + \ldots + n$ is equal to $n(n+1)/2$.

Example 3-2

Using the data given in Example 3-1 determine the depreciation schedule using the SYD depreciation model. The depreciation schedule is obtained using Eqs. (3-5) and (3-6) and is shown in Table 3-2. As examples, the depreciation amounts for the first two years are

$$D_1 = \frac{8-1+1}{8(9)/2}(100{,}000 - 10{,}000)$$
$$= \$20{,}000$$

$$D_2 = \frac{8-2+1}{8(9)/2}(100{,}000 - 10{,}000)$$
$$= \$17{,}000$$

and the book values are

$$B_1 = (100{,}000 - 10{,}000)\left(\frac{8-1}{8}\right)\left(\frac{8-1+1}{8+1}\right) + 10{,}000$$
$$= \$80{,}000$$

$$B_2 = (100{,}000 - 10{,}000)\left(\frac{8-2}{8}\right)\left(\frac{8-2+1}{8+1}\right) + 10{,}000$$
$$= \$62{,}500$$

TABLE 3-2

Sum-of-the-Years-Digits Depreciation Schedule for Example 3-2

End of Year	Depreciation Amount	Book Value
0	—	$100,000
1	$20,000	80,000
2	17,500	62,500
3	15,000	47,500
4	12,500	35,000
5	10,000	25,000
6	7,500	17,500
7	5,000	12,500
8	2,500	10,000

DECLINING-BALANCE DEPRECIATION

The declining-balance depreciation model is sometimes referred to as the *fixed-percentage* depreciation model. It is another accelerated depreciation model. In the declining-balance depreciation model the yearly depreciation amounts are determined by multiplying the book value at the beginning of the year by a constant fraction. Expressed mathematically, the depreciation amount is

$$D_j = a\, B_{j-1} \tag{3-7}$$

where a is the constant fraction. The book value at the end of year j is

$$B_j = (1-a)^j P \tag{3-8}$$

The yearly depreciation amounts can be directly determined by the equation

$$D_j = aP(1-a)^{j-1} \tag{3-9}$$

which is a result of substituting Eq. (3-8) into Eq. (3-7).

Values for a   Values for the constant fraction, a, are determined in two ways. The first way is to determine a value that will give a book value at the end of the depreciation life equal to the salvage value. Expressed mathematically, this is

$$L = (1-a)^n P$$

which is usually written as

$$a = 1 - \sqrt[n]{\frac{L}{P}} \tag{3-10}$$

Eq. (3-10) has some weaknesses. It cannot be used to depreciate an asset to a salvage value of zero. Also, if the salvage value is very small compared to the initial cost of the asset, the depreciation amounts in the early years can be unreasonably large. These weaknesses are not serious and can be partially overcome by the second method for determining values for a. A reasonable rate may be taken from tax regulations as long as the maximum yearly depreciation does not exceed an amount given by twice (200%) the straight-line rate. This implies that the maximum tax depreciation in any year is

$$\frac{2}{n}(P) \qquad \text{Double} \tag{3-11}$$
$$\text{Declining-balance}$$

since the straight-line rate is $\frac{1}{n}$. Consequently, it is common to set the value of a equal to $\dfrac{2}{n}$. If this is done, it is called a *double declining-balance* (DDB) depreciation model. Under certain circumstances specified in the tax regulations, twice the straight-line rate is not allowed. In these circumstances the rate is limited to 150% or 125% of the straight-line rate. In these cases the values of a, respectively, are $\dfrac{1.50}{n}$ and $\dfrac{1.25}{n}$.

This second method also has a weakness in that it does not guarantee that the salvage value will be obtained at the end of the depreciation life. A systematic method to overcome this weakness, when it exists, is to switch over to straight-line depreciation. The switch to straight-line is made whenever the straight-line depreciation, based on the remaining undepreciated amount and life, is greater than the depreciation amount given by the double declining-balance model. This can be expressed mathematically as

$$\frac{B_{j-1} - L}{n - (j - 1)} > aB_{j-1} \tag{3-12}$$

The basis of Eq. (3-12) is related to the present worth of taxes paid and is discussed in greater detail in the next chapter.

Example 3-3

A capital asset has an initial cost of \$100,000, a salvage value of \$20,000, and a depreciation life of eight years. Determine the depreciation schedule for this asset using the declining-balance model with the following rates:

a. The rate defined by Eq. (3-10).
b. The double declining rate.
c. The 125% rate with switch over to straight-line depreciation.

Using Eq. (3-10), the rate for Part a is

$$a = 1 - \sqrt[8]{\frac{20,000}{100,000}} = 0.18223$$

With this rate and Eqs. (3-7), (3-8), and (3-9) the depreciation schedule shown in Table 3-3 is obtained. For example, the depreciation amounts for the first two years are

$$D_1 = 0.18223\,(100,000)$$
$$= \$18,223$$

TABLE 3-3

Declining-Balance Depreciation

$a = 0.18223$

End of Year	Depreciation Amount	Book Value
0	—	$100,000
1	$18,223	81,777
2	14,902	66,875
3	12,187	54,688
4	9,966	44,722
5	8,150	36,572
6	6,665	29,907
7	5,450	24,457
8	4,457	20,000

$$D_2 = 0.18223(1 - 0.18223)^1(100,000)$$

$$= \$14,902$$

and the book values are

$$B_1 = (1 - 0.18223)(100,000)$$

$$= \$81,777$$

$$B_2 = (1 - 0.18223)^2(100,000)$$

$$= \$66,875$$

For Part b, the rate is

$$a = \frac{2}{n}$$

$$= \frac{2}{8}$$

$$= 0.2500$$

The depreciation schedule using this rate is shown in Table 3-4. Note that the depreciation amount given in year six is not the amount given by Eq. (3-7) since this equation gives

$$D_6 = 0.2500(23,730)$$

$$= \$5,933$$

If this value is used for D_6 the salvage value in year six would be less than $20,000. Consequently, the depreciation in year six is limited to the

TABLE 3-4

Double Declining-Balance Depreciation

$$a = 0.2500$$

End of Year	Depreciation Amount	Book Value
0	—	$100,000
1	$25,000	75,000
2	18,750	56,250
3	14,063	42,187
4	10,547	31,640
5	7,910	23,730
6	3,730	20,000
7	—	20,000
8	—	20,000

amount necessary to obtain the salvage value ($3,730 in this case). This implies that the asset is fully depreciated at the end of six years and no further depreciation is taken. Consequently, the asset would maintain a book value equal to its salvage value ($20,000) for the remainder of its life. Another point, quite often when DDB depreciation is used, a switch to straight-line depreciation is in order. From the standpoint of the present worth of taxes, there is no advantage in switching to straight-line depreciation if the book value at the end of an asset's depreciation life, calculated using Eq. (3-8), is less than the salvage value. Using Eq. (3-8), the book value at the end of the eighth year is

$$B_8 = (1 - 0.2500)^8 (100,000)$$

$$= \$10,011$$

which is less than the salvage value. In these cases, the approach is to adjust the depreciation in order to obtain the salvage value as shown in this example. However, if the book value at the end of the depreciation life is greater than the salvage value, there is a present worth advantage in switching to straight-line depreciation. This is the case in Part c.

The rate for Part c is

$$a = \frac{1.25}{8}$$

$$= 0.1563$$

Using this rate and Eq. (3-8), the book value at the end of the depreciation life is

$$B_8 = (1 - 0.1563)^8(100,000)$$

$$= \$25,675$$

Since this value is greater than the salvage value, a switch to straight-line depreciation is in order. As mentioned earlier, the year that this switch is made is given by Eq. (3-12). The depreciation amounts and book values for this part of the example are given in Table 3-5. This table shows that the switch to straight-line depreciation occurs in the sixth year. The declining-balance depreciation amounts are calculated using Eq. (3-9) and the straight-line amounts are calculated using the left-hand side of Eq. (3-12). For example, the straight-line amounts for the first two years are

$$\frac{100,000 - 20,000}{8} = \$10,000$$

$$\frac{84,370 - 20,000}{7} = \$\ 9,196$$

SINKING-FUND DEPRECIATION

Sinking-fund depreciation is based on a series of equal annual deposits over the depreciation life that are equal to the depreciable amount (initial

TABLE 3-5

Declining-Balance Depreciation with Switchover to Straight-Line Depreciation

$a = 0.1563$

End of Year	Depreciation Comparison		Final Depreciation	Book Value
	Declining-Balance	Straight-Line		
0	—	—	—	$100,000
1	$15,630	$10,000	$15,630	84,370
2	13,187	9,196	13,187	71,183
3	11,126	8,531	11,126	60,057
4	9,387	8,011	9,387	50,670
5	7,921	7,668	7,921	42,749
6	6,682	7,583	7,583	35,166
7	—	—	7,583	27,583
8	—	—	7,583	20,000

cost minus salvage). That is, an equal annual amount, A, that is equal to

$$A = (P - L)(A/F\ i,n) \qquad (3\text{-}13)$$

where n is the depreciation life and i is some specified interest rate. The depreciation amount in any year consists of the sinking-fund deposit given by Eq. (3-13) and interest on the accumulated fund. The resulting expression, after algebraic simplification is,

$$D_j = (P - L)(A/F\ i,n)(F/P\ i,\ (j - 1)) \qquad (3\text{-}14)$$

The book value is given by

$$B_j = P - (P - L)(A/F\ i,n)(F/A\ i,j) \qquad (3\text{-}15)$$

The sinking-fund depreciation model assumes that an asset depreciates at an increasing rate. Consequently, it is rarely used for tax computations. However, it is used on occasion by governmental agencies and thus is included in this text.

Example 3-4

Determine the depreciation schedule for an asset that has an initial cost of \$100,000, a salvage value of \$10,000, and a depreciation life of eight years using sinking-fund depreciation and an interest rate of 12%.

The depreciation schedule is calculated using Eqs. (3-14) and (3-15) and is shown in Table 3-6.

Sample calculations follow for the first two years.

$$D_1 = (100,000 - 10,000)(A/F\ 12,8)(F/P\ 12,0)$$

$$= (90,000)(0.0813)(1.000)$$

$$= \$7,317$$

TABLE 3-6

Sinking-Fund Depreciation

End of Year	Depreciation Amount	Book Value
0	—	\$100,000
1	\$ 7,317	92,683
2	8,195	84,488
3	9,176	75,312
4	10,280	65,032
5	11,517	53,515
6	12,893	40,622
7	14,444	26,178
8	16,178	10,000

$$D_2 = (100,000 - 10,000)(A/F\ 12,8)(F/P\ 12,1)$$
$$= 90,000(0.0813)(1.12)$$
$$= \$8,195$$

USAGE DEPRECIATION

In the previous depreciation models, depreciation is based entirely on time. In some instances, depreciation models are based on usage. In these instances, the yearly depreciation amount is calculated by

$$D_j = \frac{P - L}{U}(U_j) \tag{3-16}$$

where U is the total usage expected during the lifetime of the asset and U_j is the usage during the year j. The units of U and U_j depend on the type of asset. For example, earth-moving equipment often uses cubic yards. For tax purposes, depreciation amounts are calculated at the end of a particular year since U_j must be the *actual* usage. If a depreciation schedule is to be determined from the standpoint of estimating capital recovery, then yearly values for U_j must be estimated.

Example 3-5

A certain piece of earth-moving equipment has an initial cost of $75,000, a salvage value of $10,000, and an estimated lifetime usage of two million cubic yards. Determine the depreciation amount for a particular year if the usage is 80,000 cubic yards.

The depreciation amount using Eq. (3-16) is

$$D_j = \frac{75,000 - 10,000}{2,000,000}(80,000)$$
$$= \$2,600$$

DEPLETION

Depletion allowances are applicable when the consumption of natural resources (gold, silver, timber, oil, etc.) are involved. Two methods are used to determine depletion allowances: (1) cost depletion and (2) percentage depletion. Because the determination of depletion allowances is directly related to tax considerations, a detailed discussion of depletion is deferred until Chapter 4.

CAPITAL RECOVERY AND RETURN

In economic analyses the recovery of the invested capital and a return on the yearly unrecovered capital must be included. This is analogous to loaning money. The principal (invested capital) must be recovered as well as interest (a return). If it is assumed that the yearly depreciation amounts equal the yearly amounts of capital recovered, then the yearly capital recovery and return, $(CR)_j$, is

$$(CR)_j = D_j + (i)B_{j-1} \qquad (3\text{-}17)$$

where i is the rate of return on the unrecovered capital. If Eq. (3-17) and a 10% return are applied to the values given in Table 3-1, the results shown in Table 3-7 are obtained. An equivalent annual amount of the capital recovery and return ECR, is

$$\begin{aligned}
ECR &= \big(21{,}250(P/F\ 10{,}1) + 20{,}125(P/F\ 10{,}2) \\
&\quad + \ldots + 13{,}375(P/F\ 10{,}8)\big)(A/P\ 10{,}8) \\
&= (95{,}335)(0.1875) \\
&= \$17{,}875
\end{aligned}$$

If this same approach is taken with the values given in Table 3-2, the results given in Table 3-8 are obtained. The equivalent annual amount for the capital recovery and return amounts in Table 3-8 is

$$\begin{aligned}
ECR &= \big(30{,}000(P/F\ 10{,}1) + 25{,}500(P/F\ 10{,}2) \\
&\quad + \ldots + 3{,}750(P/F\ 10{,}8)\big)(A/P\ 10{,}8) \\
&= \$17{,}875
\end{aligned}$$

TABLE 3-7

Capital Recovery and Return (Straight-Line Depreciation)

End of Year	Capital Recovery (Depreciation)	Capital Unrecovered (Book Value)	Return on Unrecovered Capital	Capital Recovery and Return
0	—	$100,000	—	—
1	$11,250	88,750	$10,000	$21,250
2	11,250	77,500	8,875	20,125
3	11,250	66,250	7,750	19,000
4	11,250	55,000	6,625	17,875
5	11,250	43,750	5,500	16,750
6	11,250	32,500	4,375	15,625
7	11,250	21,250	3,250	14,500
8	11,250	10,000	2,125	13,375

TABLE 3-8

Capital Recovery and Return (SYD Depreciation)

End of Year	Capital Recovery (Depreciation)	Capital Unrecovered (Book Value)	Return on Unrecovered Capital	Capital Recovery and Return
0	—	$100,000	—	—
1	$20,000	80,000	$10,000	$30,000
2	17,500	62,500	8,000	25,500
3	15,000	47,500	6,250	21,250
4	12,500	35,000	4,750	17,250
5	10,000	25,000	3,500	13,500
6	7,500	17,500	2,500	10,000
7	5,000	12,500	1,750	6,750
8	2,500	10,000	1,250	3,750

which is the same value obtained using straight-line depreciation. Further, if the ECR is calculated using the relationship

$$\text{ECR} = (P - L)(A/P\ i,n) + L(i) \qquad (3\text{-}18)$$

the result is

$$\text{ECR} = (100,000 - 10,000)(A/P\ 10,8) + 10,000\ (.10)$$

$$= 90,000\,(0.1875) + 1,000$$

$$= \$17,875$$

which also gives the same result as the previous two cases. In fact, the same result ($17,875) is obtained regardless of the depreciation model. That is, *Eq. (3-18) is independent of the depreciation model.* Consequently, Eq. (3-18) provides a convenient method for determining the *equivalent* annual amount of capital recovery and return. Eq. (3-18) is particularly useful in making cost comparisons and replacement studies (topics discussed later). It is introduced at this point because of its relationship to depreciation.

PROBLEMS

3-1. Using straight-line depreciation, determine the depreciation schedule for an asset that has an initial cost of $80,000, a salvage value of $8,000, and a depreciation life of nine years.

3-2. Using straight-line depreciation, determine the depreciation schedule for an asset that has an initial cost of $64,000, a salvage value of zero, and a depreciation life of eight years.

3-3. Using sum-of-the-years-digits depreciation, determine the depreciation schedule for an asset that has an initial cost of $100,000, a salvage value of $10,000, and a depreciation life of nine years.

3-4. Using sum-of-the-years-digits depreciation, determine the depreciation schedule for an asset that has an initial cost of $165,000, a salvage value of zero, and a depreciation life of ten years.

3-5. Using sinking-fund depreciation, determine the depreciation schedule for an asset that has an initial cost of $90,000, a salvage value of $9,000, and a depreciation life of eight years. Assume $i = 12\%$.

3-6. Repeat Problem 3-5 using a salvage value of zero.

3-7. Using declining-balance depreciation, determine the depreciation schedule for an asset that has an initial cost of $80,000, a salvage value of $10,000, and depreciation life of ten years. Use Eq. (3-10) for the rate.

3-8. Repeat Problem 3-7 using double declining-balance depreciation and a switch to straight-line depreciation on the basis of Eq. (3-12).

3-9. Using double declining-balance depreciation, determine the depreciation schedule for an asset that has an initial cost of $80,000, a salvage value of zero, and a depreciation life of ten years. Switch to straight-line depreciation on the basis of Eq. (3-12).

3-10. Using usage depreciation and the estimated yearly usage given below, determine the depreciation schedule for an asset that has an initial cost of $100,000, a salvage value of $10,000, and an estimated lifetime usage of 5.5 million pounds.

Year	Estimated Usage (Pounds)
1	1,000,000
2	2,000,000
3	500,000
4	1,000,000
5	1,000,000

3-11. If an asset has an initial cost of $30,000, a salvage value of $6,000, and a depreciation life of 20 years, determine the depreciation amount for the fourth year using:
(a) Straight-line depreciation.
(b) Sum-of-the-years-digits depreciation.
(c) Sinking-fund depreciation with $i = 10\%$.

       (d) Declining-balance depreciation using Eq. (3-10) for the rate.

       (e) Double declining-balance depreciation.

3-12. Determine the book values at the end of the fourth year using the data given in Problem 3-11.

3-13. Determine the estimated annual amounts of capital recovery plus a 12% return for the data given in Problem 3-5. Using these results, calculate an equivalent annual amount and check this result with the value obtained from Eq. (3-18).

3-14. Repeat Problem 3-13 using the data given in Problem 3-8 and a return of 10%.

3-15. Repeat Problem 3-13 using the data given in Problem 3-9 and a return of 10%.

3-16. Repeat Problem 3-13 using the data given in Problem 3-10 and a return of 10%.

3-17. If an asset has an initial cost of $100,000, a salvage value of $10,000, and a depreciation life of ten years, determine the following:

       (a) The estimated capital recovery plus a 10% return for the fourth year assuming sum-of-the-years-digits depreciation.

       (b) The equivalent capital recovery plus a 10% return for the fourth year assuming sum-of-the-years-digits depreciation.

4

TAXES

This chapter discusses certain tax regulations that have an effect on some of the topics considered in later chapters. These discussions of tax effects are limited to corporations. Tax regulations regarding individuals are not considered.

Over the past years, there have been many changes in the procedures and rates used to compute a corporation's tax liability. There is every reason to believe that there will be more changes in the future. Consequently, it is always desirable to check current tax regulations to be sure that the procedures or rates presented in this chapter have not been changed.

FEDERAL INCOME TAXES

Beginning in 1979, federal income taxes for corporations are assessed in the following manner: 17% on the first $25,000 of taxable income, 20% on the next $25,000, 30% on the next $25,000, 40% on the next $25,000, and 46% on the taxable income above $100,000.

Example 4-1

Determine the income tax liability for a company with the following taxable incomes: (a) $20,000, (b) $30,000, (c) $60,000, (d) $90,000, and (e) $130,000.

The tax liabilities, t', for the various taxable incomes are shown below:

Part a: $t' = 20,000(0.17)$
$= \$3,400$

Part b: $t' = 25,000(0.17) + (30,000 - 25,000)(0.20)$
$= \$5,250$

Part c: $t' = 25,000(0.17) + 25,000(0.20) + (60,000 - 50,000)(0.30)$
$= \$12,250$

Part d: $t' = 25,000(0.17) + 25,000(0.20) + 25,000(0.30)$
$+ (90,000 - 75,000)(0.40)$
$= \$22,750$

Part e: $t' = 25,000(0.17) + 25,000(0.20) + 25,000(0.30)$
$+ 25,000(0.40) + (130,000 - 100,000)(0.46)$
$= \$40,550$

Example 4-1 shows the present method for calculating a company's total federal income tax liability and provides a basis for the subsequent discussion of *incremental* federal income taxes.

Change in

Incremental Federal Income Taxes The methods and procedures presented in this book for making economic analyses are based on an incremental approach. That is, the economic desirability of an investment and the comparison of alternatives are based on the *yearly incremental changes* in a company's income, costs, and taxes that are estimated to result from some particular endeavor or investment. For the purposes of this book, the yearly incremental federal income tax is determined by

$$t = (G - C - I - D_t)(T) \qquad (4\text{-}1)$$

where

t = incremental federal income tax for a particular year

G = yearly change in income (receipts, sales, savings, or revenues) as a result of some investment

C = yearly change in cost of goods sold (labor and materials) and other deductions (state and local taxes, executive salaries, advertising costs, etc.) as a result of some investment

I = yearly change in interest paid on debt obligations as a result of some investment

D_t = yearly change in the tax depreciation allowance resulting from some investment

$(G - C - I - D_t)$ = yearly incremental taxable income resulting from some investment

T = incremental federal income tax rate

The cost of goods sold should be clearly understood. It is the cost associated with the sale of those items that provided the gross income. It is not necessarily the costs for the tax period. For example, if a company produces 5,000 items in a particular year but only sells 4,000 items in the same year, then only the costs associated with the 4,000 items are deductible. The other 1,000 items enter a finished-goods inventory, and when sold their costs are then deducted. This procedure can result in an investment requiring an increase in a company's working capital requirements. Working capital is discussed in a later chapter.

The incremental federal income tax rate, T, is dependent upon a company's existing taxable income. A company having an existing taxable income in excess of $100,000 has a tax rate of 46% (see Example 4-1) on any additional increment of taxable income. For companies with existing taxable incomes less than $100,000, the incremental tax rate depends on the existing taxable income and whether the incremental change in taxable income changes the rate. The incremental tax rates for various taxable income are shown in Table 4-1.

Example 4-2

A company's current taxable income is $120,000. If this company undertakes an investment that increases gross income by $20,000 per year, costs by $5,000 per year, interest by $1,000 per year, and depreciation by $1,500 per year, determine the following:

a. The yearly increase in taxes resulting from the investment.
b. Repeat Part a if the company's current taxable income is $80,000.
c. Repeat Part a if the company's current taxable income is $90,000.

TABLE 4-1
Incremental Tax Rates

Corporate Taxable Income	Incremental Tax Rate, %
$0 –$ 25,000	17
25,001– 50,000	20
50,001– 75,000	30
75,001– 100,000	40
greater than 100,000	46

The increase in taxable income resulting from the investment is

$$(20{,}000 - 5{,}000 - 1{,}000 - 1{,}500) = \$12{,}500$$

Therefore, the yearly increase in taxes for Part a is

$$t = (12{,}500)(0.46)$$
$$= \$5{,}750 \text{ per year}$$

An incremental tax rate of 46% is used since the current taxable income is above \$100,000. In Part b the incremental tax rate is 40% since the current taxable income (\$80,000) and the increase in taxable income (\$12,500) remain within the 40% tax rate range. Therefore, the yearly increase in taxes is

$$t = (12{,}500)(0.40)$$
$$= \$5{,}000 \text{ per year}$$

The solution to Part c is not as direct as the solution to Parts a and b because the taxable income plus the change in taxable income changes the tax rate. There is a change from a tax rate of 40% to 46%. Where the incremental tax rate is changed, the incremental taxes must be determined by calculating the taxes for the two taxable incomes and then taking the difference. In this example, the taxes for a taxable income of \$90,000 are

$$t' = 25{,}000(0.17) + 25{,}000(0.20) + 25{,}000(0.30)$$
$$+ (90{,}000 - 75{,}000)(0.40)$$
$$= \$22{,}750$$

and for a taxable income of \$102,500 (\$90,000 plus \$12,000) the taxes are

$$t' = 25{,}000(0.17) + 25{,}000(0.20) + 25{,}000(0.30)$$
$$+ 25{,}000(0.40) + (102{,}500 - 100{,}000)(0.46)$$
$$= \$27{,}900$$

Consequently, the incremental taxes are

$$t = 27{,}900 - 22{,}750$$
$$= \$5{,}150$$

and, as an extension, the incremental tax rate is

$$\frac{5{,}150}{12{,}500} = 0.412$$
$$= 41.2\%$$

CAPITAL GAINS AND LOSSES

Federal tax laws provide special treatment for the gains and losses resulting from the sales and exchanges of qualified capital assets. In general, a capital asset is any property. However, these same tax laws *exclude* the following types of property:

1. Raw material inventories.
2. Property held primarily for sale to customers in the ordinary course of a taxpayer's trade or business.
3. Notes or accounts receivable acquired in the ordinary course of trade or business.
4. Depreciable business property.
5. Copyrights.

Examples of capital assets that do qualify for the special tax treatment are bonds, stocks, and similar securities *provided they are held for investment.* Debt obligations sold or exchanged by financial institutions do not qualify. Also, stocks held by a dealer in securities do not qualify unless they are held for investment.

If a capital asset is sold for more or less than its original cost, the result is a capital gain or loss. If the capital asset is held for over one year, it is a *long-term* capital gain or loss. If it is held for one year or less, it is a *short-term* capital gain or loss. Short-term gains and losses are determined for each sale of a capital asset and then added to obtain a net short-term gain or loss. Long-term gains and losses are treated in a similar manner. These results are then merged to determine the tax treatment of the net gains and losses. This merger of the net gains and losses can give various combinations of gains and losses. These combinations and their tax treatment are given in Table 4-2.

For corporations a net result indicated as a capital gain in Table 4-2 can be treated in two ways for tax purposes. The choice is up to the corporation. The first way is to treat the net result as ordinary income, and the second way is to tax the net result at a rate of 28%. Obviously corporations with tax rates less than 28% will choose to treat the capital gain as ordinary income, while corporations with tax rates in excess of 28% will choose the 28% rate.

A net result indicated as a capital loss in Table 4-2 can be carried back to each of the three years preceding the loss and used to offset gains. Any remaining excess may be carried forward for five years. *When carried back or forward the loss is treated as a short-term loss regardless of whether it was a short-term or long-term loss when it occurred.*

TABLE 4-2
Tax Treatment of Capital Gains and Losses

Result of Long-Term Transactions	Result of Short-Term Transactions	Net Result	Tax Treatment		
			Capital Gain	Capital Loss	Ordinary Income
Long-term loss	None	Long-term loss		X	
	Short-term gain	Long-term loss		X	
		or			
		Short-term gain			X
	Short-term loss	Long-term loss		X	
		and			
		Short-term loss		X	
Long-term gain	None	Long-term gain	X		
	Short-term gain	Long-term gain	X		
		and			
		Short-term gain			X
	Short-term loss	Long-term gain	X		
		or			
		Short-term loss		X	
None	Short-term gain	Short-term gain			X
	Short-term loss	Short-term loss		X	

Example 4-3

During a particular tax year, a corporation has the transactions shown in Table 4-3. Assuming these transactions qualify for the special tax treatment given capital gains and losses, determine the following:

    a. The incremental taxes resulting from the transactions in Table 4-3 if the corporation's taxable income before consideration of these transactions is $40,000.

    b. Repeat Part a if the corporation's taxable income is $90,000.

    c. Repeat Part a if the corporation's taxable income is $150,000.

    d. Repeat Part c if the purchase price for the eighth transaction is changed from $6,000 to $2,000.

The first step in this example is to convert the data given in Table 4-3 to the form shown in Table 4-4. This table is obtained by subtracting the purchase price from the selling prices given in Table 4-3. The values in parentheses indicate losses. The long-term or short-term classification depends on the time held given in Table 4-3. Combining the totals of the long-term transactions, $6,000, and the short-term transactions ($1,200), gives a net result of a $4,800 long-term capital gain (see Table 4-2).

TABLE 4-3
Data for Example 4-3

Transaction	Selling Price	Purchase Price	Time Held in Months
1	$10,000	$ 8,000	24
2	6,000	7,000	36
3	5,000	5,000	8
4	15,000	12,000	24
5	9,000	7,000	6
6	7,000	5,000	15
7	12,000	12,500	6
8	4,000	6,000	4
9	6,000	6,700	9

For Part a the incremental taxes are

$$t = 4,800\,(0.20)$$

$$= \$960$$

A 20% tax rate is used in this part because the taxable income ($40,000) indicates a rate lower than the 28% rate. Consequently, a corporation would choose to treat the capital gain of $4,800 as ordinary income.

For Part b the incremental taxes are

$$t = 4,800\,(0.28)$$

$$= \$1,344$$

TABLE 4-4
Capital Gains and Losses for Example 4-3

Transaction	Long-Term	Short-Term
1	$ 2,000	—
2	(1,000)	—
3	—	$ 0
4	3,000	—
5	—	2,000
6	2,000	—
7	—	(500)
8	—	(2,000)
9	—	(700)
Total	$ 6,000	$(1,200)

The maximum rate of 28% is used in this part because taxable income ($90,000) indicates an incremental rate greater than 28%.

The solution to Part c is the same as Part b and for the same reason.

With the change in purchase price given in Part d, the total of the long-term transactions is a gain of $6,000 and the total of the short-term transactions is a gain of $2,800. Therefore, the incremental taxes are

$$t = 6,000\,(0.28) + 2,800\,(0.46)$$

$$= \$2,968$$

An incremental tax rate of 28% is applied to the long-term capital gain because of the incremental tax rate (46%) implied by the taxable income. The 46% is applied to the short-term gain because it is treated as ordinary income (see Table 4-2).

DEPRECIABLE PROPERTY AND BUSINESS REAL ESTATE TAXES

The tax treatment of the gains and losses resulting from the disposal of depreciable business property and business real estate is largely based on three sections of the tax laws: Section 1245, Section 1250, and Section 1231.

Section 1245 property is depreciable property that is used as an integral part of manufacturing, production, extraction, or the furnishing of transportation, communications, electrical energy, gas, water or sewage disposal services. It does *not* include buildings or their structural components.

A gain (selling price minus book value) on the sale of Section 1245 property is taxable as ordinary income *to the extent of the depreciation deducted*. A loss on the sale of Section 1245 property is a Section 1231 loss. If Section 1245 property is sold for an amount that is greater than the original purchase price (initial cost), the difference between the selling price and initial cost is a Section 1231 gain. The remainder of the gain (initial cost minus book value) is taxed as ordinary income. These relationships are shown in Figure 4-1 where S_1, S_2, and S_3 refer to various selling prices.

Section 1231 provides for a special tax treatment of the gains and losses on the disposition of Section 1245 property, Section 1250 property, and business real estate (land). This section states that after the gains and losses have been determined for these types of property, the gains and losses are combined. If the gains exceed the losses, then each gain and loss is treated as though it was derived from the sale of a long-term capital

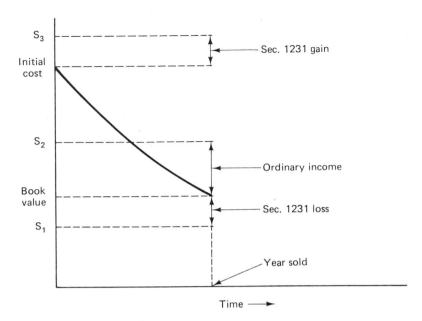

FIGURE 4-1   Gains and Losses from Section 1245 Property

asset (assuming the asset was held for more than one year). If the gains do not exceed the losses, each gain and loss is treated as though it was *not* derived from the sale of a capital asset. This results in treating the net loss as a fully deductible business expense (a reduction in ordinary income).

Example 4-4

A company purchased a Section 1245 asset for $120,000, and after five years the same asset had a book value of $80,000. If the company's current taxable income is $150,000 before consideration of the gains and losses from the sale of this asset, determine the company's total taxes for the following selling prices of the 1245 asset: (a) $100,000, (b) $70,000, and (c) $200,000.

The taxes on the current taxable income are

$$t = 25,000\,(0.17) + 25,000\,(0.20) + 25,000\,(0.30)$$
$$+ 25,000\,(0.40) + (150,000 - 100,000)\,(0.46)$$

$$= \$49,750$$

For Part a, a selling price of $100,000 means a gain of

$$100,000 - 80,000 = \$20,000$$

This gain is treated as ordinary income (see Figure 4-1). Consequently, the total taxes are

$$t' = 49{,}750 + 20{,}000\,(0.46)$$
$$= \$58{,}950$$

An incremental tax rate of 46% is used since the company's current taxable income is greater than $100,000.

For Part b, a selling price of $70,000 means a loss of

$$80{,}000 - 70{,}000 = \$10{,}000$$

Since this is Section 1245 property, Section 1231 applies and this loss can be taken as an ordinary loss. Consequently, the company's taxes are

$$t' = 49{,}750 - (10{,}000)\,(0.46)$$
$$= \$45{,}150$$

For Part c, a selling price of $200,000 means a Section 1231 gain of

$$200{,}000 - 120{,}000 = \$80{,}000$$

and ordinary income of

$$120{,}000 - 80{,}000 = \$40{,}000$$

Consequently the company's taxes are

$$t' = 49{,}750 + 40{,}000\,(0.46) + 80{,}000\,(0.28)$$
$$= \$90{,}550$$

The Section 1231 gain of $80,000 is taxed at a 28% rate since it qualifies as a long-term capital gain. The difference between the original cost ($120,000) and the book value ($80,000) is taxed as ordinary income due to the requirements of Section 1245.

In this example, the taxes are calculated on the basis that only one Section 1245 asset was sold. If more than one is sold, the Section 1231 gains and losses are combined to determine the tax treatment. Also, this example is worked on the basis of single asset item depreciation. The procedures in this example are not necessarily applicable in the case of group depreciation (discussed later).

Section 1250 property is depreciable property that is not included in Section 1245. It includes buildings and their structural components. Section 1250 states that any excess depreciation is taxed as ordinary income and any remaining amount is a Section 1231 gain. Losses on the disposal of Section 1250 property, as previously mentioned, are classified as Section 1231 losses.

Example 4-5 _____

A Section 1250 asset has an initial cost of $700,000, a salvage value of $50,000, and a depreciation life of 25 years. If sum-of-the-years-digits depreciation is used for tax purposes, determine the incremental tax effects of selling this asset after five years, assuming a taxable income in excess of $100,000, for the following selling prices: (a) $550,000, (b) $620,000, (c) $400,000.

The first step is to calculate the yearly depreciation amounts using SYD depreciation. These results are shown in Table 4-5. The next steps are to calculate the straight-line depreciation amounts and the excess depreciation amounts. These results are also shown in Table 4-5.

Now, the book value of the asset is the initial cost minus the total depreciation; namely,

$$B_5 = 700,000 - 230,000$$
$$= \$470,000$$

Therefore in Part a the gain with a selling price of $550,000 is

$$550,000 - 470,000 = \$80,000$$

This amount is taxed as ordinary income since it is less than the total excess depreciation ($100,000). Consequently, the incremental taxes are

$$t = 80,000\,(0.46)$$
$$= \$36,800$$

With the selling price in Part b, the gain is

$$620,000 - 470,000 = \$150,000$$

TABLE 4-5
Data for Example 4-5

End of Year	SYD Depreciation	Straight-Line Depreciation	Excess Depreciation
1	$50,000	$26,000	$24,000
2	48,000	26,000	22,000
3	46,000	26,000	20,000
4	44,000	26,000	18,000
5	42,000	26,000	16,000
Total	230,000	130,000	100,000

In this case $100,000 is taxed as ordinary income, and the remaining $50,000 is a Section 1231 gain. Consequently, the incremental taxes are

$$t = 100,000\,(0.46) + 50,000\,(0.28)$$
$$= \$60,000$$

In Part c, a selling price of $400,000 means a loss of

$$470,000 - 400,000 = \$70,000$$

which is a Section 1231 loss. Consequently, the incremental taxes are

$$t = -70,000\,(0.46)$$
$$= \$-32,200$$

where the negative sign implies a reduction in taxes.

In Example 4-4 as in Example 4-5 the taxes are calculated on the basis of the sale of only one asset and single asset depreciation. In the case of the sales of both Section 1245 and Section 1250 property, the Section 1231 gains are combined and the Section 1231 losses are combined. Then these results are combined to determine if there is a net Section 1231 gain or loss. If there is ordinary income involved in the sales of several Section 1245 and 1250 assets, the total amount of this income is taxed as ordinary income regardless of the net result of the combination of 1231 gains and losses.

Example 4-6

A company has disposed of certain Section 1245 and 1250 properties. The resulting Section 1231 gains, losses, and ordinary income are shown in Table 4-6. Using these results and assuming the company's taxable income is well in excess of $100,000, determine the incremental taxes resulting from these transactions.

The incremental taxes are

$$t = 7,000\,(0.46) + (5,000 - 2,000)\,(0.28)$$
$$= \$4,060$$

In determining this result, it should be noted that the Section 1231 gain and loss are combined and the net result, $3,000, is taxed as a capital gain (28%). It is *incorrect* to calculate the incremental taxes in the following manner:

$$t = 7,000\,(0.46) + 5,000\,(0.28) - 2,000\,(0.46)$$
$$= \$3,700$$

TABLE 4-6
Data for Example 4-6

Transaction	Ordinary Income	Section 1231 Gain	Section 1231 Loss
1	$4,000	$5,000	—
2	$3,000	—	—
3	—	—	$2,000

As an extension to this example, if the Section 1231 loss of $2,000 in Table 4-6 is changed to a loss of $6,000, the incremental taxes are

$$t = 7,000\,(0.46) - 1,000\,(0.46)$$

$$= \$2,760$$

since the combination of the Section 1231 gain and loss results in a net loss of $1,000 and this loss under Section 1231 is taken as an *ordinary loss*.

Example 4-6 points out that the appropriate tax rate for a particular Section 1231 transaction cannot be determined without knowledge of gains and losses from other Section 1231 transactions that occur in the same tax year. Unless, of course, there is only one transaction. If there is information about other Section 1231 transactions it should be used. However, the usual situation is that such information is unknown because most economic evaluations involve an estimation of *future* economic events. An estimation of future Section 1231 gains and losses is difficult (if not impossible). Consequently, the approach taken in this text is to approximate the tax effects of Section 1231 gains and losses on the basis of a single transaction. This approach is used in the case of replacement studies considered later in this text.

The discussion of Section 1245, Section 1250, and Section 1231 gains and losses up to this point is applicable when *single asset (item) depreciation* accounts are used and an asset is retired. It may or may not be applicable in the cases of exchanges of equipment or when *multiple asset depreciation* accounts are used. In general, the gains and losses resulting from *unlike* exchanges are recognized (taxes are paid on gains and tax benefits from losses are received) when single asset depreciation accounts are used. In the case of *like-kind* exchanges, gains and losses are in general not recognized (with some qualifications). By far, the usual case in economic evaluations is a like-kind exchange. Consequently, the case of unlike exchanges is not considered in this discussion. Basically, a like-kind exchange occurs when property (equipment) of the same nature or character (not its grade or quality) is exchanged. From the standpoint of future discussions, the important case is the like-kind exchange of property (equipment) used for *productive purposes*. For example, when old equipment is traded for new equipment to be used for the same productive purpose, no gain or loss is recognized since this is a like-kind exchange.

Example 4-7

A company exchanged an old machine, used for productive purposes, which had a salvage value of $20,000, for a similar new machine with a list price of $35,000. In addition, the company paid $12,000 cash (referred to as boot in tax terminology). In this case the realized gain of

$$35,000 - (20,000 + 12,000) = \$3,000$$

is not recognized (taxes are not paid on the gain of $3,000) since this is a like-kind exchange. Also, the basis of the new machine (first cost for depreciation purposes) is $32,000 (the sum of the salvage value and cash paid).

If the list price of the new equipment had been $30,000, the loss of

$$(20,000 + 12,000) - 30,000 = \$2,000$$

is not recognized (no tax benefit). The basis in this case is still the sum of the salvage and cash paid ($32,000).

Example 4-7 only presents the tax situation from the standpoint of the company that purchased the new machine. It does not consider the tax situation of the seller of the new machine. In the case of the seller, *assuming he produces the machine for sale purposes* (not used for production purposes), the $12,000 is income and the old machine enters the seller's inventories at its fair market value (not necessarily its book salvage value or its trade-in value). In the case of a like-kind exchange where both parties use the exchanged equipment for productive purposes, the basic tax rule is, no gain or loss is recognized when boot (cash) is *given*. When boot is *received*, gain is recognized only to the extent of the boot received and losses are not recognized.

Example 4-8

Suppose two parties, X and Y, make a like-kind exchange of used property that both hold for productive purposes. The current adjusted basis (book salvage value) of X's property is $3,000 and Y's property is $3,700. In addition, X gives Y $600 in cash. For the sets of fair market values

(FMV) given below, determine the tax treatment of the gains and losses. Also, determine the basis of the equipment received.

a. $(FMV)_X = \$3,100$ and $(FMV)_Y = \$3,600$
b. $(FMV)_X = \$3,000$ and $(FMV)_Y = \$3,800$
c. $(FMV)_X = \$3,800$ and $(FMV)_Y = \$3,500$

The gains and losses realized by X for Parts a, b, and c, respectively, are

$$\text{gain} = (3,000 + 600) - 3,600$$
$$= \$0$$
$$\text{gain} = 3,800 - (3,000 + 600)$$
$$= \$200$$
$$\text{loss} = (3,000 + 600) - 3,500$$
$$= \$100$$

These gains and losses are not recognized since X gave boot of $600. The basis of the property acquired by X for each part is $3,600 (the sum of the adjusted basis and boot given). For Y, the gains and losses are

$$\text{gain} = (3,100 + 600) - 3,700$$
$$= \$0$$
$$\text{loss} = 3,700 - (3,000 + 600)$$
$$= \$100$$
$$\text{gain} = (3,800 + 600) - 3,700$$
$$= \$700$$

There is no recognition of the loss or, of course, the zero gain. However, in the case of the $700 gain, the gain is recognized (taxes paid) on $600 of the gain since this is the extent of the boot *received*. The additional $100 gain is not recognized. From the standpoint of receiving boot in a like-kind exchange, the basis of the property received is the adjusted basis of the property transferred minus cash received plus gain recognized or minus loss recognized. Consequently, the basis for Parts a and b is $3,100; the adjusted basis of $3,700 minus the money received ($600). In Part c, the basis is $3,700: the adjusted basis of $3,700 minus the money received ($600) plus the gain recognized ($600).

Multiple Asset Depreciation Accounts   When a number of assets are combined with the same or different depreciation lives and depre-

ciated using a single rate, this is called *multiple asset depreciation*. This type of depreciation accounting uses group, composite, and classified accounts. These accounts are often separated on the basis of location, acquisition dates, and use. Group accounts contain similar assets with approximately the same average life. Composite accounts contain assets regardless of their character or lives. Classified accounts are established on the basis of their use without regard to the useful life of individual components.

In group and composite accounts the life used in determining yearly depreciation amounts is established in one of two ways: (1) an average of the asset lives in the account or (2) the longest-lived asset in the account. The average life is *not* simply an arithmetic average. Rather it is roughly a weighted average of the depreciation amounts of the individual components in the account. The depreciation amounts are determined using straight-line depreciation.

In retiring or exchanging assets that are components within a multiple asset account, the recognition of gains and losses is dependent on whether the account uses an average life or the longest-lived asset approach and whether the retirement or exchange is classified as normal or abnormal. In general, a retirement or exchange is normal if the retirement or exchange occurs within the range of component lives used to establish the multiple account depreciation life. If an asset is retired prior to this range, it is an abnormal retirement. Also, retirements due to casualty or *extraordinary* obsolescence are classified as abnormal. In the case of an average life account and normal retirement, losses are not recognized. Gains, in general, are also not recognized. However, if a gain when added to the depreciation reserve (account) causes the reserve to exceed the unadjusted basis of the account, the excess above the unadjusted basis is recognized. If the retirement is classified as abnormal, gains and losses are recognized. In the case of a longest-lived account, gains and losses are recognized for both normal and abnormal retirements, with certain limitations on the amount of the gain recognized in cases of exchanges (replacements) resulting from casualty.

Exchanges of components within a multiple asset account are handled in the same manner as a single asset account except for the computation of the adjusted basis (book value) of a particular component. In the case of an average life account and normal retirement, the adjusted basis is the salvage value of the component. In an abnormal retirement, the adjusted basis is computed as if it were a single asset account using the average life. In the case of a longest-lived account, the adjusted basis for a component is computed as if it were a single asset using the longest life for both normal and abnormal retirements.

In the final analysis, the inclusion of some of the aspects involved in multiple asset depreciation accounts into economic analysis is not possible for the same reason mentioned earlier. That is, the precise inclusion of many tax effects requires a knowledge of the future.

Classified Accounts   The Class Life Asset Depreciation (ADR) System is a classified account. It is a relatively new (June 1971) development in depreciation accounting for tax purposes. The ADR System is designed to reduce disputes regarding depreciation life, salvage values, and the separation of repair expenses from capitalized expenses. This is attempted by allowing lower depreciation lives, a zero salvage value when computing depreciation allowances, and establishing an allowable repair allowance.

The ADR System establishes broad classes of industrial assets and specifies an asset guideline period, an asset depreciation range, and an alloowable repair percentage. Examples of various classes are shown in Table 4-7. The ADR System allows the taxpayer to choose for a particular class of asset, any depreciation life in half-year increments that is in the given asset depreciation range. For example, the depreciation life for class 28.0 can be chosen from 9 through 13 years.

The election to use the ADR System is an annual one. However, if the ADR System is used in a particular year, all eligible property put in service in the same year must use the ADR System. The eligible property is put in vintage accounts. These accounts can be either single asset or multiple asset accounts, but Section 1245 and 1250 property must be kept in separate accounts and depreciation reserves must be maintained for each account.

The guideline repair allowance percentage provided in the ADR System (see Table 4-7) provides a taxpayer with the option of capitalizing or using the repair allowance. For example, the repair allowance in Class 30.1 is 5.0%. This means that if the total (unadjusted) cost of the vintage account is $200,000, then of the yearly expenses associated with this account up to $10,000 can be taken each year as a reduction in ordinary income. Any remaining expenses are put in a new vintage account and treated as capitalized expenditures. If the taxpayer desires, all expenses can be capitalized.

The ADR System allows the use of double declining-balance (for new property), sum-of-the-years-digits, and straight-line depreciation methods. Under the ADR System, permission from the Internal Revenue Service is not required to convert from double declining-balance or sum-of-the-years-digits to straight-line depreciation. As mentioned previously, salvage values are not considered when computing depreciation amounts. However, the total cost cannot be depreciated beyond "a reasonable salvage value."

TABLE 4-7
*Examples of ADR Classes**

| Asset Guideline Class | Description of Assets | Asset Depreciation Range (in Years) | | | Annual Asset Guideline Repair Allowance Percentage |
		Lower Limit	Asset Guideline Period	Upper Limit	
26.2	Manufacture of paper and paper board	9.5	12	14.5	5.5
27.0	Printing, publishing, and allied industries	9	11	13	5.5
28.0	Manufacture of chemicals and allied products	9	11	13	5.5
30.1	Manufacture of rubber products	11	14	17	5.0
.					
.					
.					
35.0	Manufacture of machinery, except electrical and transportation equipment	8	10	12	11.0
35.1	Manufacture of metalworking machinery	9.5	12	14.5	5.5
35.2	Manufacture of other machines	9.5	12	14.5	5.5
.					
.					
.					
	Electric generating equipment:				
40.51	Hydraulic	40	50	60	1.5
40.52	Nuclear	16	20	24	3.0
40.53	Steam	22.5	28	33.5	2.5
40.54	Steam, compressed air, and other power plant equipment	22.5	28	33.5	7.5

* From 1980 tax regulations.

Retirements under the ADR System are classified as either *ordinary or extraordinary retirements*. All retirements of Section 1245 property are ordinary except in cases of casualty or termination of income-producing assets. In the case of casualty, the retirement is extraordinary provided the taxpayer consistently treats such retirements as extraordinary. In the case of termination of income-producing assets, the retirement is considered extraordinary if the total original value of the retired assets is greater than 20% of the total original value of *all* accounts having the same class and vintage. *All retirements of Section 1250 property are extraordinary.*

Under the ADR System, Section 1245 gains and losses are in general not recognized for multiple asset accounts. However, if the proceeds from the gains and losses result in the depreciation reserve exceeding the depreciable amount (cost minus salvage), the excess is recognized as a gain in the year in which it occurs (Section 1245 ordinary income). Losses are not recognized until the last item in the multiple asset account is retired. In the case of *single asset accounts*, gains and losses are recognized. However, if the single asset accounts are essentially multiple asset accounts (single asset accounts with the same class and vintage), the gains and losses are treated as though they are a multiple asset account.

As mentioned earlier all Section 1250 retirements are extraordinary. Consequently, Section 1250 and Section 1231 tax regulations become involved in cases of single asset depreciation accounts. For Section 1250 multiple asset accounts, the retired asset is removed from the vintage account and the depreciation reserve is reduced by the total accumulated depreciation due to the retired asset. The amount of accumulated depreciation is determined using the depreciation method and life established for the total vintage account. This calculation also serves as the basis for determining gain or loss on the retirement of the asset.

It should be noted that in this discussion of the ADR System the emphasis is on *retirements* of assets as opposed to *exchanges* of assets. Under the ADR System, the rules previously discussed concerning the exchange of assets are still applicable.

THE INVESTMENT TAX CREDIT

A federal income tax credit is allowed when investments in certain qualified properties are made. Qualified property is Section 38 property which includes Section 1245 property. Buildings and their components do not qualify unless they are "special buildings." The basic amount that is allowed as a tax credit for *new property* is 10% of the qualified investment. Under certain circumstances (employee stock ownership plans), this investment tax credit can be increased to 11.5%. The approach in this text is to use 10% for the investment tax credit unless otherwise specified. The full 10% (or 11.5%) deduction is only available for investments with a depreciation life of seven years or greater. For depreciation lives less than seven years only a proportion of the full allowance can be used. Table 4-8 shows the proportion for various depreciation lives. The amount of the investment tax credit taken in any one year is limited. The tax credit is applied to the first $25,000 of tax liability, plus 90%

TABLE 4-8
Investment Tax Credit Proportions

Life	Proportion
Less than three years	0
Three and four years	⅓
Five and six years	⅔
Seven or more years	1

(beginning in 1982) of the tax liability exceeding $25,000. Any part of the investment tax credit that is not used because of the limitations can be carried back three years and carried over for seven years. For *used property*, the cost of the property for the basis of computing the investment tax credit is limited to $100,000.

Example 4-9

A taxpayer has a tax liability of $200,000 without consideration of the investment tax credit. He puts in service property that costs $3,000,000 and has a depreciation life of ten years. If the property qualifies for the investment tax credit, what is the taxpayer's final tax liability?

The maximum investment tax credit that can be taken is

$$25,000 + (0.9)(200,000 - 25,000) = \$182,500$$

The investment tax credit is 10% of $3,000,000, or $300,000. Consequently, the final tax liability is

$$200,000 - 182,500 = \$17,500$$

The remaining amount of the investment tax credit

$$300,000 - 182,500 = \$117,500$$

is subject to the carry back and carry over provisions.

There is the possibility of an *investment tax penalty* if Section 38 property is disposed of earlier than its originally estimated depreciation life. This penalty is the difference between the investment tax credit originally taken and the investment tax credit that should have been taken.

Example 4-10

An asset that cost $150,000 was put into service five years ago. It was estimated at that time to have a depreciation life of ten years, and consequently the full investment tax credit of $15,000 was taken. If the asset is now sold, what is the investment tax penalty?

The investment tax credit that should have been taken is two-thirds of the full amount since the life is only five years. Therefore the investment tax penalty is

$$15,000 - \frac{2}{3}(15,000) = \$5,000$$

In cases of like-kind (nontaxable) exchanges of equipment, the application of the investment tax credit is dependent upon whether the exchange is for new or used assets. For example, the basis for determining the investment tax credit for *new equipment* received in a like-kind exchange is the adjusted basis of the transferred property plus any boot (money) given.

Example 4-11

A taxpayer traded in an old asset with an adjusted basis of $15,000 for a *new similar* asset. In addition, the taxpayer paid $5,000.

The basis for the calculation of the investment tax credit in this case is $20,000. Namely, the adjusted basis of the old machine plus the boot ($5,000).

In the case of like-kind exchanges of *used property*, the basis for determining the investment tax credit is equal to its adjusted basis excluding any part of the adjusted basis used in the basis of other property (subject to the $100,000 limitation).

Example 4-12

A taxpayer trades in a *used asset* with an adjusted basis of $6,000 for a used asset. In addition, the taxpayer paid $5,000. The basis of the received asset is $11,000. However, the basis for determining the investment tax credit is $5,000; namely, the $11,000 basis minus the adjusted basis of $6,000 of the traded asset.

As an extension of the case of used property exchanges, a taxpayer sells an asset with an adjusted basis of $7,000 and then buys a used replacement asset for $10,000. The basis for determining the investment tax credit is $3,000 ($10,000 minus $7,000).

DEPLETION

In general, depletion is to the owner of a natural resource (oil, gas, minerals, timber, etc.) property what depreciation is to the owner of depreciable property. Depletion is a procedure for recovering the cost of the property over its life. From a tax standpoint, depreciation and depletion are also similar in their result; namely, a reduction in tax liability.

There are two methods for determining depletion allowances: cost depletion and percentage depletion. Cost depletion is determined using the following relationships:

$$\begin{pmatrix} \text{cost depletion} \\ \text{allowance} \end{pmatrix} = \frac{\text{cost of property}}{\substack{\text{number of units} \\ \text{in property}}} \begin{pmatrix} \text{units sold} \\ \text{during the year} \end{pmatrix} \quad (4\text{-}2)$$

The result determined using Eq. (4-2) is a deduction in determining taxable income. It is important to note that in Eq. (4-2) it is the number of units *sold* not extracted.

Example 4-13

A taxpayer buys a copper mine for $800,000, and it is estimated that the mine contains 1,500,000 tons of ore. The estimated value of the associated land, excluding the ore, is $50,000. If the taxpayer extracts 125,000 tons of ore and sells 100,000 tons of ore, the cost depletion using Eq. (4-2) is

$$\left(\frac{800,000 - 50,000}{1,500,000} \right) (100,000) = \$50,000$$

Percentage depletion (not available for timber) is based, with certain limitations, on a constant percentage of the gross sales of the natural resource. Some of these percentages are listed in Table 4-9 (not a com-

TABLE 4-9
Examples of Percentage Depletion Values

Percentage	Resource
22%	Sulfur, asbestos, uranium produced in the U.S.A.
22%	Regulated natural gas deposits sold under fixed contract
15%	Gold, silver, copper deposits in the U.S.A.
10%	Coal, lignite
5%	Gravel, sand

prehensive list). In general, percentage depletion is not allowed for oil and gas wells. The limitations are (1) the deduction for percentage depletion cannot exceed 50% of the taxable income (without the percentage depletion) and (2) cost depletion must be used if it is greater than percentage depletion. It is interesting to note that this allows the depletion of a natural resource beyond its cost. That is, after the cost of the property is reduced to zero, either through the use of cost or percentage depletion, it is still possible to use percentage depletion.

Example 4-14

A taxpayer owns a uranium mine that was purchased for $10 million. The mine was estimated to have five million tons of uranium ore and the value of the land was zero. Using the data given in Table 4-10, determine the tax liability for Cases A, B, and C.

For Case A, the cost depletion is

$$\frac{10,000,000}{5,000,000}(50,000) = \$100,000$$

and the percentage depletion is

$$(0.22)(250,000) = \$55,000$$

Consequently, the cost depletion is used. Using Eq. (4-1) and substituting the depletion allowance for the depreciation deduction, the incremental taxes are

$$t = (250,000 - 100,000 - 100,000)(0.48)$$

$$= \$24,000$$

In Case B the cost depletion is

$$\frac{10,000,000}{5,000,000}(20,000) = \$40,000$$

TABLE 4-10
Data for Example 4-14

| | Case | | |
	A	B	C
Gross sales	$250,000	$250,000	$400,000
Operating costs and interest	$100,000	$100,000	$250,000
Amount of ore sold (tons)	50,000	20,000	20,000
Tax rate—%	48	48	48

and the percentage depletion is the same as in Case A ($55,000). Since the percentage depletion is greater, a check must be made to be sure that it does not exceed the limitation of 50% of the taxable income which is

$$(0.50)(250,000 - 100,000) = \$75,000$$

Since this is greater than the percentage depletion, the incremental taxes are

$$t = (250,000 - 100,000 - 55,000)(0.48)$$

$$= \$45,600$$

In Case C the cost depletion ($40,000) and the limitation ($75,000) are the same as in Case B. However, the percentage depletion is

$$(0.22)(400,000) = \$88,000$$

Therefore, the incremental taxes are

$$t = (400,000 - 250,000 - 75,000)(0.48)$$

$$= \$36,000$$

TAXES AND INTEREST

As mentioned earlier, interest payments resulting from externally borrowed money are a deduction in computing taxable income. Since interest is a tax deduction, the actual cost of borrowed funds is reduced. For example, if a company has an incremental increase in taxable income of $500,000 as a result of some new investment and its incremental tax rate is 48%, the company's incremental tax increase is

$$t = 500,000\,(0.48)$$

$$= \$240,000$$

Now, if the company also had an incremental increase in interest expense of $100,000 its taxes are

$$t = (500,000 - 100,000)(0.48)$$

$$= \$192,000$$

Consequently, the actual interest expense is

$$100,000 - (240,000 - 192,000) = \$52,000$$

which could also be determined by

$$100,000\,(1 - 0.48) = \$52,000$$

TAXES AND DEPRECIATION

It was implied in Chapter 3 that some depreciation considerations are tax related. This is true. Accelerated depreciation models do provide an economic advantage. This economic advantage lies in the *present worth of taxes paid*. The advantage is not in the *total taxes paid*. In effect, accelerated depreciation models allow the postponement of tax payments. These points can be shown by considering Tables 4-11 and 4-12. In these tables the taxes are calculated using straight-line depreciation, sum-of-the-years-digits depreciation, and the same taxable income before depreciation. They show that the total taxes paid over the eight-year period are the same. However, the present worth of taxes paid is less for sum-of-the-years-digits depreciation which, of course, is more desirable. The same amount for the total taxes paid ($110,400) would be obtained if a different depreciation model had been used. However, the present worth of the taxes paid will vary with the depreciation model. Some generalizations are possible in regard to which depreciation model will provide the lower present value of taxes. For example, sum-of-the-years-digits will always provide a smaller tax present worth than straight-line. Declining-balance is always better than straight-line provided the constant percentage (a) is greater than the reciprocal of the depreciation life. Double declining-balance with optimal switching is always better than straight-line depreciation. (An excellent discussion of depreciation

TABLE 4-11
Income Taxes and Straight-Line Depreciation

End of Year	Taxable Income before Depreciation	Depreciation (See Table 3-1)	Taxable Income after Depreciation	Taxes T = 48%
0	—	—	—	—
1	$40,000	$11,250	$28,750	$13,800
2	40,000	11,250	28,750	13,800
3	40,000	11,250	28,750	13,800
4	40,000	11,250	28,750	13,800
5	40,000	11,250	28,750	13,800
6	40,000	11,250	28,750	13,800
7	40,000	11,250	28,750	13,800
8	40,000	11,250	28,750	13,800

$$\sum \text{taxes} = 8(13,800) = \$110,400$$

$$\text{PW}_t = 13,800(P/A\ 10,8) = \$73,622$$

TABLE 4-12
Income Taxes and Sum-of-the-Years-Digits Depreciation

End of Year	Taxable Income before Depreciation	Depreciation (See Table 3-1)	Taxable Income after Depreciation	Taxes T = 48%
0	—	—	—	—
1	$40,000	$20,000	$20,000	$ 9,600
2	40,000	17,500	22,500	10,800
3	40,000	15,000	25,000	12,000
4	40,000	12,500	27,500	13,200
5	40,000	10,000	30,000	14,400
6	40,000	7,500	32,500	15,600
7	40,000	5,000	35,000	16,800
8	40,000	2,500	37,500	18,000

$$\text{total taxes} = \sum_{x=1}^{8} t_x = \$110,400$$

$$PW_t = \sum_{x=1}^{8} t_x \, (P/F \; 10, x) = \$70,450$$

strategies is presented in L. E. Bussey's *The Economic Analysis of Industrial Projects*.)

Values for the Constant Percentage   In Chapter 3 it is stated that the values for the constant percentage (a) used in the declining-balance depreciation method are sometimes based on the tax laws. For determining tax depreciation amounts, the value of $2/n$ for the constant is limited to *new* tangible property with a depreciation life of three or more years. A value of $1.5/n$ is the limit for *used* tangible property with a depreciation life of three years of more. The value of $1.25/n$ is the limit for *used residential* property with a depreciation life of 20 years or more purchased after July 24, 1969.

Additional First Year Depreciation   In the present tax laws (1981) there is a provision for an additional depreciation allowance. This allowance is 20% of the cost of the qualifying asset. However, it is limited to the first $10,000 of the cost of the asset. This means that the maximum additional depreciation amount is $2,000. Further, this allowance is limited to the taxpayer. That is, a taxpayer can only take the additional depreciation allowance once per tax year.

The allowance cannot be taken for each asset purchased in the same year. Also, the basis of the acquired property is reduced by the amount of the additional depreciation allowance for purposes of calculating yearly depreciation amounts. In general it is advantageous for a taxpayer to use this additional depreciation allowance. However, since it is limited to the taxpayer and has little effect when depreciation amounts are relatively large, the additional first year depreciation amount is not included in later topics.

Salvage Value Adjustment   Under present tax laws the taxpayer may elect to reduce the salvage value (but not below zero) of qualified property by 10% of the basis of the property. This reduced salvage value is then used in calculating depreciation amounts. Qualified property is depreciable personal property acquired after October 16, 1962 having a life of three years or more. The election of this salvage value adjustment is, of course, to the taxpayer's advantage. In future discussions, this salvage value adjustment is not explicitly considered. It is assumed that a given salvage value has already been adjusted for the 10% reduction.

OTHER TAXES

Up to this point the discussion of taxes has been centered on federal tax considerations. There are, of course, other tax considerations which warrant mentioning.

State Income Taxes   It is not possible to generalize state income taxes because rates vary from state to state as well as the computation of the taxable base (income). For example, some states allow the deduction of federal taxes in computing the state tax base; others do not. Some state taxes are based on the federal tax base; others are not. The usual approach taken in economic analysis is to include the effects of state income taxes by defining a composite incremental rate that reflects both the state and federal rates. (The procedures used to define a composite rate are shown in G. T. Stevens' *Economic and Financial Analysis of Capital Investments*.) For the purposes of this text, it is assumed that the given tax rates have been adjusted to take into account state income taxes.

Property Taxes (Ad Valorem Taxes)   States, counties, cities, and school districts impose taxes on the basis of a company's assessed value. A company's assessed value may or may not be its total investment depending on nontaxable items that may be included in the total investment. The usual procedure in economic studies is to estimate incremental property taxes on the basis of a constant percentage of the initial cost of the property. This percentage is dependent upon the location of the property.

Payroll Taxes   A company's payroll is subject to taxes for workmen's compensation, Social Security, and unemployment insurance. These taxes are a significant part of labor overhead. These taxes are implicitly included in economic studies through the estimation of the overall yearly costs, a portion of which is overhead.

Franchise Taxes   Franchise taxes are assessed on the basis of constant percentage of the gross income. They are often omitted in economic studies either because they are not applicable or they are sufficiently small so as not to affect an economic study.

Sales Taxes   Companies usually are assessed sales taxes on their purchases of material and equipment. They are usually implicitly included in economic studies through the estimation of the costs of material and equipment.

SUMMARY

In this chapter many tax considerations have been presented. Some of these tax considerations are used in later discussions, others are not. For those tax considerations not used, their discussion is presented on the basis that they may be usable for investigations and studies into more advanced topics. Also, these discussions provide the reader with some of the "tax language" that might be encountered at some later time.

REFERENCES

Bussey, Lynn E. *The Economic Analysis of Industrial Projects.* Englewood Cliffs, N.J.: Prentice-Hall, 1978.

Federal Tax Course, 1981. Englewood Cliffs, N.J.: Prentice-Hall, 1981.

Stevens, G. T., Jr. *Economic and Financial Analysis of Capital Investments.* New York: John Wiley & Sons, 1979.

United States Master Tax Guide. New York: Commerce Clearing House, 1981.

PROBLEMS

4-1.   Determine a company's tax liability for the following taxable income: (a) $40,000, (b) $80,000, and (c) $150,000.

4-2. In Problem 4-1, determine the effective tax rates for each taxable income.

4-3. A company is considering a project that is estimated to increase its gross income by $150,000 per year, increase costs by $40,000 per year, increase interest payments by $10,000, and increase depreciation by $30,000 per year. If the company's current taxable income is (a) $40,000, (b) $80,000, and (c) $150,000, what will be the increase in taxes as a result of this project? What is the incremental tax rate for the additional taxable income?

4-4. For a particular tax year, a company has the long-term and short-term transactions shown in the table below and a taxable income, before consideration of the long- and short-term transactions, of $200,000. Determine the following:

(a) The total tax liability if all the transactions are gains.

(b) Repeat Part (a) changing the $3,000 and $5,000 short-term gains to losses.

(c) Repeat Part (a) changing the $5,000 and $6,000 long-term gains to losses.

(d) Repeat Part (a) changing all long-term gains to losses.

Transaction	Long-Term	Short-Term
1	5,000	—
2	6,000	—
3	2,000	—
4	3,000	—
5	—	3,000
6	—	5,000
7	—	1,000
8	—	2,000

4-5. Five years ago, a company purchased a Section 1245 asset for $100,000. A single asset depreciation account was established for this asset on the basis of a salvage value of $10,000, a life of 15 years, and SYD depreciation. If the company's taxable income, without consideration of the sale of the Section 1245 asset, is $200,000, determine the following:

(a) The company's tax liability if the asset is sold for $58,000 and there are no other gains or losses from Section 1245 or Section 1250 properties.

(b) Repeat Part (a) for a selling price of $45,000.

(c) Repeat Part (b) for a selling price of $110,000.

4-6. Repeat Problem 4-5 with the exception that the asset is classified as Section 1250.

4-7. Repeat Problem 4-5 on the basis that straight-line depreciation is used and the asset is classified as Section 1250 property.

4-8. A company's taxable income is $500,000 exclusive of the data given in the tables below:

Section 1245 Transactions

Transaction	Purchase Price	Selling Price	Book Value
1	$ 50,000	$25,000	$20,000
2	100,000	46,000	40,000
3	80,000	42,000	60,000
4	70,000	75,000	60,000

Section 1250 Transactions

Transaction	Purchase Price	Selling Price	Book Value	Accumulated SL Depreciation
1	$ 60,000[a]	$33,000	$30,000	$30,000
2	85,000[a]	36,000	34,000	34,000
3	75,000[b]	31,000	20,000	48,000
4	110,000[b]	45,000	40,000	60,000

[a] Assume straight-line depreciation.
[b] Assume SYD depreciation.

Determine the company's tax liability assuming there are no other long- or short-term gains or losses.

4-9. Repeat Problem 4-8, only change the selling price of Transaction #1 under Section 1250 Transactions from $33,000 to $45,000.

4-10. Repeat Problems 4-8 and 4-9 with the additional information that the sum of the long- and short-term transactions not qualifying as Section 1245 or 1250 property are as follows:

(a) The sum of the long-term transactions is a gain of $60,000; the sum of the short-term transactions is a loss of $40,000.

(b) The sum of the long-term transactions is a gain of $50,000; the sum of the short-term transactions is a loss of $60,000.

4-11. A company exchanges an existing machine used for productive purposes for a similar new machine. The current salvage value of the existing machine is $60,000, and the list price of the new machine is $200,000. The company also paid $120,000. Determine the following:

(a) The gain on the exchange.

(b) The taxes paid on the exchange.

(c) The first cost of the new machine for tax depreciation purposes.

4-12. Two taxpayers, A and B, make a like-kind exchange of used property that both use for productive purposes. The current book value of A's property is $48,000, and the book value of B's property is $65,000. In addition, A gives B $10,000 cash. For the sets of fair market values (FMV) given below, determine the tax treatment of the gains and losses from the standpoints of both A and B. Also, determine the basis of the equipment received.

(a) $FMV_A = \$50,000$ and $FMV_B = \$63,000$

(b) $FMV_A = \$61,000$ and $FMV_B = \$56,000$

4-13. Five years ago, a company purchased an asset for $150,000. At that time, it was estimated to have a life of ten years. Assuming the company had enough taxable income to take the full investment tax credit in the year the asset was purchased, determine the following:

(a) The investment tax credit taken five years ago.

(b) The investment tax penalty if the asset is sold now.

4-14. A company has purchased certain deposits of sulfur that cost $15 million. The estimated value of the associated land is $1 million. It is estimated that there are two million tons of sulfur available in these deposits. Determine the following:

(a) The cost depletion if 90,000 tons of sulfur are sold in a particular year.

(b) The percentage depletion if the gross income is $1.5 million and the taxable income before depletion is $1 million.

(c) Repeat Part (b) only assume that the taxable income before depletion is $500,000.

(d) Considering Parts (a) and (b) what would the company's depletion allowance be for the year?

4-15. A company has a yearly equal payment for a loan of $10,000. If in a particular year $2,000 of this payment is principal and the other $8,000 is interest, determine the after-tax payment using an incremental tax rate of 46%.

4-16. Determine the total taxes and present worth of taxes paid for the following set of conditions: (1) initial cost of asset is $72,000, (2) depreciation life is eight years, and (3) the salvage value is zero. Use a taxable income before depreciation of $40,000 per year for ten years, a discount rate of 12%, a tax rate of 46%, and the following depreciation methods:

(a) Straight-line.

(b) SYD.

(c) DDB with optimal switching to straight-line.

5

THE ECONOMIC EVALUATION OF A SINGLE PROJECT

This chapter discusses various methods for determining the economic desirability of a *single* project (investment). That is, the decision alternative is either *accept* or *not accept* the project. Methods for choosing alternatives in problems that involve a comparison (ranking) of competing projects (cost comparisons, replacement analysis, and capital budgeting) are discussed in later chapters.

The specific methods discussed in this chapter for determining the economic desirability of a project are internal rate of return (IRR), net present value (NPV), and payout (payback) period. There are other methods proposed to economically evaluate projects such as the benefit-cost ratio. A review of some of these methods is also presented in this chapter.

Basically the methods for evaluating the economic desirability of a single investment are very similar to the evaluation of a loan. A company loans money, usually called *invested capital,* to a project, and the project, in turn, returns the monetary surplus of the incomes and various costs resulting from the project's activities to the company. This monetary surplus is called *net cash flow.* The net cash flow and invested capital are transformed into a rate of return (or some other criterion). This rate of return is then compared to a *required* rate of return called the *minimum acceptable (attractive) rate of return* (MARR) or *the hurdle rate.* In general, if MARR is less than the project's rate of return, the project is economically desirable.

THE MINIMUM ACCEPTABLE RATE OF RETURN

A company obtains its capital (funds) to invest in projects from primarily two sources: (1) debt sources and (2) equity sources. Debt capital is obtained by borrowing money from institutions (banks and insurance companies) *external* to the company and from the sale of company bonds. Equity capital is obtained through the sale of common stock and retained earnings (profits not paid in the form of dividends to stockholders). Each of these two types of capital has an associated cost. These costs are referred to as the *cost of debt capital* and the *cost of equity capital* and are usually expressed as an interest rate. In general, the cost of equity capital is larger than the cost of debt capital. These two costs of capital are combined to define a *weighted before-tax cost of capital*. Expressed mathematically, this weighted cost of capital is

$$k_b = w_e k_e + w_d k_d \qquad (5\text{-}1)$$

where

k_b = before-tax weighted cost of capital

k_e = cost of equity capital

k_d = cost of debt capital

w_e = proportion of equity capital

w_d = proportion of debt capital

Since the interest paid on debt capital is a tax deduction, a weighted after-tax cost of capital, k_a, can be defined as

$$k_a = w_e k_e + (1-T) w_d k_d \qquad (5\text{-}2)$$

where T is the company's incremental tax rate. *From the standpoint of evaluating proposed (new) projects*, the costs of capital and proportions indicated in Eqs. (5-1) and (5-2) should be based on a company's plans for raising capital to finance new projects over some finite planning period. The basis should not be current or past values unless current proportions and capital costs are considered to be a true representation of future financing policy. When Eq. (5-2) is used as a basis for establishing a MARR value that is to be used in the economic evaluation of projects, the inclusion of the term $(1-T)$ implies certain assumptions regarding the method of debt payment. These assumptions are discussed later.

Eqs. (5-1) and (5-2) are often written in terms of a debt ratio (c) where the debt ratio is the proportion of debt capital to be raised for a group of projects. That is, c is substituted for w_d and since only two sources of capital are considered

$$w_d + w_e = 1.00 \qquad (5\text{-}3)$$

and therefore

$$w_e = 1 - c \qquad (5\text{-}4)$$

consequently, Eq. (5-1) can be written as

$$k_b = (1 - c)\,k_e + ck_d \qquad (5\text{-}5)$$

and similar substitutions can be made in Eq. (5-2).

An Important Point (Assumption)   The previous discussion of cost of capital and debt ratio provides in part a foundation for a discussion of the debt ratio as it relates to the manner in which a *particular* project is financed. A *particular project* may be financed entirely by debt capital, entirely by equity capital, or some combination of debt and equity capital that is *not in agreement* with the debt ratio of the total monies being obtained for *a group of new projects*. In these cases, the question is, what debt ratio should be used for puposes of evaluating the economic desirability of a particular project? One answer might be the debt ratio of the project, and another might be the planned debt ratio of the total capital being raised for all new projects. In actuality, both answers are correct. For a company could obtain, for a period of time, the debt ratio of the total capital funds required for a group of projects by financing early projects entirely by debt and later projects by equity (or vice versa). Or a company could finance each project strictly in accordance with the debt ratio of the total capital being raised. Both approaches give the same result; namely, the desired debt ratio of the total capital committed to a group of projects at the end of some period of time. However, many times capital used to finance new projects is raised in "blocks" of money, and the proportions of debt and equity money used to finance a particular project are not known. In these cases the planned debt ratio of the total capital funds should be used in the evaluation of a particular project so long as the debt ratio remains constant. If the debt ratio is changed at some point in time (when another block of money is obtained), a revised debt ratio is used. Since using the debt ratio of the total capital avoids the problem of determining how a particular project is financed, the convention taken in this text is to use the debt ratio that represents the planned debt ratio of the total capital being raised for all projects. In capital budgeting problems that involve the comparison of acceptable projects this convention is highly desirable. It allows the comparison of projects on an equitable basis, namely, the same debt ratio. In practice the debt ratio is not difficult to determine because many companies raise money in accordance with their existing debt ratios. This approach of using a planned debt ratio does not preclude the actual use of a different combination of debt and equity capital once a project is determined to be acceptable (assuming there are no undesirable short-term effects such as interim dividend payments).

The Cost of Debt Capital   The cost of debt capital is the interest rate paid for externally borrowed money. It is relatively easy to determine since it is usually explicitly stated when a loan is made or it can be calculated knowing the amount borrowed and the payment schedule (see Examples 2-20 and 2-22). Some care must be taken when determining the cost of debt capital. It must be the *actual* cost of the debt capital. Many times, the stated interest rate on a loan and the actual rate being paid are not the same due to the procedure of discounting loans. Also, the cost of debt capital should be expressed as an effective annual rate since it is in this context that it is most often used.

The Cost of Equity Capital   The cost of equity capital is more conceptual than the cost of debt capital. Furthermore, a great deal of controversy exists concerning the determination of the cost of equity capital, and it appears unlikely that complete unanimity will ever exist. However, it is generally accepted that there *is* a cost of equity capital and its purpose is to make economic decisions in the best interest of the stockholders. It is used to achieve one of the basic objectives of a company's management; namely, the maximization of the stockholders' wealth. One often cited approximation for determining the cost of equity capital is the Gordon-Shapiro growth model. (See References at the end of the chapter.) This model is a dividend valuation model that incorporates a growth factor and can be expressed mathematically as

$$k_e = \frac{d}{p} + br \qquad (5\text{-}6)$$

where

k_e = cost of equity capital

d = current dividends per share of common stock

p = current market value per share of common stock

b = proportion of earnings retained $= \dfrac{y - d}{y}$

y = after-tax earnings per share

r = return on book value $= \dfrac{y}{B}$

B = book value per share of common stock

br = growth factor

Example 5-1

A company is currently paying a dividend of $5.00 per share, and the current market value for a share of its common stock is $40.00. In addition, the company's current financial report shows the following data:

$$
\begin{array}{lr}
\text{after-tax earnings} & = \ \$\ 3{,}500{,}000 \\
\text{total assets} & = \$20{,}000{,}000 \\
\text{liabilities} & = \ \$\ 5{,}000{,}000 \\
\text{number of common stock} & = \quad 500{,}000
\end{array}
$$

Determine the company's cost of equity capital.

The earnings per share are

$$
y = \frac{3{,}500{,}000}{500{,}000}
$$

$$
= \$7.00
$$

and the book value per share is

$$
B = \frac{\$20{,}000{,}000 - 5{,}000{,}000}{500{,}000}
$$

$$
= \$30.00
$$

The return on book value is

$$
r = \frac{7.00}{30.00}
$$

$$
= 0.233
$$

and the proportion of retained earnings is

$$
b = \frac{7.00 - 5.00}{7.00}
$$

$$
= 0.286
$$

Using Eq. (5-6), the return on equity is

$$
k_e = \frac{5}{40} + (0.286)(0.233)
$$

$$
= 0.195
$$

$$
= 19.5\%
$$

The cost of capital serves as a practical foundation upon which the MARR is based. In practice the cost of capital is adjusted (increased) to obtain the MARR. This adjustment is a result of risk considerations. The amount of the adjustment is often a result of the type of project under consideration. Consequently, it is not unusual to find a company with different MARR values for different types of projects. For example, a company might have a higher MARR value for projects involving new products than the MARR value for the expansion of existing production facilities.

The previous discussion of the cost of capital and MARR is not meant to be a comprehensive discussion. In actuality the theories and methods for determining the cost of capital and MARR are far beyond the scope of this text. In this text the discussion of cost of capital introduces the concepts of debt and equity capital to show how they are involved in the economic analysis of projects, once their cost values are determined. For an in-depth discussion of cost of capital the references at the end of this chapter should be consulted.

NET CASH FLOW

All of the methods mentioned earlier for evaluating the economic desirability of a project are related to the concept of net cash flow. It is important at this point to define net cash flow. From the standpoint of evaluating a project, the net cash flow is the algebraic sum of money estimated to flow in and out of a company over some period of time as a result of a particular project. *Incremental* cash flows occur as a result of the project. The sign convention used in this chapter is to designate cash inflows positive and cash outflows negative. The net cash flows are usually evaluated for each year of the project's life. It is then assumed that these yearly amounts occur as discrete amounts at the end of their respective year (end-of-year convention). This assumption allows the use of discrete interest factors and introduces very little, if any, error in the evalution.

Net cash flows can be defined in two ways. The first way defines the cash flows on the basis of returns to *equity capital*, and the second way defines the cash flows on the basis of returns to the *total investment*. Both ways, under certain circumstances, can be used to evaluate the economic desirability of projects. The basic difference between the two definitions of cash flow is whether or not *explicit* provision is made for the recovery of debt capital. Mathematically, the equity net cash flows can be defined as

$$X_{ej} = (G_j - C_j - I_j) - (G_j - C_j - I_j - D_j)\,T$$
$$- K_j + L_j + B_j - P_j \pm W_j \tag{5-7}$$

and the total cash flows can be defined as

$$X_j = (G_j - C_j) - (G_j - C_j - D_j)\,T$$
$$- K_j + L_j \pm W_j \qquad (5\text{-}8)$$

The components in Eqs. 5-7 and 5-8 are defined as follows:

X_{ej} = *net equity cash flow and* X_j = *net total cash flow at the end of year j.* As mentioned earlier, the basic difference between Eqs. (5-7) and (5-8) is that Eq. (5-7) provides for the explicit recovery of debt capital while Eq. (5-8) seemingly (but not in actuality) omits debt capital considerations.

G_j = *gross income (savings, receipts, revenues) at the end of year j.* Gross income could be the result of the selling price per unit multiplied by the expected volume of sales in year j. It should be clearly understood that the G_j, as used in Eqs. (5-7) and (5-8), is the cash flows that are expected to be *actually realized.* They are subject to taxation after applicable tax deductions (interest, depreciation, costs, etc.). In Eqs. (5-7) and (5-8), G_j does *not represent potential gross income* such as in finished-goods inventories, which are a working capital consideration (discussed later).

C_j = *the total yearly cost associated with the gross income* (G_j). As used in Eqs. (5-7) and (5-8), the yearly cost *does not include depreciation* since it is not a cash flow. It includes such items as labor, material, and applicable overhead expenses that are associated with the realization of the corresponding income (G_j). The value used for a C_j is not necessarily the total of all the costs incurred in the year j. For example, some of the costs incurred in a given year might be the result of the purchase of raw materials expected to be needed by the project under consideration in later years. In this case only the cost of the raw materials associated with G_j is included in C_j. The remaining amount is a working capital consideration. Also, *debt interest is not included* in C_j since it is considered separately.

W_j = *net increase (or decrease) in working capital in year j.* This value is negative if a particular project requires a net increase in working capital. It is positive if a project results in a net decrease in working capital or if there is a recovery of working capital. Many types of projects require significant changes in working capital as a result of meeting payrolls, paying other current costs, accounts receivable, and inventories (raw materials, in-process, and finished goods). The usual case is to have working capital requirements increase cash outflows in the beginning years of a project. The exception is to have some project that decreases working capital requirements as a result of increased efficiency. The inclusion of working capital considerations in Eqs. (5-7) and (5-8) is important since its omission can lead to incorrect conclusions regarding the desirability of a project.

$I_j = debt\ interest\ paid\ in\ year\ j$. This is the increase in debt interest as a result of the project under consideration. It is directly related to the amount borrowed (B_j) to finance the project and the principal payments (P_j). This text considers four methods for the repayment of borrowed money. They are (1) a single payment of principal and interest, (2) a constant interest payment, (3) a constant principal payment, and (4) one single payment of interest and principal. In order to use Eq. (5-7) the specific yearly amounts of interest and principal must be separated and known since interest is a tax deductible item and principal is not tax deductible. In order to show the four methods for repayment of debt the following example is worked.

Example 5-2 _____

If $40,000 is borrowed for five years at an interest rate of 10%, determine the yearly interest and principal payments for the following methods of repayment:

    a. Single payment of principal and interest.
    b. Constant interest payment.
    c. Constant principal payment.
    d. Constant payment.

In Part a the total payment at the end of five years is

$$40,000\ (F/P\ 10,5)$$

$$40,000\ (1.611) = \$64,400$$

which means that the interest and principal payment in year five are

$$P_5 = \$40,000$$

$$I_5 = \$64,400 - 40,000$$

$$= \$24,400$$

and the interest and principal payments in years one through four are zero. The interest and principal payment schedule is shown in Table 5-1.

In Part b, the constant interest paid in years one through five is

$$40,000\ (0.10) = \$4,000$$

and the principal is paid in one lump sum ($40,000) in year five. The interest and principal payment schedule is shown in Table 5-1.

TABLE 5-1
Four Methods for Debt Repayment

End of Year	Interest Payment	Principal Payment	Total Payment	End of Year	Interest Payment	Principal Payment	Total Payment
0	$0	$0	$0	0	$0	$0	$0
1	0	0	0	1	4,000	0	4,000
2	0	0	0	2	4,000	0	4,000
3	0	0	0	3	4,000	0	4,000
4	0	0	0	4	4,000	0	4,000
5	24,400	40,000	64,400	5	4,000	40,000	44,000

a. Single Payment of Debt and Interest   b. Constant Interest Payment

End of Year	Interest Payment	Principal Payment	Total Payment	End of Year	Interest Payment	Principal Payment	Total Payment
0	$0	$0	$0	0	$0	$0	$0
1	4,000	8,000	12,000	1	4,000	6,552	10,552
2	3,200	8,000	11,200	2	3,345	7,207	10,552
3	2,400	8,000	10,400	3	2,624	7,928	10,552
4	1,600	8,000	9,600	4	1,831	8,721	10,552
5	800	8,000	8,800	5	959	9,593	10,552

c. Constant Principal Payment   d. Constant Payment

In Part c, the constant principal payment is

$$\frac{40,000}{5} = \$8,000 \text{ per year}$$

and the interest is assessed on the unpaid principal. Consequently, the interest for years one and two are

$$I_1 = 40,000 \ (0.10)$$

$$= \$4,000$$

$$I_2 = (40,000 - 8,000)(0.10)$$

$$= \$3,200$$

The method used in determining the specific yearly interest and principal payment for Part d is basically the same as the method used for house mortgages (see Example 2-21). However, in this example it is done on a yearly basis rather than the monthly basis used in the house mortgage example. The total constant yearly payment of interest and principal is

$$40,000 \ (A/P \ 10,5)$$

$$40,000 \ (0.2638) = \$10,552$$

The interest for the first year is

$$40,000 \ (0.10) = \$4,000$$

and the principal payment is

$$10,553 - 4,000 = \$6,553$$

Similarly, the interest for the second year is

$$(40,000 - 6,553)(0.10) = \$3,345$$

and the principal paid is

$$10,553 - 3,345 = \$7,207$$

The remaining values for principal and interest are given in Table 5-1.

D_j = *tax depreciation amount for year j.* The tax depreciation schedule must be determined. Various depreciation models are discussed in Chapter 3.

K_j = *total capital expenditure (investment, cost) in year j.* This is the total amount of money spent on capital assets that are required by the project in year j.

T = *incremental tax rate.* In Eqs. (5-7) and (5-8) the tax rate is assumed to be constant over the life of the project. This is the usual assumption. However, this assumption is not required. The tax rate could be varied if considered applicable. In practice the tax rate is often adjusted in order to approximate both federal and state income taxes.

L_j = *salvage value received in year j.* This is the salvage values of the capital assets. It is usually assumed that these values are recoverable at the end of the depreciation period except in cases where the tax depreciation period is shorter than the life of the project. In these cases another convention is used. This convention is shown and discussed in a later example.

B_j = *the amount of borrowed money received in year j.* This is the amount of money borrowed from external sources (loans from bank, sale of company bonds, etc.) used to finance the capital expenditure. As mentioned earlier, in the context of evaluating the incremental equity cash flows, B_j is directly related to I_j and P_j. B_j is often referred to as the *debt capital* required by the project. The *equity capital* required by the project in year j, K_{ej}, is the difference between the total capital, K_j, and the borrowed money. That is,

$$K_{ej} = K_j - B_j \qquad (5\text{-}9)$$

P_j = *the principal payment provision in year j.* This is often referred to as the recovery of the debt capital (B_j) required by the project. In actuality the payment (reduction) of the principal may or may not be made. This is a management decision. However, a provision for the recovery of the debt capital must be *explicitly* included in the definition of net cash flow if *equity* cash flows are used.

c = *debt ratio.* This is not specifically included in Eqs. (5-7) and (5-8); however, it is implied. The debt ratio expresses the amount of total capital (K_j) that is financed by debt as a percentage. That is,

$$B_j = cK_j \qquad (5\text{-}10)$$

and, consequently,

$$K_{ej} = (1 - c)\, K_j \qquad (5\text{-}11)$$

Eqs. (5-10) and (5-11) imply the convention mentioned previously regarding the debt ratio; that is, to use the debt ratio of the total capital funds as the basis for separating debt and equity capital when evaluating a particular project.

THE INTERNAL RATE OF RETURN

The internal rate of return (IRR) is the interest rate that makes the sum of the discounted cash flows equal zero. This definition is true for both definitions of net cash flow [(Eqs. (5-7) and (5-8)]. However, the interpretation of the IRR is different for the two definitions of cash flow (discussed later). Mathematically, the IRR is determined from the equation

$$0 = \sum_{j=0}^{n} \frac{X'_j}{(1 + i)^j} \qquad (5\text{-}12)$$

where

X'_j = net cash flow in year j defined by either Eq. (5-7) or (5-8)

n = number of years of cash flow

j = the year in which the cash flow, X'_j, occurs

i = IRR = the internal rate of return

Example 5-3 _____

A company is considering a project that has an initial expenditure of $100,000 and a salvage value of $10,000 at the end of ten years. It is estimated that this initial expenditure will increase gross incomes and costs by, respectively, $40,000 and $10,000 per year for the next ten years. The company's tax rate is 52%; and for tax purposes the initial expenditure will be depreciated on a straight-line basis. Assuming no working capital considerations or investment tax credit, determine the following:

a. The yearly total cash flows and the corresponding internal rate of return.

b. The yearly equity cash flows and the corresponding internal rate of return. Assume the debt ratio is 40% and the debt is to be paid in ten equal principal installments with interest assessed on the unpaid balance at a cost of 10%.

For Part a, Eq. (5-8) is used to define the cash flows. Since straight-line depreciation is specified, the tax depreciation is a constant yearly value of

$$D_j = \frac{100,000 - 10,000}{10}$$

$$= \$9,000$$

Applying Eq. (5-8) to the data gives the cash flow for year zero (the beginning of the first year) as

$$X_0 = -\$100,000$$

For year one, the cash flow is

$$X_1 = (40,000 - 10,000) - (40,000 - 10,000 - 9,000)(.52)$$

$$= \$19,080$$

The remaining cash flows are given in Table 5-2. In order to solve for the internal rate of return, Eq. (5-12) is applied to the cash flows in Table 5-2.

$$0 = -100,000 + 19,080 (1 + i)^{-1} + \ldots + 19,080 (1 + i)^{-10} + 10,000 (1 + i)^{-10}$$

Since in this case most of the cash flows are constant, a more efficient way to solve for the internal rate of return is by the formulation

$$0 = -100,000 + 19,080 (P/A\ i,10) + 10,000 (P/F\ i,10)$$

which gives

$$i = IRR = 14.59\%$$

TABLE 5-2
Total Net Cash Flows for Example 5-3

End of Year	Capital Expenditure and Salvage	Gross Income	Costs	Depreciation	Total Cash Flows
0	$100,000	—	—	—	−$100,000
1	—	$40,000	$10,000	$9,000	19,080
2	—	40,000	10,000	9,000	19,080
3	—	40,000	10,000	9,000	19,080
4	—	40,000	10,000	9,000	19,080
5	—	40,000	10,000	9,000	19,080
6	—	40,000	10,000	9,000	19,080
7	—	40,000	10,000	9,000	19,080
8	—	40,000	10,000	9,000	19,080
9	—	40,000	10,000	9,000	19,080
10	10,000	40,000	10,000	9,000	19,080 + 10,000

In order to obtain this value (14.59%) a trial-and-error procedure is used. This procedure involves "bracketing" the internal rate of return. That is, determining two interest rates that give positive and negative results for Eq. (5-12) and then using linear interpolation to obtain the IRR. Of course, the closer these two interest rates are, the better the approximation. Using this case as an example, 12% gives

$$-100,000 + 19,080 \ (P/A \ 12,10) + 10,000 \ (P/F \ 12,10) = \$11,026$$

and 15% gives

$$-100,000 + 19,080 \ (P/A \ 15,10) + 10,000 \ (P/F \ 15,10) = \$-1,769$$

Therefore, the IRR is between 12% and 15% and using linear interpolation, the IRR is

12%	11,026
IRR	0
15%	−1,769

$$IRR = 12 + \frac{11,026 \ (3)}{12,795}$$

$$= 14.59\%$$

For Part b, Eq. (5-7) is used to define the cash flows. The problem statement indicates that the amount of borrowed money is

$$B_0 = 100,000 \ (0.4)$$

$$= \$40,000$$

Therefore, the principal payments in years one through ten are

$$P = \frac{40,000}{10}$$

$$= \$4,000$$

and the interest amounts for the first two years are

$$I_1 = 40,000 \, (0.10)$$

$$= \$4,000$$

$$I_2 = (40,000 - 4,000)(0.10)$$

$$= \$3,600$$

The interest payments for the remaining years are given in Table 5-3. With this data and the depreciation schedule obtained in Part a, the equity cash flows are determined. For example, the equity cash flows in years zero and one are

$$X_{e0} = -100,000 + 40,000$$

$$= -\$60,000$$

$$X_{e1} = (40,000 - 10,000 - 4,000)$$

$$-(40,000 - 10,000 - 4,000 - 9,000)(.52) - 4,000$$

$$= \$13,160$$

TABLE 5-3
Net Equity Cash Flows for Example 5-3

End of Year	Capital Expenditure and Salvage	Gross Income	Costs	Depre- ciation	Borrowed Money	Principal Payments	Interest	Equity Cash Flows
0	$100,000	—	—	—	$40,000	—	—	$-60,000
1	—	$40,000	$10,000	$9,000	—	4,000	4,000	13,160
2	—	40,000	10,000	9,000	—	4,000	3,600	13,352
3	—	40,000	10,000	9,000	—	4,000	3,200	13,544
4	—	40,000	10,000	9,000	—	4,000	2,800	13,736
5	—	40,000	10,000	9,000	—	4,000	2,400	13,928
6	—	40,000	10,000	9,000	—	4,000	2,000	14,120
7	—	40,000	10,000	9,000	—	4,000	1,600	14,312
8	—	40,000	10,000	9,000	—	4,000	1,200	14,504
9	—	40,000	10,000	9,000	—	4,000	800	14,696
10	10,000	40,000	10,000	9,000	—	4,000	400	24,888[a]

[a] includes $10,000 salvage value

The remaining equity cash flows are given in Table 5-3. The internal rate of return is

$$0 = -60,000 + 13,160 \, (P/F \, i,1) + \ldots + 24,888 \, (P/F \, i,10)$$

where

$$i = \text{IRR}$$
$$= 19.71\%$$

Decision Criterion for the IRR   The economic desirability of a project (capital investment) is determined by making a comparison of the IRR and the MARR. In making this comparison a very important point must be realized. *The correct MARR value to use in the comparison and the definition of cash flow are dependent.* The MARR value could be based on a weighted cost of capital as defined either by Eq. (5-1) or Eq. (5-2). The MARR value could also be based strictly on the cost of equity capital (k_e). If equity cash flows are used, Eq. (5-7), the resulting IRR is the *return on equity capital*. Consequently, it must be compared with a MARR that is based on the *required* return on equity (equity cost of capital). If total cash flows, Eq. (5-8), are used, the resulting IRR is the return on the *total investment* and should be compared to a MARR value based on a cost of capital defined by Eq. (5-2). However, if Eq. (5-2) is used in conjunction with total cash flows, certain assumptions, suggested earlier, are implied as a result of the $(1-T)$ term included in Eq. (5-2). The implied assumptions are (1) the payment of the debt obligation is spread over the life of the project and (2) the interest is a constant yearly amount. Consequently, the after-tax cost of capital defined by Eq. (5-2) is only an *approximation* for other methods of debt payment. This point must be realized since the return on equity does vary with the manner in which debt payments (interest and principal) are made. It is possible, therefore, for the return on equity and return on total investment to give conflicting results regarding the acceptability of a project. A project that is acceptable on the basis of return on equity will be acceptable on the basis of return on total investment. However, the convese is not necessarily true. A project can be acceptable using return on total investment but unacceptable from the standpoint of return on equity. This is especially true when the debt is paid over a period less than the life of the project. This dependency between the definitions of cash flow and MARR must be clearly understood. Otherwise, incorrect decisions can be made regarding the desirability of a project.

The manner in which the MARR and IRR values are compared for decision purposes depends on the form of the cash flow series under consideration. This book chooses to distinguish between a traditional and a nontraditional cash flow series. A *traditional cash flow series* is defined as a series of cash flows comprised of at least one negative cash flow *followed* by at least one positive cash flow and whose algebraic total, at a discount rate of zero, is positive. Note that this definition of a traditional cash flow series allows only *one sign change* in the cash flow series. A *nontraditional cash flow series* is defined as a series of cash flows that do not qualify as a traditional cash flow series. Although the definition of a traditional cash flow series may appear limiting, a series of traditional cash flows is by far the most usual case in the analysis of capital investments. For decision purposes an investment giving a series of traditional cash flows is considered acceptable if the IRR is equal to or greater than MARR (IRR $\geq$ MARR). Otherwise, the investment is unacceptable. This decision criterion does imply the assumption (condition) that the capital required by the investment could be invested in other economic endeavors and earn the value of MARR. The decision criterion for a nontraditional cash flow series is discussed later.

This text takes the point of view that *equity cash flows* should be the basic criterion for the evaluation of capital projects either from the standpoint of IRR or net present value (discussed later). This point of view is taken because, as previously stated, the principal objective of a company's management is to maximize the equity shareholder's wealth (in conjunction with the objective of survival). Consequently, the critical figure in the economic analysis of investments is the *return on equity capital*. It is true that the use of equity cash flows requires some knowledge (approximation) regarding the manner in which the debt obligation is paid. However, this is not a difficult problem. Any one of the methods for debt payment shown in Table 5-1 could be used. Some might be more appropriate than others. For example, if the debt funds are largely a result of a bond issue, then the constant interest method might be applicable. If the debt funds are largely a result of borrowing from institutions (banks, insurance companies) or mortgages, then the constant payment or constant principal methods might be applicable. In general, it would be a rare circumstance for the single payment method to be applicable except in cases of short-term debt obligations. From the combined standpoints of separating and calculating interest and principal payments and providing for an *annual* recovery of the debt capital, the constant principal method is perhaps the easiest and the most appropriate.

A final point in regard to Example 5-3. The IRR for the equity cash flows (19.71%) is higher than the IRR for the total cash flows (14.59%). This result can be generalized. That is, if the quantities G_j, C_j, D_j, K_j, and L_j remain the same, the return on equity will be higher. This also implies that as the debt ratio increases, the return on equity will increase. This is one reason why companies are inclined to use some mix of debt and equity capital to finance projects even though the companies might have the money to finance projects entirely by equity funds.

Another Interpretation of the IRR   Eq. (5-12) provides a mathematical definition of the IRR. A better insight to the meaning of the IRR is obtained by considering the calculations in Table 5-4. If the IRR is calculated for the cash flows in Table 5-4, the result is

$$0 = -20,000 + 4,463 \ (P/A \ i,6) + 1,000 \ (P/F \ i,6)$$

$$i = \text{IRR}$$

$$= 10\%$$

Using this IRR as the return on the yearly unrecovered capital, the total capital is recovered over the six-year period as shown in Table 5-4. Thus, another interpretation of the IRR is that it is the rate of return earned each year on the unrecovered capital which allows for the full recovery of the capital over the life of the project. Another way of interpreting the IRR is that it is the rate of return earned on the company's "loan" of $20,000 to the project and the project's return of the net cash flows to the company.

There exists a persistent misconception regarding the IRR. Namely, that in order to earn the IRR, the cash flows must be reinvested at the IRR. This is an incorrect statement. By comparison, if a person loans $20,000 and is paid back the cash flows in Table 5-4, the person earns 10% on his or her loan regardless of what is done with the yearly cash flows. This is what happens when a company invests in a project. In effect a company "loans" money (capital) to the project, and the project in turn returns money in the form of positive cash flows to the company. Consequently, there is no assumption regarding the reinvestment of *the cash flows*. The IRR is generated internally as a result of the cash flows. This is the reason the word *internal* is used in conjunction with the words

TABLE 5-4
The Meaning of the Internal Rate of Return

End of Year	Net Cash Flow	Return on Unre- covered Capital	Capital Recovered	Unrecovered Capital
0	−$20,000	—	—	$−20,000
1	4,463	0.1(−20,000) = $−2,000	4,463−2,000 = $2,463	−20,000+2,463 = −17,537
2	4,463	0.1(−17,537) = −1,754	4,463−1,754 = 2,709	−17,537+2,709 = −14,828
3	4,463	0.1(−14,828) = −1,483	4,463−1,483 = 2,980	−14,828+2,980 = −11,848
4	4,463	0.1(−11,848) = −1,185	4,463−1,185 = 3,278	−11,848+3,278 = − 8,570
5	4,463	0.1(− 8,570) = − 857	4,463− 857 = 3,606	− 8,570+3,606 = − 4,964
6	1,000[a] +4,463	0.1(− 4,964) = − 496	5,463[c]− 496 = 4,967	− 4,964+4,967 = 0[b]

[a] Salvage value.
[b] Actual difference is +3 which is due to rounding-off error.
[c] Includes salvage value.

rate of return. As stated previously, the investment assumption that is made is that the required capital could be invested at the value of **MARR** in other economic endeavors.

CASH FLOW EXTENSIONS AND CONVENTIONS

Determining the cash flows in Example 5-3 was a relatively simple matter since there was only one capital expenditure and most of the variables were constants. Also there were no working capital or investment tax credit considerations. In this section a more comprehensive cash flow example is worked and certain conventions used in generating cash flows are discussed.

Example 5-4 _____

For a particular project the data shown in Tables 5-5 and 5-6 has been estimated. Determine the equity cash flows using the additional information given below:

1. The tax rate is 52%.
2. The investment tax credit is applicable.
3. Depreciation for tax purposes is straight-line.
4. The debt ratio is 40%.
5. All debt capital is to be paid back in ten equal principal installments, and the cost of debt capital is 10% on the unpaid principal.

The first step in generating the equity cash flows is to determine the yearly tax depreciation amounts for each depreciable asset. These amounts are shown in Table 5-7. The convention used in Table 5-7 is to

TABLE 5-5
Capital Requirement Data for Example 5-4

End of Year	Capital Requirement	Use	Tax Depreciation Life in Years	Salvage	Working Capital Requirement
0	$ 500,000	Land	—	—	—
1	2,000,000	Building	25	200,000	600,000
2	3,000,000	Equipment	15	300,000	800,000
3	6,000,000	Equipment	15	600,000	1,000,000

TABLE 5-6
Gross Income and Cost Data for Example 5-4

End of Year	Gross Income	Costs	G − C
0	—	—	—
1	—	—	—
2	—	—	—
3	—	—	—
4	500,000	1,000,000	−500,000
5	1,500,000	1,000,000	500,000
6	5,000,000	1,000,000	4,000,000
·	·	·	·
·	·	·	·
·	·	·	·
20	5,000,000	1,000,000	4,000,000

TABLE 5-7
Depreciation Amounts for Example 5-4

End of Year	Building $2(10)^6$	Equipment $3(10)^6$	Equipment $6(10)^6$	Total Depreciation
0	—	—	—	—
1	—	—	—	—
2	72,000	—	—	72,000
3	72,000	180,000	—	252,000
4	72,000	180,000	360,000	612,000
5	72,000	180,000	360,000	612,000
6	72,000	180,000	360,000	612,000
7	72,000	180,000	360,000	612,000
8	72,000	180,000	360,000	612,000
9	72,000	180,000	360,000	612,000
10	72,000	180,000	360,000	612,000
11	72,000	180,000	360,000	612,000
12	72,000	180,000	360,000	612,000
13	72,000	180,000	360,000	612,000
14	72,000	180,000	360,000	612,000
15	72,000	180,000	360,000	612,000
16	72,000	180,000	360,000	612,000
17	72,000	180,000	360,000	612,000
18	72,000	—	360,000	432,000
19	72,000	—	—	72,000
·	·	·	·	·
·	·	·	·	·
26	72,000	—	—	72,000

begin the depreciation amounts following the year in which the capital expenditure (K_j) occurs. There is another convention that is sometimes used in determining the yearly tax depreciation amounts. In this other way, the depreciation begins after the entire payment is completed. This would imply the depreciation amounts shown in Table 5-8. In this table the building and equipment depreciation amounts all begin in year four. The depreciation schedules for the building and equipment are separated because they have different lives. Also, the building is, in all probability, Section 1250 Property and the equipment is Section 1245 Property. The depreciation lives are decided by tax regulations. Both of the depreciation conventions shown in Tables 5-7 and 5-8 are correct under certain circumstances. The question from the standpoint of tax regulations is, Are the assets ready for service? If an asset is ready for service, depreciation deductions can start as shown in Table 5-7. If assets are dependent (the entire facility must be completed before it is ready for use), then the depreciation convention in Table 5-8 is more applicable. It should be noted that the tax regulation is based on *ready* for service. It is not based on being in actual use. In general the depreciation convention shown in Table 5-7 is used in this text. Also, this example uses straight-line depreciation for tax purposes. This is merely for convenience. In practice the tax depreciation model would most likely be an accelerated depreciation model (DDB, SYD).

TABLE 5-8
Another Depreciation Schedule for Example 5-4

End of Year	Building $2(10)^6$	Equipment $9(10)$	Total Depreciation
0	—	—	—
1	—	—	—
2	—	—	—
3	—	—	—
4	72,000	540,000	612,000
5	72,000	540,000	612,000
6	72,000	540,000	612,000
·	·	·	·
·	·	·	·
·	·	·	·
18	72,000	540,000	612,000
19	72,000	—	72,000
·	·	·	·
·	·	·	·
·	·	·	·
28	72,000	—	72,000

The next step is to calculate the amount of borrowed money and corresponding principal and interest payments. As mentioned earlier, the approach taken in this text is to use the convention that the amount of borrowed money is a function of the debt ratio. Therefore, the debt money for each year is

$$B_0 = (0.4)(500,000)$$

$$= \$200,000$$

$$B_1 = (0.4)(2,000,000 + 600,000)$$

$$= \$1,040,000$$

$$B_2 = (0.4)(3,000,000 + 800,000)$$

$$= \$1,520,000$$

$$B_3 = (0.4)(6,000,000 + 1,000,000)$$

$$= \$2,800,000$$

where the values in parentheses are the capital expenditures and working capital requirements given in Table 5-5. The principal payments and interest charges are shown in Table 5-9. Note that the principal and interest payments start in the year following the borrowed amount and are based, as stated in the problem, on ten equal principal installments with interest (10%) assessed on the unpaid balance. With the data in Tables 5-5, 5-6, 5-7, 5-9, and Eq. (5-7), it is possible to determine the annual net equity cash flows. The calculations and results are shown in

TABLE 5-9
Principal and Interest Payments for Example 5-4

End of Year	$B_0 = \$200,000$ Principal	Interest	$B_1 = \$1,040,000$ Principal	Interest	$B_2 = \$1,520,000$ Principal	Interest	$B_3 = \$2,800,000$ Principal	Interest	Total Principal	Interest
0	—	—	—	—	—	—	—	—	—	—
1	$20,000	$20,000	—	—	—	—	—	—	$ 20,000	$ 20,000
2	20,000	18,000	$104,000	$104,000	—	—	—	—	124,000	122,000
3	20,000	16,000	104,000	93,600	$152,000	$152,000	—	—	276,000	261,600
4	20,000	14,000	104,000	83,200	152,000	136,800	$280,000	$280,000	556,000	514,000
5	20,000	12,000	104,000	72,800	152,000	121,600	280,000	252,000	556,000	458,400
6	20,000	10,000	104,000	62,400	152,000	106,400	280,000	224,000	556,000	402,800
7	20,000	8,000	104,000	52,000	152,000	91,200	280,000	196,000	556,000	347,200
8	20,000	6,000	104,000	41,600	152,000	76,000	280,000	168,000	556,000	291,600
9	20,000	4,000	104,000	31,200	152,000	60,800	280,000	140,000	556,000	236,000
10	20,000	2,000	104,000	20,800	152,000	45,600	280,000	112,000	556,000	180,400
11	—	—	104,000	10,400	152,000	30,400	280,000	84,000	536,000	124,800
12	—	—	—	—	152,000	15,200	280,000	56,000	432,000	71,200
13	—	—	—	—	—	—	280,000	28,000	280,000	28,000

Table 5-10. In determining the cash flows in Table 5-10 certain conventions are used. A discussion of these conventions follows:

1. Land is not depreciable. However, it does represent a negative cash flow when it is purchased. In this example, the land is purchased in year zero. The usual convention is to assume that money spent for land is recoverable in the year that the cash flows resulting from the project end. Consequently, in this example, the value of the land ($500,000) is added in year 26.

2. It is assumed in generating the cash flows that there are sufficient incomes from other company endeavors to allow for the full deductions of costs and depreciation amounts in years where the project itself is not generating sufficient incomes to cover these items. Also, the building will continue to be depreciated after the gross income stops.

3. The investment tax credit (10%) is taken in the years following the associated capital expenditures. For example, the investment tax credit for the $3,000,000 worth of equipment purchased in year 2 is taken in year 3. This is merely the convention used in this text. Valid arguments can be made for taking the investment tax credit in the same year as the year in which the equipment is purchased. The full 10% credit is taken since the life of the equipment is over seven years. No investment tax credit is provided for the land or building. In general, land and buildings do not qualify for the investment tax credit.

4. The net increases in working capital are deducted in the appropriate years. The usual convention is to assume that the increases in working capital required by a project are recovered in the last year of the gross income. Consequently, the total working capital ($2,400,000) is added to the cash flow in year 20. If it is estimated that the working capital is recovered over some period of years, then the yearly amounts should be added in the appropriate years. Note that the working capital is taken in year 20 as an equity cash flow since the recovery of the debt-financed portion of the working capital is provided for in the principal payments.

5. The two equipment salvage values are added in year 20. It might be argued that these values should be added in the year when the asset is fully depreciated. In this example this would be year 17 for the $3,000,000 equipment and year 18 for the $6,000,000 equipment. This text takes the point of view that it is more realistic to assume that the earliest these salvage values can be realized is in the year the gross income ceases since this implies that production stops at that time. If there is an estimated decrease in production activity and this makes possible the realization of salvage values, then the appropriate salvage values should be added in the years in which they can be realized. If an

TABLE 5-10
Equity Cash Flows for Example 5-4

End of Year		
0	$X_0 = -500{,}000 + 200{,}000$	$= \$-300{,}000$
1	$X_1 = (-20{,}000) - (-20{,}000)(0.52) - 2{,}000{,}000 - 600{,}000 + 1{,}040{,}000 \\ - 20{,}000$	$= -1{,}589{,}600$
2	$X_2 = (-122{,}000) - (-122{,}000 - 72{,}000)(0.52) - 3{,}000{,}000 - 800{,}000 \\ + 1{,}520{,}000 - 124{,}000$	$= -2{,}425{,}120$
3	$X_3 = (-261{,}600) - (-261{,}600 - 252{,}000)(0.52) - 6{,}000{,}000 \\ - 1{,}000{,}000 + 2{,}800{,}000 - 276{,}000 + 300{,}000^a$	$= -4{,}170{,}528$
4	$X_4 = (-500{,}000 - 541{,}600) - (-500{,}000 - 541{,}600 - 612{,}000)(0.52) \\ - 556{,}000 + 600{,}000^a$	$= -137{,}728$
5	$X_5 = (500{,}000 - 458{,}400) - (500{,}000 - 458{,}400 - 612{,}000)(0.52) \\ - 556{,}000$	$= -217{,}792$
6	$X_6 = (4{,}000{,}000 - 402{,}800) - (4{,}000{,}000 - 402{,}800 - 612{,}000)(0.52) \\ - 556{,}000$	$= 1{,}488{,}896$
7	$X_7 = (4{,}000{,}000 - 347{,}200) - (4{,}000{,}000 - 347{,}200 - 612{,}000)(0.52) \\ - 556{,}000$	$= 1{,}515{,}584$
8	$X_8 = (4{,}000{,}000 - 291{,}600) - (4{,}000{,}000 - 291{,}600 - 612{,}000)(0.52) \\ - 556{,}000$	$= 1{,}542{,}272$
9	$X_9 = (4{,}000{,}000 - 236{,}000) - (4{,}000{,}000 - 236{,}000 - 612{,}000)(0.52) \\ - 556{,}000$	$= 1{,}568{,}960$
10	$X_{10} = (4{,}000{,}000 - 180{,}400) - (4{,}000{,}000 - 180{,}400 - 612{,}000)(0.52) \\ - 556{,}000$	$= 1{,}595{,}648$
11	$X_{11} = (4{,}000{,}000 - 124{,}800) - (4{,}000{,}000 - 124{,}800 - 612{,}000)(0.52) \\ - 536{,}000$	$= 1{,}642{,}336$
12	$X_{12} = (4{,}000{,}000 - 71{,}200) - (4{,}000{,}000 - 71{,}200 - 612{,}000)(0.52) \\ - 432{,}000$	$= 1{,}772{,}064$
13	$X_{13} = (4{,}000{,}000 - 28{,}000) - (4{,}000{,}000 - 28{,}000 - 612{,}000)(0.52) \\ - 280{,}000$	$= 1{,}944{,}800$
14	$X_{14} = (4{,}000{,}000) - (4{,}000{,}000 - 612{,}000)(0.52)$	$= 2{,}238{,}240$
15	$X_{15} = (4{,}000{,}000) - (4{,}000{,}000 - 612{,}000)(0.52)$	$= 2{,}238{,}240$
16	$X_{16} = (4{,}000{,}000) - (4{,}000{,}000 - 612{,}000)(0.52)$	$= 2{,}238{,}240$
17	$X_{17} = (4{,}000{,}000) - (4{,}000{,}000 - 612{,}000)(0.52)$	$= 2{,}238{,}240$
18	$X_{18} = (4{,}000{,}000) - (4{,}000{,}000 - 432{,}000)(0.52)$	$= 2{,}144{,}640$
19	$X_{19} = (4{,}000{,}000) - (4{,}000{,}000 - 72{,}000)(0.52)$	$= 1{,}957{,}440$
20	$X_{20} = (4{,}000{,}000) - (4{,}000{,}000 - 72{,}000)(0.52) + 300{,}000^b + 600{,}000^c \\ + 2{,}400{,}000^d$	$= 5{,}257{,}440$
21	$X_{21} = -(-72{,}000)(0.52)$	$= 37{,}440$
22	$X_{22} = -(-72{,}000)(0.52)$	$= 37{,}440$
23	$X_{23} = -(-72{,}000)(0.52)$	$= 37{,}440$
24	$X_{24} = -(-72{,}000)(0.52)$	$= 37{,}440$
25	$X_{25} = -(-72{,}000)(0.52)$	$= 37{,}440$
26	$X_{26} = -(-72{,}000)(0.52) + 200{,}000^e + 500{,}000^f$	$= 737{,}440$

[a] Investment tax credit $= (0.10)(3{,}000{,}000) = \$300{,}000$.
[a] Investment tax credit $= (0.10)(6{,}000{,}000) = \$600{,}000$.
[b] Salvage value.
[c] Salvage value.
[d] Working capital recovery.
[e] Salvage value of building.
[f] Recovery of land.

asset becomes fully depreciated *after* the gross income stops, the convention used in this text is to assume the salvage value can be realized in the year in which the asset becomes fully depreciated. It must be remembered that depreciation lives for tax purposes are dictated by tax regulations. These regulations may or may not agree with the expected life of the project. Also in relation to the recovery of salvage values and the land, it should be understood that the project can provide these cash flows to the company. Whether or not the company actually realizes these cash flows is dependent upon the alternatives and situation at the time it is possible to retire the assets. For example, some of the equipment might be used for another project or other purposes. However, the project under consideration does provide these cash flows. Consequently, the project should be credited with these cash flows regardless of the actual disposition of these assets.

6. In this example the tax salvage values are given (estimated) for each depreciable component (building and equipment) of the total investment. Salvage values for each investment component are not always known or estimated. Often, only the total salvage values for similar components of the capital investment are estimated. For example, a salvage value for the building might be estimated and only a total salvage value for all the equipment might be estimated. This is consistent since in this example the building is considered to be Section 1250 Property and the equipment is considered to be Section 1245 Property, and thus separate depreciation accounts are required under the ADR System. If depreciation begins after the total equipment expenditure as shown in Table 5-8, there is no problem with a total salvage value for the total equipment expenditures. However, if depreciation begins following the expenditure of a particular capital component as shown in Table 5-7 (this implies separate depreciation accounts), the total salvage value must be allocated to the various investment components. This allocation of the total salvage value between various investment components is usually assumed to be in direct proportion to the dollar expenditure of the investment component. That is,

$$L_x = \frac{K_x}{K_T} (L_T) \qquad (5\text{-}13)$$

where

L_x = salvage value for investment component x

K_x = investment expenditure of component x

K_T = total capital investment

L_T = total salvage for K_T

Suppose in Example 5-4 that only a total salvage value of $900,000 is given for the total equipment investment ($9,000,000). The salvage value for the $3,000,000 equipment component using Eq. (5-13) is

$$L_x = \frac{3,000,000}{9,000,000}(900,000)$$
$$= \$300,000$$

This is the same value given in Table 5-5. However, it should *not* be concluded, because these salvage values are the same, that the salvage values for each investment component should always be in direct proportion to the investment component. Eq. (5-13) is simply a *convenient method* for determining component salvage values *when only the total salvage value is estimated*. If salvage values are estimated independently for each component, Eq. (5-13) does not necessarily have to be satisfied. Also, Eq. (5-13) is only applicable if the various components have the same depreciation life. It is not applicable if the depreciation lives of the components are different since this requires different depreciation accounts, which in turn would require the determination of salvage values for each component (depreciation account).

7. The assumption is implied, in regard to salvage values and the land, that no gains or losses occur. That is, the value actually realized from the disposition of these assets exactly equals the tax salvage value. Consequently, there are no gains or losses and therefore no possible tax effects. This is the usual assumption (convention) for cash flow calculations because of the problem of estimating actual realizable salvage values that occur in the distant future. This assumption can also be usually justified on the practical consideration that any difference between actual realizable salvage values and tax salvage values and the possible resulting tax effects contribute very little in the economic evaluation of a project due to the discounting process. That is, in the usual practical situation, salvage values are discounted over a long period of time and consequently have little effect in determining the internal rate of return or net present value.

8. Mathematically, it is not difficult to determine the IRR. However, this example does suggest that determining the IRR for a series of cash flows such as those given in Table 5-10 could be tedious. A computer program for determining the IRR is provided in the appendices.

Some Additional Tax Effects in Cash Flow Calculations   In spite of the practical arguments for disregarding possible differences between actual realizable salvage values and tax salvage values presented in Example 5-4, this section presents a method for including (approximating) tax effects in the cash flows calculations when there are estimated differences between actual realizable salvage values and tax salvage values. This presentation is provided for purposes of completeness and providing a project evaluator with an appreciation for the possible magnitude of these effects.

Salvage values used in determining *tax* depreciation amounts are based on tax considerations and regulations. They may or may not be representative of the actual realizable salvage value. When there are estimated differences between the realizable salvage value and tax salvage value, it may be necessary to include the tax effects. Whether or not these tax effects should be included in the cash flow calculations is dependent upon the classification of the retirement. If retirements are classified as normal under group depreciation or as ordinary under the ADR System, there are no tax effects because gains and losses are in general not recognized. If retirements are classified as abnormal or extraordinary, then tax effects should be included when there are gains or losses. For example, suppose in Example 5-4 that the *actual* realizable salvage values for the equipment available for retirement in year 20 are $240,000 and $600,000 for, respectively, K_2 and K_3. With these values and assuming normal or ordinary retirements, the cash flow for year 20 is

$$X_{20} = (4,000,000) - (4,000,000 - 72,000)(0.52)$$
$$+ 240,000 + 600,000 + 2,400,000$$

$$= \$5,197,440$$

For the case of abnormal or extraordinary retirements assuming Section 1245 Property, the cash flow is

$$X_{20} = (4,000,000) - (4,000,000 - 72,000)(0.52)$$
$$+ 240,000 + (300,000 - 240,000)(0.52)$$
$$+ 600,000 + 2,400,000$$

$$= \$5,228,640$$

The term

$$+ (300,000 - 240,000)(0.52)$$

is included because the loss of $(300,000 - 240,000)$ is a Section 1231 loss and therefore a reduction in ordinary income with a tax rate of 52%. If there is a gain, then there is an increase in taxes. Consequently, the cash flow must be reduced by the increased taxes. For example if the actual realizable salvage is $350,000 instead of $240,000, the cash flow for year 20 is

$$
\begin{aligned}
X_{20} &= (4{,}000{,}000) - (4{,}000{,}000 - 72{,}000)(0.52) \\
&\quad + 350{,}000 + 600{,}000 + 2{,}400{,}000 \\
&= \$5{,}307{,}440
\end{aligned}
$$

for the case of normal or ordinary retirements. For the case of abnormal or extraordinary retirements, the cash flow is

$$
\begin{aligned}
X_{20} &= (4{,}000{,}000) - (4{,}000{,}000 - 72{,}000)(0.52) \\
&\quad + 350{,}000 - (350{,}000 - 300{,}000)(0.52) \\
&\quad + 600{,}000 + 2{,}400{,}000 \\
&= \$5{,}281{,}440
\end{aligned}
$$

where the term

$$
- (350{,}000 - 300{,}000)(0.52)
$$

represents a reduction in cash flow since taxes are increased. Note that no tax adjustment is made to the $600,000 tax salvage value since the actual realizable salvage value is the same. In situations where there is more than one tax salvage value different from the actual salvage value, the gains and losses should be combined in accordance with the procedure discussed in Chapter 4 and then the net tax effect is included in the cash flow. In actuality the same result (cash flow) is obtained either by combining the gains or losses or by treating the gains and losses separately *as long as all gains and losses are changes in ordinary income*. However, if some of the gains are long-term capital gains, then these gains and any losses must be combined before the correct tax effect can be determined. This point is also made in Chapter 4. For example, suppose in year 26 the retirements are classified as abnormal or extraordinary and the actual realizable salvage values of $150,000 for the building and $600,000 for the land. These values imply the gains and losses shown in Table 5-11. Using the values in Table 5-11, the cash flow for year 26 is

$$
\begin{aligned}
X_{26} &= - (-72{,}000)(0.52) + 750{,}000 - (100{,}000 - 50{,}000)(0.28) \\
&= \$773{,}440
\end{aligned}
$$

It would be *incorrect* to calculate the cash flow as

$$
\begin{aligned}
X_{26} &= - (-72{,}000)(0.52) + 750{,}000 - 100{,}000\,(0.28) + 50{,}000\,(0.52) \\
&= \$785{,}440
\end{aligned}
$$

since this calculation treats the gain and loss separately. It should be

TABLE 5-11
Tax Treatment of Salvage Values

	Tax Salvage	Actual Salvage	Gain	Loss	Tax Treatment
Building	$200,000	$150,000	—	$50,000	Section 1231 loss
Land	500,000	600,000	$100,000	—	Section 1231 gain

noted that in these calculations a *reduction in taxes* is a *cash inflow*, while an *increase in taxes* is a *cash outflow*.

As another example, suppose the realizable salvage value of the land is $550,000 and $110,000 for the building. In this case the cash flow is

$$X_{26} = -(-72,000)(0.52) + 650,000 + (100,000 - 50,000)(0.52)$$
$$= \$713,440.$$

The previous calculation of cash flows that include tax effects are approximations since the true tax effects would depend on gains and losses from the disposal of other assets in the same year. That is, the tax effects are based on the assumption that they are the *only* gains and losses occurring during the year.

NET PRESENT VALUE

The net present value is the algebraic sum of the net cash flows discounted at the minimum acceptable rate of return (MARR), to time zero. Mathematically, the net present value is

$$\text{NPV} = \sum_{j=0}^{n} \frac{X'_j}{(1+k)^j} \tag{5-14}$$

where

NPV = net present value

X'_j = net cash flow in year j defined by either Eq. (5-7) or (5-8)

n = number of years of cash flow

j = the year in which the cash flow, X'_j, occurs

k = MARR = the minimum acceptable rate of return

As in the case of the IRR, k is dependent upon the definition used for the cash flows. If equity cash flows are used, it must be based on an acceptable (required) return on *only* equity funds. If total cash flows are used, it must be based on an acceptable return on the *combined total* of debt and equity funds.

Example 5-5

Calculate the net present value for the cash flows given in Tables 5-2 and 5-3 assuming the minimum acceptable rate of return is 12% for total cash flows.

Using Eq. (5-14), the net present value for total cash flows is

$$NPV = -100,000 + 19,080 \ (P/A \ 12,10) + 10,000 \ (P/F \ 12,10)$$

$$= \$11,026$$

Since the MARR for total (debt and equity) funds is 12%, this implies that the MARR for equity funds, k_e, based on Eq. (5-2) is

$$12 = (0.60) \ k_e + (1 - .52)(0.40)(10)$$

where

$$k_e = 16.8\%$$

Therefore, the net present value for the equity funds is

$$NPV = -60,000 + 13,160 \ (P/F \ 16.8,1) + 13,352 \ (P/F \ 16.8,2)$$
$$+ \ 13,544 \ (P/F \ 16.8,3) + \ldots + 24,888 \ (P/F \ 16.8,10)$$

$$= \$6,816$$

Decision Criterion for the NPV Using the net present value, a project is economically desirable if the NPV ≥ 0 and undesirable if NPV < 0. Consequently, in Example 5-5, the project is acceptable for both cash flow definitions. However, the result that both cash flow definitions gave the same decision *should not* be generalized. As mentioned in the discussion of the decision criterion for the IRR, equity cash flows can give a different decision than total cash flows as a result of the manner in which the debt obligation is paid.

The NPV decision criterion makes the same investment assumption that is stated in the discussion of the IRR decision criterion. That is, the capital required by a particular project could be invested in some other economic endeavor that would earn the value of MARR (NPV = 0).

Another Interpretation of the NPV If the cash flows given in Table 5-4 are used and the MARR is equal to 8%, the net present value is

$$NPV = -20,000 + 4,463 \ (P/A \ 8,6) + 1,000 \ (P/F \ 8,6)$$

$$= \$1,262$$

Now if the procedure shown in Table 5-4 is repeated with the exception that the MARR is used in place of the IRR, the results in Table 5-12 are obtained. The results in Table 5-12 indicate that all the capital is recovered somewhere between the fifth and six year with a yearly return of 8% on the unrecovered capital. Also a surplus of $2,003 is realized in the sixth year. If this surplus is discounted to time zero at the MARR, the result is

$$2,003 \; (P/F \; 8,6) = \$1,262$$

which is the NPV. Consequently, a *positive* NPV can be interpreted as a surplus or a "bonus," measured in present dollars, that a project provides in addition to the recovery of all capital and a return of MARR on the unrecovered capital. A negative NPV indicates the amount of capital not recovered, in present dollars, at the value of MARR. If equity cash flows are used to calculate the net present value, a positive NPV "belongs" to the equity stockholder (an increase in wealth). If total cash flows are used, the NPV is a return to the combined pool of debt and equity capital.

THE RELATIONSHIP BETWEEN THE NPV AND THE IRR

The internal rate of return and net present value give the same decision regarding the economic desirability of a *single project with traditional cash flows*. That is, a project that is acceptable using the IRR criterion is also acceptable using the NPV criterion. Conversely, if it is unacceptable using the IRR, it is unacceptable using the NPV. This relationship can

TABLE 5-12
The Meaning of the Net Present Value

End of Year	Net Cash Flow	Return on Unrecovered Capital	Capital Recovered	Unrecovered Capital
0	−20,000	—	—	−20,000
1	4,463	0.08(−20,000) = $−1,600	4,463 − 1,600 = $2,863	−20,000 + 2,863 = $−17,137
2	4,463	0.08(−17,137) = −1,371	4,463 − 1,371 = 3,092	−17,137 + 3,092 = −14,045
3	4,463	0.08(−14,045) = −1,124	4,463 − 1,124 = 3,339	−14,045 + 3,339 = −10,706
4	4,463	0.08(−10,706) = − 856	4,463 − 856 = 3,607	−10,706 + 3,607 = − 7,099
5	4,463	0.08(− 7,099) = − 568	4,463 − 568 = 3,895	− 7,099 + 3,895 = − 3,204
6	1,000[a] + 4,463	0.08(− 3,204) = − 256	5,463[b] − 256 = 5,207	− 3,204 + 5,207 = + 2,003

[a] Salvage value.
[b] Includes salvage value.

be seen by plotting the net present value profile for a series of *traditional cash flows*. The net present value profile for a series of traditional cash flows is shown in Figure 5-1. This figure is basically a plot of the NPV and the MARR (indicated as *i* in Figure 5-1). It is obtained for a particular series of cash flows by assuming various MARR values, calculating the corresponding NPV, and plotting these results.

If Figure 5-1 is considered, it can be seen that if MARR is i_1 the NPV is positive, which indicates that the MARR is less than the IRR. If MARR is i_2, the NPV is negative, which indicates that the MARR is greater than the IRR. These results substantiate the earlier statement that the IRR and NPV give the same decision. However, it should be noted that this is *only true for traditional cash flows*.

NONTRADITIONAL CASH FLOWS

A series of nontraditional cash flows can give multiple rates of return. This occurrence is a result of Descartes "rule of signs" which states that the number of real positive roots is never greater than the number of sign changes for an nth-degree polynomial. The applicability of this rule to finding a rate of return can be seen by expanding Eq. (5-12). That is,

$$0 = X_0 + aX_1 = a^2X_2 + \ldots + a^nX_n \tag{5-15}$$

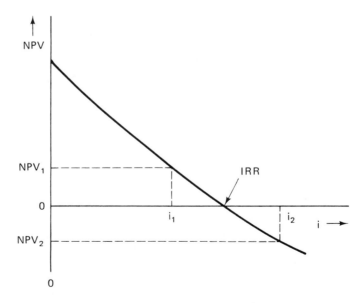

FIGURE 5-1   Net Present Value Profile for Traditional Cash Flows

where

$$a = \frac{1}{(1 + i)} \tag{5-16}$$

Eq. (5-15) is an nth-degree polynomial. Therefore, if the number of sign changes in Eq. (5-15) is two or more, then there *may* be more than one rate of return. Two or more sign changes in the cash flows is a *necessary* condition but not a *sufficient* condition for the existence of more than one rate of return. There are numerous examples of cash flows that give more than one rate of return. Some of these examples are given in G. T. Stevens' *Economic and Financial Analysis of Capital Investments* (see References). When more than one rate of return exists for a series of cash flows, the net present value and its related decision criterion should be used to determine the economic desirability of the cash flows.

Example 5-6 _____

For the series of cash flows shown in Table 5-13, determine the net present value profile and determine under what circumstances the cash flows are acceptable.

Calculating the net present values for various interest rates gives the results shown in Table 5-14. Plotting these results gives Figure 5-2. Figure 5-2 indicates that the series of cash flows given in Table 5-13 is acceptable if the MARR is between 0% and 20% or between 50% and 100%.

THE PAYBACK PERIOD

A method that is sometimes used for the economic evaluation of a project is the payback period (or payout period). The payback period is the number of years required for incoming cash flows to balance the cash outflows. Expressed mathematically, the payback period, p, is

$$0 = \sum_{j=0}^{p} X'_j \tag{5-17}$$

TABLE 5-13
Cash Flows for Example 5-6

End of Year	Cash Flow
0	−500
1	2,350
2	−3,600
3	1,800

TABLE 5-14
Net Present Values for Example 5-6

i	NPV
0	50
10	13
20	0
30	−3
50	0
70	3
100	0

Eq. (5-17) is one definition of the payback period. There is another definition that employs a discounting procedure. However, Eq. (5-17) is the definition most often used in practice.

Example 5-7 _____

Determine the payback period for the series of cash flows given in Table 5-15.

Using Eq. (5-17), the sum of the cash flows for the first five years is

$$-20{,}000 - 7{,}000 - 5{,}000 + 8{,}000 + 9{,}000 + 9{,}000 = \$-6{,}000$$

and for the first six years is

$$-20{,}000 - 7{,}000 - 5{,}000 + 8{,}000 + 9{,}000 + 9{,}000 + 10{,}000 = \$4{,}000$$

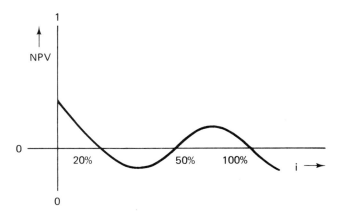

FIGURE 5-2 Net Present Value Profile for Example 5-6

TABLE 5-15
Cash Flows for Example 5-7

End of Year	Net Cash Flow
0	−20,000
1	− 7,000
2	− 5,000
3	8,000
4	9,000
5	9,000
6	10,000
7	10,000
8	10,000

which implies the payback period is between five and six years. Using linear interpolation the payback period is

$$p = 5 + \frac{6,000}{10,000}$$

$$= 5.6 \text{ years}$$

Decision Criterion   The usual approach used with the payback period is to compare a project's payback period with some predetermined payback period. If a project's payback period is equal to or less than the predetermined period, the project is acceptable. Otherwise, the project is unacceptable.

There are serious drawbacks to using the payback period as a procedure for evaluating the economic desirability of a project. It is a simple task to provide examples of cash flows that are acceptable using the IRR or NPV but are unacceptable using the payback criterion. Conversely, examples are possible where a series of cash flows is acceptable based on the payback period but are unacceptable from the standpoints of the IRR and NPV. These conflicts occur because the payback period does not consider the time value of money nor does it consider what the cash flows are after the payback period.

The payback period may have some merit as a secondary criterion. Once a project is considered acceptable on the basis of NPV or IRR, the payback might be used as a rough indicator of a project's effect on a company's liquidity requirements.

INFLATIONARY EFFECTS

For clarity's sake the previous discussions in this chapter did not explicitly include inflationary effects. However, it can be assumed that inflationary effects were included in some correct manner. That is, the estimates of gross incomes, costs, and other variables in the cash flow equation are in terms of either real or actual dollars (at this point, the section on inflation in Chapter 2 should be reviewed).

In order to explicitly include inflationary effects in economic evaluation of a project, each component in the cash flow equation must be estimated (calculated) on a consistent basis of either *real* or *actual* dollars. If this is done, the evaluation will give the same results for either real or actual dollars. This can be shown by considering the data in Table 5-3 as real dollars and the discount rate of 16.8% used in calculating the NPV ($6,816) as a rate unadjusted for inflation. If a constant yearly inflation rate, e, of 8% is used to convert the real dollar cash flow components (gross income, costs, depreciation, etc.) in Table 5-3 to actual dollars, each component value must be multiplied by the appropriate $(F/P\ e, j)$ factor. Then, the cash flows can be calculated in terms of actual dollars. However, since every cash flow component occurring in the same year is multiplied by the same $(F/P\ e, j)$ factor, it is only necessary to multiply the net cash flow in real dollars by the appropriate $(F/P\ e, j)$ factor to obtain the net cash flows in actual dollars. This procedure is shown in Table 5-16. If the discount rate (MARR) is adjusted for inflation, the result, using Eq. (2-7), is

$$f = 0.168 + 0.08 + (0.168)(0.08)$$

$$= .26144$$

$$= 26.144\%$$

TABLE 5-16

Conversion of Real Dollar Cash Flows to Actual Dollar Cash Flows

End of Year	Real Dollar Cash Flows	Factor $(F/P\ 8, j)$	Actual Dollar Cash Flows
0	−$60,000	1.0000	−$60,000
1	13,160	1.0800	14,213
2	13,352	1.1664	15,574
3	13,544	1.2597	17,061
4	13,736	1.3605	18,688
5	13,928	1.4693	20,464
6	14,120	1.5869	22,407
7	14,312	1.7138	24,528
8	14,504	1.8509	26,845
9	14,696	1.9990	29,377
10	24,888	1.1589	53,731

and calculating the NPV of the actual dollar cash flows in Table 5-16 gives

$$\text{NPV} = -60{,}000 + 14{,}213\,(P/F\ 26.144{,}1) + 15{,}574\,(P/F\ 26.144{,}2)$$
$$+17{,}061\,(P/F\ 26.144{,}3) + \ldots + 53{,}731\,(P/F\ 26.144{,}10)$$
$$= \$6{,}816$$

which is the same result obtained using real dollars and a discount rate unadjusted for inflation.

A basic point that must be remembered, from the standpoint of including inflationary effects in the economic evaluation of a project, is the maintenance of a consistent relationship between the cash flows and the discount (MARR) rate. That is, if the cash flows are in real dollars, the discount rate used in association with the IRR or NPV is unadjusted for inflation. If actual dollars are used, the discount rate is adjusted for inflation. Another point that should be remembered, in estimating the cash flow components, is that certain components are unresponsive to inflation. Such items as interest payments, depreciation, and leasing costs are unresponsive to inflation because of their contractual nature and consequently are in terms of actual dollars.

OTHER MEASURES OF A PROJECT'S ECONOMIC WORTH

In addition to the methods already presented in this chapter for evaluating the economic desirability of a project, there are other methods that are sometimes proposed. Some of these methods are (1) proceeds per dollar of outlay, (2) average proceeds per dollar of outlay, (3) average income on investment, and (4) average income on average book value. None of these methods consider the time value of money and are not acceptable as measures of a project's economic worth. Hence, they are not discussed further.

The Benefit-Cost Ratio   Another method for the evaluation of projects is the benefit-cost ratio (B/C). This method has received wide attention particularly in the evaluation of projects in the public (government) sector. For a particular project, the basic definition of the B/C ratio is

$$\text{B/C} = \frac{\displaystyle\sum_{j=0}^{n} B_j\,(1+k)^j}{\displaystyle\sum_{j=0}^{n} C_j\,(1+k)^j} \tag{5-18}$$

where

$$B_j = \text{project benefits in the year } j$$

$$C_j = \text{project costs in the year } j$$

$$k = \text{MARR}$$

The decision criterion used in conjunction with the B/C ratio defined by Eq. (5-18) is to accept the project if the B/C ratio is equal to or greater than one and reject the project if the ratio is less than one. Now, there is a problem with the B/C ratio. This problem revolves around the definitions of benefit and cost and can be shown numerically by considering the data in Table 5-17. This table shows cash flow data for a particular project. In applying Eq. (5-18) to the data in Table 5-17, one approach might be to define the benefits as positive net cash flows and the costs as negative net cash flows. That is, assuming MARR equals 15%, the discounted benefits and costs are

$$B = 59,000 \, (P/A \; 15,3)(P/F \; 15,1) + 69,000 \, (P/F \; 15,5)$$

$$= \$151,450$$

$$C = 100,000 + 31,000 \, (P/F \; 15,1)$$

$$= \$126,958$$

which gives a B/C ratio of

$$B/C = \frac{151,450}{126,958}$$

$$= 1.193$$

TABLE 5-17
Cash Flow Data for B/C Ratio

End of Year	Capital Investments	Salvage Value	Total Depreciation[b]	Gross Income	Annual Costs	Taxes (T = 50%)	Net Cash Flows[c]
0	−$100,000	—	—	—	—	—	−$100,000
1	− 80,000	—	$18,000	$100,000	$20,000	$31,000	−$ 31,000
2	—	—	38,000	100,000	20,000	21,000	59,000
3	—	—	38,000	100,000	20,000	21,000	59,000
4	—	—	38,000	100,000	20,000	21,000	59,000
5	—	$10,000[a]	38,000	100,000	20,000	21,000	69,000[d]

[a] The salvage value for K_0 is $10,000 and for K_1 zero.
[b] Straight-line depreciation is used for both K_0 and K_1 with depreciation lives of five and four years, respectively.
[c] Based on Eq. (5-8).
[d] Includes $10,000 salvage.

Another approach might be to define the denominator of the B/C ratio in terms of the required capital investments (K_0 and K_1) and omit the capital investment in the cash flow result. With this approach the discounted benefits and costs are

$$B = 49{,}000\ (P/F\ 15{,}1) + 59{,}000\ (P/A\ 15{,}3)(P/F\ 15{,}1)$$
$$+ 69{,}000\ (P/F\ 15{,}5)$$

$$= \$194{,}060$$

$$C = 100{,}000 + 80{,}000\ (P/F\ 15{,}1)$$

$$= \$169{,}568$$

and the B/C ratio is

$$B/C = \frac{194{,}060}{169{,}568}$$

$$= 1.144$$

A third approach, and the final one considered, is to define all positive (inflow) cash flow components as benefits and all negative (outflow) components as costs. This approach gives

$$B = 100{,}000\ (P/A\ 15{,}5) + 10{,}000\ (P/F\ 15{,}5)$$

$$= \$340{,}192$$

$$C = 100{,}000 + 80{,}000\ (P/F\ 15{,}1) + 20{,}000\ (P/A\ 15{,}5)$$
$$+ 31{,}000\ (P/F\ 15{,}1) + 21{,}000\ (P/A\ 15{,}4)(P/F\ 15{,}1)$$

$$= \$315{,}707$$

and a B/C ratio of

$$B/C = \frac{340{,}192}{315{,}707}$$

$$= 1.078$$

These three approaches all give different values and point out that the B/C ratio depends on how the benefits and costs are defined. It is true that if the B/C ratio is greater than one for a particular project, the NPV for the same project is positive. However, since the B/C ratio does not provide any computational advantages over the NPV and since it is weakened by its dependency on the definitions of benefits and costs, it is not used further in this text.

REFERENCES

Gordon, M. J. *The Investment, Financing, and Valuation of the Corporation.* Homewood, Ill.: Richard D. Irwin, 1962.

Gordon, M. J., and Shapiro, E. "Capital Equipment Analysis: The Required Rate of Profit." *Management Science* 3 (October 1956): 102–10.

Haley, C. W., and Schall, L. D. *The Theory of Financial Decisions.* New York: McGraw-Hill Book Co., 1973.

Lewellen, Wilbur G. *The Cost of Capital.* Belmont, Calif.: Wadsworth Publishing Co., 1969.

Robichek, A. A., and Myers, S. C. *Optimal Financial Decisions.* Englewood Cliffs, N.J.: Prentice-Hall, 1965.

Stevens, G. T., Jr. *Economic and Financial Analysis of Capital Investments.* New York: John Wiley & Sons, 1979.

Solomon, Ezra. "Measuring a Company's Cost of Capital." *Journal of Business* (October 1955).

VanHorne, James C. *Financial Management and Policy.* 2d ed. Englewood Cliffs, N.J.: Prentice-Hall, 1971.

Weston, J. F., and Brighan, E. F. *Essentials of Managerial Finance.* 3d ed. Hinsdale, Ill.: Dryden Press, 1974.

PROBLEMS

5-1. For the net cash flows given below, determine the following:

(a) The net present value if MARR equals 12%.

(b) The internal rate of return.

(c) The payback period.

End of Year	Net Cash Flow
0	−200,000
1	−300,000
2	100,000
3	100,000
4	100,000
5	100,000
6	100,000
7	100,000
8	100,000
9	100,000
10	100,000

5-2. For the net cash flows given below, determine the following:

(a) The net present value if MARR equals 15%.

(b) The internal rate of return.

(c) The payback period.

End of Year	Net Cash Flow
0	− 50,000
1	− 70,000
2	−100,000
3	30,000
4	50,000
5	70,000
6	100,000
7	100,000
8	100,000
9	100,000
10	100,000
11	100,000
12	100,000

5-3. A company uses a minimum acceptable rate of return of 20% for total cash flows. If the company's debt ratio is 40%, tax rate is 52%, and the cost of debt capital is 15%, what is the company's implied required return on equity capital?

5-4. A company is considering certain modifications to one of its production systems. The modifications will require an initial expenditure of $500,000 for equipment. It is estimated that the modifications will provide gross savings of $300,000 per year for ten years and the annual costs for operating the new equipment are a total of $100,000 per year. For tax purposes, the company uses straight-line depreciation, a salvage value of zero, and a life of ten years for evaluating projects of this type. The company's tax rate is 52% and the investment tax credit is to be neglected. If the minimum acceptable rate of return is 20% for total cash flows, are the modifications economically justified?

5-5. Repeat Problem 5-4 on the basis of equity cash flows. Assume the debt ratio is 40%, the cost of debt is 15%, and the debt obligation is to be paid back in ten equal installments of principal with interest payments assessed on the unpaid balance.

5-6. Repeat Problem 5-5 using the following methods of debt payment:

(a) Constant principal payment over a five-year period.
(b) Constant interest.
(c) Cost and yearly payment of interest and principal.

5-7. Based on the results obtained in the solutions to Problems 5-4, 5-5, and 5-6 what generalizations are possible in relation to the use of equity and total cash flows in determining the acceptability of a project? Suppose in Problem 5-4 a debt ratio of zero is used. What does this imply? What would the cash flows be?

5-8. Determine the yearly interest and principal payments using the four methods of debt payment shown in Table 5-1 if the amount borrowed is $100,000, the loan is to be paid back in eight years, and the loan interest rate is 10%. Also determine the total present value of principal and interest for the four methods using the following discount rates: (a) 5%, (b) 10%, and (c) 15%. Using these results, are any generalizations possible?

5-9. A particular investment requires a capital expenditure of $300,000. It is expected that this investment will provide a gross income of $200,000 per year for ten years and costs of $100,000 for the same period of time. The tax depreciation is based on a straight-line model, a life of ten years, and a salvage value of zero. The tax rate is 52%. Determine the following:

(a) The net present value profile for the total cash flows.
(b) The net present value profile for the equity cash flows assuming a debt ratio of 30%, a 10% cost of debt capital, and the debt is paid back in ten equal installments of principal with interest assessed on the unpaid principal.

5-10. Repeat Problem 5-9 but use the following depreciation models for tax purposes:

(a) Sum-of-the-years-digits.
(b) Double declining-balance with switch over to straight-line.

5-11. Based on the results obtained in the solution of Problems 5-9 and 5-10, what generalizations are possible?

5-12. A company is considering certain modifications to one of its manufacturing processes. The equipment necessary for these modifications has an initial cost of $600,000 and qualifies for a 10% investment tax credit. It is estimated that these modifications will result in gross savings of $420,000 per year for ten years but will increase yearly costs by $200,000 per year for the same period of time. For tax purposes the company will depreciate the equipment over a ten-year period using a straight-line model and a salvage value of $60,000. The company's tax rate is 52%. The company's present debt ratio is 20%, and this ratio is not expected to change in the future. The major source of the company's borrowed money is through the sale of company bonds that mature in ten years. These bonds pay 15%. Determine if the modifications are economically justified on the basis of a required return on equity of 25%.

5-13. For cash flows given below plot the net present value profile.

End of Year	Cash Flows
0	—
1	80
2	80
3	80
4	80
5	80
6	−1,400
7	200
8	200
9	200
10	200
11	200
12	200

5-14. A company is considering a project with the data and conditions given below. Determine if the project is acceptable if the required return on equity is 15%.

Capital Investment and Working Capital Requirements

End of Year	Capital Investment	Working Capital
0	—	—
1	$1,000,000	—
2	2,000,000	—
3	4,000,000	—
4	2,000,000	$2,000,000
5	1,000,000	2,000,000

Gross Income and Costs

End of Year	Gross Income	Cost
0	—	—
1	—	—
2	—	—
3	—	—
4	—	—
5	—	—
6	$10,000,000	$3,000,000
.	.	.
.	.	.
.	.	.
25	10,000,000	3,000,000

Conditions:

1. The project cannot provide service until the entire capital investment ($10,000,000) is made. For tax purposes, the depreciation is based on a straight-line model with a life of 20 years and a zero salvage value.
2. The company plans to maintain a constant debt ratio of 30%, and its tax rate is 52%.
3. All debt financing is to be obtained through the sale of bonds. The interest rate paid on the bonds is 12% and the bonds mature in 20 years.

5-15. A company is considering a new product line. It is estimated that this new product line will require the following capital expenditures and increases in working capital:

End of Year	Capital Expenditure	Use	Depreciation Life	Salvage Value	Working Capital
0	$200,000	Land	—	—	—
1	500,000	Building	20	40,000	100,000
2	800,000	Equipment	15	50,000	150,000
3	500,000	Equipment	15	20,000	200,000

As a result of this new product line, it is estimated that gross incomes and costs will increase by the amounts shown below:

End of Year	Gross Income	Cost
0	—	—
1	—	$400,000
2	—	400,000
3	$300,000	400,000
4	500,000	400,000
5	1,000,000	400,000
6	1,000,000	400,000
7	1,000,000	400,000
8	1,000,000	400,000
9	1,000,000	400,000
10	1,000,000	400,000
11	1,000,000	400,000
12	1,000,000	400,000
13	1,000,000	400,000
14	1,000,000	400,000
15	1,000,000	400,000

Determine if this new product line is economically justified assuming the company's required return on equity is 15% and the following additional points are considered:

1. The company's debt ratio is 30%, and this is not expected to change.
2. All debt funds are to be paid back in ten equal installments of principal with interest paid yearly on the unpaid principal at a rate of 10%.
3. Tax depreciation for each capital expenditure component begins immediately following the capital and is based on a straight-line depreciation model.
4. The investment tax credit (10%) is applicable for the equipment.
5. The tax rate is 52%.
6. There is sufficient taxable income from the company's other activities to take advantage of any depreciation or interest deductions that are not offset by the taxable incomes from this project.

5-16. A project requires an initial expenditure of $70,000. For tax purposes straight-line depreciation is used with a life of five years and a zero salvage value. The tax rate is 52%. The gross income and costs per year for five years are, respectively, $40,000 and $10,000 in terms of *actual dollars*. Using total cash flows, determine the following:

(a) Is the project acceptable if the MARR is 15% for total cash flows and the inflation rate is 10%?
(b) What are the yearly total cash flows in terms of real dollars?

5-17. Repeat Problem 5-16 and assume that 50% of the initial expenditure is from debt sources. The payment of debt money is based on a constant principal payment over the life of the project, and the cost of the debt is 12% assessed on the unpaid balance.

5-18. A project requires an initial expenditure of $100,000. For tax purposes straight-line depreciation is used with a life of five years and a zero salvage value. The tax rate is 52%. The gross income and costs per year for five years are, respectively, $65,000 and $20,000 in terms of *real dollars*. Using total cash flows, determine the following:

(a) Is the project acceptable if the MARR is 15% for total cash flows and the inflation rate is 10%?
(b) What are the cash flows in terms of actual dollars?

5-19. Repeat Problem 5-18 only assume that 50% of the initial expenditure is from debt sources. The payment of debt money is based on a constant principal payment over the life of the project, and the cost of the debt is 12% assessed on the unpaid balance.

5-20. A company is considering a project that has an initial cost of $3 million. This initial cost is divided between a building that costs $1 million and equipment that costs $2 million. The company uses the ADR system and consequently must maintain separate depreciation accounts for the building (Section 1250 Property) and the equipment (Section 1245 Property). The building will be depreciated on the basis of a straight-line model with a life of ten years and a salvage value of $200,000. It is expected that this project will provide gross savings of $2 million per year for 20 years and increase costs by $800,000 per year for the same period of time. Determine the following:

(a) The total cash flows.
(b) The total cash flow for year 20 if the building and equipment are disposed of at this time for their respective salvage values.
(c) Repeat Part (b) if the building and equipment are disposed of for $150,000 and $100,000 respectively.
(d) Repeat Part (b) if the building and equipment are disposed of for $120,000 and $250,000 respectively.
(e) Determine the cash flow for year 15 on the basis that all cash flows are terminated at this point and the disposal prices of the building and equipment are $300,000 and $100,000 respectively. Assume that the depreciation schedules are fixed by tax regulations and consequently remain the same as in Part (a).

6

MINIMUM ANNUAL REVENUE REQUIREMENTS

Minimum annual revenue requirements provide another method for the economic evaluation of a project. In addition, they can be used to make cost comparisons and analyze replacement alternatives. Basically, minimum annual revenue requirements are the *minimum* yearly gross incomes that provide for the recovery of invested capital, all costs, and a return on the yearly unrecovered capital.

Minimum annual revenue requirements can be expressed mathematically as

$$R_j = D_{bj} + F_{ej} + I_j + C_j + t_j \qquad (6\text{-}1)$$

The components in Eq. (6-1) are defined as follows:

R_j = *the minimum annual revenue requirement for year j.* This can also be considered as the minimum gross income or the annual costs with a required return on equity.

D_{bj} = *the total capital recovered in year j.* This is the amount of the total investment (capital) recovered in year j. It is usually estimated on the basis of a depreciation model and is often referred to as the book depreciation. The book depreciation may or may not be the same as the tax depreciation. There is no requirement that they be the same. Since the book depreciation is based on the total investment (not just the equity portion), the assumption is implied in generating revenue requirements that any debt portion of the investment is being recovered over the book depreciation life. Further, the capital recovered (book depreciation) in

139

the year j is proportional between the recovery of the debt capital, D_{dj}, and equity capital, D_{ej}, in accordance with the debt ratio, c. That is,

$$D_{dj} = cD_{bj} \tag{6-2}$$

$$D_{ej} = (1 - c)D_{bj} \tag{6-3}$$

The recovery of the debt capital can be considered as the recovery of the principal involved in any borrowed money.

F_{ej} = *return on equity in year j.* Mathematically, this is determined by

$$F_{ej} = (1 - c)(k_e)(B_{j-1}) \tag{6-4}$$

where, k_e is the minimum acceptable return (MARR) on equity and B_{j-1} is the book value for the year $(j - 1)$ based on the book depreciation method. The value of k_e is usually assumed to be a constant over the life of the project.

I_j = *debt interest cost in year j.* Mathematically, this is determined by the equation

$$I_j = (c)(k_d)(B_{j-1}) \tag{6-5}$$

where k_d is the cost of debt capital and assumed to be constant over the life of the project. Eqs. (6-4) and (6-5) are sometimes added to define an overall return, F_{oj}, as

$$F_{oj} = F_{ej} + I_j = \left[(1 - c)k_e + ck_d\right]B_{j-1} \tag{6-6}$$

Using Eq. (5-5), Eq. (6-6) can be written as

$$F_{oj} = k_b(B_{j-1}) \tag{6-7}$$

This text prefers to keep the returns on equity and debt interest separate and not use Eq. (6-7) since separation of these quantities facilitates an understanding of minimum annual revenue requirements.

C_j = *annual costs in year j.* These are the annual costs of operation and maintenance. They could also be the costs of labor and materials, but they do not include depreciation.

t_j = *taxes paid in year j.* An expression for the annual taxes can be obtained by considering the basic equation for the incremental taxes; namely,

$$t_j = (G_j - C_j - I_j - D_j)T \tag{6-8}$$

Since the minimum annual revenue requirements are the minimum gross incomes, Eq. (6-1) is substituted in Eq. (6-8) for G_j. The result is

$$t_j = (D_{bj} + F_{ej} - D_j + t_j)T \tag{6-9}$$

which can be written as

$$t_j - t_j T = (D_{bj} + F_{ej} - D_j)T \tag{6-10}$$

and rearranged to give

$$t_j = \frac{T}{1-T}(D_{bj} + F_{ej} - D_j) \tag{6-11}$$

Levelized Minimum Annual Revenue Requirements   This is simply another name for an *equivalent annual amount* of the minimum annual revenue requirements. It is often used in determining the economic desirability of a project. This equivalent annual amount, E, is obtained by

$$E = \left[\sum_{j=1}^{n} R_j(P/F\ k_b,j) \right](A/P\ k_b,n) \tag{6-12}$$

It should be noted that the discount rate, k_b, in Eq. (6-12) is the weighted cost of capital given by Eq. (5-5). The use of Eq. (5-5) to define the discount rate k_b is discussed in greater detail later in this chapter.

Example 6-1

Using the data given below, generate the annual revenue requirements and determine the levelized revenue requirement:

$$\text{initial cost of the project} = \$100,000$$

$$\text{book depreciation} = \text{straight-line model}$$

$$\text{salvage} = \$20,000$$

$$\text{life} = 10 \text{ years}$$

$$\text{tax depreciation} = \text{sum-of-the-years-digits model}$$

$$\text{salvage} = \$10,000$$

$$\text{life} = 8 \text{ years}$$

$$\text{required return on equity} = 30\%$$

$$\text{cost of debt capital} = 15\%$$

$$\text{debt ratio} = \tfrac{1}{3}$$

$$\text{tax rate} = 52\%$$

$$\text{total costs} = \$7,000 \text{ per year}$$

The minimum annual revenue requirements for this data are given in Table 6-1. Some sample calculations follow:

The book depreciation amounts are

$$D_b = \frac{100,000 - 20,000}{10}$$

$$= \$8,000$$

since straight-line depreciation is specified. The tax depreciation amounts for the first two years are

$$D_1 = \frac{8}{36}(100,000 - 10,000)$$

$$= \$20,000$$

$$D_2 = \frac{7}{36}(100,000 - 10,000)$$

$$= \$17,500$$

It should be noted that in generating the minimum annual revenue requirements it is not required that the tax and book depreciation models, including life and salvage, be the same.

TABLE 6-1
Minimum Annual Revenue Requirements for Example 6-1

End of Year	Book Depreciation D_b	Tax Depreciation D	Book Value B	Equity Return F_e	Debt Interest I	Tax t	Annual Cost C	Minimum Annual Revenue Requirement R
0	—	—	$100,000	—	—	—	—	—
1	$8,000	$20,000	92,000	$20,000	$5,000	$ 8,666	$7,000	$48,666
2	8,000	17,500	84,000	18,400	$4,600	9,641	7,000	47,641
3	8,000	15,000	76,000	16,800	4,200	10,616	7,000	46,616
4	8,000	12,500	68,000	15,200	3,800	11,591	7,000	45,591
5	8,000	10,000	60,000	13,600	3,400	12,566	7,000	44,566
6	8,000	7,500	52,000	12,000	3,000	13,541	7,000	43,541
7	8,000	5,000	44,000	10,400	2,600	14,516	7,000	42,516
8	8,000	2,500	36,000	8,800	2,200	15,491	7,000	41,491
9	8,000	—	28,000	7,200	1,800	16,466	7,000	40,466
10	8,000	—	20,000	5,600	1,400	14,733	7,000	36,733

The equity returns for the first two years using Eq. (6-4) are

$$F_{e1} = \left(1 - \frac{1}{3}\right)\left(0.30\right)\left(100{,}000\right)$$

$$= \$20{,}000$$

$$F_{e2} = \left(1 - \frac{1}{3}\right)\left(0.30\right)\left(92{,}000\right)$$

$$= \$18{,}400$$

and debt interest for the first two years, using Eq. (6-5) are

$$I_1 = \left(\frac{1}{3}\right)\left(0.15\right)\left(100{,}000\right)$$

$$= \$5{,}000$$

$$I_2 = \left(\frac{1}{3}\right)\left(0.15\right)\left(92{,}000\right)$$

$$= \$4{,}600$$

Using Eq. (6-11), the taxes for the first two years are

$$t_1 = \frac{0.52}{1 - 0.52}(8{,}000 + 20{,}000 - 20{,}000)$$

$$= \$8{,}666$$

$$t_2 = \frac{0.52}{1 - 0.52}(8{,}000 + 18{,}400 - 17{,}500)$$

$$= \$9{,}641$$

The revenue requirements for the first two years, using Eq. (6-1), are

$$R_1 = 8{,}000 + 20{,}000 + 5{,}000 + 7{,}000 + 8{,}666$$

$$= \$48{,}666$$

$$R_2 = 8{,}000 + 18{,}400 + 4{,}600 + 7{,}000 + 9{,}641$$

$$= \$47{,}641$$

It is instructive at this point to see if the taxes given by Eq. (6-11) are the same as the taxes given by Eq. (6-8). Using the R_j values as the gross incomes, the taxes given by Eq. (6-8) for the first two years are

$$t_1 = (48{,}666 - 7{,}000 - 5{,}000 - 20{,}000)(0.52)$$

$$= \$8{,}666$$

$$t_2 = (47{,}641 - 7{,}000 - 4{,}600 - 17{,}500)(0.52)$$

$$= \$9{,}641$$

which are the same as the taxes given by Eq. (6-11).

Using Eq. (6-12), the levelized revenue requirement is

$$E = [48{,}666\,(P/F\ 25{,}1) + 47{,}641\,(P/F\ 25{,}2) + \ldots$$
$$+ 36{,}733\ (P/F\ 25{,}10)]\,(A/P\ 25{,}10)$$

$$= \$45{,}723 \text{ per year}$$

Decision Criterion for Minimum Annual Revenue Requirements

The basic decision criterion is to compare the minimum annual revenue requirements with the expected (actual) revenues (gross incomes). If the minimum revenue requirements are less than or equal to the expected revenues, the project is acceptable. Otherwise, the project is unacceptable. This decision criterion allows a comparison of minimum and actual revenues on an *attribute basis* as opposed to an actual numerical comparison. That is, are the minimum annual revenue requirements less than the expected gross revenues (incomes)? A yes or no answer to this question provides a decision regarding the acceptability of a project. This decision criterion is based on the fact that if the levelized (equivalent annual) amount of the revenue requirements is less than the levelized (equivalent annual) amount of the expected gross revenues, the IRR of the implied cash flows is larger than MARR which also means that the NPV is positive. Similarly if the levelized revenue requirement is greater than the levelized expected gross revenues, this implies that the IRR is less than MARR and the NPV is negative. These relationships are shown numerically in a later discussion.

Revenue requirements provide another dimension from the standpoint of evaluating a particular project. They allow a comparison of *yearly* revenues. Or, as this text chooses to call it, a comparison of the *short-term effects* as well as a comparison of the *long-term effects*. The long-term effects are the levelized amounts of the minimum revenue requirements and the expected annual revenues. For example, suppose in Example 6-1, the expected annual revenues are constant values of $60,000, $35,000, $47,000, and $43,000. In the case of the $60,000 value, the project is acceptable since this value is greater than all the minimum revenue requirements given in Table 6-1. This also implies that the levelized minimum annual revenue requirement ($45,723) is less than the levelized amount of the expected revenues ($60,000 in this case since it is a constant amount). Similarly in the case of the $35,000 amount, the project is unacceptable since this value is less than all the revenue requirements. In the case of the $47,000 value, the decision is not quite as clear since this value is less than R_1 and R_2 and greater than all other R_j values. However, it is greater than the levelized revenue requirement. The basic question in this case is: Do the short-term effects (the yearly R values) outweigh the long-term effects (the levelized amount)? If in a particular year the actual gross income is less than the required minimum, this might have an undesirable effect upon a company's financial position from the standpoint of such things as availability of funds for investment and dividend payments. If these short-term effects, or others, are considered critical, it is possible that the project might be rejected even though the levelized expected revenues are greater than the levelized minimum annual revenue requirements. In the case of the $43,000 amount, the project is rejected because the levelized revenue requirement is lower than the levelized expected amount; and the yearly revenue requirements are, for the most part, larger than the expected revenues. The possible conflict between the short-term and long-term effects occurs in cases where the levelized expected revenue is greater than the levelized minimum revenue requirements but some of the yearly minimum revenue requirements are greater than the yearly expected revenues. In these cases, the decision-maker must ultimately make a choice between the short-term and long-term effects.

The Investment Tax Credit   In the formulation of the annual revenue requirements, a provision for the investment tax credit is not included. This was done, initially, to facilitate the presentation. However, it is a relatively easy matter to include a provision for the investment tax credit. This is accomplished by adding the term

$$- \frac{V}{1-T} \qquad (6\text{-}13)$$

to the revenue requirements (or the tax equation) *for just the first year.* The value V is the investment tax credit. Eq. (6-13) is based on the fact that for a decrease in taxes, the equivalent reduction in gross income is $G(1-T)$. As an example of the use of Eq. (6-13), suppose a 10% investment tax credit is applicable in Example 6-1. The revenue requirement in year one is changed to

$$R_1 = 48{,}666 - \frac{100{,}000\,(0.10)}{1-0.52}$$

$$= \$27{,}833$$

and the other revenue requirements are the same as those given in Table 6-1. Another approach to including the investment tax credit is to add Eq. (6-13) to Eq. (6-11). That is,

$$t_1 = \frac{0.52}{1 - 0.52}(8{,}000 + 20{,}000 - 20{,}000) - \frac{100{,}000\,(0.10)}{1 - 0.52}$$

$$= -\$12{,}167$$

Either approach gives the same answer for R_1. As a check, the taxes for year one with the investment tax credit and using Eq. (6-8) are

$$t_1 = (27{,}833 - 7{,}000 - 5{,}000 - 20{,}000)(0.52) - 10{,}000$$

$$= -\$12{,}167$$

The negative result for the taxes simply implies the assumption that there is sufficient income from other company operations to take the full investment tax credit. It shows that the investment tax credit can have a significant short-term effect and can be a definite factor in the decision process.

The Levelized Revenue Requirement   A simple procedure for determining *just* the levelized revenue requirement (the equivalent annual amount of the revenue requirements) can be developed if a certain simplifying assumption is made; namely, that the tax and book depreciation are exactly the same. With this assumption $D_{bj} = D_j$ and Eq. (6-11) can be written as

$$t_j = \frac{T}{1 - T}(F_{ej}) \tag{6-14}$$

Substituting Eq. (6-4) into Eq. (6-14) gives

$$t_j = (1 - c)k_e \frac{T}{1 - T}(B_{j-1}) \tag{6-15}$$

A levelized (equivalent annual) amount of the taxes, E_t, based on Eq. (6-15) is

$$E_t = (1 - c)k_e \frac{T}{1 - T} \left[\sum_{j=1}^{n} B_{j-1}\,(P/F\ k_b,j) \right](A/P\ k_b,n) \tag{6-16}$$

In Chapter 3, Eq. (3-18) is given for determining an equivalent annual amount of capital recovery and return using i as the rate of return. For levelized revenue requirements, this return is k_b as defined by Eq. (5-5). Consequently, the levelized capital recovery and return, E_c, can be written as

$$E_c = (P - L)(A/P\ k_b,n) + L(k_b) \tag{6-17}$$

and, finally, the levelized revenue requirement can be written as

$$E = E_c + E_t + C \qquad (6\text{-}18)$$

where C is the annual cost which is assumed to be constant in Eq. (6-18). The use of Eq. (6-18) is shown in the following example.

Example 6-2

Determine the levelized revenue requirement for the following data:

$$\text{initial cost of project} = \$10,000$$

$$\text{book depreciation and tax depreciation} = \text{SYD}$$

$$\text{salvage value} = \$1,000$$

$$\text{life} = 5 \text{ years}$$

$$\text{required return on equity} = 25\%$$

$$\text{cost of debt capital} = 10\%$$

$$\text{debt ratio} = 1/3$$

$$\text{annual costs} = \$500$$

$$\text{tax rate} = 52\%$$

Using Eq. (5-5), the overall rate of return is

$$k_b = \left(\frac{1}{3}\right)\left(10\right) + \left(\frac{2}{3}\right)\left(25\right)$$

$$= 20\%$$

The levelized capital recovery is

$$E_c = (10,000 - 1,000)(A/P\ 20,5) + 1,000(0.20)$$

$$= \$3,210$$

The book values using SYD depreciation are

$$B_0 = \$10,000$$

$$B_1 = 7,000$$

$$B_2 = 4,600$$

$$B_3 = 2,800$$

$$B_4 = 1,600$$

$$B_5 = 1,000$$

The levelized amount of the taxes using Eq. (6-16) is

$$E_t = \left(1 - \frac{1}{3}\right) (0.25) \frac{0.52}{1 - 0.52} \left[10,000 \, (P/F \, 20,1) \right.$$

$$\left. + \, 7,000 \, (P/F \, 20, \, 2) + \ldots + 1,600 \, (P/F \, 20,5) \right] (A/P \, 20,5)$$

$$= (0.18055)(17,850)(0.3344)$$

$$= \$1,078$$

Therefore the levelized revenue requirement is

$$E = 3,210 + 1,078 + 500$$

$$= \$4,788$$

As a check on this answer the annual requirements are determined and shown in Table 6-2. The levelized amount of the revenue requirement in Table 6-2 is

$$E = \left[7,306 \, (P/F \, 20,1) + 5,564 \, (P/F \, 20,2) \right.$$

$$\left. + \ldots + 1,709 \, (P/F \, 20,5) \right] (A/P \, 20,5)$$

$$= \$4,788$$

which is the same result obtained using Eq. (6-18). As a further check, the

TABLE 6-2
Minimum Revenue Requirements for Example 6-2

End of Year	Book Depreciation D_b	Tax Depreciation D_t	Book Value B	Equity Return F_e	Debt Interest I	Tax t	Annual Cost C	Minimum Annual Revenue Requirement R
0	—	—	$10,000	—	—	—	—	—
1	$3,000	$3,000	7,000	$1,667	$333	$1,806	$500	$7,306
2	2,400	2,400	4,600	1,167	233	1,264	500	5,564
3	1,800	1,800	2,800	767	153	831	500	4,051
4	1,200	1,200	1,600	467	93	506	500	2,766
5	600	600	1,000	267	53	289	500	1,709

levelized amount of the taxes given in Table 6-2 are

$$E_t = \left[1,806\,(P/F\ 20,1) + \ldots + 289\,(P/F\ 20,5) \right](A/P\ 20,5)$$

$$= \$1,078$$

which is the same result given by Eq. (6-16).

In Example 6-2, the investment tax credit is not considered. If the investment tax credit is applicable, then Eq. (6-19)

$$-\frac{V}{1-T}\,(P/F\ k_b,1)(A/P\ k_b,n) \tag{6-19}$$

is added to Eq. (6-18). For example, if the investment tax credit is applicable in Example 6-2, the levelized revenue requirement is

$$E = \$4,788 - \frac{667}{1-0.52}\,(P/F\ 20,\ 1)(A/P\ 20,\ 5)$$

$$= \$4,400$$

Only \$667 is used for the investment tax credit, V, in this calculation because the tax depreciation life is five years (see Table 4-8).

THE RELATIONSHIP BETWEEN MINIMUM REVENUE REQUIREMENTS AND EXPECTED REVENUES

The basis of the decision criterion given previously of comparing minimum revenue requirements and expected revenues can be shown by some examples. These same examples also show *numerically* the relationships between the definitions of cash flow and MARR discussed in Chapter 5.

If the revenue data given in Table 6-2 are used as the yearly gross incomes and the total cash flows are determined using Eq. (5-8), the results shown in Table 6-3 are obtained. As sample calculations, the total cash flows for years 0, 1, and 2 are

$$X_0 = -\$10,000$$

$$X_1 = (7,306 - 500) - (7,306 - 500 - 3,000)(0.52)$$

$$= \$4,827$$

$$X_2 = (5,564 - 500) - (5,564 - 500 - 2,400)(0.52)$$

$$= \$3,679$$

TABLE 6-3
Total Cash Flows

End of Year	Total Cash Flows
0	−$10,000
1	4,827
2	3,679
3	2,640
4	1,712
5	1,892[a]

[a] Includes salvage value.

calculating the internal rate of return, IRR, for the cash flows in Table 6-3 gives

$$0 = -10,000 + 4,827\,(P/F\ i,1) + \ldots + 1,892\,(P/F\ i,5)$$

where

$$i = \text{IRR}$$
$$= 0.1827$$
$$= 18.27\%$$

which is exactly equal to the MARR defined by Eq. (5-2); namely,

$$\left(\frac{1}{3}\right)\left(10\right)\left(1 - 0.52\right) + \left(\frac{2}{3}\right)\left(25\right) = 18.27\%$$

Taking the same approach only calculating the equity net cash flows, defined by Eq. (5-7), the results shown in Table 6-4 are obtained. In order to obtain the values in Table 6-4, the yearly principal payments (recovery

TABLE 6-4
Equity Cash Flows

End of Year	Net Equity Cash Flow
0	−$6,667
1	3,667
2	2,767
3	1,967
4	1,267
5	1,334

of debt capital) must be determined. The principal payments are determined in accordance with Eq. (6-2) and are

$$P_1 = \left(\frac{1}{3}\right)\left(3{,}000\right)$$

$$= \$1{,}000$$

$$P_2 = \left(\frac{1}{3}\right)\left(2{,}400\right)$$

$$= \$\ \ 800$$

$$P_3 = \left(\frac{1}{3}\right)\left(1{,}800\right)$$

$$= \$\ \ 600$$

$$P_4 = \left(\frac{1}{3}\right)\left(1{,}200\right)$$

$$= \$\ \ 400$$

$$P_5 = \left(\frac{1}{3}\right)\left(600\right)$$

$$= \$\ \ 200 + \left(\frac{1}{3}\right)\left(1{,}000\right)$$

$$= \$\ \ 533$$

The term $\left(\frac{1}{3}\right)(1{,}000)$ in P_5 is a result of considering the salvage value as the recovery of debt and equity capital proportioned in accordance with the debt ratio. With these principal payments, the equity cash flows are

$$X_0 = -\ 10{,}000 + 3{,}333$$

$$= -\ \$6{,}667$$

$$X_1 = (7{,}306 - 500 - 333)$$

$$-\ (7{,}306 - 500 - 333 - 3{,}000)(0.52) - 1{,}000$$

$$= \$3{,}667$$

$$X_2 = (5{,}564 - 500 - 233)$$

$$-\ (5{,}564 - 500 - 233 - 2{,}400)(0.52) - 800$$

$$= \$2{,}767$$

$$X_5 = (1{,}709 - 500 - 53)$$

$$- (1{,}709 - 500 - 53 - 600)(0.52) - 533 + 1{,}000$$

$$= \$1{,}334$$

Calculating the IRR for the equity cash flows gives

$$0 = -6{,}667 + 3{,}667\,(P/F\ i{,}1) + \ldots + 1{,}334\,(P/F\ i{,}5)$$

where

$$i = \text{IRR}$$

$$= 25\%$$

which is exactly the required return on equity capital.

Now, the results of IRR = 18.27% for the total cash flows, and an IRR = 25% for equity cash flows are not surprising. In fact these results are expected since these returns are "built into" the minimum revenue requirements in Table 6-2. The results do show the basis of the decision criterion used with minimum annual revenue requirements. If the expected revenues are less than those minimum revenue requirements or if the levelized expected revenue is less than the levelized minimum revenue amount, this will give an IRR less than MARR or a negative NPV. Further, these results show the *dependency between the definitions of cash flow and MARR*. In both cases the NPV equals zero since IRR = MARR. However, an NPV of zero is not obtained if a cash flow definition is used with an incorrect definition of MARR.

Another Definition of Cash Flow   In addition to the two definitions of net cash flow given in Chapter 5 and used in the previous discussion, there is another definition of net cash flow that is sometimes used. It is important at this point to consider this additional definition of cash flow because it provides insight as to when the term $(1 - T)$ should be included in the definition of the cost of capital. This additional definition of net cash flows is

$$X_{jb} = (G_j - C_j) - (G_j - C_j - D_j - I_j)\,T - K_j + L_j \qquad (6\text{-}20)$$

In this text, the net cash flows defined by Eq. (6-20) are called the *net operating cash flows*. Eq. (6-20) is very similar to the total cash flows defined by Eq. (5-8) except that in Eq. (6-20) the debt interest (I_i) is explicitly included in the tax term.

If the revenue data in Table 6-2 are used as the yearly gross incomes and cash flows are calculated using Eq. (6-20), the results given in Table 6-5 are obtained. For example, the cash flows for years zero through two are

$$X_{0b} = -\$10,000$$

$$X_{1b} = (7{,}306 - 500) - (7{,}306 - 500 - 3{,}000 - 333)(0.52)$$

$$= \$5{,}000$$

$$X_{2b} = (5{,}564 - 500) - (5{,}564 - 500 - 2{,}400 - 233)(0.52)$$

$$= \$3{,}800$$

Calculating the IRR using the cash flows in Table 6-5 gives

$$0 = -10{,}000 + 5{,}000\,(P/F\ i,1) + \ldots + 1{,}920\,(P/F\ i,5)$$

where

$$i = \text{IRR}$$

$$= 20\%$$

which is the same cost of capital value defined by Eq. (5-5); namely,

$$k_b = \frac{1}{3}\left(10\right) + \left(1 - \frac{1}{3}\right)\left(25\right)$$

$$= 20\%$$

These results suggest an important point. That is, the term $(1 - T)$ in the cost of capital definition is an adjustment for deductibility of interest in computing taxes. Consequently, if interest is not explicitly included in the tax term, the term $(1 - T)$ should be included in the cost of capital definition. If interest is explicitly included in the tax term, as in Eq. (6-20), then the term $(1 - T)$ should not be included in the cost of capital definition. An adjustment of the cost of capital by the term $(1 - T)$ *and the inclusions of interest in the tax term are incorrect* since this is equivalent to counting the tax deduction of interest expense *twice*.

TABLE 6-5
Cash Flows Using Eq. (6-20)

End of Year	Net Operating Cash Flows
0	−$10,000
1	5,000
2	3,800
3	2,720
4	1,760
5	1,920[a]

[a] Includes $1,000 salvage value.

From a practical standpoint, Eq. (6-20) is of little use as a definition of cash flow because it requires that the yearly interest payment schedule be known in order to evaluate the tax term. If the interest payment schedule is known, the principal payments are also known or, at least, implied. Consequently, the equity cash flows should be determined using Eq. (5-7). The primary reason for considering Eq. (6-20) as a cash flow definition is to show, numerically, the *dependency* between the definitions of cash flows given by Eqs. (5-8) and (6-20) and the cost of capital definitions given by Eqs. (5-5) and (5-2). Also, Eq. (6-20) provides a basis for the discussion of the discount rate used to determine the levelized revenue requirements.

The Levelized Revenue Requirement Discount Rate   There

seems to be some controversy on the correct discount rate used to determine the levelized requirements. This controversy centers around whether or not the $(1 - T)$ term should be included in defining the discount rate. That is, should the discount rate used in determining the levelized revenue requirements be based on k_a, Eq. (5-2), or on k_b, Eq. (5-5)? Before proceeding further with this question, the meaning of the levelized revenue requirements and their uses must be clearly understood. The annual revenue requirements are the required minimum *gross incomes* and, as such, are before-tax amounts. It is true that taxes are explicitly included in determining the revenue requirements. However, the revenue requirements are *still before-tax amounts*. Levelized revenue requirements are compared with the levelized *expected* gross incomes (revenues or savings) in determining the acceptability of a project. These expected gross incomes are also before-tax amounts. Consequently, *before-tax amounts are* being compared. As a result, the discount rate should not be adjusted for tax considerations and therefore Eq. (5-5) should be the basis of the discount rate.

The use of Eq. (5-5) as the basis for the discount rate used in determining the levelized revenue requirements can also be defended by making the substitution

$$t_j = (R_j - C_j - D_j - I_j)T \tag{6-21}$$

into Eq. (6-1) which gives

$$R_j = D_{bj} + F_{ej} + I_j + C_j + (R_j - C_j - D_j - I_j)T \tag{6-22}$$

It should be remembered that from the standpoint of revenue requirements the gross income (G_j) is the revenue requirement (R_j).

Rearranging Eq. (6-22) gives

$$R_j = D_{bj} + F_{ej} + I_j(1 - T) + C_j + t_j' \tag{6-23}$$

where

$$t_j^{'} = (R_j - C_j - D_j)T \tag{6-24}$$

The terms $F_{ej} + I_j(1 - T)$ can be combined into an overall return,

$$f_j^{'} = F_{ej} + I_j(1 - T), \tag{6-25}$$

which can be written as

$$f_i^{'} = \left[(1 - c)k_e + c(1 - T)k_d\right]B_{j-1} \tag{6-26}$$

Eq. (6-23) can now be written as

$$R_j = D_{bj} + f_j^{'} + C_j + t_j^{'} \tag{6-27}$$

and substituting this equation into Eq. (6-24) gives

$$t_j^{'} = (f_j^{'} + t_j^{'})T$$

$$t_j^{'} = \frac{T}{1 - T}(f_j^{'}) \tag{6-28}$$

assuming the tax and book depreciation are the same.

Using the data in Example 6-2, Eq. (6-27), and Eq. (6-28), the minimum revenue requirements shown in Table 6-6 are obtained. Note that the revenue requirements in Table 6-2 and 6-6 are the same (slight differences are rounding errors). However, the total returns in Table 6-2 $(F_{ej} + I_j)$ and in Table 6-6 are different. Also, the taxes are different. These differences are due to the inclusion of the $(1 - T)$ term in the equation for the total return [see Eq. (6-26)]. Now if the levelized revenue requirements are calculated on the basis of a discount rate given by

TABLE 6-6

Minimum Annual Revenue Requirements Using Eqs. (6-27) and (6-28)

(Data from Example 6-2)

End of Year	Book Depreciation D_b	Tax Depreciation D	Book Value B	Total Return f'	Tax t'	Annual Cost C	Minimum Annual Revenue Requirement R
0	—	—	$10,000	—	—	—	—
1	$3,000	$3,000	7,000	$1,827	1,979	500	$7,306
2	2,400	2,400	4,600	1,279	1,386	500	5,565
3	1,800	1,800	2,800	840	910	500	4,050
4	1,200	1,200	1,600	512	555	500	2,767
5	600	600	1,000	292	316	500	1,708

Eq. (5-2), which in this case is 18.27%, this would imply that the tax deduction of *interest expense is being accounted for twice*. This is incorrect. Consequently, the correct discount rate should be based on Eq. (5-5), which is 20% in this case.

A MINIMUM REVENUE REQUIREMENT EXTENSION

In the previous discussions of minimum annual revenue requirements, a convention is used where the total investment (capital expenditure) required by the project occurs at one point in time ($j = 0$). This convention is satisfactory for projects requiring a short construction period. However, there are many cases where the total capital expenditure is spread over several years. This is particularly true for major projects. In these cases, this convention becomes unacceptable. Consequently, it is the purpose of this section to provide a method for determining minimum annual revenue requirements for the case of extended construction periods. There are two methods presented. The method to use is dependent upon how the capital recovery (book depreciation) and tax depreciation schedules are approached. One depreciation approach is to begin the depreciation amount the year after a particular capital expenditure. This is the approach used for the depreciation amount in Table 5-7. The other approach is to begin the depreciation schedules after the total amount of capital is expended. This is the approach used for the depreciation amounts in Table 5-8. As mentioned in the discussion of these two different depreciation schedules in Chapter 5, the basic question is, When are the components represented by the associated capital expenditure ready for service? If they are ready for service after each capital expenditure, then the approach given in Table 5-7 is applicable. If service can only begin after the commitment of all capital, the approach in Table 5-8 is applicable. The methods for determining the minimum annual revenue requirements for these two depreciation approaches are shown in the following example.

Example 6-3

Determine the minimum annual revenue requirements for the data given below assuming the following:

a. Depreciation amounts begin after each expenditure of capital.

b. Depreciation begins after all the capital is expended.

capital expenditure at $j = 0$ is \$100,000

book depreciation = straight-line

life = 10 years

salvage = \$20,000

tax depreciation = SYD

life = 8 years

salvage = \$10,000

capital expenditure at $j = 1$ is \$80,000

book depreciation = straight-line

life = 10 years

salvage = \$4,000

tax depreciation = SYD

life = 8 years

salvage = \$8,000

capital expenditure at $j = 2$ is \$60,000

book depreciation = straight-line

life = 10 years

salvage = \$5,000

tax depreciation = SYD

life = 8 years

salvage = \$6,000

required return on equity = 30%

cost of debt capital = 15%

debt ratio = 1/3

tax rate = 52%

annual costs = \$7,000

For Part a, the most straightforward method is to determine the minimum annual revenue requirements, *excluding the annual costs* for each capital expenditure component, as though they are independent. Then combine these results in the appropriate years. At this point, the annual costs are also added in the years that are estimated to be appropriate. The minimum annual revenue requirements, excluding annual costs, for each of the capital expenditure components are given in Tables 6-7, 6-8, and 6-9.

In adding the component revenue requirements to obtain the total revenue requirements for the project, it must be remembered that the revenue requirement in year one for the capital expenditure occurring in year one actually occurs in year two. Similarly, the revenue requirement in year one for the capital expenditure occurring in year two actually occurs in year three. The addition of the revenue requirements and annual costs is shown in Table 6-10. In Table 6-10, the annual costs are added in years three through twelve. This is arbitrary. In actuality, the years in which the annual costs are applicable must be estimated for the particular project under consideration.

In this example, the tax and book salvage values are given (estimated) for each component of the total capital investment ($240,000). As pointed out in Chapter 5, these values are not always given (estimated). Often, only the total salvage value is given (estimated). The usual approach in these cases is the same as that discussed in Chapter 5. That is, allocate the total salvage value to the various capital expenditure components using Eq. (5-13).

TABLE 6-7

Minimum Annual Revenue Requirements for the Capital Expenditure at $j = 0$

End of Year	Book Depreciation D_b	Tax Depreciation D_t	Book Value B	Equity Return F_e	Debt Interest I	Tax t	Cost C	Minimum Annual Revenue Requirement R
0	—	—	$100,000	—	—	—	—	—
1	$8,000	$20,000	92,000	$20,000	$5,000	$ 8,666	—	$41,666
2	8,000	17,500	84,000	18,400	4,600	9,641	—	40,641
3	8,000	15,000	76,000	16,800	4,200	10,616	—	39,616
4	8,000	12,500	68,000	15,200	3,800	11,591	—	38,591
5	8,000	10,000	60,000	13,600	3,400	12,566	—	37,566
6	8,000	7,500	52,000	12,000	3,000	13,541	—	36,541
7	8,000	5,000	44,000	10,400	2,600	14,516	—	35,516
8	8,000	2,500	36,000	8,800	2,200	15,491	—	34,491
9	8,000	—	28,000	7,200	1,800	16,466	—	33,466
10	8,000	—	20,000	5,600	1,400	14,733	—	29,733

TABLE 6-8

Minimum Annual Revenue Requirements for the Capital Expenditure at $j = 1$

End of Year	Book Depreciation D_b	Tax Depreciation D_t	Book Value B	Equity Return F_e	Debt Interest I	Tax t	Cost C	Minimum Annual Revenue Requirement R
0	—	—	$80,000	—	—	—	—	—
1	$7,600	$16,000	72,400	$16,000	$4,000	$ 8,233	—	$35,833
2	7,600	14,000	64,800	14,480	3,620	8,753	—	34,453
3	7,600	12,000	57,200	12,960	3,240	9,273	—	33,073
4	7,600	10,000	49,600	11,440	2,860	9,793	—	31,693
5	7,600	8,000	42,000	9,920	2,480	10,313	—	30,313
6	7,600	6,000	34,400	8,400	2,100	10,833	—	28,933
7	7,600	4,000	26,800	6,880	1,720	11,353	—	27,553
8	7,600	2,000	19,200	5,360	1,340	11,873	—	26,173
9	7,600	—	11,600	3,840	960	12,393	—	24,793
10	7,600	—	4,000	2,320	580	10,746	—	21,246

TABLE 6-9

Minimum Annual Revenue Requirements for the Capital Expenditure at $j = 2$

End of Year	Book Depreciation D_b	Tax Depreciation D_t	Book Value B	Equity Return F_e	Debt Interest I	Tax t	Cost C	Minimum Annual Revenue Requirement R
0	—	—	$60,000	—	—	—	—	—
1	$5,500	$12,000	54,500	$12,000	$3,000	$5,958	—	$26,458
2	5,500	10,500	49,000	10,900	2,725	6,391	—	25,516
3	5,500	9,000	43,500	9,800	2,450	6,825	—	24,575
4	5,500	7,500	38,000	8,700	2,175	7,258	—	23,633
5	5,500	6,000	32,500	7,600	1,900	7,691	—	22,691
6	5,500	4,500	27,000	6,500	1,625	8,125	—	21,750
7	5,500	3,000	21,500	5,400	1,350	8,558	—	20,808
8	5,500	1,500	16,000	4,300	1,075	8,991	—	19,866
9	5,500	—	10,500	3,200	800	9,425	—	18,925
10	5,500	—	5,000	2,100	525	8,233	—	16,358

TABLE 6-10

Total Minimum Revenue Requirements for Example 6-3

End of Year	Minimum Annual Revenue Requirements for Capital Expenditures at $j = 0$	$j = 1$	$j = 2$	Cost C	Total Minimum Revenue Requirement
0	—	—	—	—	—
1	$41,666	—	—	—	$ 41,666
2	40,641	$35,833	—	—	76,474
3	39,616	34,453	$26,458	$7,000	107,527
4	38,591	33,073	25,516	7,000	104,180
5	37,566	31,693	24,575	7,000	100,834
6	36,541	30,313	23,633	7,000	97,487
7	35,516	28,933	22,691	7,000	94,140
8	34,491	27,553	21,750	7,000	90,794
9	33,466	26,173	20,808	7,000	87,447
10	29,733	24,793	19,866	7,000	81,392
11	—	21,246	18,925	7,000	47,171
12	—	—	16,358	7,000	23,358

For Part b, the method for determining the minimum annual revenue requirements is different from the method used in Part a. The depreciation amounts begin in the year after the total amount of capital is expended and are based on the total investment and total salvage. In the example, this is year three and the book depreciation is

$$D_b = \frac{240,000 - 29,000}{10}$$

$$= \$21,100$$

for years three through twelve. The tax depreciation amounts for years three and four are

$$D_{t_3} = \frac{8}{36}(240,000 - 24,000)$$

$$= \$48,000$$

$$D_{t_4} = \frac{7}{36}(240,000 - 24,000)$$

$$= \$42,000$$

The remaining tax depreciation amounts are given in Table 6-11.

The book values given in Table 6-11 are the cumulative totals of the capital expenditure components. These values do not begin to decrease until year three when the recovery of capital (book depreciation) begins. The other values given in Table 6-11 are determined using the equations previously given in this chapter. For example, the equity returns for years one and two, using Eq. (6-4), are

$$F_{e_1} = \left(\frac{2}{3}\right)\left(0.30\right)\left(100,000\right)$$

$$= \$20,000$$

$$F_{e_2} = \left(\frac{2}{3}\right)\left(0.30\right)\left(180,000\right)$$

$$= \$36,000$$

and the debt interest for the same years, using Eq. (6-5), are

$$I_1 = \left(\frac{1}{3}\right)\left(0.15\right)\left(100,000\right)$$

$$= \$5,000$$

TABLE 6-11

Minimum Annual Revenue Requirements for Part b of Example 6-3

End of Year	Book Depreciation D_b	Tax Depreciation D_t	Book Value B	Equity Return F_e	Debt Interest I	Tax t	Cost C	Minimum Annual Revenue Requirement R
0	—	—	$100,000	—	—	—	—	—
1	—	—	180,000	$20,000	$ 5,000	$21,666	—	$ 46,666
2	—	—	240,000	36,000	9,000	38,999	—	83,999
3	$21,100	$48,000	218,900	48,000	12,000	22,858	$7,000	110,958
4	21,100	42,000	197,800	43,780	10,945	24,786	7,000	107,611
5	21,100	36,000	176,700	39,560	9,890	26,714	7,000	104,264
6	21,100	30,000	155,600	35,340	8,835	28,642	7,000	100,917
7	21,100	24,000	134,500	31,120	7,780	30,571	7,000	97,571
8	21,100	18,000	113,400	26,900	6,725	32,499	7,000	94,224
9	21,100	12,000	92,300	22,680	5,670	34,427	7,000	90,877
10	21,100	6,000	71,200	18,460	4,615	36,356	7,000	87,531
11	21,100	—	50,100	14,240	3,560	38,284	7,000	84,184
12	21,100	—	29,000	10,020	2,505	33,712	7,000	74,337

$$I_2 = \left(\frac{1}{3}\right)\left(0.15\right)\left(180{,}000\right)$$
$$= \$9{,}000$$

Using Eq. (6-11), the taxes for the first two years are

$$t_1 = \frac{0.52}{1-0.52}(20{,}000)$$
$$= \$21{,}666$$

$$t_2 = \frac{0.52}{1-0.52}(36{,}000)$$
$$= \$38{,}999$$

and using Eq. (6-1), the minimum annual revenue requirements for the first two years are

$$R_1 = 20{,}000 + 5{,}000 + 21{,}666$$
$$= \$46{,}666$$

$$R_2 = 36{,}000 + 9{,}000 + 38{,}999$$
$$= \$83{,}999$$

The costs (\$7,000) are not added in determining these two values because it is assumed that these costs begin in year three. As in Part a, this is arbitrary. Where the annual costs begin must be estimated.

INFLATION AND REVENUE REQUIREMENTS

The discussion of minimum annual revenue requirements, up to this point, does not specifically consider inflation. This is done in order to simplify the discussion. However, inflationary effects can be included in the revenue requirements by using the relationship

$$R_j' = R_j(F/P\ e,j) \tag{6-29}$$

where

R_j' = actual dollar minimum revenue requirements in year j

R_j = real dollar minimum revenue requirements in year j

e = yearly constant inflation rate

As an example, consider the data given in Table 6-12 as estimates in

TABLE 6-12
Minimum Annual Revenue Requirements in Real Dollars

End of Year	Book Depreciation D_b	Tax Depreciation D	Book Value B	Equity Return F_e	Debt Interest I	Tax t	Annual Cost C	Minimum Annual Revenue Requirement R
0	—	—	$10,000	—	—	—	—	—
1	$1,800	$3,000	8,200	$1,500	$400	$325	$500	$4,525
2	1,800	2,400	6,400	1,230	328	682	500	4,540
3	1,800	1,800	4,600	960	256	1,040	500	4,556
4	1,800	1,200	2,800	690	184	1,397	500	4,571
5	1,800	600	1,000	420	112	1,755	500	4,587

terms of real dollars. The values in Table 6-12 are calculated in the same manner as previously discussed and are based on the following:

initial cost of project = $10,000

book depreciation = straight-line model

salvage = $1,000

life = 5 years

tax depreciation = sum-of-years-digits depreciation

salvage = $1,000

life = 5 years

required return on equity
excluding inflation = 25%

cost of debt capital = 10%

debt ratio = 40%

tax rate = 52%

total costs = $500 per year

The conversion of the real dollar minimum annual revenue requirements in Table 6-12 to actual dollar revenue requirements is accomplished by using Eq. (6-29) with an annual inflation rate of 8%. The results of these conversions are shown in Table 6-13.

If it is desired to correct the various components involved in the revenue requirements (D_b, D, F_e, I, t, C) to actual dollar values, there

TABLE 6-13

Conversion of Real to Actual Minimum Revenue Requirements

Year	Real R_j	$F/P\,8,j$	Actual R_j'
1	4,525	1.080	4,887
2	4,540	1.166	5,294
3	4,556	1.260	5,741
4	4,571	1.360	6,217
5	4,587	1.469	6,738

are two methods possible. The first method is to multiply each of the components given in real dollar values by the appropriate $(F/P\ e\,,j)$ factor. This approach is shown in Table 6-14 for the third-year components.

If the components are given in actual dollars, the conversion of the components to real dollars is accomplished by using the appropriate $(P/F\ e\,,j)$ factor.

The second approach is to adjust certain components for inflation by using the appropriate $(F/P\ e\,,j)$ factor and then calculating the remaining components using Eqs. (6-1), (6-4), (6-5), and (6-11). Again, if the components are given in actual dollars, an appropriate $(P/F\ e\,,j)$ factor is used to convert the components to real dollars. The components that require adjustment using the $(F/P\ e\,,j)$ factor, or $(P/F\ e\,,j)$ factor in the case of actual dollars, are the book depreciation, tax depreciation, and the annual costs. However, if this second method is used, another component must be added. This component is called the chargeable book value. For the

TABLE 6-14

Conversion of Real Dollar Components to Actual Dollar Components

Component in Real Dollars		$F/P\,8,3$	Component in Actual Dollars
D_b :	1,800	1.260	2,268
D :	1,800	1.260	2,268
F_e :	960	1.260	1,210
I :	256	1.260	323
t :	1,040	1.260	1,310
C :	500	1.260	630
R :	4,556	1.260	5,741

year j, it is designated as B'_{cj} and is used to compute the return on equity and debt interest using the relationships

$$F'_{ej} = (1 - c)(k_e)(B'_{c(j-1)}) \tag{6-30}$$

$$I'_j = (c)k_d(B'_{c(j-1)}) \tag{6-31}$$

where the primes denote the components in actual dollars. The chargeable book value is a result of yearly increases in book values as a result of inflation. However, it is only for *purposes of computing the equity return and debt interest*. In general, a company's financial accounting procedures do not take into account the effect of inflation on book values since this effect is not recognized by the Internal Revenue Service or regulatory agencies. In this example, the book value at the beginning of the first year ($t = 0$) to the end of the first year grows as a result of inflation to the value

$$10,000 \ (F/P \ 8,1) = \$10,800$$

This value is the chargeable investment for year zero (B'_{c0}). It is the basis for calculating the equity return and debt interest for the first year as indicated in Eqs. (6-30) and (6-31). The book value at the end of the first year in actual dollars is

$$B'_1 = 10,800 - 1,944$$

$$= \$8,856$$

Therefore, the *chargeable book value* for the first year is

$$B'_{c1} = 8,856 \ (F/P \ 8,1)$$

$$= \$9,564$$

In general, the chargeable book value for the year j is given by

$$B'_{cj} = (1+e)\left[K(F/P \ e,j) - \sum_{m=1}^{j} D'_{b,m}(F/P \ e,(j-m)) \right] \tag{6-32}$$

where K is the initial investment at $j = 0$ and the quantity inside the brackets is the book value in actual dollars (B'_j) at the end of the jth year. For example, the chargeable book value for the third year is

$$B'_{c3} = (1 + .08) \ [10,000 \ (F/P \ 8,3) - 1,944 \ (F/P \ 8,2)$$
$$- 2,099 \ (F/P \ 8,1) - 2,268]$$

$$= (1.08)(5,798)$$

$$= \$6,262$$

All of the chargeable book values are given in Table 6-15.

With the chargeable book values, the book depreciation, the tax depreciation, and the annual costs in terms of actual dollars, the revenue requirements can be calculated in actual dollars. For example, the required equity returns for the first two years using Eq. (6-30) are

$$F'_{e1} = (1 - 0.4)(0.25)(10,800)$$

$$= \$1,620$$

$$F'_{e2} = (1 - 0.4)(0.25)(9,564)$$

$$= \$1,435$$

and the debt interest for the first two years using Eq. (6-31) are

$$I'_1 = (0.40)(0.10)(10,800)$$

$$= \$432$$

$$I'_2 = (0.40)(0.10)(9,564)$$

$$= \$383$$

The taxes in actual dollars, using Eq. (6-11), for the first two years are

$$t'_1 = (1,944 + 1,620 - 3,240)\left(\frac{0.52}{1 - 0.52}\right)$$

$$= \$351$$

$$t'_2 = (2,099 + 1,435 - 2,798)\left(\frac{0.52}{1 - 0.52}\right)$$

$$= \$797$$

and the revenue requirements, using Eq. (6-1), are

$$R'_1 = 1,944 + 1,620 + 432 + 351 + 540$$

$$= \$4,887$$

$$R'_2 = 2,099 + 1,435 + 383 + 797 + 583$$

$$= \$5,297$$

The remaining values for all components are given in Table 6-15. Some of the corresponding values given in Tables 6-13, 6-14, and 6-15 and by Eq. (6-32) are slightly different. This is due to rounding off error.

TABLE 6-15

Minimum Annual Revenue Requirements in Actual Dollars

End of Year	Book Depre- ciation D_b'	Tax Depre- ciation D'	Book Value B'	Charge- able Book Value B_c'	Equity Return F_e'	Debt Interest I'	Tax t'	Annual Cost C'	Minimum Annual Revenue Require- ment R'
0	—	—	$10,000	$10,800	—	—	—	—	—
1	$1,944	$3,240	8,856	9,564	$1,620	$432	$ 351	540	$4,887
2	2,099	2,798	7,465	8,062	1,435	383	797	583	5,297
3	2,268	2,268	5,794	6,258	1,209	322	1,310	630	5,739
4	2,448	1,632	3,810	4,115	939	250	1,901	680	6,218
5	2,644	881	1,471	—	617	165	2,578	735	6,739

If the approach of defining a chargeable investment is used to convert the revenue components from actual to real dollars, Eq. (6-32) must be modified to

$$B_{cj} = \frac{1}{(1+e)}\left[K(P/F\,e,j) - \sum_{m=1}^{j} D_{b,m}(P/F\,e,(j-m)) \right] \quad (6\text{-}33)$$

which gives the chargeable investment in terms of real dollars. Also Eqs. (6-30) and (6-31) are changed to

$$F_{ej} = (1-c)(k_e)\left(B_{c,(j-1)}\right) \quad (6\text{-}34)$$

$$I_j = (c)(k_d)\left(B_{c,(j-1)}\right) \quad (6\text{-}35)$$

Note that in Eq. (6-33) the book depreciation $(D_{b,m})$ is in terms of real dollars.

Levelized Minimum Annual Revenue Requirements   When inflation is included, Eq. (6-12) can be used to determine the levelized minimum annual revenue requirements, provided certain modifications are made. These modifications are dependent upon whether the revenue requirements are in terms of real or actual dollars. If the revenue requirements are in terms of real dollars, Eq. (6-12) can be used without modification. For example, the levelized revenue requirements for the data in Table 6-12 are

$$E = \left[4{,}525\,(P/F\ 19{,}1) + 4{,}540\,(P/F\ 19{,}2)\right.$$

$$\left. + \ldots + 4{,}587\,(P/F\ 19{,}5)\right](A/P\ 19{,}5)$$

$$E = \left[13{,}911\right](0.3271)$$

$$= \$4{,}550$$

The interest rate used in this calculation is the weighted cost of capital. That is,

$$k_b = (1 - 0.4)(0.25) + (0.40)(0.10)$$

$$= 0.19$$

$$= 19\%$$

If the revenue requirements are in actual dollars, the interest rate in Eq. (6-12) must be modified to include the inflation rate. That is, k_b in Eq. (6-12) is replaced with k_b' where

$$k_b' = k_b + e + (k_b)(e) \qquad (6\text{-}36)$$

Also, the revenue requirements in Eq. (6-12) are in terms of actual dollars. For example, the levelized revenue requirements for the data in Table 6-15 are

$$E' = \left[4{,}887\,(P/F\ 28.52{,}1) + 5{,}297\,(P/F\ 28.52{,}2)\right.$$

$$\left. + \ldots + 6{,}739\,(P/F\ 28.52{,}5)\right](A/P\ 28.52{,}5)$$

$$= \left[13{,}911\right](0.3990)$$

$$= \$5{,}550$$

where the interest rate is determined using Eq. (6-36).

That is,

$$k_b' = 0.19 + 0.08 + (0.19)(0.08)$$

$$= 0.2852$$

$$= 28.52\%$$

Note that the value in the brackets (\$13,911) is the same for both real and actual dollars. This is consistent since the value in the brackets represents the present value of the revenue requirements.

Decision Criterion   If the minimum annual revenue requirements are determined in terms of either real or actual dollars, an important point must be remembered in regard to determining the acceptability of a

project. That is, the comparison between revenue requirements and expected gross revenues must be on the same basis. Revenue requirements in real dollars must be compared to expected gross revenues in real dollars, and revenue requirements in actual dollars must be compared to expected gross revenues in actual dollars; to do otherwise, may lead to incorrect decisions.

SOME ADDITIONAL INSIGHTS INTO INFLATIONARY EFFECTS

Some additional insights to the effects of inflation on cash flow definitions (discussed in Chapter 5) and the related MARR value can be obtained using the results of the previous section. If the revenue requirements in Table 6-12 are used as the gross incomes, the total cash flows in real dollars can be calculated using Eq. (5-8). For example, the cash flows for years 0, 1, and 5 are

$$X_0 = -\$10,000$$

$$X_1 = (4,525 - 500) - (4,525 - 500 - 3,000)(0.52)$$

$$= \$3,492$$

$$X_5 = (4,587 - 500) - (4,587 - 500 - 600)(0.52) + 1,000$$

$$= \$3,274$$

The remaining values are given in Table 6-16. Now using these cash flows, the IRR is

$$0 = -10,000 + 3,492(P/F\ i,1) + \ldots + 3,274(P/F\ i,5)$$

TABLE 6-16
Total Cash Flows in Real Dollars

End of Year	Total Cash Flow
0	−$10,000
1	3,492
2	3,187
3	2,883
4	2,578
5	3,274

where

$$i = \text{IRR}$$
$$= 0.1692$$
$$= 16.92\%$$

This IRR is exactly equal to the MARR defined by Eq. (5-2); namely,

$$(1 - 0.4)(0.25) + (0.4)(0.10)(1 - 0.52) = .1692 = 16.92\%$$

If the same approach is taken with the data in Table 6-15, the total cash flows in terms of actual dollars for years 0, 1, and 5 are

$$X_0 = -\$10,000$$
$$X_1 = (4,887 - 540) - (4,887 - 540 - 3,240)(0.52)$$
$$= \$3,771$$
$$X_5 = (6,739 - 735) - (6,739 - 735 - 881)(0.52) + 1,471$$
$$= \$4,811$$

The remaining values are given in Table 6-17. The IRR for the cash flows in Table 6-17 is

$$0 = -10,000 + 3,771 (P/F\ i,1) + \ldots + 4,811\ (P/F\ i,5)$$

where

$$i = \text{IRR}$$
$$= 0.2627$$
$$= 26.27\%$$

TABLE 6-17
Total Cash Flows in Actual Dollars

End of Year	Total Cash Flows
0	−$10,000
1	3,771
2	3,718
3	3,632
4	3,507
5	4,811

which is exactly equal to the value given by Eq. (6-36). That is,

$$k'_b = 0.1692 + 0.08 + (0.1692)(0.08)$$

$$= 0.2627$$

$$= 26.27\%$$

Now calculating the real dollar equity cash flows using Eq. (5-7) and the data in Table 6-12 gives

$$X_0 = -10,000 + 4,000$$

$$= -\$6,000$$

$$X_1 = (4,525 - 500 - 400) - (4,525 - 500 - 400 - 3,000)(0.52) - 720$$

$$= \$2,580$$

$$X_5 = (4,587 - 500 - 112) - (4,587 - 500 - 112 - 600)(0.52)$$
$$- 720 + (0.6)(1,000)$$

$$= \$2,100$$

where the $720 value is the principal payment obtained from the debt ratio multiplied by the book depreciation

$$(0.04)(1,800) = \$720$$

and the $(0.6)(1,000)$ term is the portion of the salvage value that is considered part of the recovery of equity capital. The remaining $400 of the salvage is the recovery of a part of the debt capital. The remaining equity cash flows are given in Table 6-18. The IRR for the net cash flows in Table 6-18 is 25% which is exactly the required return on equity capital.

TABLE 6-18
Equity Cash Flows in Real Dollars

End of Year	Equity Cash Flows
0	−$6,000
1	2,580
2	2,310
3	2,040
4	1,770
5	2,100

If the actual dollar equity cash flows are determined using the data in Table 6-15, the results for years 0, 1, and 5 are

$$X_0 = -\$10,000 + 4,000$$

$$= -\$6,000$$

$$X_1 = (4,887 - 540 - 432) - (4,887 - 540 - 432 - 3,240)(0.52) - 778$$

$$= \$2,786$$

$$X_5 = (6,739 - 735 - 165) - (6,739 - 735 - 165 - 881)(0.52)$$
$$- 1,058 + (0.6)(1,471)$$

$$= \$3,086$$

where the values of 778 and 1,058 are the principal payments in actual dollars. They are obtained by multiplying the principal payments in real dollars (\$720) by the appropriate $(F/P\ e\ j)$ factor. The value 1,471 is the salvage value in actual dollars. The remaining equity cash flows are given in Table 6-19. The IRR for the cash flows in Table 6-19 is 35%. This IRR is exactly equal to the required return on equity adjusted for inflation. That is,

$$0.25 + 0.08 + 0.25(0.08) = 0.35$$

$$= 35\%$$

The calculations in this section again point out the dependency between the definition of cash flow and MARR. In addition, they show that it must be clearly understood whether the cash flows are in terms of real or actual dollars in order to determine if the required MARR should be adjusted by the inflation rate. For if the cash flows (total or equity) are in terms of real dollars, the MARR value (weighted average or equity) is not adjusted for inflation. If the cash flows are in terms of actual dollars, the required

TABLE 6-19
Equity Cash Flows in Actual Dollars

End of Year	Equity Cash Flows
0	−\$6,000
1	2,786
2	2,694
3	2,570
4	2,407
5	3,086

MARR value should be adjusted for inflation in the manner shown in this section.

SUMMARY

This chapter has presented the concept of minimum annual revenue requirements for purposes of evaluating a single project (investment). The generation of revenue requirements for this purpose is not difficult. However, it can be tedious, especially when the capital recovery period (book depreciation life) is more representative (longer) than the periods used in this chapter's examples. A computer program is provided in the appendices for generating the minimum annual revenue requirements. In addition to evaluating a single project, revenue requirements may be used for purposes of making cost comparisons. This use of revenue requirements is discussed in a later chapter.

The method given in this chapter for generating revenue requirements is known as the *flow-through method* because it follows the concept of cash flow from the standpoint of accounting for costs and incomes at the time of their estimated occurrence. Another method, not discussed in this book, for generating revenue requirements is possible. This method is known as the *normalizing method* and is widely used by public utility companies because of its similarities to their accounting procedures. A detailed discussion of the normalizing method is given in reference [6] listed in Chapter 5.

PROBLEMS

6-1. Determine the minimum annual revenue requirements for the following data:

$$\text{initial investment} = \$60,000$$
$$\text{book depreciation} = \text{straight-line}$$
$$\text{life} = 8 \text{ years}$$
$$\text{salvage} = \$4,000$$
$$\text{tax depreciation} = \text{sum-of-years-digits}$$
$$\text{life} = 5 \text{ years}$$
$$\text{salvage} = \$0$$
$$\text{debt ratio} = 25\%$$
$$\text{cost of debt capital} = 12\%$$
$$\text{required return on equity} = 20\%$$
$$\text{tax rate} = 52\%$$
$$\text{annual costs} = \$5,000$$
$$\text{inflation rate} = 0\%$$

6-2. What are the minimum revenue requirements in Problem 6-1 if the investment tax credit is applicable?

6-3. Determine the levelized minimum annual revenues for the data in Problem 6-1.

6-4. Repeat Problem 6-1 but assume that the tax depreciation model is double declining-balance with a switch-over to straight-line depreciation at the most optimum point. Also, determine the levelized revenue requirement.

6-5. Calculate the minimum annual revenue requirements and the levelized revenue requirement for the data given below. Also, check the levelized amount using Eq. (6-18).

$$\text{initial cost} = \$40,000$$
$$\text{tax and book depreciation} = \text{sum-of-years-digits}$$
$$\text{life} = 8 \text{ years}$$
$$\text{salvage value} = \$4,000$$
$$\text{annual costs} = \$3,000$$
$$\text{required return on equity} = 25\%$$
$$\text{cost of debt} = 15\%$$
$$\text{debt ratio} = 40\%$$
$$\text{inflation rate} = 0\%$$
$$\text{tax rate} = 52\%$$

6-6. Derive an expression for the levelized (equivalent) annual amount of taxes based on the assumptions that the tax and book depreciation are the same and both use the straight-line model. Show that this derivation is correct using the data in Problem 6-5 with these assumptions.

6-7. Using the data given below, determine the minimum annual revenue requirements on the basis that the book and tax depreciation begins in the year following a particular capital expenditure:

$$\text{total investment} = \$250,000$$
$$\text{capital expenditure at } j = 0 \text{ is } \$40,000$$
$$\text{capital expenditure at } j = 1 \text{ is } \$160,000$$
$$\text{capital expenditure at } j = 2 \text{ is } \$50,000$$
$$\text{total salvage value for both}$$
$$\text{tax and book purposes} = \$50,000$$
$$\text{required return on equity} = 20\%$$
$$\text{debt interest} = 10\%$$
$$\text{debt ratio} = 40\%$$
$$\text{tax rate} = 52\%$$

life for both tax and book
depreciation purposes = 8 years
depreciation method for
tax purposes = sum-of-years-digits
depreciation method for book
(capital recovery) purposes = straight-line
annual costs = $10,000 beginning in the third
year and ending in year ten

6-8. Repeat Problem 6-7 but assume that the depreciation begins after the total capital is expended.

6-9. If the estimated annual gross revenues (income) in Problem 6-1 are (a) $30,000, (b) $17,000, (c) $25,000, and (d) $20,000, is the project acceptable?

6-10. Suppose in Problem 6-1 that the estimated gross revenues are as shown below. Is the project acceptable?

End of Year	Estimated Gross Revenues
1	$18,000
2	20,000
3	24,000
4	24,000
5	25,000
6	30,000
7	30,000
8	30,000

6-11. Calculate the levelized revenue requirements for Problems 6-7 and 6-8.

6-12. A company is considering buying a particular machine for $840,000. It is estimated that the annual cost of operating (power and labor) this machine is $50,000. The company's practice is to depreciate this type of machine for tax purpose on the basis of sum-of-the-years-digits, a seven-year life, and a zero salvage value. For capital recovery purposes, the company uses straight-line depreciation and the same life and salvage as that used for tax depreciation. For this type of machine, the company's required return on equity is 25%. The company believes that a 15% cost of debt capital and a tax rate of 52% are applicable for the next seven years. The company currently operates with a 30% debt ratio and does not expect this ratio to change in the future. If the company can lease the same machine for $250,000 per year, should the company purchase or lease the machine?

6-13. A company is considering revising their current materials-handling system over the next two years. The total cost of the equipment for the contemplated revisions is $600,000 which is estimated to be split in the following manner: an initial expenditure of $200,000, an expenditure of $250,000 one year from now, and an expenditure of $150,000 two years from now. It is estimated that the annual cost of operating and maintaining the new equipment is $25,000. The company requires a return on equity capital of 30% and uses a 15% interest rate for debt capital. It currently has a debt ratio of one-third, and this ratio is expected to be maintained in the future. The company uses the same depreciation model for tax and capital recovery purposes. For this equipment sum-of-the-years-digits depreciation is used with a total salvage value of $60,000 and a life of eight years. Because of the nature of materials-handling equipment, service of the equipment cannot be realized until all the revisions are made. All new materials-handling equipment required by this project is eligible for the investment tax credit (10%), and the company's tax rate is 50%. Calculate the minimum annual revenue requirements for this project and determine if the project is economically desirable assuming that the annual gross savings resulting from this project are $400,000 a year for the first eight years the project is in service.

6-14. Using the data given in Problem 6-13, determine the yearly total cash flows and the internal rate of return.

6-15. Using the data given in Problem 6-13, determine the yearly equity cash flows and the internal rate of return. In determining the cash flows use Eq. (6-2) to determine the principal payments which begin in year three. Interest is assessed on any unpaid balance. Also in determining the cash flows, a portion (the debt ratio) of the salvage value should be considered as the recovery of debt capital.

6-16. Assuming the revenue requirements obtained in the solution of Problem 6-1 are in terms of real dollars, determine the following assuming an inflation rate of 10%:
(a) The revenue requirements in actual dollars.
(b) The levelized revenue requirement in actual dollars.
(c) The levelized revenue requirement in real dollars.
(d) The revenue requirement components (book depreciation, return on equity, taxes, costs, etc.) for the third year in terms of actual dollars.

6-17. Assuming the revenue requirements obtained in the solution of Problem 6-1 are in terms of actual dollars, determine the following assuming an inflation rate of 10%:

(a) The revenue requirements in real dollars.

(b) The levelized revenue requirement in real dollars.

(c) The levelized revenue requirement in actual dollars.

(d) The revenue requirement components (book depreciation, return on equity, taxes, costs, etc.) for the third year in terms of real dollars.

7

CAPITAL BUDGETING

In Chapters 5 and 6 the primary concern is the acceptability of a *single* project (investment). In this chapter the concern is with the problem of choosing a single project or group of projects from a larger group of *individually acceptable* projects. This problem is referred to as the *capital budgeting problem.* It is a result of a group of acceptable projects competing for some restricted (constrained) resource (capital, manpower, materials, etc.) that does not allow all the projects to be chosen.

Before a solution to the capital budgeting problem can be formulated, a correct criterion for ranking projects must be established. In this text, this criterion is based on the financial objective of maximizing the wealth of the stockholders. Also in establishing this criterion two conditions are imposed that are consistent with this financial objective. These conditions are (1) every additional requirement of capital must be justified and (2) an acceptable project today is preferred over the speculation that a better project might be available in the future.

For the discussions in this chapter, the initial starting point is with the cash flows already determined for each project. This is done to facilitate these discussions. However, it should be understood that determining the cash flows for each project is, in actuality, the first step. These cash flows are determined in accordance with the procedures discussed in Chapter 5. In the capital budgeting problem, a relative comparison of the projects' cash flows is made. The cash flows for each project must be determined on a consistent basis in order to insure an equitable comparison. The following points must be maintained when comparing cash flows:

1. The cash flows for all projects must be either in terms of real or actual dollars if inflationary effects are included in the cash flows. It is not acceptable to have some cash flows in terms of actual dollars and others in terms of real dollars.

2. The cash flows for all projects must be expressed as either total or equity cash flows. It is not acceptable to have some projects with total cash flows and others with equity cash flows in the same capital budgeting problem. Also, it must be remembered that it is assumed that any debt obligation is recovered over the life of the project if total cash flows are used (this point is made in Chapter 5).

3. If equity cash flows are used, the debt ratio should be the same for all projects. This is *only for purposes of providing a consistent basis* for the comparison of the projects in a particular capital budgeting problem. It does not preclude a particular project, once selected, from being financed in some manner that is not in accordance with the debt ratio used in the analysis. This point and approach are discussed in Chapter 5.

4. Since the NPV and IRR for equity cash flows vary with the method used to pay the debt obligation, the debt payment method in a particular capital budgeting problem should be the same for each project. This debt payment method should be based on the manner in which a company has decided to obtain a majority of its new debt capital. This point is similar to the situation discussed in Chapter 5 in regard to a single project.

In addition to the preceding four points, two other conditions are imposed on the discussions of capital budgeting problems in this chapter. These two conditions are (1) risk is not a consideration and (2) the projects in a particular capital budgeting problem are all independent.

Because it is stated in Chapter 5 that the NPV and IRR give the same decision regarding the acceptability of a project, it might be assumed that either the NPV or IRR is acceptable as a ranking criterion. This is not the case. In capital budgeting problems, the NPV and IRR can give different rankings. This can be seen by considering the four projects in Table 7-1. If the projects in Table 7-1 are ranked on the basis of IRR, the result is 1-3-2-4. If the same projects are ranked on the basis of NPV, the result is 3-2-4-1. These rankings are not the same and point out the ranking inconsistency that exists between the NPV and the IRR. In contrast to this result, it is sometimes stated in the literature that the IRR and NPV give a consistent choice of projects in capital budgeting problems. This is a correct statement *provided its full meaning is clearly understood.* The

TABLE 7-1

Internal Rates of Return and Net Present Values

End of Year	Cash Flows			
	Project 1	*Project 2*	*Project 3*	*Project 4*
0	−$50,000	−$100,000	−$120,000	−$200,000
1	14,000	24,000	30,000	40,000
2	14,000	24,000	30,000	40,000
3	14,000	24,000	30,000	40,000
4	14,000	24,000	30,000	40,000
5	14,000	24,000	30,000	40,000
6	14,000	24,000	30,000	40,000
7	14,000	24,000	30,000	40,000
8	14,000	24,000	30,000	40,000
9	14,000	24,000	30,000	40,000
10	14,000	24,000	30,000	40,000
IRR	25.00%	20.21%	21.55%	15.11%
NPV (10%)	$36,024	$47,470	$64,338	$45,784

full meaning of this statement centers around a condition previously stated. That is, every additional requirement of capital must be justified. This condition can best be explained by considering a special case of the capital budgeting problem; namely, the case of mutually exclusive projects. Also by considering mutually exclusive projects, a ranking criterion for the capital budgeting problem can be established.

MUTUALLY EXCLUSIVE PROJECTS

Projects are mutually exclusive when the choice of one project precludes the choice of any other project. This implies that *only one* project is chosen from a group of acceptable projects. This is not an unusual situation. An example of mutually exclusive projects is the situation where there are several methods of making a new product. Each method has different initial costs, gross incomes, yearly costs, etc. The question is, Which method should be chosen? The answer to this question is, the method with the greatest economic advantage. Or, to be consistent with one of the basic conditions, the method that provides the greatest wealth to the stockholders.

The solution to the mutually exclusive capital budgeting problem involves a comparison of the return earned on an incremental amount of capital with the MARR value or a comparison of the NPV for each project. These two solution methods are discussed in the following example.

Example 7-1

Determine which project should be chosen if the projects in Table 7-1 are mutually exclusive and MARR equals 10%.

The first step is to determine if all projects have an IRR that is equal or greater than MARR. This step has already been done and the results are given in Table 7-1. These results indicate that all projects are acceptable. If a project has an IRR that is less than MARR, it should be eliminated from further consideration.

The next step is to determine the rate of return earned on each additional increment of required capital. A comparison of Project 1 to doing nothing indicates a rate of return of 25% (Table 7-1) which is larger than MARR. Consequently, Project 1 is better than doing nothing. A comparison of Projects 1 and 2 (the yearly cash flows of Project 2 minus the yearly cash flows of Project 1) gives a rate of return, RR, of

$$0 = -100,000 + 50,000 + (24,000 - 14,000)\,(P/A\ i,10)$$

where

$$i = RR$$

$$= 15.11\%$$

Since this result is greater than MARR, it indicates that the additional capital required ($50,000) by Project 2 is justified by the yearly increase in cash flow ($10,000). Consequently, Project 2 is preferred over Project 1. A comparison of Project 2 and 3 gives

$$0 = -120,000 + 100,000 + (30,000 - 24,000)\,(P/A\ i,10)$$

where

$$i = RR$$

$$= 27.50\%$$

This result is larger than MARR. Consequently, Project 3 is preferred over Project 2. A comparison of Projects 3 and 4 gives

$$0 = -200,000 + 120,000 + (40,000 - 30,000)\,(P/A\ i,10)$$

where

$$i = RR$$

$$= 4.28\%$$

which indicates Project 3 is preferred to Project 4 since the RR is smaller than MARR and consequently the final choice is Project 3. *Note that Project 3 is the choice if the decision were based on the largest NPV.*

Some Important Comments   The results obtained in Example 7-1 can be generalized. The incremental RR approach will give the same choice of project as the project with the highest NPV. This is an important point because it serves as the basis for determining a solution to a more general form of the capital budgeting problem. The question sometimes arises, why use the RR approach when the NPV is computationally easier? The answer to this question is, the RR in a practical situation is, in all probability, not used. The RR approach is presented here to show the basis of the statement given previously that the IRR and NPV give a consistent choice of projects in the capital budgeting problems. Example 7-1 shows that this statement is correct *provided* the internal rate of return approach is used in a correct manner. That is, an incremental approach is used. This statement *does not imply* that the project with the largest IRR should be chosen. It is sometimes erroneously argued that the project with the highest IRR should be chosen and money could be "saved" and used for "better investments" that might occur in the future. A problem with this statement is that "better investments" might *not* occur at that time. Also, if a better investment does occur in the future, then it should be undertaken (theoretically at least). Otherwise the wealth of the stockholders is not being maximized.

In Example 7-1, the cash flows are constant for each project. This is not a requirement. The cash flows can vary yearly (and often do). However, the basic procedure is the same for determining the RR on the increment but is computationally more involved. In cases of cash flows that vary yearly, the most direct way is to determine the NPV for each project. Sometimes, a present value of the incremental cash flows is calculated to determine if the incremental cash flows have an RR greater than MARR. This method has decided computational advantages over the incremental RR approach. For example, a comparison of Projects 1 and 2 in Example 7-1 on the basis of incremental present value, IPV, is

$$IPV = -100,000 + 50,000 + (24,000 - 14,000)\,(P/A\ 10,10)$$

$$= \$11,446$$

Since this value is positive, it implies that the RR is greater than MARR. As in Example 7-1, Project 2 is preferred over Project 1.

Different Lives   In Example 7-1, the cash flows for each project extended over the same period of time (ten years). This is not always the case. It is possible for the projects in capital budgeting problems to have cash flows that extend over different periods of time.

In general, any comparison of projects must be made over *the same period of time.* Otherwise, the comparison is questionable. In the comparison of projects with cash flows over different periods of time, certain assumptions are necessary in order to provide for a comparison that is over the same period of time. There are three basic assumptions that can be made. They are as follows:

1. For a period of time equal to the longest project, make specific estimates about future investment alternatives that occur in the period of time between the end of an alternative's life and the life of the longest project.

2. For a period of time equal to the longest project, assume that the cash flows for all projects will be invested at MARR.

3. Assume that each project's cash flows cycle for a period of time equal to the least common multiple (LCM) of all the projects' lives.

The meaning of these three assumptions is shown in the following example. Also, this example shows that these three assumptions can give different results (decisions).

Example 7-2

Using the cash flows given in Table 7-2 and the three assumptions for the comparison of projects with unequal lives, determine the net present values for each project if MARR equals 15%.

If Assumption 1 is used, this means that it is necessary to estimate specific investment opportunities that will be available at the end of the tenth year and their resulting cash flows through year twenty. From a practical standpoint, this is a rather difficult task. Obviously, the NPV of Project 1 will vary with the estimated investment opportunities. The NPV for Project 2 is

$$NPV_2 = -150,000 + 35,000 \, (P/A \, 15,20)$$

$$= \$69,076$$

If Assumption 2 is used, the positive cash flows for each project are invested at MARR through year twenty. This means that the future worth, F, resulting from these positive cash flows at the end of year twenty is

$$F_1 = (32,000) \, (F/A \, 15,10) \, (F/P \, 15,10)$$

$$F_2 = (35,000) \, (F/A \, 15,20)$$

TABLE 7-2

Projects with Different Lives

End of Year	Cash Flows	
	Project 1	Project 2
0	−$100,000	−$150,000
1	32,000	35,000
2	32,000	35,000
3	32,000	35,000
4	32,000	35,000
5	32,000	35,000
6	32,000	35,000
7	32,000	35,000
8	32,000	35,000
9	32,000	35,000
10	32,000	35,000
11	—	35,000
12	—	35,000
13	—	35,000
14	—	35,000
15	—	35,000
16	—	35,000
17	—	35,000
18	—	35,000
19	—	35,000
20	—	35,000

and the NPV for each project with this assumption is

$$\text{NPV}_1 = -100{,}000 + [32{,}000 \ (F/A \ 15{,}10) \ (F/P \ 15{,}10)] \ (P/F \ 15{,}20)$$

$$= \$60{,}602$$

$$\text{NPV}_2 = -150{,}000 + [35{,}000 \ (F/A \ 15{,}20)] \ (P/F \ 15{,}20)$$

$$= \$69{,}076$$

The same net present values are obtained if the difference in project lives is *seemingly* disregarded. That is,

$$\text{NPV}_1 = -100{,}000 + 32{,}000 \ (P/A \ 15{,}10)$$

$$= \$60{,}602$$

$$\text{NPV}_2 = -150{,}000 + 35{,}000 \ (P/A \ 15{,}20)$$

$$= \$69{,}076$$

This is an important point since this result can be generalized. That is, with Assumption 2 the NPV for each project can be calculated without *explicit* consideration of the difference in project lives provided this assumption is considered applicable.

If Assumption 3 is used, there is a second cycle of Project 1 as shown in Table 7-3. With this assumption, the net present values for the two projects are

$$NPV_1 = -100,000 - 100,000 \ (P/F \ 15,10) + 32,000 \ (P/A \ 15,20)$$

$$= \$75,578$$

$$NPV_2 = -150,000 + 35,000 \ (P/F \ 15,20)$$

$$= \$69,076$$

Note that the net present values for Project 1 are different from Assumptions 2 and 3. In fact, a different choice of project is indicated if the

TABLE 7-3

Recycling Assumption

End of Year	Cash Flows		Project 2
	Project 1		
0	-$100,000		-$150,000
1	32,000		35,000
2	32,000		35,000
3	32,000		35,000
4	32,000		35,000
5	32,000		35,000
6	32,000		35,000
7	32,000		35,000
8	32,000		35,000
9	32,000		35,000
10	32,000	-100,000	35,000
11		32,000	35,000
12		32,000	35,000
13		32,000	35,000
14		32,000	35,000
15		32,000	35,000
16		32,000	35,000
17		32,000	35,000
18		32,000	35,000
19		32,000	35,000
20		32,000	35,000

projects are mutually exclusive. If Assumption 1 is used, this could also give an NPV that is different from either Assumption 2 or 3 depending on what estimate is made regarding future investment opportunities for Project 1.

Assumption for Unequal Lives Example 7-2 shows that the three different assumptions for comparing projects with different lives can give different results. The question is, What assumption should be used? This text uses Assumption 2. The use of Assumption 2 is based on the combined consideration of plausibility, computational advantage, practicality, and theoretical correctness for the comparison of projects *with different earnings (gross incomes)*. A different assumption is used later in the comparison of projects *with equal earnings* (cost comparisons and replacement analysis). Assumption 1 has decided theoretical merit. However, it is not used in this text because of the difficulty (practicality) of estimating investment opportunities far into the future.

Assumption 3 is a popular assumption (especially in cost comparisons and replacement analysis). However, there are problems in regard to its plausibility and computational requirements. The idea that projects with identical cash flows are available in later years (the cycling requirement) is not very plausible, especially in the case of projects with different earnings. Consider two projects with lives of 15 and 25 years. The least common multiple of their lives is 75 years and implies a total of five cycles for the project with a life of 15 years and a total of three cycles for the project with a life of 25 years. This idea of project cycles is very difficult to justify on grounds of practicality and plausibility. Although the computational disadvantages with Assumption 3 are not insurmountable, they do increase as the number of cycles increases.

Assumption 2 has some merit since it does not suffer from plausibility or practicality considerations nor does it have computational disadvantages. If a broad view is taken in regard to the assumption that the cash flows are invested at MARR, Assumption 2 has theoretical merit. That is, the cash flows can be "invested" (theoretically at least) in retiring debt obligations and paying dividends to stockholders. These considerations make Assumption 2 a good choice for capital budgeting problems.

THE CAPITAL BUDGETING PROBLEM

One solution to the capital budgeting problem can be obtained by applying the procedures used to solve the mutually exclusive problem. This solution involves arranging all the possible combinations of projects into mutually exclusive "bundles" and then choosing the bundle that maximizes the NPV and does not violate any restrictions (constraints) placed on the solution. For example, if the projects in Table 7-1 are assumed to be independent and arranged in mutually exclusive "bundles" the results shown in Table 7-4 are obtained. If a restriction is imposed that only a certain amount of money can be spent for new projects (a capital expenditure budget), then those bundles with total capital expenditures exceeding this amount are eliminated from further consideration. For example, a capital expenditure budget of $450,000 means that bundle 14 (Projects 2, 3, 4) is chosen since it maximizes the NPV and does not exceed the limitation of $450,000. As two further examples, a budget restriction of $300,000 gives bundle 11 (Projects 1, 2, 3) as the choice, and a budget restriction of $250,000 gives bundle 8 (Projects 2, 3) as the choice. This approach to the capital budgeting problem has a computational disadvantage since the number of possible combinations (bundles) is $2^n - 1$, where n is the number of projects. For example if there are ten projects, there are 1,023 possible combinations (bundles). One way to avoid this computational disadvantage is to formulate the capital budgeting problem in a mathematical programming format. That is,

$$\text{maximize: } z = \sum_{i=1}^{n} (\text{NPV})_i x_i \qquad (7\text{-}1)$$

TABLE 7-4

Projects Arranged in Mutually Exclusive Bundles

Bundle	Projects	Capital Expenditure	Annual Cash Flow	NPV (10%)	IRR (%)
1	1	$ 50,000	$ 14,000	$ 36,204	25.00
2	2	100,000	24,000	47,470	20.21
3	3	120,000	30,000	64,338	21.55
4	4	200,000	40,000	45,784	15.11
5	1,2	150,000	38,000	83,494	23.25
6	1,3	170,000	44,000	100,362	24.36
7	1,4	250,000	54,000	81,808	19.29
8	2,3	220,000	54,000	111,808	21.57
9	2,4	300,000	64,000	93,254	17.00
10	3,4	320,000	70,000	110,122	17.71
11	1,2,3	270,000	68,000	147,832	22.94
12	1,2,4	350,000	78,000	129,278	18.22
13	1,3,4	370,000	84,000	146,146	18.72
14	2,3,4	420,000	94,000	157,592	18.33
15	1,2,3,4	470,000	108,000	193,616	19.04

subject to:

$$\sum_{i=1}^{n} K_i x_i \leq B \tag{7-2}$$

$$x_i = 0 \text{ or } 1 \text{ for all } i \tag{7-3}$$

where

$(NPV)_i$ = net present value for Project i

K_1 = capital expenditure (investment) required by Project i

n = number of projects

x_i = decision variable for Project i

B = budget (capital expenditure) restriction

In mathematical programming vocabulary, Eq. (7-1) is referred to as the *objective* equation and Eqs. (7-2) and (7-3) are referred as the *restrictions* (constraints). Eq. (7-3) is a mathematical expression of the fact that a project is either accepted ($x_i = 1$) or rejected ($x_i = 0$). That is, the projects are not divisible.

The use of Eqs. (7-1), (7-2), and (7-3) is demonstrated in the following formulation using the data in Table 7-1 and a budget restriction of $250,000.

$$\text{maximize: } z = 36{,}204x_1 + 47{,}470x_2 + 64{,}338x_3 + 45{,}784x_4 \tag{7-4}$$

subject to:

$$50{,}000x_1 + 100{,}000x_2 + 120{,}000x_3 + 200{,}000x_4 \leq 250{,}000 \tag{7-5}$$

$$x_{1,2,3,4} = 0 \text{ or } 1 \tag{7-6}$$

Because of the small number of projects involved in this formulation, Eqs. (7-4), (7-5), and (7-6) can be solved by inspection. The solution is $x_1 = 0, x_2 = 1, x_3 = 1,$ and $x_4 = 0$. This is the same solution obtained using the bundle approach shown earlier. When there is a large number of projects, specialized algorithms are necessary. These algorithms are beyond the scope of this text and will not be discussed further. The formulation of the capital budgeting problem expressed by Eqs. (7-1), (7-2), and (7-3) can be extended to include certain other considerations that may be applicable to capital budgeting problems.

Mutually Exclusive Projects   A subset, m, of mutually exclusive projects in a capital budgeting problem can be accommodated by adding the restriction

$$\sum_m x_m \leq 1 \qquad (7\text{-}7)$$

to the mathematical formulation. As an example suppose that in some particular capital budgeting problem, Projects 2, 6, 8, and 9 are mutually exclusive. Using Eq. (7-7), the restriction

$$x_2 + x_6 + x_8 + x_9 \leq 1 \qquad (7\text{-}8)$$

is added to the mathematical formulation of the problem. Sometimes there is a tendency to choose the project with the highest NPV from a subset of mutually exclusive projects and include only this chosen project in the overall formulation of a capital budgeting problem. This is incorrect. It is possible to have some other mutually exclusive project with a lower net present value and lower capital investment that, when combined with some other project not in the mutually exclusive set, can give a higher total net present value.

Interdependent Projects   It is possible in the capital budgeting problem to have projects that are interdependent. In this case, the equation

$$x_r - x_s \leq 0 \qquad (7\text{-}9)$$

is added to mathematical programming formulation. Eq. (7-9) expresses the situation that if Project r is done then Project s must be done. However, Project s can be done without Project r. Also, neither Project r or s need be done.

Labor and Material Restrictions   There are situations where the total available labor and / or materials are limited. These situations can be included in the formulation of the capital budgeting problem by adding a set of restrictions, m, of the form

$$\sum_m m_{ij}x_i \leq M_j \qquad (7\text{-}10)$$

where

m_{ij} = materials (labor) required by Project i in year j

x_i = decision variable for Project i

M_j = total materials (labor) available in year j

Multiperiod Budgets   It is shown in Chapter 5 that the total expenditure required by a project can be expended over a several year period. Consequently, it is not unusual to have budget restrictions established for future years. In this case, a set of budget restrictions, m, replaces the single budget restriction. That is, the budget set

$$\sum_m K_{ij} x_i \leq B_j \qquad (7\text{-}11)$$

replaces the single budget restriction defined by Eq. (7-2) where K_{ij} is the capital expenditure required by Project i in year j.

Example 7-3 _____

Using the data given in Table 7-5 and the following conditions, formulate the capital budgeting problem in a mathematical programming format and solve it by inspection.

1. The budget restriction for $j = 0$ is \$100,000.
2. The budget restriction for $j = 1$ is \$80,000.
3. The budget restriction for $j = 2$ is \$50,000.
4. Projects 2, 6, and 7 are mutually exclusive.
5. Projects 1 and 3 are interdependent: if Project 1 is done, Project 3 must be done; but Project 3 can be done without Project 1.

TABLE 7-5

Capital Budgeting Problem

Project Number	Capital Expenditure $j = 0$	Capital Expenditure $j = 1$	Capital Expenditure $j = 2$	Net Present Value
1	\$30,000	\$20,000	\$ 5,000	\$10,000
2	15,000	10,000	8,000	7,000
3	10,000	–	5,000	2,000
4	20,000	10,000	–	6,000
5	18,000	15,000	–	8,000
6	30,000	–	15,000	9,000
7	10,000	10,000	10,000	8,000
8	28,000	20,000	15,000	12,000
9	12,000	–	20,000	5,000
10	9,000	15,000	9,000	8,000

The mathematical programming format is to maximize:

$$z = 10{,}000x_1 + 7{,}000x_2 + 2{,}000x_3 + 6{,}000x_4 + 8{,}000x_5 + 9{,}000x_6$$
$$+ 8{,}000x_7 + 12{,}000x_8 + 5{,}000x_9 + 8{,}000x_{10}$$

subject to:

$$30{,}000x_1 + 15{,}000x_2 + 10{,}000x_3 + 20{,}000x_4 + 18{,}000x_5 + 30{,}000x_6$$
$$+ 10{,}000x_7 + 28{,}000x_8 + 12{,}000x_9 + 9{,}000x_{10} \leq 100{,}000$$

$$20{,}000x_1 + 10{,}000x_2 + 10{,}000x_4 + 15{,}000x_5 + 10{,}000x_7$$
$$+ 20{,}000x_8 + 15{,}000x_{10} \leq 80{,}000$$

$$5{,}000x_1 + 8{,}000x_2 + 5{,}000x_3 + 15{,}000x_6 + 10{,}000x_7 + 15{,}000x_8$$
$$+ 20{,}000x_9 + 9{,}000x_{10} \leq 50{,}000$$

$$x_2 + x_6 + x_7 \leq 1$$

$$x_1 - x_3 \leq 0$$

$$x_i = 0 \text{ or } 1 \text{ for } i = 1, 2, \ldots, 10$$

The solution to this problem is

$x_1 = 0$	$x_6 = 0$
$x_2 = 0$	$x_7 = 1$
$x_3 = 1$	$x_8 = 1$
$x_4 = 1$	$x_9 = 0$
$x_5 = 1$	$x_{10} = 1$

$$z = \$44{,}000$$

Some Incorrect Proposals Certain incorrect methods are some-times proposed to solve the capital budgeting problem. There are two particular incorrect methods that seem to be persistently proposed. The first method involves listing the project on the basis of highest rates of return and keeping a cumulative total of the capital expenditures. Once the cumulative total of the capital expenditures exceeds a given budget, the projects included in this listing are the ones selected. An example of this method using the projects in Table 7-1 is shown in Table 7-6. The results in Table 7-6 indicate that for a budget of $400,000, Projects 1, 2, and 3 are selected. This selection gives a total NPV of $147,832. However if the NPV is maximized, the selected projects are 2, 3, and 4 with a total NPV of $157,592. The latter answer (Projects 2, 3, and 4) is the *correct solution* since it maximizes the NPV. It is true that this method can give

TABLE 7-6

Project Ranking by Rate of Return

Project	Rate of Return (%)	Cumulative Capital Required ($)
1	25.00	50,000
3	21.55	170,000
2	20.21	270,000
4	15.11	470,000

correct answers to the capital budgeting problem. However, as shown in this example, it is not possible to determine if the answers given by this method do, in fact, maximize the NPV. Consequently, this method is not recommended.

A second method sometimes proposed to solve the capital budgeting problem is similar to the first method. Except in this second method, the projects are listed on the basis of NPV. This method is shown in Table 7-7 using the data given in Table 7-1. The results in Table 7-7 indicate Projects 2 and 3 should be selected for a budget restriction of $400,000 which gives a total NPV of $111,808. However, the correct solution is to choose Projects 1, 3, and 4 which give a total NPV of $146,146. This second method is not recommended since it too does not guarantee that the NPV is maximized.

The only two methods that guarantee that the NPV is maximized are the bundling approach and the mathematical programming approach. They are the methods recommended here.

TABLE 7-7

Projects Ranking by Net Present Value

Project	NPV $	Cumulative Capital Required ($)
3	64,338	120,000
2	47,470	220,000
4	45,784	420,000
1	36,024	470,000

PROBLEMS

7-1. The four projects listed below are mutually exclusive. Determine the following using an incremental rate of return approach:
(a) Which project should be selected if MARR equals 12%.
(b) Which project should be selected if MARR equals 20%.

	Project			
	1	*2*	*3*	*4*
Capital investment, $	40,000	50,000	70,000	100,000
Annual cash flow, $	8,000	10,000	13,000	18,000
Life, years	10	10	10	10

7-2. Using the data in Problem 7-1, which project should be selected using the maximization of NPV as the criterion?

7-3. If the four projects listed below are mutually exclusive, determine the following using an incremental rate of return approach:
(a) Which project should be selected if MARR equals 15%.
(b) Which project should be selected if MARR equals 25%.

	Project			
	1	*2*	*3*	*4*
Capital investment, $	20,000	35,000	40,000	50,000
Annual cash flow, $	3,600	5,800	7,200	8,600
Life, years	15	15	15	15

7-4. Using the data in Problem 7-3, which project should be selected using the maximization of NPV as the criterion?

7-5. If the four projects listed below are mutually exclusive, determine the following:
(a) Which project should be selected if MARR equals 15% and a rate of return approach is used.
(b) Which project should be selected if MARR equals 15% and the NPV criterion is used.
 HINT It is first necessary to determine how to calculate rate of return and NPV with an infinite life.

	Project			
	1	*2*	*3*	*4*
Capital investment, $	60,000	75,000	80,000	90,000
Annual cash flow, $	10,000	12,000	14,000	15,000
Life, years	∞	∞	∞	∞

7-6. If the projects listed below are mutually exclusive, determine which project should be selected using an incremental approach and MARR equal to 12%.

End of Year	Cash Flows			
	Project 1	Project 2	Project 3	Project 4
0	−$40,000	−$48,000	−$59,000	−$75,000
1	8,000	9,000	14,000	16,000
2	8,000	9,000	14,000	16,000
3	8,000	9,000	14,000	16,000
4	8,000	9,000	14,000	16,000
5	8,000	9,000	10,000	16,000
6	8,000	10,000	10,000	12,000
7	6,000	10,000	10,000	12,000
8	6,000	10,000	10,000	12,000
9	6,000	10,000	10,000	12,000
10	6,000	10,000	10,000	12,000

7-7. Repeat Problem 7-6, only use the NPV criterion.

7-8. Assuming the projects in Problem 7-7 are independent and not mutually exclusive, which projects should be selected if:
(a) A capital expenditure restriction of $200,000 is imposed?
(b) A capital expenditure restriction of $150,000 is imposed?

7-9. The four projects listed below are mutually exclusive. Determine which project should be selected using an incremental approach and MARR equal to 15%. Also what assumption(s) are implied in your answer?

	Project			
	1	2	3	4
Capital investment, $	100,000	130,000	150,000	190,000
Annual cash flow, $	24,000	26,000	42,000	43,000
Life, years	8	10	6	8

7-10. Repeat Problem 7-9, only use NPV as the basis of selecting a project.

7-11. Determine which project(s) should be accepted using the data given below and a MARR equal to 15% if:
(a) The projects are mutually exclusive.
(b) The projects are independent, and there is a budget restriction of $400,000.

Assume that the cash flows in year zero are the capital expenditures.

End of Year	Project Cash Flows				
	1	2	3	4	5
0	−80,000	−100,000	−150,000	−170,000	−200,000
1	19,000	24,000	36,000	40,000	46,000
2	19,000	24,000	36,000	40,000	46,000
3	19,000	24,000	36,000	40,000	46,000
4	19,000	24,000	36,000	40,000	46,000
5	19,000	24,000	36,000	40,000	46,000
6	19,000	24,000	36,000	40,000	46,000
7	19,000	24,000	36,000	40,000	46,000
8	19,000	24,000	36,000	40,000	46,000

7-12. Using the data and conditions given below, write the mathematical programming format needed to determine which project should be done.

Project	Capital Expenditure $j = 0$	Capital Expenditure $j = 1$	Capital Expenditure $j = 2$	Net Present Value
1	$20,000	$7,000	$8,000	$6,000
2	3,000	–	2,000	2,000
3	4,000	4,000	–	4,000
4	10,000	6,000	–	7,000
5	8,000	5,000	4,000	5,000
6	6,000	–	3,000	2,000
7	9,000	8,000	7,000	3,000
8	7,000	5,000	–	8,000
9	10,000	7,000	5,000	6,000

Conditions

1. Budget restriction for $j = 0$ is $70,000.
2. Budget restriction for $j = 1$ is $40,000.
3. Budget restriction for $j = 2$ is $20,000.
4. Projects 6 and 8 are mutually exclusive.
5. Projects 2 and 3 are interdependent: Project 3 can be done without Project 2, but Project 2 must accompany Project 3.

7-13. For the data and conditions given below, determine the following:

    (a) The project that should be chosen if the projects are mutually exclusive.

    (b) The project(s) that should be chosen if the projects are independent and the budget for total capital expenditures in year $j = 0$ is \$250,000 and in year $j = 1$ \$200,000.

Conditions

1. The debt ratio is 30%.
2. The debt obligation is paid on the basis of constant interest over the life of the project at a cost of 10%.
3. Depreciation begins after the total capital expenditure is made, and for tax purposes a straight-line model is used with a life of ten years and a zero salvage value.
4. The MARR for equity is 20%.
5. The tax rate is 52%.

End of Year	Project 1			Project 2			Project 3		
	Capital Investment	Gross Income	Costs	Capital Investment	Gross Income	Costs	Capital Investment	Gross Income	Costs
0	100,000	—	—	120,000	—	—	150,000	—	—
1	70,000	—	—	80,000	—	—	100,000	—	—
2		100,000	40,000		130,000	50,000		150,000	60,000
.		.	.		.	.		.	.
.		.	.		.	.		.	.
.		.	.		.	.		.	.
15		100,000	40,000		130,000	50,000		150,000	60,000

8

BREAK-EVEN MODELS

Break-even models provide a method for understanding the basic relationships between profit and costs. Break-even models can also provide an understanding of the relationship between profit and net cash flow.

LINEAR BREAK-EVEN MODELS

In break-even models, the relationship between profit and costs can be either linear or nonlinear. For the linear case, the relationship between profit and costs is

$$P = (sV - cV - F - D_b - I) - (sV - cV - F - D - I)T \qquad (8\text{-}1)$$

where

P = after-tax profit per unit of time

V = volume of sales per unit of time

s = selling price per unit

c = variable cost per unit

F = fixed costs per unit of time, *excluding* book depreciation and debt interest expense

D_b = book depreciation (capital recovery) per unit of time. This is sometimes referred to as the company's depreciation

I = debt interest expense per unit of time

D = tax depreciation per unit of time. In general, $D_b \neq D$

T = tax rate

sV = gross income (revenues) per unit of time

cV = variable costs per unit of time

$s - c$ = the contribution per unit. This difference is the portion of the selling price that contributes to paying the fixed costs

Sometimes in break-even models, an overall fixed cost, F', is defined in the following manner

$$F' = F + D_b + I \qquad (8\text{-}2)$$

and if it is assumed that $D_b = D$, Eq. (8-1) can be written as

$$P = (sV - cV - F')(1 - T) \qquad (8\text{-}3)$$

Or, if $D_b \neq D$, Eq. (8-1) can be written as

$$P = (sV - cV - F')(1 - T) + (D - D_b)T \qquad (8\text{-}4)$$

Although Eqs. (8-3) and (8-4) are more concise than Eq. (8-1), they are not used to any extent in this chapter. Eq. (8-1) provides greater insights into the relationships between profits, costs, and net cash flows. Eq. (8-1) implies certain assumptions. First, sales and production volumes (V) are the same. Second, fixed costs are independent of the production volume. Third, variable costs and gross income are both linear functions of the production (sales) volume. In practice the usual time unit in Eq. (8-1) is one year. That is, profit and other time dependent variables are often defined on an annual basis.

Variable Costs

These costs over a period of time (cV) are proportional to the volume of production. The variable cost per unit (c) comprises such costs as: raw material, direct labor, direct supplies, direct supervision and direct maintenance.

Fixed Costs

These costs are independent of the volume of production. In actuality, this is only true over a range of production. If the production volume continues beyond this range, fixed expenses will increase because additional equipment must be purchased, new buildings built, etc. However, for most break-even models, the assumption that the fixed costs are constant is adequate since the time period over which the profits and costs are usually considered is short (one year). Fixed costs include such items as depreciation, debt interest, property taxes, rent, insurance, and executive salaries.

Break-even models obtain their name from the determination of the point at which the profit and, consequently, the income taxes are zero. Two break-even points usually are of particular interest. The first break-even point is the volume of production (sales) at which the profit is zero. This point, V_b, can be determined by substituting zero for the profit and tax term in Eq. (8-1) which gives

$$V_b = \frac{F + D_b + I}{s - c} \tag{8-5}$$

The second point is the unit sales price at which the profit is zero, s_b, which, for a given volume of sales (V), is

$$s_b = c + \frac{F + D_b + I}{V} \tag{8-6}$$

Note in Eq. (8-6) that as the volume of sales (V) increases, the break-even selling price decreases.

Break-even models can be portrayed graphically. A generalized model is shown in Figure 8-1. The slope of the gross income line in Figure 8-1 is s, and the slope of the total cost line is c. Note that the total cost line begins at the fixed costs. In this way, the total costs are portrayed. The profit after tax is obtained using Eq. (8-1), and the profit before tax, P_b, is obtained using the equation

$$P_b = (sV - cV - F - D_b - I) \tag{8-7}$$

Example 8-1

A product sells for $70 per unit. Labor, material, and direct overhead costs are $15, $10, and $15 per unit respectively. The company's book depreciation is $50,000 per year, and debt interest is $10,000 per year. Other fixed expenses amount to $100,000 per year. Determine the following if the company's volume of sales is 10,000 units per year and tax rate is 52%.

a. The annual before-tax profit.
b. The annual after-tax profit if the tax depreciation is $60,000 per year.
c. The break-even volume of sales.

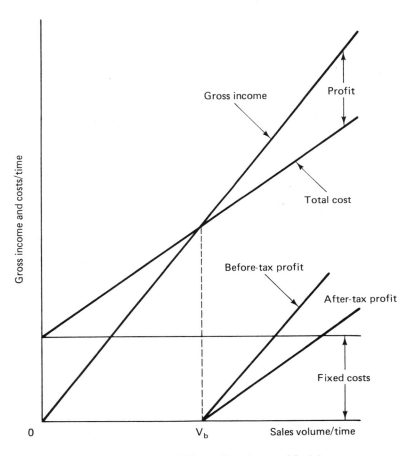

FIGURE 8-1 A Linear Break-even Model

   d. The break-even selling price per unit.

   e. Plot a break-even chart for the data in this example.

For this example the variable cost per unit is

$$c = 15 + 10 + 15$$
$$= \$40$$

Using Eq. (8-7), the profit before tax for Part a is

$$P_b = 70(10,000) - 40(10,000) - 100,000 - 50,000 - 10,000$$
$$= \$140,000 \text{ per year}$$

For Part b, the after-tax profit using Eq. (8-1) is

$$P = [70(10,000) - 40(10,000) - 100,000 - 50,000 - 10,000]$$
$$- [70(10,000) - 40(10,000) - 100,000 - 60,000 - 10,000](0.52)$$
$$= \$72,400 \text{ per year}$$

For Part c, the break-even volume of sales using Eq. (8-5) is

$$V_b = \frac{100,000 + 50,000 + 10,000}{70 - 40}$$
$$= 5,333 \text{ units per year}$$

For Part d, the break-even selling price using Eq. (8-6) is

$$s_b = 40 + \frac{100,000 + 50,000 + 10,000}{10,000}$$
$$= \$56 \text{ per unit}$$

The break-even chart for this example is shown in Figure 8-2.

NONLINEAR BREAK-EVEN MODELS

Nonlinear break-even models occur when one or more components in the profit equation are not linear. The basic approach is the same as in linear models. That is, profit is equal to the gross income minus the total costs. Usually, nonlinear break-even models require some use of calculus. A nonlinear break-even model is discussed in the next example.

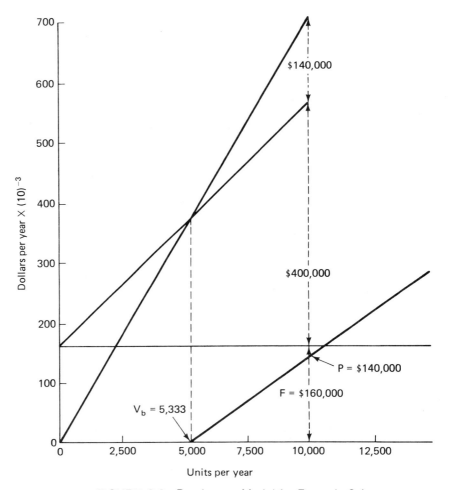

FIGURE 8-2 Break-even Model for Example 8-1

Example 8-2

It has been determined that the weekly sales, V, is related to the unit selling price, s, by the equation

$$s = (180 - 0.5V) \tag{8-8}$$

The weekly total costs, C, have also been determined to be related to the weekly sales by the equation

$$C = -0.25V^2 + 120V + 200 \tag{8-9}$$

The following information is required:

a. The volume of weekly sales for maximum profit.
b. The maximum weekly profit.
c. The break-even point.

For Part a, the profit equation, using Eqs. (8-8) and (8-9), is

$$P = (180 - 0.5V)V - (-0.25V^2 + 120V + 200) \tag{8-10}$$

which simplifies to

$$P = -0.25V^2 + 60V - 200 \tag{8-11}$$

Taking the derivative of Eq. (8-11) and setting it equal to zero gives the volume of sales for maximum profit.

$$\frac{dP}{dV} = 0 = -0.5V + 60$$

$$V = 120 \text{ units per week}$$

For Part b, the result of Part a is substituted into Eq. (8-11) which gives for the maximum profit

$$P = -0.25(120)^2 + 60(120) - 200$$

$$= \$3,400 \text{ per week}$$

The break-even point required in Part c is obtained using the quadratic formula and the coefficients in Eq. (8-11).

$$V_b = \frac{-60 \pm \sqrt{(60)^2 - 4(-0.25)(-200)}}{2(-0.25)}$$

$$= \frac{-60 \pm 58.31}{-0.5}$$

$$= 3.38 \text{ and } 236.62 \text{ units per week}$$

In this case there are two break-even points. A break-even chart for this example is given in Figure 8-3.

An Additional Note   Economic theory states that maximum profit occurs when marginal income (revenue) equals marginal cost. In the context of Example 8-2, the marginal income is

$$\frac{dI}{dV} = \frac{d\,[180V - 0.5V^2\,]}{dV} \qquad (8\text{-}12)$$

$$= 180 - V$$

The marginal cost is

$$\frac{dC}{dV} = \frac{d\,[\,-0.25V^2 + 120V + 200]}{dV} \qquad (8\text{-}13)$$

$$= -0.5V + 120$$

Setting Eq. (8-12) equal to Eq. (8-13) gives

$$180 - V = -0.5V + 120$$

$$V = 120 \text{ units per week}$$

Which is the same result obtained in Example 8-2.

PROFIT AND NET CASH FLOW

In general, profit and net cash flow are not equal but they are related. The basic difference between profit and net cash flow is due to book (the company's) depreciation. In determining profit, the book depreciation is deducted as part of the fixed costs. It is a provision for recovering the capital investment. However, in determining net cash flows, the book depreciation is not deducted. Depreciation amounts stay within the company (actually, depreciation amounts become a source of investment funds; i.e., they are not "paid" to anyone). Consequently, depreciation is not a cash flow.

The relationship between yearly profits and net cash flows can be seen by considering the equity cash flow equation given in Chapter 5 and the profit equation, Eq. (8-1). For comparison purposes, the equation for net equity cash flows, Eq. (5-7), is repeated here as Eq. (8-14):

$$X_e = (G - C - I\,) - (G - C - I - D\,)T$$

$$- K + L + B - P \pm W \qquad (8\text{-}14)$$

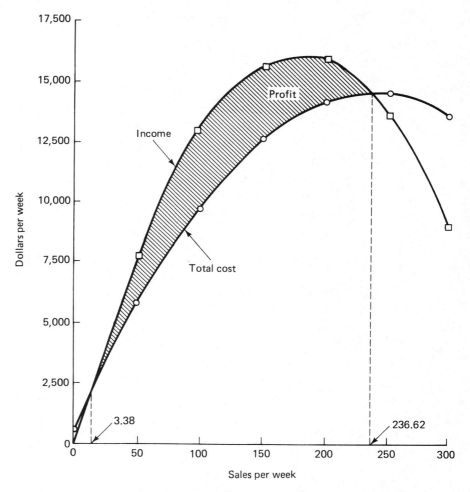

FIGURE 8-3 Nonlinear Break-even Chart (Example 8-2)

For convenience, the subscript, j, used in Eq. (5-7) has been omitted in Eq. (8-14). In order to make Eq. (8-1) more clearly resemble Eq. (8-14), the substitution $G = sV$ is made since the selling price multiplied by the volume of sales is the gross income. In Eq. (8-14), C is the *total costs excluding depreciation.* Consequently, the C in Eq. (8-14) is equal to $cV + F$ in Eq. (8-1). Making these substitutions, Eq. (8-1) can be written as

$$P = (G - C - D_b - I) - (G - C - D - I)T \qquad (8\text{-}15)$$

and some of the similarities between Eq. (8-14) and (8-15) are discernible. Some of the variables included in Eq. (8-14) are not included in the profit equation. The reasons for not including these variables in Eq. (8-15) are given in the following explanations:

1. Capital expenditures, K, are not considered in determining profits. They are an increase in the company's assets.
2. Salvage values, L, do not contribute to profit as long as the actual realizable salvage equals the book salvage value.
3. The borrowed money, B, is not a part of profit. It is a liability and is offset by the increase in capital assets purchased with the borrowed money.
4. Principal payments, P, are not a part of profits. The book depreciation, D_b, is based on the *total capital* expenditure. Consequently, the recovery of the debt capital (principal) is implied in the book depreciation.
5. Increases or decreases in working capital do not change profits. They are changes in a company's assets.

If the last five variables (K, L, B, P, and W) in Eq. (8-14) are zero, then the following relationship between profit and net cash flow is true

$$P = X_e - D_b \qquad (8\text{-}16)$$

Eq. (8-16) supports the statement made earlier that the *basic* difference between profit and net cash flow is the book depreciation.

Example 8-3

In this example, the data in Example 5-3 is used to determine the incremental yearly changes in after-tax profit that are expected to result from the profit under consideration in Example 5-3. It is assumed that the tax and book depreciation are equal. However, this is not generally necessary. In practice the book and tax depreciation schedules usually are different.

Most of the data needed to determine the yearly incremental profits are available in Table 5-3. Using Eq. (8-15), some selected yearly profits are

$$P_0 = 0$$

$$P_1 = (40,000 - 10,000 - 9,000 - 4,000)$$
$$- (40,000 - 10,000 - 9,000 - 4,000)(0.52)$$
$$= \$8,160$$

$$P_5 = (40,000 - 10,000 - 9,000 - 2,400)$$
$$- (40,000 - 10,000 - 9,000 - 2,400)(0.52)$$
$$= \$8,928$$

$$P_{10} = (40,000 - 10,000 - 9,000 - 400)$$
$$- (40,000 - 10,000 - 9,000 - 400)(0.52)$$
$$= \$9,888$$

The remaining yearly profits are given in Table 8-1.

TABLE 8-1

Yearly Incremental Profits

(Example 8-3)

End of Year	Incremental Profit
0	0
1	8,160
2	8,352
3	8,544
4	8,736
5	8,928
6	9,120
7	9,312
8	9,504
9	9,696
10	9,888

PROBLEMS

8-1. A company is producing a particular unit that has the following data:

$$\text{volume of sales per year} = 80,000 \text{ units}$$
$$\text{selling price per unit} = \$50$$

$$\text{variable cost per unit} = \$30$$
$$\text{fixed costs per year} = \$900,000$$
$$\text{tax rate} = 52\%$$

Using this data, determine the following:

(a) The before-tax profit.

(b) The after-tax profit assuming the tax and book depreciation are equal.

(c) The yearly sales volume in order to break even.

(d) The unit selling price in order to break even.

(e) Plot a break-even chart for this problem.

8-2. A company sells a product for $25 per unit. Material, labor, and direct overhead costs are respectively $4, $6, and $5 per unit. The company's book depreciation is $1,000,000 per year and debt interest is $200,000 per year. Other fixed expenses are $4,800,000 per year. The volume of sales per year is 1,000,000 units. If the company's tax rate is 52%, determine the following:

(a) The company's before-tax profit.

(b) The company's after-tax profit.

(c) The break-even yearly volume of sales.

(d) The break-even unit selling price.

8-3. A company is currently producing three products, X, Y, and Z, having the data shown in the following tables.

Product	Selling Price Per Unit	Variable Cost Per Unit	Volume of Sales Per Year
X	$50	$28	40,000
Y	20	11	70,000
Z	30	16	60,000

Product	Fixed Costs Per Year	Book Depreciation Per Year	Debt Interest Per Year
X	$100,000	$100,000	$ 50,000
Y	300,000	100,000	150,000
Z	100,000	200,000	100,000

The company is considering eliminating product Y and replacing it with product Q having the following data:

Product	Selling Price Per Unit	Variable Cost Per Unit	Volume of Sales Per Year
Q	$35	$20	50,000

If the company's tax rate is 52% and the tax and book depreciation are equal, should the company make this change?
(a) Assume the fixed costs do not change.
(b) Assume the current fixed costs increase by $500,000.
(c) In Parts (a) and (b) what is the increase (decrease) in after-tax profits if product Q replaces product Y?

8-4. A company is considering two methods for manufacturing a particular product. Both methods provide the same gross income. Using the data given in the following table, determine the range of yearly sales needed to choose (a) method X and (b) method Y.

Method	Variable Cost Per Unit	Fixed Costs Per Year
X	$40	$900,000
Y	80	500,000

8-5. A company has a product that sells for $400 per unit. The total yearly before-tax cost of producing this product is given by the equation

$$C = n^2 - 2,000n + 1,000,000$$

where n is the number of units sold yearly. Determine the following:
(a) The yearly fixed costs.
(b) The number of units per year for maximum profit.
(c) The maximum profit per year after tax assuming the tax rate is 52% and the tax and book depreciation are the same.
(d) The break-even point.
(e) Plot a break-even chart.

8-6. Using the economic concept mentioned in this chapter that maximum profit occurs when marginal revenue equals marginal costs and the data in Problem 8-5, show that the volume of production for maximum profit is the same as that obtained in the solution to Problem 8-5.

8-7. The weekly volume of sales of a particular unit is related to the unit selling price, S, by the function $(200\text{-}S)$. The total weekly costs are given by

$$500 + 100n + \frac{0.5n^2}{2}$$

where n is the weekly volume of sales. Determine the following:
(a) The unit selling price for weekly maximum profit.
(b) The maximum weekly profit.
(c) The weekly volume of sales for maximum profit.
(d) The break-even unit selling prices.

8-8. Repeat Problem 8-6, only use the data in Problem 8-7.

8-9. Determine the yearly incremental changes in after-tax profit resulting from the project described in Example 5-4. Assume the tax and book depreciation are equal.

8-10. Determine the yearly incremental changes in after-tax profit using the data in Example 6-1 assuming the minimum annual revenue requirements are the gross incomes. It should be noted that the tax and book depreciation are not equal.

9

COST COMPARISONS

Basically, cost comparisons are mutually exclusive capital budgeting problems with certain modifications. In cost comparisons, the gross incomes (revenues) are considered to be the same for all alternatives. Or stated another way, the alternatives are considered to provide equal service. Consequently, a comparison of the alternatives is based on their costs and the alternative with the least total cost is selected. The alternative of "doing nothing" is not a feasible alternative in cost comparisons since there is an implied need for service (use) that must be satisfied by one of the alternatives.

This text considers two approaches for making cost comparisons. The first approach is to generate the yearly minimum annual revenue requirements for each alternative and then make a comparison of these yearly amounts as well as a comparison of the levelized (equivalent) annual revenue (cost) requirement. The second approach, which in this text is the *conventional approach*, is concerned with determining only a levelized (equivalent) annual cost of the alternatives and then making a comparison. This latter approach is subdivided into before-tax and after-tax cost comparisons. In actuality the revenue and conventional approaches are directly related. The relationship between these two approaches is sometimes not fully recognized. *The most inclusive and direct method for making cost comparisons is the minimum annual revenue requirement approach.* The conventional approach to cost comparisons is included to show the relationships between these two approaches and to point out their advantages and disadvantages. The discussion in this chapter presupposes the same condition regarding inflationary effects mentioned in Chapter 7. That is, all cash flows are consistently expressed in either real or actual dollars.

THE REVENUE REQUIREMENT APPROACH

As previously stated, this approach requires that the minimum annual revenue requirements for each alternative be determined and then compared. Remember that annual revenue requirements are annual costs with a required return on equity from the standpoint of cost comparisons. Consequently, *the terms annual revenue requirements and annual costs are used interchangeably.*

In the initial discussions of cost comparisons in this chapter, it is assumed that the lives of the alternatives are equal and the period of need for the service provided by the alternatives is at least equal to the lives of the alternatives. It is also assumed that the actual salvage value realized at the end of an alternative's life is equal to the tax salvage value. Consequently, there are no gains or losses and no tax effects in the last year of an alternative's life. These assumptions are relaxed in later discussions in this chapter.

Example 9-1

Using a minimum annual revenue approach and the data in Table 9-1, make a cost comparison of the two alternatives and determine which alternative should be chosen.

TABLE 9-1

Data for Example 9-1

	Alternative 1	Alternative 2
Initial cost	$100,000	$150,000
Annual cost of operation and maintenance	$ 20,000	$ 5,000
Book depreciation	SL	SL
Salvage value	$ 8,000	$ 10,000
Life, years	8	8
Tax depreciation	SL	SL
Salvage value	$ 8,000	$ 10,000
Life, years	8	8
Cost of debt capital	12.5%	12.5%
Cost of equity capital	25%	25%
Debt ratio	40%	40%
Tax rate	52%	52%
Investment tax credit	0%	0%

The first step is to determine the annual costs (revenue requirements) for each alternative in accordance with the procedures given in Chapter 6. The annual costs for the two alternatives are given in Tables 9-2 and 9-3. The next step is to compare these annual costs and choose the alternative with the least cost. In making this comparison *both the long-term and short-term effects must be considered.* Long-term effects refer to the levelized (equivalent) annual cost, and short-term effects refer to the specific yearly annual costs. The levelized annual costs for the two alternatives are

$$E_1 = [67,750 \ (P/F\ 20,\ 1) + 63,581 \ (P/F\ 20,\ 2)$$
$$+ \ldots + 38,569 \ (P/F\ 20,\ 8)\,]\,(A/P\ 20,\ 8)$$

$$= [218,717]\,(0.2606)$$

$$= \$57,011$$

$$E_2 = [76,874 \ (P/F\ 20,\ 1) + 70,531 \ (P/F\ 20,\ 2)$$
$$+ \ldots + 32,469 \ (P/F\ 20,\ 8)\,]\,(A/P\ 20,\ 8)$$

$$= [232,295]\,(0.2606)$$

$$= \$60,536$$

If only these levelized amounts are compared, Alternative 1 is the choice. However, if the annual costs for the two alternatives are compared year by year, there is a conflict. The annual costs for Alternative 1 are smaller than the annual costs for Alternative 2 during the first five years but are

TABLE 9-2

Annual Costs for Alternative 1

(Example 9-1)

End of Year	Book Depreciation D_b	Tax Depreciation D	Book Value B	Equity Return F_e	Debt Interest I	Tax t	Operation and Maintenance C	Minimum Annual Revenue Requirement R
0	—	—	$100,000	—	—	—	—	—
1	$11,500	$11,500	88,500	$15,000	$5,000	$16,250	$20,000	$67,750
2	11,500	11,500	77,000	13,275	4,425	14,381	20,000	63,581
3	11,500	11,500	65,500	11,550	3,850	12,512	20,000	59,412
4	11,500	11,500	54,000	9,825	3,275	10,643	20,000	55,243
5	11,500	11,500	42,500	8,100	2,700	8,775	20,000	51,075
6	11,500	11,500	31,000	6,375	2,125	6,906	20,000	46,906
7	11,500	11,500	19,500	4,650	1,550	5,037	20,000	42,737
8	11,500	11,500	8,000	2,925	975	3,169	20,000	38,569

TABLE 9-3

Annual Costs for Alternative 2

Example (9-2)

End of Year	Book Depreci- ation D_b	Tax Depreci- ation D	Book Value B	Equity Return F_e	Debt Interest I	Tax t	Operation and Maintenance C	Minimum Annual Revenue Requirement R
0	—	—	$150,000	—	—	—	—	—
1	$17,500	$17,500	132,500	$22,500	$7,500	$24,374	$5,000	$76,874
2	17,500	17,500	115,000	19,875	6,625	21,531	5,000	70,531
3	17,500	17,500	97,500	17,250	5,750	18,687	5,000	64,187
4	17,500	17,500	80,000	14,625	4,875	15,843	5,000	57,843
5	17,500	17,500	62,500	12,000	4,000	13,000	5,000	51,500
6	17,500	17,500	45,000	9,375	3,125	10,156	5,000	45,156
7	17,500	17,500	27,500	6,750	2,250	7,312	5,000	38,812
8	17,500	17,500	10,000	4,125	1,375	4,469	5,000	32,469

larger for the last three years. In this example, it is perhaps safe to say that Alternative 1 is the choice as a result of the magnitude of the annual costs, the magnitude of the differences between the annual costs and levelized amounts, and the timing of these differences.

Decision Criteria Using Revenue Requirements   In Example 9-1 it is shown that it is possible to have a conflict between the short-term and long-term effects. This conflict can be further illustrated by assuming that an investment tax credit of 10% is applicable to the alternatives in Example 9-1. With the investment tax credit, the first year annual cost for Alternative 1 is

$$R_1 = 67,750 - \frac{100,000\,(0.10)}{1 - 0.52}$$

$$= \$46,917$$

and for Alternative 2 is

$$R_1 = 76,874 - \frac{150,000\,(0.10)}{1 - 0.52}$$

$$= \$45,624$$

The annual costs for years two through eight are the same as given in Tables 9-2 and 9-3. This implies the comparison of the annual costs (short-term effects) shown in Table 9-4 and a comparison of the levelized

TABLE 9-4

Comparison of Short-Term Effects for Example 9-1 with the Investment Tax Credit Included

End of Year	Annual Costs	
	Alternative 1	Alternative 2
0	—	—
1	$46,917	$45,624
2	63,581	70,531
3	59,412	64,187
4	55,243	57,844
5	51,075	51,500
6	46,906	45,156
7	42,737	38,812
8	38,569	32,469

annual costs (long-term effects) which are

$$E_1 = [46,917 \, (P/F \; 20, \; 1) + 63,581 \, (P/F \; 20, \; 2)$$
$$+ \ldots + 38,569 \, (P/F \; 20, \; 8)] \, (A/P \; 20, \; 8)$$

$$= [201,406] \, (0.2606)$$

$$= \$52,486$$

$$E_2 = [45,624 \, (P/F \; 20, \; 1) + 70,531 \, (P/F \; 20, \; 2)$$
$$+ \ldots + 32,469 \, (P/F \; 20, \; 8)] \, (A/P \; 20, \; 8)$$

$$= [206,244] \, (0.2606)$$

$$= \$53,749$$

Again, if only these levelized annual costs are considered, Alternative 1 is the choice. However, if both the short-term effects (Table 9-4) and long-term effects are considered, the choice is not so apparent. There may be circumstances that make Alternative 2 more attractive because of its lower cost in the first year and in years six through eight. The ultimate choice of an alternative will depend on a balance between the short-term and long-term effects, the magnitude of the costs, the magnitude of the difference between the annual costs and levelized annual costs, and the timing of these differences. In this case there is no clear-cut decision.

Example 9-1 and the previous discussion point out that a comparison of the short-term and long-term effects does not always give a clear yes or no decision regarding the choice of an alternative. There are situations that might be termed *gray areas* in choosing an alternative. These gray areas occur because of conflicts between the short-term and long-term effects. There are many patterns of annual costs that lead to these conflicts. Some of the more common patterns are shown in Table 9-5. In Case A, the decision is clear-cut. Alternative 1 is the correct choice since all of its annual costs are less than the annual costs of Alternative 2. This also implies that the levelized annual cost for Alternative 1 (E_1) is less than the levelized annual cost for Alternative 2 (E_2).

In Case B, the choice of an alternative is not clear. This is the situation in Example 9-1. The usual tendency in this case, with the condition $E_1 < E_2$, is to choose Alternative 1. The condition $E_1 > E_2$ for this case is unusual but can occur when the operation and maintenance costs (C) are not a constant but increase in later years for the alternatives. The decision with $E_1 > E_2$ is a situation that requires a definite assessment of the relative importance of the short-term and long-term effects.

Cases C and D usually occur when the investment tax credit is applicable and the initial cost of Alternative 2 is larger than the initial cost of Alternative 1. As in Case B, these situations require a definite assessment of the relative importance of the short-term and long-term effects.

It is unfortunate that simple decision rules cannot be given when making cost comparisons using the revenue requirements approach. However, this is the usual situation; rarely, are economic decisions a

TABLE 9-5

Various Patterns of Annual Costs

End of Year	Case A alt. 1	Case A alt. 2	Case B alt. 1	Case B alt. 2	Case C alt. 1	Case C alt. 2	Case D alt. 1	Case D alt. 2
0	—	—	—	—	—	—	—	—
1	R_1	$< R_1$	R_1	$< R_1$	R_1	$> R_1$	R_1	$> R_1$
2	R_2	$< R_2$	R_2	$< R_2$	R_2	$< R_2$	R_2	$< R_2$
3	R_3	$< R_3$	R_3	$< R_3$	R_3	$< R_3$	R_3	$< R_3$
.	.	.	.	.	.	.	.	.
.	.	.	.	.	.	.	.	.
.	.	.	.	.	.	.	.	.
t	R_t	$< R_t$	R_t	$> R_t$	R_t	$> R_t$	R_t	$< R_t$
.	.	.	.	.	.	.	.	.
.	.	.	.	.	.	.	.	.
.	.	.	.	.	.	.	.	.
n	R_n	$< R_n$	R_n	$> R_n$	R_n	$> R_n$	R_n	$< R_n$
Condition 1	E_1	$< E_2$	E_1	$< E_2$	E_1	$< E_2$	E_1	$< E_2$
Condition 2	—		E_1	$> E_2$	E_1	$> E_2$	E_1	$> E_2$

simple yes or no decision. On the other hand, the revenue requirement approach to cost comparisons does allow the determination of the specific yearly costs and, consequently, an assessment of the short-term effects of the alternatives.

CONVENTIONAL METHODS FOR MAKING COST COMPARISONS

Conventional methods for making cost comparisons center around the determination of a single amount for each alternative. This single amount usually takes the form of an equivalent annual amount, a single present amount, or what is referred to as a capitalized amount. The equivalent annual amount is the most popular. The determination of this amount employs either a before-tax or after-tax approach. The phrases *before-tax* and *after-tax* are often misunderstood. A before-tax cost comparison takes taxes into account *implicitly* by adjusting the MARR value. An after-tax cost comparison takes tax considerations into account *explicitly*. By these definitions *minimum annual revenue requirements provide an after-tax analysis even though the revenue requirements are before-tax amounts*.

Before-Tax Cost Comparisons   A before-tax cost comparison involves an adjustment of the MARR value for tax considerations. The cost values obtained are before-tax amounts. The MARR value used in a before-tax cost comparison, k'_b, is defined as

$$k'_b = ck_d + \frac{(1-c)k_e}{(1-T)}$$

(9-1)

where the variables in Eq. (9-1) are defined in Chapter 5. The value given by Eq. (9-1) is used as the required rate of return in Eq. (3-18) to determine the equivalent annual amount of capital recovery and return (see Chapter 3). The total equivalent annual cost for an alternative is then obtained by adding the annual cost of operation and maintenance to the capital recovery and return. This assumes the annual cost of operation and maintenance is a constant. When it is not a constant, the concept of an economic life becomes involved. Determining the economic life of an asset and the use of an economic life in cost comparisons are discussed in the next chapter. For the purposes of this chapter, a constant annual operation and maintenance cost is used.

The basis of Eq. (9-1) can be shown by considering the total (equity and debt) return plus taxes for a particular year (S_j). The sum of these three components, using the nomenclature of Chapter 6, is

$$S_j = I_j + F_{ej} + t_j \qquad (9\text{-}2)$$

Substituting Eq. (6-11) for the tax term in Eq. (9-2), which *assumes the tax and book depreciation amounts are equal*, gives

$$S_j = I_j + F_{ej} + \frac{T}{1-T}[F_{ej}] \qquad (9\text{-}3)$$

which can be written as

$$S_j = I_j + \frac{F_{ej}}{1-T} \qquad (9\text{-}4)$$

Substituting Eqs. (6-4) and (6-5) into Eq. (9-4) and rearranging gives

$$S_j = B_{j-1}\left[ck_d + \frac{(1-c)K_e}{1-T}\right] \qquad (9\text{-}5)$$

The terms within the brackets in Eq. (9-5) are the same as those in Eq. (9-1). On this basis Eq. (9-1) is used to define the before-tax return (k'_b).

Example 9-2 _____

Using the data in Example 9-1, make a before-tax cost comparison of the alternatives.

Eq. (9-1) gives a before-tax required return of

$$k'_b = (0.4)(12.5) + \frac{(1-0.4)(25)}{1-0.52}$$
$$= 36.25\%$$

Using this result (36.25%) and Eq. (3-18), the before-tax equivalent annual costs, E'_i for the two alternatives are

$$E'_1 = (100{,}000 - 8{,}000)(A/P\ 36.25, 8)$$
$$+\ 8{,}000\ (0.3625) + 20{,}000$$

$$= \$59{,}316$$

$$E'_2 = (150{,}000 - 10{,}000)(A/P\ 36.25, 8)$$
$$+\ 10{,}000\ (0.3625) + 5{,}000$$

$$= \$64{,}041$$

These results are before-tax amounts and indicate that Alternative 1 should be chosen since it has the smaller cost.

Comments Regarding Examples 9-1 and 9-2. It can be seen be seen by comparing the equivalent annual cost of alternatives that the before-tax analysis in Example 9-2 overstates the after-tax analysis in Example 9-1. Consequently, *the before-tax analysis is an approximation* of the actual (after-tax) equivalent annual cost. This is one of the reasons that the revenue requirement approach is preferred for cost comparisons.

It is pointed out in Chapter 6 that the levelized (equivalent annual) revenue requirements can also be obtained by adding the capital recovery and return, the annual cost of operation and maintenance, and the equivalent annual amount of taxes. This is formulated in Eq. (6-18). As an example, this amount for Alternative 1 in Example 9-1 is

$$E_1 = (100,000 - 8,000)(A/P \; 20, 8)$$
$$+ \; 8,000 \; (0.20) + 20,000 + 11,436$$
$$= \$57,011$$

where the value $11,436 is the equivalent annual amount of the taxes (E_t). It is calculated in the following manner using the yearly tax data in Table 9-2:

$$E_t = [16,250 \; (P/F \; 20, 1) + 14,381 \; (P/F \; 20, 2)$$
$$+ \ldots + 3,169 \; (P/F \; 20, 8)] \; (A/P \; 20, 8)$$
$$= [43,884] \; (0.2606)$$
$$= \$11,436$$

Since the tax and book depreciation are the same in this case, the equivalent annual amount of the taxes can be calculated using Eq. (6-16).

$$E_t = (1 - 0.4)(0.25) \left(\frac{0.52}{1 - 0.52} \right) [100,000 \; (P/F \; 20, 1)$$
$$+ \; 88,500 \; (P/F \; 20, 2)$$
$$+ \ldots + 19,500 \; (P/F \; 20, 8)] \; (A/P \; 20, 8)$$
$$= (0.15)(1.0833) \; [270,060] \; (0.2606)$$
$$= \$11,436$$

In addition to these methods for determining the equivalent annual cost, another method is sometimes used. This method uses the relationship

$$E_i = \frac{(P - L)(A/P \; k_b, n) + L(k_b)}{1 - T} + C$$
$$- \frac{E_d(T)}{1 - T} - \frac{E_I(T)}{1 - T} \tag{9-6}$$

where the nomenclature is previously defined and

E_d = equivalent annual amount of the tax depreciation computed using k_b as the discount rate

E_I = equivalent annual amount of debt interest
computed using k_b as the discount rate

If Eq. (9-6) is used to calculate the equivalent annual cost of Alternative 1 in Table 9-1, the result is

$$E_1 = \frac{(100{,}000 - 8{,}000)(A/P\ 20,\ 8) + 8{,}000\,(0.20)}{1 - 0.52} + 20{,}000$$

$$- \frac{11{,}500\,(0.52)}{1 - 0.52} - \frac{3{,}519\,(0.52)}{1 - 0.52}$$

$$= \$57{,}011$$

This is the same value determined using Eq. (6-18). The approach used by Eq. (9-6) is to convert all values to *before-tax amounts*. However, by the definitions used in this text, this is an *after-tax analysis* since the tax considerations of debt interest and depreciation are explicitly included in determining the equivalent annual cost ($57,011).

Equivalent annual *after-tax amounts* are sometimes used in the cost comparison of alternatives. These after-tax amounts are based on the various definitions of cash flow given in Chapters 5 and 6. The cash flow definitions are modified for cost comparisons by omitting the gross income (G_j) term and, for convenience, reversing the sign convention (cash outflows are positive and cash inflows are negative). For example, the cash definition given by Eq. (6-20) *for cost comparisons*, X'_{bj}, is

$$X'_{bj} = C_j - (C_j + D_j + I_j)\,T + K_j - L_j \tag{9-7}$$

Using Eq. (9-7) and the data in Table 9-2, the cash flows in Table 9-6

TABLE 9-6

Cash Flows for Alternative 1

(Example 9-1)

End of Year	Investment and Salvage K and L	Operation and Maintenance C	Depreciation D	Interest I	Tax t	Net Cash Flow X'_b
0	K = $100,000	—	—	—	—	$100,000
1		$20,000	$11,500	$5,000	$18,980	1,020
2		20,000	11,500	4,425	18,681	1,319
3		20,000	11,500	3,850	18,382	1,618
4		20,000	11,500	3,275	18,083	1,917
5		20,000	11,500	2,700	17,784	2,216
6		20,000	11,500	2,125	17,485	2,515
7		20,000	11,500	1,550	17,186	2,814
8		20,000	11,500	975	16,887	3,113
8	L = 8,000					−8,000

are obtained. The equivalent annual after-tax amount of the cash flows (costs), E_a, in Table 9-6 is

$$E_a = 100{,}000\ (A/P\ 20,\ 8) + [1{,}020 + 299\ (A/G\ 20,\ 8)]$$
$$-\ 8{,}000\ (A/F\ 20,\ 8)$$

$$=\ \$27{,}365$$

Note that a return of 20% is used in determining the equivalent annual cost. It is shown in Chapter 6 that Eq. (6-20) defines the cash flows, then Eq. (5-5) defines the required return. Eq. (5-5), for the data in Table 9-1, gives

$$k_b = (0.6)(25) + (0.4)(12.5)$$

$$=\ 20\%$$

A value for the after-tax amount (E_a), based on the cash flows defined by Eq. (9-7), can be directly calculated using the relationship

$$E_a = (K - L)(A/P\ k_b,n) + L\ (k_b)$$
$$+\ C\ (1 - T) - E_d\ (T) - E_I\ (T) \qquad (9\text{-}8)$$

For example, Eq. (9-8) gives

$$E_a = (100{,}000 - 8{,}000)(A/P\ 20,8) + 8{,}000\ (0.20)$$
$$+\ 20{,}000\ (1 - 0.52) - 11{,}500\ (0.52) - 3{,}519\ (0.52)$$

$$=\ \$27{,}365$$

It should be noted that if Eq. (9-8) is divided by the term $(1 - T)$ the result is Eq. (9-6) or

$$E_a = (1 - T)\ E_i \qquad (9\text{-}9)$$

Another approach is to base the cost comparison on the definition of equity cash flows given by Eq. (5-7). In terms of a cost comparison, Eq. (5-7) can be written as

$$X'_{ej} = C_j + I_j - (C_j + I_j + D_j)\ T + K_j - B_j - L_j + P_j \qquad (9\text{-}10)$$

If Eq. (9-10) is used to define the cash flows for the data in Table 9-2, the results in Table 9-7 are obtained. The equivalent annual after-tax amount of these equity cash flows, E_e, is

$$E_e = 60{,}000\ (A/P\ 25,\ 8) + [10{,}620 - 276\ (A/G\ 25,\ 8)]$$
$$-\ 4{,}800\ (A/F\ 25,\ 8)$$

$$=\ \$27{,}743$$

TABLE 9-7

Equity Cash Flow for Alternative 1

(Example 9-1)

End of Year	Investment and Salvage K and L	Operation and Maintenance C	Depre- ciation D	Interest I	Tax t	Borrowed Money B	Principal Payment P	Net Cash Flow X'_{ej}
0	K = $100,000	—	—	—	—	$40,000	—	$60,000
1		$20,000	$11,500	$5,000	$18,980	—	$4,600	10,620
2		20,000	11,500	4,425	18,681	—	4,600	10,344
3		20,000	11,500	3,850	18,382	—	4,600	10,068
4		20,000	11,500	3,275	18,083	—	4,600	9,792
5		20,000	11,500	2,700	17,784	—	4,600	9,516
6		20,000	11,500	2,125	17,485	—	4,600	9,240
7		20,000	11,500	1,550	17,186	—	4,600	8,964
8		20,000	11,500	975	16,887	—	4,600	8,688
8								+3,200
8	L = 8,000							−8,000

Note that the equivalent annual cost is calculated using the required return on equity (25%). That is, since equity cash is being used, the return is defined as the required return on equity (k_e). The equivalent annual equity cost can also be calculated from the relationship

$$E_e = (K_e - L_e)(A/P \ k_e, n) + L_e (k_e) + C (1 - T) \\ + E'_I (1 - T) - E'_d (T) + E_p \qquad (9\text{-}11)$$

where

K_e = equity capital = $(1 - c)(K)$

L_e = equity salvage = $(1 - c)(L)$

E'_I = equivalent annual interest computed using k_e as the discount rate

E'_d = equivalent annual tax depreciation computed using k_e as the discount rate

E_p = equivalent annual principal payment computed using k_e as the discount rate

For example, Eq. (9-11) gives

$$E'_{e1} = [100,000 \ (0.6) - 8,000 \ (0.6)] \ (A/P \ 25, 8) \\ + (0.6)(8,000)(0.25) \\ + 20,000 \ (1 - 0.52) + 3,627 \ (1 - 0.52) \\ - 11,500 \ (0.52) + 4,600 \\ = \$27,743$$

In most of the previous discussions of determining the equivalent annual cost, only one alternative is considered. This is done in order to facilitate these discussions. Obviously, if a cost comparison is being made, the equivalent annual cost of all alternatives must be determined before a decision is possible.

Present Worth Cost Comparisons The previous section considered the equivalent annual cost as a basis for making cost comparisons. Another procedure is to make a present worth cost comparison. A present worth cost comparison is made by discounting all the cash flows for each alternative to the present and then comparing these amounts. Or in the case of revenue requirements, the revenue requirements are discounted to the present. For example, an after-tax present worth cost, P_i, comparison of the alternatives in Tables 9-2 and 9-3 is

$$P_1 = [67,750 \, (P/F \, 20, 1) + 63,581 \, (P/F \, 20, 2) \\ + \ldots + 38,569 \, (P/F \, 20, 8)]$$

$$= \$218,717$$

$$P_2 = [76,874 \, (P/F \, 20, 1) + 70,531 \, (P/F \, 20, 2) \\ + \ldots + 32,469 \, (P/F \, 20, 8)]$$

$$= \$232,295$$

which indicates that Alternative 1 is the choice since it has the smaller value. This is the same decision given by a comparison of *only* the equivalent annual costs (a combined comparison of the specific yearly costs and the equivalent annual costs might, in some cases, indicate a different decision). It is always true that a present worth and equivalent annual cost comparison gives the same choice of an alternative since a definite relationship exists between these two methods for making cost comparisons. This relationship, in general, is

$$E_i = P_i \, (A/P \, k,n) \qquad\qquad (9\text{-}12)$$

where

$$E_i = \text{equivalent annual cost for Alternative } i$$

$$P_i = \text{present worth cost for Alternative } i$$

$$k = \text{discount rate}$$

$$n = \text{the length of the comparison period}$$

As an additional example, a before-tax present worth comparison of the alternatives in Example 9-2 is

$$P'_1 = 100,000 - 8,000 \, (P/F \, 36.25, 8) + 20,000 \, (P/A \, 36.25, 8)$$

$$= \$149,852$$

$$P'_2 = 150{,}000 - 10{,}000 \, (P/F \, 36.25, \, 8) + 5{,}000 \, (P/A \, 36.25, \, 8)$$
$$= \$161{,}789$$

In actuality, present worth cost comparisons provide no advantages over equivalent annual cost comparisons. In fact, present worth cost comparisons have a definite computational disadvantage when the lives of the alternatives are different.

COST COMPARISONS WITH DIFFERENT LIVES

In Examples 9-1 and 9-2, the cost comparisons are based on a period of eight years which is also the life of each alternative. These cost comparisons imply the assumption that the need for the service provided by the alternatives is at least eight years. In actuality, there is no requirement that the lives of the alternatives equal the period of service (need). Therefore, it is the purpose of this section to consider cost comparisons of alternatives with different lives.

In making cost comparisons, there are two basic conditions that must be satisfied. These two conditions are (1) the alternatives must be compared over an *equal period of time* and (2) this period of time must equal the service life. The basis assumption made in comparing *cost alternatives* (not projects with explicit gross incomes as in Chapter 7) is that the cost data for each alternative cycles over a period of time equal to the service life, or, in some cases, over a period of time equal to the least common multiple (LCM) of the lives of the alternatives. This assumption is reasonable once it is understood that it does not imply that a selected alternative must be kept until the end of its life. Theoretically a selected alternative can be replaced at any point in time by another alternative that provides an economic advantage. The service life can be either infinite or finite.

Infinite Service Life   With an infinite service life, the annual costs and the equivalent annual cost for each alternative are determined using the life of the particular alternative. With the cycling assumption, these annual costs cycle to infinity and a comparison of the alternatives is possible over the same service life (infinity).

Example 9-3

Make a cost comparison for the two alternatives given in Table 9-8 using a revenue requirement (annual cost) approach and assuming an infinite need.

TABLE 9-8

Cost Data for Example 9-3

	Alternative 1	Alternative 2
Initial cost	$40,000	$60,000
Annual cost of operation and maintenance	$ 4,000	$ 3,000
Book depreciation	SL	SL
Salvage value	$ 2,000	$ 4,000
Life, years	4	7
Tax depreciation	SYD	SYD
Salvage value	$ 2,000	$ 4,000
Life, years	4	7
Cost of debt capital	12.5%	12.5%
Cost of equity capital	25%	25%
Debt ratio	40%	40%
Tax rate	52%	52%
Investment tax credit	10%	10%

The first step is to calculate the revenue requirements for each alternative using the procedures given in Chapter 6. The results of this step are given in Tables 9-9 and 9-10.

TABLE 9-9

Annual Costs for Alternative 1

(Example 9-3)

End of Year	Book Depreciation D_b	Tax Depreciation D	Book Value B	Equity Return F_e	Debt Interest I	Tax t	Operation and Maintenance C	Minimum Annual Revenue Requirement R
0	—	—	$40,000	—	—	—	—	—
1	$9,500	$15,200	30,500	$6,000	$2,000	−$2,452 [a]	$4,000	$19,048
2	9,500	11,400	21,000	4,575	1,525	2,898	4,000	22,498
3	9,500	7,600	11,500	3,150	1,050	5,471	4,000	23,171
4	9,500	3,800	2,000	1,725	575	8,044	4,000	23,844

[a] Includes the value $-\dfrac{(0.10)(40,000)}{3(1-0.52)} = -\$2,777$ for the investment tax credit. Only one-third of the full amount is taken since the tax depreciation life is four years.

TABLE 9-10

Annual Costs for Alternative 2

(Example 9-3)

End of Year	Book Depreciation D_b	Tax Depreciation D	Book Value B	Equity Return F_e	Debt Interest I	Tax t	Operation and Maintenance C	Minimum Annual Revenue Requirement R
0	—	—	$60,000	—	—	—	—	—
1	$8,000	$14,000	52,000	$9,000	$3,000	−$9,250[a]	$3,000	$13,750
2	8,000	12,000	44,000	7,800	2,600	4,117	3,000	25,517
3	8,000	10,000	36,000	6,600	2,200	4,983	3,000	24,783
4	8,000	8,000	28,000	5,400	1,800	5,850	3,000	24,050
5	8,000	6,000	20,000	4,200	1,400	6,716	3,000	23,316
6	8,000	4,000	12,000	3,000	1,000	7,583	3,000	22,583
7	8,000		4,000	1,800	600	8,450	3,000	21,850

[a] Includes the value $-\dfrac{(0.10)(60,000)}{1-0.52} = -\$12,500$ for the investment tax credit.

The equivalent annual cost for each alternative is

$$E_1 = [19,048 \ (P/F \ 20, \ 1) + 22,498 \ (P/F \ 20, \ 2) + 23,171 \ (P/F \ 20, \ 3)$$
$$+ \ 23,844 \ (P/F \ 20, \ 4) \,] \,(A/P \ 20, \ 4)$$

$$= [56,405] \ (0.3863)$$

$$= \$21,789$$

$$E_2 = [13,750 \ (P/F \ 20, \ 1) + 25,517 \ (P/F \ 20, \ 2) + 24,783 \ (P/F \ 20, \ 3)$$
$$+ \ \ldots \ + 21,850 \ (P/F \ 20, \ 7) \,] \,(A/P \ 20, \ 7)$$

$$= [78,150] \ (0.2774)$$

$$= \$21,679$$

It may appear that these calculations and Tables 9-9 and 9-10 ignore the difference in the lives of the two alternatives. This is not the case. The actual comparison that is implied is shown in Table 9-11. This table shows the result of the cycling assumption previously mentioned. That is, since the cost data for each alternative cycles, the annual costs cycle for each alternative and consequently the equivalent annual cost is the same each year.

The actual choice of an alternative in this example is a "gray area decision" since there is conflict between the short-term and long-term effects. However, in this example, it is probably safe to say that Alter-

TABLE 9-11

Cost Comparison for an Infinite Need

(Example 9-3)

End of Year	Alternative 1		Alternative 2	
	Annual Cost	Equivalent Annual Cost	Annual Cost	Equivalent Annual Cost
1	$19,048	$21,789	$13,750	$21,679
2	22,498	21,789	25,517	21,679
3	23,171	21,789	24,783	21,679
4	23,844	21,789	24,050	21,679
5	19,048	21,789	23,316	21,679
6	22,498	21,789	22,583	21,679
7	23,171	21,789	21,850	21,679
8	23,844	21,789	13,750	21,679
9	19,048	21,789	25,517	21,679
10	22,498	21,789	24,783	21,679
11	23,171	21,789	24,050	21,679
12	23,844	21,789	23,316	21,679
13	19,048	21,789	22,583	21,679
14	22,498	21,789	21,850	21,679
.	.	.	.	.
.	.	.	.	.
.	.	.	.	.
∞	.	21,789	.	21,679

native 2 should be the choice. Of course, if only the long-term effects are considered, Alternative 2 is clearly the choice.

Capitalized Cost Comparisons

If the service life is considered to be infinite, another method for making cost comparisons is sometimes used. This method is called a *capitalized cost comparison* and is defined as a single amount at the present that is equivalent to a series of cash flows that are repeated forever. In part, this definition requires the same cycling assumption made for an infinite service life. In Example 9-3, it is shown that this cycling assumption results in an equivalent annual cost that extends from year one through infinity. Consequently by its definition, the capitalized cost (CC) is

$$(CC) = E \ (P/A \ k,n) \tag{9-13}$$

where n is infinity. The limit of the P/A factor in Eq. (9-13) as n approaches infinity is

$$\lim_{n \to \infty} \left[(P/A \ k,n) \right] = \lim_{n \to \infty} \left[\frac{1}{k} - \frac{1}{k(1+k)^n} \right] = \frac{1}{k} \qquad (9\text{-}14)$$

Consequently, a capitalized amount, in general, is

$$(CC) = \frac{E}{k} \qquad (9\text{-}15)$$

A capitalized cost comparison for the data in Example 9-3 is

$$(CC)_1 = \frac{21{,}789}{0.20}$$

$$= \$108{,}945$$

$$(CC)_2 = \frac{21{,}679}{0.20}$$

$$= \$108{,}395$$

Based on these results, Alternative 2 is the choice, which is the same result given by a comparison of the equivalent annual costs. This is always the case. A capitalized cost comparison should always give the same decision as an equivalent annual cost comparison. It should be noted that by its definition, a capitalized cost comparison is only applicable for an infinite service life. Consequently, it is not discussed later when the service life is finite.

Present Worth Comparisons   The basic procedure for making a present worth comparison has been given previously. However, it is desirable to reexamine a present worth cost comparison when the lives of the alternatives are different and the service life is infinite. It was stated previously that in order to be valid, a cost comparison of alternatives must be over the same period of time and this period of time must equal the service life. If these two requirements are strictly adhered to, the result is a capitalized cost comparison when the service life is infinite. Consequently, one of these requirements is relaxed for *present worth cost comparisons over an infinite service life* to meet the requirement that the cost comparison must be over an equal period of time. *This period of time is the least common multiple (LCM) of the lives of the alternatives.*

Two approaches are possible for making present worth comparisons. The first approach is to find the equivalent annual costs for the alternatives based on their respective lives and then multiply these results by a P/A factor that is based on the LCM of the lives of the alternatives. The second approach is to cycle the cost data over the LCM and then directly calculate the present worth of these costs. Both approaches give the same result. However, the second approach has a computational disadvantage which can be shown by making a before-tax present worth comparison of the alternatives given in Table 9-12. Using the first approach, the equivalent annual costs for the two alternatives in Table 9-12 are

$$E'_1 = (50,000 - 5,000)\,(A/P\ 36.25,\ 4) + 5,000\,(0.3625) + 4,000$$

$$= (45,000)\,(0.5107) + 1813 + 4,000$$

$$= \$28,795$$

$$E'_2 = (70,000 - 7,000)\,(A/P\ 36.25,\ 7) + 7,000\,(0.3625) + 2,000$$

$$= 63,000\,(0.4095) + 2,538 + 2,000$$

$$= \$30,336$$

where the return 36.25% is obtained using Eq. (9-1) and the data in Table 9-12. The LCM of the two alternatives in Table 9-12 is 28 years, and therefore the present worth comparison is

$$P'_1 = 28,795\,(P/A\ 36.25,\ 28)$$

$$= 28,795\,(2.7580)$$

$$= \$79,417$$

$$P'_2 = 30,336\,(P/A\ 36.25,\ 28)$$

$$= 30,336\,(2.7580)$$

$$= \$83,667$$

TABLE 9-12

Cost Data

	Alternative 1	Alternative 2
Initial cost	$50,000	$70,000
Life, years	4	7
Salvage value	$ 5,000	$ 7,000
Annual cost of operation and maintenance	$ 4,000	$ 2,000
Cost of debt capital	12.5%	12.5%
Cost of equity capital	25%	25%
Debt ratio	40%	40%

TABLE 9-13

An Example of the Cycling Assumption for a Present Worth Cost Comparison

End of Year	Alternative 1		Alternative 2	
0	50,000		70,000	
1		4,000		2,000
2		4,000		2,000
3		4,000		2,000
4	50,000; L = 5,000	4,000		2,000
5		4,000		2,000
6		4,000		2,000
7		4,000	70,000; L = 7,000	2,000
8	50,000; L = 5,000	4,000		2,000
9		4,000		2,000
10		4,000		2,000
11		4,000		2,000
12	50,000; L = 5,000	4,000		2,000
13		4,000		2,000
14		4,000	70,000; L = 7,000	2,000
15		4,000		2,000
16	50,000; L = 5,000	4,000		2,000
17		4,000		2,000
18		4,000		2,000
19		4,000		2,000
20	50,000; L = 5,000	4,000		2,000
21		4,000	70,000; L = 7,000	2,000
22		4,000		2,000
23		4,000		2,000
24	50,000; L = 5,000	4,000		2,000
25		4,000		2,000
26		4,000		2,000
27		4,000		2,000
28	L = 5,000	4,000	L = 7,000	2,000

If the second approach is used, the present worth of the cost data in Table 9-13 must be determined (remembering that salvage values are negative). These present worths for the two alternatives are

$$P'_1 = 50,000 \, [1 + (P/F \ 36.25, \ 4) + (P/F \ 36.25, \ 8)$$
$$+ \, (P/F \ 36.25, \ 12) + (P/F \ 36.25, \ 16)$$
$$+ \, (P/F \ 36.25, \ 20) + (P/F \ 36.25, \ 24) \,]$$
$$-5,000 \, [(P/F \ 36.25, \ 4) + (P/F \ 36.25, \ 8)$$
$$+ \, (P/F \ 36.25, \ 12) + (P/F \ 36.25, \ 16)$$

$$+ (P/F\ 36.25,\ 20) + (P/F\ 36.25,\ 24)$$
$$+ (P/F\ 36.25,\ 28)\ ]$$
$$+ 4{,}000\ (P/A\ 36.25,\ 28)$$

$$P'_1 = 50{,}000\ (1.4086) - 5{,}000\ (0.4087)$$
$$+ 4{,}000\ (2.7580)$$

$$= \$79{,}417$$

$$P'_2 = 70{,}000\ [1 + (P/F\ 36.25,\ 7) + (P/F\ 36.25,\ 14)$$
$$+ (P/F\ 36.25,\ 21)\ ]$$
$$-7{,}000\ [(P/F\ 36.25,\ 7) + (P/F\ 36.25,\ 14)$$
$$+ (P/F\ 36.25,\ 21) + (P/F\ 36.25,\ 28)\ ]$$
$$+2{,}000\ (P/A\ 36.25,\ 28)$$

$$= 70{,}000\ (1.1294) - 7{,}000\ (0.1296)$$
$$+ 2{,}000\ (2.7580)$$

$$= \$83{,}667$$

These numerical examples show that a present worth cost comparison does have a computational disadvantage if an equivalent annual cost comparison is not made first. Basically, the capitalized and present worth cost comparisons offer no advantages over an equivalent annual cost comparison. In fact, as just demonstrated, they have a computational disadvantage. Consequently, further discussions of cost comparisons (and replacement analysis) are limited to only equivalent annual cost comparisons.

Tax Effects In all of the previous examples, it is assumed that the salvage values for the tax and book depreciation schedule are the same. It is further assumed that these values are also equal to the actual salvage values that can be realized at the end of a particular alternative's life. Consequently, there are no tax effects included in the last year of an alternative's life. By far, these are the usual assumptions made in cost comparisons. However, it is not difficult to include possible tax effects resulting from differences between realizable and tax salvage values when it is considered to be appropriate. If these possible tax effects are considered appropriate, they can be included in the revenue requirement of an alternative's last year by using the relationship

$$\pm\ \frac{\text{tax effect}}{1 - T} \tag{9-16}$$

The plus or minus sign in Eq. (9-16) is dependent upon the tax effect. If the tax effect is an increase in taxes, the plus sign is correct. If it is a decrease in taxes, the negative sign is correct. The calculation of the tax effect is accomplished in the same manner as discussed in Chapter 5. As an example, suppose the actual realizable salvage value for Alternative 1 in Example 9-3 is $500. Since the tax salvage value is $2,000, this means a loss of $1,500. Assuming that Alternative 1 is Section 1245 Property and the tax rate is 52%, this means, under certain conditions, a reduction in taxes of

$$(1,500)(0.52) = \$780$$

The revenue requirement for year four (see Table 9-9) becomes, with this tax effect, the following:

$$R_4 = 23,844 - \frac{780}{1 - 0.52}$$

$$= \$22,219$$

This value is then used in the cost comparison in place of the originally determined value of $23,844. The revenue requirements for years one through three are the same as those given in Table 9-9. As another example, if the net realizable salvage value is $2,800, the revenue requirement for the fourth year is

$$R_4 = 23,844 + \frac{800(0.52)}{1 - 0.52}$$

$$= \$24,711$$

The inclusion of this type of tax effect is a cost comparison based on several considerations (estimates). For example, it is possible to have any gain or loss resulting from the disposal of a particular alternative offset by gains and losses from the disposal of other assets. Also if the asset is part of a multiple asset depreciation account, it is highly unlikely that any tax is actually paid on a gain or any tax benefit actually received on a loss. Further, the cycling assumption implies the replacement of an asset by an asset with the same cost data *for the same service*. Consequently, it is most probable that this is a like-kind exchange and there are in general no tax effects (see Chapter 4). It is a result of the uncertainties surrounding these considerations and for practical convenience reasons that the assumption is usually made that the book and tax salvage values are equal, and these salvage values are in turn equal to the actual realizable salvage values.

In some of the past examples, the book and tax depreciation lives are the same. This is not required *if* the revenue requirement approach is used. In fact, it is highly likely that these lives are different. The tax depreciation life and tax salvage values are based on tax regulations and the fact that a shorter tax depreciation life and smaller tax salvage value are desirable from a tax standpoint. The book depreciation life and salvage are based on capital recovery considerations and their effect on the unit cost of the items being produced. Revenue requirements can easily be determined for differences in book and depreciation lives and salvage values as shown in Example 6-1. In practice it is highly likely that the tax depreciation life is the same for all cost comparison alternatives since the alternatives are for the same type of service and are classified for tax purposes as the same type of equipment. Also, it is highly likely that the book depreciation life is the same for all alternatives since the same type of equipment is involved in a cost comparison and most companies have established capital recovery periods (book depreciation lives) for various types of equipment. All of these considerations plus tax effects can be explicitly included in the yearly revenue requirements. These are some of the reasons that the revenue requirement approach to cost comparisons is emphasized in this text.

Finite Service Life   When the service life is determined (estimated) to be some finite period of time, any cost comparison should be based on this same period of time. A finite service life implies, in this text, that there is no need for an asset after the service life and the involved equipment could be sold, used for some other service, or discarded (scrapped). Relative to an infinite service life, a finite service life is unusual. By far, in practice, most cost comparisons are based on an infinite service life because of its computational convenience and the difficulties in estimating a finite service life. The assumption of a very long (infinite) service life is the usual approach. However, on occasion, a finite service life can occur. Therefore, it is considered in this section.

The approach for making a cost comparison with a finite service life is dependent upon the LCM of the lives of the alternatives and the service life. There are three possibilities. They are

> (1) LCM = service life
>
> (2) LCM < service life
>
> (3) LCM > service life

When the LCM equals the service life, the cost comparison is numerically the same as the case of an infinite service life because of the cycling assumption. For example if the service life in Example 9-3 is 28 years, the equivalent annual costs for Alternative 1 and Alternative 2, respectively, are $21,789 and $21,679.

When the LCM is less than the service life, the cost comparison is again numerically the same as the case of an infinite service life. This is based on the cycling assumption for the period of time from the present to the LCM and on an additional assumption regarding the period of time from the LCM to the service life. This additional assumption is that the most economical (least cost) choice of an alternative is made for the period of time between the LCM and the service life. This merely implies that the decision-maker is rational and will choose the least cost alternative. This is considered to be a reasonable assumption. As an example, suppose the service life for Example 9-3 is 35 years. This implies, *from the standpoint of equivalent annual costs,* the cost comparison shown in Table 9-14 where E_s represents the equivalent annual cost of the best (least cost) alternative that is available for the period of years 29 through 35. This alternative may or may not be related to Alternatives 1 and 2 in Table 9-8. Also, specific numerical values are not required for E_s; all that is required is the assumption that it is the best (cheapest) alternative for the years remaining after the LCM (years 29 through 35). With this assumption it can be seen that, by choosing the alternative with the least equivalent annual cost (using only equivalent annual costs as the decision criterion) over the LCM, the costs over the service period are minimized. From a computational standpoint, all that is required is an infinite service life cost comparison in order to choose an alternative.

When the LCM is greater than the service life, it is necessary to estimate for each alternative the costs and salvage values that are expected to occur at particular points in time over the service life. The approach taken in this text, *for cost comparison and this case,* is to estimate these costs and salvage values on the basis that the cost data for

TABLE 9-14

Cost Comparison with LCM < Service LIfe

(Example 9-3 Data)

End of Year	Equivalent Annual Costs Alternative	
	1	2
1	$21,789	$21,679
2	21,789	21,679
•	•	•
•	•	•
•	•	•
28	21,789	21,679
29		E_s
•		•
•		•
•		•
35		E_s

each alternative cycles. For partial cycles that may occur just prior to the service life, salvage values are estimated for the implied period of use. With these salvage values, it is possible to generate the revenue requirements over the partial cycle. For example, if the service life for the alternatives in Table 9-8 is ten years, this implies the cost comparison shown in Table 9-15. The revenue requirements in years one through eight for Alternative 1 are the revenue requirements from Table 9-9 and show the cycling assumption. The revenue requirements for alternative one in years nine and ten must be determined. They are determined, in this text, on the basis of the original data given in Table 9-8 for Alternative 1 and an estimated realizable salvage after two years of service. For example, using a realizable salvage value of $20,000, the revenue requirements for two years of service are shown in Table 9-16. These values are Alternative 1's revenue requirements for years nine and ten in Table 9-15. In determining the revenue requirements in Table 9-16, the net realizable salvage value is used as the basis for calculating the book depreciation amounts. That is,

$$D_b = \frac{40,000 - 20,000}{2}$$

$$= \$10,000$$

for years one and two since straight-line depreciation is specified for the book depreciation. The remaining values are calculated using the procedures given in Chapter 6. It should be noted that no investment tax credit is taken in Table 9-16 since the implied use life is only two years. Also,

TABLE 9-15

Cost Comparison with LCM > Service Life

(Example 9-3 Data)

End of Year	Revenue Requirements Alternative 1	Alternative 2
1	$19,048	$13,750
2	22,498	25,517
3	23,171	24,783
4	23,844	24,050
5	19,048	23,316
6	22,498	22,583
7	23,171	21,850
8	23,844	R_8
9	R_9	R_9
10	R_{10}	R_{10}

TABLE 9-16

Revenue Requirements for Two Years of Service

(Alternative 1)

End of Year	Book Depreci- ation D_b	Tax Depreci- ation D	Book Value B	Equity Return F_e	Debt Interest I	Tax t	Operation and Maintenance C	Minimum Annual Revenue Requirement R
0	—	—	$40,000	—	—	—	—	—
1	$10,000	$15,200	30,000	$6,000	$2,000	$ 867	$4,000	$22,867
2	10,000	11,400	20,000	4,500	1,500	3,358	4,000	23,358

it should be noted that the tax depreciation schedule does not change from the schedule given in Table 9-9 since tax regulations dictate the tax depreciation life. Consequently, assuming the four-year tax depreciation life and salvage specified in Table 9-8 are in agreement with tax regulations, the tax depreciation schedule is the same.

Since there is a difference between the estimated realizable salvage value and the tax salvage value at the end of two years of service, it is possible that there is a tax effect applicable to the revenue requirement for year two in Table 9-16 (actually, year ten in Table 9-15). The tax book value at the end of year two is

$$D_t = 40,000 - (15,200 + 11,400)$$
$$= \$13,400$$

implying a gain of $6,600 ($20,000 minus $13,400). If the tax effect is applicable (and it may not be), then the value

$$R_2 = 23,358 + \frac{6,600\,(0.52)}{1 - 0.52}$$

$$= 23,358 + 7,150$$

$$= \$30,508$$

replaces the value $23,358. This assumes that alternative one is Section 1245 Property.

Sometimes, another approach is taken with the investment tax credit. This approach takes the maximum investment tax credit possible, as determined by the tax depreciation life, and then takes the investment tax penalty. For example, since the tax depreciation life is four years for Alternative 1, one-third of the full investment tax credit is applicable. Therefore, the revenue requirement for the first year in Table 9-16 (year nine in Table 9-14) using this approach is

$$R_1 = 22{,}867 - \frac{(0.10)(40{,}000)}{3(1-0.52)}$$

$$R_1 = \$20{,}089$$

and the revenue requirement for the second year in Table 9-16 (year ten in Table 9-15) is

$$R_2 = 23{,}358 + \frac{(0.10)(40{,}000)}{3(1-0.52)}$$

$$R_2 = \$26{,}136$$

assuming there are no other tax effects. If there are other tax effects due to the salvage value, they are computed and added as previously discussed.

A common assumption, made primarily for convenience in estimating the net realizable salvage value, is to assume it equals the book value, determined by the book depreciation schedule, at the end of the use period. In this way the revenue requirements are basically the same as those determined using the entire book depreciation life except for possible tax effects (investment tax credit and salvage value differences). For example using this assumption, the realizable salvage value is $21,000 at the end of two years of use for Alternative 1 (see Table 9-9). Consequently, the revenue requirements for years one and two in Table 9-16 are

$$R_1 = \$19{,}048$$

$$R_2 = 22{,}498 + \frac{(0.10)(40{,}000)}{3(1-0.52)}$$

$$= \$25{,}276$$

These values use the approach of taking the maximum investment tax credit and the investment tax penalty and also assume no other tax effects. If the other approach of taking only the allowable investment tax credit in the first year is used, then the revenue requirements are

$$R_1 = 19{,}048 + \frac{(0.10)(40{,}000)}{3(1-0.52)}$$

$$= \$21{,}825$$

$$R_2 = \$22{,}498$$

The investment tax credit is eliminated from the revenue requirement for year one since only two years of use is implied. These values also assume there are no other tax effects. It should be noted that the values of $19,048 and $22,498 are taken directly from Table 9-9. All of these approaches to the investment tax credit (penalty), estimating the realizable salvage values and possible tax effects regarding salvage values can be considered correct under various circumstances. In the final analysis, a decision must be made as to what approaches best represent future events.

The revenue requirements for three years of use for Alternative 2 in Table 9-8 are given in Table 9-17 using a realizable salvage value at the end of three years of $30,000. In Table 9-17 only one-third of the full investment tax credit is taken since the implied life is only three years. The other approach is to take the full investment tax credit, since the tax depreciation life is seven years, and assess the investment tax penalty (two-thirds of the full amount) in the third year. Also in Table 9-17, it is assumed there are no tax effects resulting from the differences in salvage values. The values indicated in Table 9-17 are the revenue requirements for years eight, nine, and ten for Alternative 2 in Table 9-15. The final cost comparison is summarized in Table 9-18 using the results of Tables 9-16 and 9-17. In order to complete the cost comparison the equivalent annual costs are calculated using the data in Table 9-18.

$$
\begin{aligned}
E_1 &= [19{,}048\,(P/F\ 20{,}1) + 22{,}498\,(P/F\ 20{,}2) \\
&\quad + 23{,}171\,(P/F\ 20{,}3) + \ldots \\
&\quad + 23{,}358\,(P/F\ 20{,}10)]\,(A/P\ 20{,}10) \\
&= [91{,}813]\,(0.2385) \\
&= \$21{,}897 \\
E_2 &= [13{,}750\,(P/F\ 20{,}1) + 25{,}517\,(P/F\ 20{,}2) \\
&\quad + 24{,}783\,(P/F\ 20{,}3) + \ldots \\
&\quad + 27{,}500\,(P/F\ 20{,}10)]\,(A/P\ 20{,}10) \\
&= [94{,}308]\,(0.2385) \\
&= \$22{,}494
\end{aligned}
$$

TABLE 9-17

Revenue Requirements for Three Years of Service

(Alternative 2)

End of Year	Book Depreciation D_b	Tax Depreciation D	Book Value B	Equity Return F_e	Debt Interest I	Tax t	Operation and Maintenance C	Minimum Annual Revenue Requirement R
0	—	—	$60,000	—	—	—	—	—
1	$10,000	$14,000	50,000	$9,000	$3,000	$1,250	$3,000	$26,250
2	10,000	12,000	40,000	7,500	2,500	5,958	3,000	28,958
3	10,000	10,000	30,000	6,000	2,000	6,500	3,000	27,500

These values and the values in Table 9-18 indicate that a definite assessment of the long-term and short-term effects must be made before an alternative can be selected.

PURCHASE VERSUS LEASE

Sometimes, leasing equipment is an alternative to purchasing equipment. Leasing equipment has an appeal because of its possible tax advantages and because leasing can avoid long-term commitments of capital. In actuality leasing may or may not provide a tax advantage. It depends on the depreciation amounts, operating costs, and investment tax credit of the purchase alternative. In any event, all purchase-lease decisions should be determined by an actual cost comparison. Basically, a cost comparison involving a leasing alternative is made in the same manner as any other cost comparison. One point to be remembered from the standpoint of inflationary effects is that leasing costs are always in terms of *actual dollars*. Consequently, care must be exercised to insure that the costs of the leasing and purchase alternatives are in consistent (real or actual) dollars.

Leasing and purchase alternatives involve the comparison of their

TABLE 9-18

Cost Comparison with LCM > Service Life

(Example 9-3 data)

End of Year	Revenue Requirements	
	Alternative 1	Alternative 2
1	$19,048	$13,750
2	22,498	25,517
3	23,171	24,783
4	23,844	24,050
5	19,048	23,316
6	22,498	22,583
7	23,171	21,850
8	23,844	26,250
9	22,867	28,958
10	23,358	27,500

respective costs over an infinite or finite service life. If the service life is infinite, it is necessary to determine the leasing costs over a time period that is equal to the book depreciation (capital recovery) life of the purchase alternative. This leasing cost is then compared to the minimum revenue requirements of the purchase alternative, and the smaller-cost alternative is selected. If the leasing alternative is selected, this procedure implies that at the end of the leasing period the cost of continuing with a lease arrangement, at either a higher or lower cost, is compared with the revenue requirements of some future purchase alternative. On the other hand, if the purchase alternative is selected, the purchased alternative can be disposed of at some future time, if a leasing arrangement becomes more economically desirable.

If the service life is finite, it is necessary to determine the leasing costs over the service life and compare them to the revenue requirements for the same period of time. Since a finite service life implies that there is no need for service after this period of time, it is highly likely that a leasing arrangement is desirable since it avoids the long-term commitment of capital.

Example 9-4

If Alternative 2 in Example 9-3 is the purchase alternative, make a cost comparison under the following conditions:

a. The service life is infinite and the leasing costs are $25,000 per year for seven years.

b. The service life is four years and the leasing costs are $25,000 per year for four years. Assume that the net realizable salvage value for the purchase alternative is $20,000 at the end of four years.

For Part a the minimum annual revenue requirements must be determined for the purchase alternative. This has been done previously, and the values are given in Table 9-10. A comparison of the costs (long-term and short-term) is shown in Table 9-19. This comparison indicates that the purchase alternative is the best even though in year two the revenue requirement is slightly larger than the leasing cost. This decision is fairly clear. However, in many purchase-lease comparisons, the decision is not clear because of conflicts between the short-term and long-term effects as well as questions concerning the commitment of capital to long-term ventures. In the final analysis, a decision-maker must balance all of these considerations.

For Part b, the revenue requirements must be determined using four years as the capital recovery period and an assumed salvage value of $20,000. The revenue requirements are given in Table 9-20. It is

TABLE 9-19

A Purchase-Lease Comparison with an Infinite Service Life

(Example 9-4)

End of Year	Purchase Alternative		Lease Alternative	
	Annual Cost	Equivalent Cost	Annual Cost	Equivalent Cost
0	–	–	–	–
1	$13,750	$21,679	$25,000	$25,000
2	25,517	21,679	25,000	25,000
3	24,783	21,679	25,000	25,000
4	24,050	21,679	25,000	25,000
5	23,316	21,679	25,000	25,000
6	22,583	21,679	25,000	25,000
7	21,850	21,679	25,000	25,000

assumed in Table 9-20 that there are no tax effects resulting from differences in the net realizable salvage value and the tax book value in year four. If tax effects are considered applicable, they can be included as previously discussed. Also in Table 9-20, only one-third of the maximum investment tax credit is taken because of the four-year life. However, a company might be willing to take the full investment tax credit in year one with the realization of an investment tax penalty in the fourth year. This is possible since the tax depreciation life for Alternative 2 is seven years and, presumably, this has been established by tax regulations. This

TABLE 9-20

Revenue Requirements for a Four-Year Service Life

(Example 9-4)

End of Year	Book Depreciation D_b	Tax Depreciation D	Book Value B	Equity Return F_e	Debt Interest I	Tax t	Operation and Maintenance C	Minimum Annual Revenue Requirement R
0	–	–	$60,000	–	–	–	–	–
1	$10,000	$14,000	50,000	$9,000	$3,000	$1,250	$3,000	$26,250
2	10,000	12,000	40,000	7,500	2,500	5,958	3,000	28,958
3	10,000	10,000	30,000	6,000	2,000	6,500	3,000	27,500
4	10,000	8,000	20,000	4,500	1,500	7,041	3,000	26,041

has been discussed previously. The equivalent annual revenue requirement for the annual costs in Table 9-20 is

$$
\begin{aligned}
E &= [26,250 \, (P/F \, 20, \, 1) + 28,958 \, (P/F \, 20, \, 2) \\
&\quad + 27,500 \, (P/F \, 20, \, 3) + 26,041 \, (P/F \, 20, \, 4)] \, (A/P \, 20, \, 4) \\
&= [70,457] \, (0.3863) \\
&= \$27,217
\end{aligned}
$$

A comparison of the costs is shown in Table 9-21 and indicates that the leasing alternative is the best selection.

Some comments are needed in regard to the basic assumptions made in this chapter. The cycling assumption is a common assumption for cost comparisons. It is usually made by default. That is, there is no evidence or estimates to the contrary. Also, from the practical standpoint of numerical calculations, the cycling assumption is convenient. The assumption made in this text for partial cycles that may occur when the LCM is larger than the service life is not, of course, the only assumption. It is possible to assume (estimate) some completely independent alternatives for partial cycles. For that matter, in theory at least, it is possible to assume alternatives that have no relationship to the initial alternatives for any part of the service life that remains after the lives of the initial alternative. In the final analysis, a decision must be made between the difficulties of estimating and the convenience of the assumptions used in this chapter.

TABLE 9-21

A Purchase-Lease Comparison with an Infinite Service Life

(Example 9-4)

End of Year	Purchase Alternative		Lease Alternative	
	Annual Cost	Equivalent Cost	Annual Cost	Equivalent Cost
0	—	—	—	—
1	$26,250	$27,217	$25,000	$25,000
2	28,958	27,217	25,000	25,000
3	27,500	27,217	25,000	25,000
4	26,041	27,217	25,000	25,000

PROBLEMS

9-1. A company is considering the purchase of one of the two alternatives shown below:

	Alternative	
	1	2
Initial cost	$60,000	$80,000
Book depreciation	SL	SL
Salvage value	$ 6,000	$ 8,000
Life, years	8 years	8 years
Tax depreciation	SYD	SYD
Salvage value	$ 6,000	$ 8,000
Life, years	8	8
Annual cost of operation and		
maintenance	$ 7,000	$ 4,000
Cost of debt capital	15%	15%
Cost of equity capital	25%	25%
Debt ratio	40%	40%
Tax rate	52%	52%
Investment tax credit	0%	0%

Assuming the service life is infinite and there are no tax effects, make a cost comparison using a revenue requirement approach.

9-2. Repeat Problem 9-1 assuming the investment tax credit is applicable.

9-3. If the alternatives in Problem 9-1 are needed for only 12 years and the net realizable salvage values after four years of use for Alternatives 1 and 2 are, respectively, $18,000 and $30,000, make a cost comparison under the following conditions. Assume the alternatives are Section 1245 Property and the investment tax credit is applicable.
 (a) There are no tax effects and the investment tax credit is taken so that there is no investment tax penalty.
 (b) There are tax effects, and the maximum investment tax credit is taken regardless of its penalty.

9-4. If in Problem 9-1 the given data for the two alternatives are in real dollars and the inflation rate is 10%, what is the effect on the cost comparison?

9-5. Using the data in Problem 9-1, determine the before-tax equivalent annual costs of the two assets if the service life is greater than eight years.

9-6. For the two alternatives shown in the following table and assuming an infinite service life, determine the following:
(a) An equivalent annual before-tax cost comparison.
(b) A present worth before-tax cost comparison.
(c) A capitalized before-tax cost comparison.

	Alternative	
	1	2
Initial cost	$100,000	$150,000
Salvage value	$ 10,000	$ 20,000
Life (capital recovery period), years	8	12
Required before-tax return	20%	20%
Annual cost of operation and maintenance	$ 8,000	$ 4,000

9-7. Using a revenue requirement approach, make a cost comparison of the two assets shown in the following table and on the basis of:
(a) An infinite need.
(b) A need that is greater than eight years.

	Asset	
	1	2
Initial cost	$60,000	$75,000
Annual cost of operation and maintenance	$ 8,000	$ 5,000
Tax depreciation	SYD	SYD
Salvage value	$ 0	$ 0
Life, years	5	5
Book depreciation	SL	SL
Salvage value	$ 0	$ 3,000
Life, years	8	8
Tax rate	52%	52%
Debt ratio	40%	40%
Return on equity	25%	25%
Cost of debt	15%	15%
Investment tax credit	10%	10%

9-8. Using the data in Problem 9-7, make a cost comparison for a service life of four years under the following conditions:

(a) The net realizable salvage value for Asset 1 after four years of use is $6,000.

(b) The net realizable salvage value for Asset 2 after four years of use is $3,000.

(c) All possible tax effects are to be included and the assets are Section 1245 Property.

(d) The maximum allowable investment tax credit is taken and any possible penalty is paid at the end of the service life.

9-9. Using a cash flow approach defined by Eq. (9-7), make a cost comparison of the two alternatives in Problem 9-7 assuming a service life greater than eight years and no tax effects.

9-10. Make a cost comparison of the two alternatives given in the following table using a revenue approach. It should be noted that Alternative 1 in this problem is the same as Alternative 2 in Problem 9-7. Assume that the maximum allowable investment tax credit indicated by the tax depreciation life is taken for any partial cost cycles, and any investment tax penalties are taken in the last year of a partial cost cycle. Also assume that there are no tax effects resulting from the disposal of the alternatives, and the actual realizable salvage values of the two alternatives at any point in time are equal to their respective book values given by the book depreciation schedule at the same point in time. Make the cost comparison for service lives of (a) infinity, (b) 30 years, and (c) 20 years.

| | Alternative | |
	1	2
Initial cost	$75,000	$90,000
Annual cost of operation		
and maintenance	$ 5,000	$ 3,000
Tax depreciation	SYD	SYD
Salvage value	$ 0	$ 0
Life, years	5	5
Book depreciation	SL	SL
Salvage value	$ 3,000	$ 6,000
Life, years	8	12
Tax rate	52%	52%
Debt ratio	40%	40%
Return on equity	25%	25%
Cost of debt	15%	15%
Investment tax credit	10%	10%

9-11. Repeat Problem 9-10, except in this problem assume that tax effects are recognized as Section 1245 gains and losses resulting from the disposal of the alternatives.

9-12. A company can lease or purchase certain needed equipment. The cost data for purchasing the equipment is listed below:

Initial cost	$2,000,000
Annual cost of operation and maintenance	$ 50,000
Tax depreciation	SYD
Life, years	5
Salvage value	$200,000
Book depreciation	SL
Life, years	10
Salvage value	$200,000
Required debt return	15%
Required equity return	25%
Tax rate	52%
Debt ratio	30%
Investment tax credit	0%

If the annual cost of leasing the equipment for ten years is (a) $500,000, (b) $900,000, (c) $750,000, and (d) $650,000, should the equipment be purchased or leased?

10

REPLACEMENT ANALYSIS

Replacement analysis basically involves the economic evaluation of two alternatives. One alternative is to keep some existing asset (sometimes referred to as the *defender*). The second alternative is to replace the existing asset with some new asset (sometimes referred to as the *challenger*). This situation usually occurs as a result of some inadequate performance on the part of the existing asset. In this chapter, the economic evaluation is based on the costs of the alternatives. Consequently, the economic evaluations assume that *the assets provide equal service*. Two approaches are presented in this chapter for the economic evaluation of replacement alternatives. The first approach is called the *conventional* approach and the second approach involves the use of *minimum annual revenue requirements*.

THE CONVENTIONAL APPROACH

In this text, the conventional approach to replacement analysis involves the determination of a before-tax (as defined in Chapter 9) equivalent annual cost for each alternative. This approach is further explained in the following example.

Example 10-1

Seven years ago, an asset was purchased and installed to provide some needed service. At that time, the data given in Table 10-1 was estimated and determined to be applicable for this existing asset. However, experience with this asset indicates that some of the original estimates were incorrect. Consequently, the replacement of the existing asset with a new asset is now being considered.

As a result of past experience, it is estimated that the annual cost of operation and maintenance is $7,000 for the remaining life of the existing asset which is estimated to be five years. The salvage value at the end of five years is now estimated to be $5,000. The present realizable salvage value for the existing asset is $30,000. Further, the future debt ratio is considered to be the same as the one originally used (40%). However, the cost of debt capital is now considered to be 17.5% and the required return on equity 30%.

A new asset is now available that provides equal service and has the estimated cost data given in Table 10-2. It is desired to compare the existing and new assets on the basis of a before-tax comparison assuming the need for the service is infinite (a finite service life is considered later).

It is desirable in replacement analysis to portray the applicable data as shown in Table 10-3. Since a before-tax comparison is desired, it is

TABLE 10-1

Original Data for Existing Asset

(Example 10-1)

Initial cost	$90,000
Annual cost of operation and maintenance	$ 3,000
Tax depreciation	SYD
Salvage value	$ 0
Life, years	5
Book depreciation	SL
Salvage value	$ 6,000
Life, years	12
Tax rate	52%
Debt ratio	40%
Return on equity	25%
Cost of debt	15%
Investment tax credit	0%

TABLE 10-2

Cost Data for New Asset

(Example 10-1)

Initial cost	$60,000
Annual cost of operation and maintenance	$ 4,000
Tax depreciation	SYD
Salvage value	$ 0
Life, years	5
Book depreciation	SL
Salvage value	$ 6,000
Life, years	10
Tax rate	52%
Debt ratio	40%
Return on equity	30%
Cost of debt	17.5%
Investment tax credit	0%

necessary to determine a before-tax rate of return. Using Eq. (9-1), this return is

$$k'_b = (0.40)(0.175) + \frac{(0.60)(.30)}{1 - 0.52}$$

$$= 0.445$$

$$= 44.5\%$$

The equivalent annual cost for the existing asset, E'_d, using Eq. (3-18) is

$$E'_d = (30,000 - 5,000)(A/P\ 44.5,5) + 5,000(0.445) + 7,000$$

$$= \$22,450$$

and the equivalent annual cost of the new asset, E'_n, is

$$E'_n = (60,000 - 6,000)(A/P\ 44.5,10) + 6,000(0.445) + 4,000$$

$$= \$31,321$$

A comparison of these values indicates that the existing asset should be kept. This decision implies an assumption since the lives of the two alternatives are different. This assumption is discussed in the following comments.

TABLE 10-3

Cost Data for Example 10-1

End of Year	Existing Asset		End of Year	New Asset	
−7	$K=\$90,000;\ n=12;\ L=\$6,000$		−7	—	
−6	—		−6	—	
•			•		
•			•		
•			•		
0	$30,000		0	$60,000	
1		$7,000	1		$4,000
2		•	2		$4,000
3		•	3		$4,000
4		•	•		•
5	$L=\$5,000$	$7,000	•		•
			•		•
			10	$L=\$6,000$	$4,000

Comments   In Example 10-1, it may appear that the solution ignores the difference in the lives of the alternatives. This is not the case. A certain assumption is being made in the solution. Specifically, this assumption is that the new asset is the best (least cost) possible replacement available at the present time. Consequently, the new asset replaces the existing asset at the end of its life and the cost data for the new asset then cycles out to the service life (infinity in Example 10-1) for the alternative of keeping the existing asset. The alternative of purchasing the new asset involves the assumption that its cost data cycles out to the service life. As in cost comparisons (Chapter 9), the comparison of replacement alternatives must be over the same period of time. This time period is the service life which can be either finite or infinite. Using the equivalent annual cost values obtained in Example 10-1 and an infinite service life, these assumptions imply the cost comparison shown in Table 10-4. This table shows that, with these assumptions, the equivalent annual costs are the same after the fifth year for the two alternatives. As a result, *if the service life is infinite*, all that is needed from a computational standpoint for a before-tax comparison of the alternatives are the equivalent annual costs of the existing and new assets, where the equivalent annual costs are computed on the basis of their respective lives. Another assumption that is sometimes made in replacement studies is to assume that the cost data for existing and new assets both cycle out to the service life. For example, using the data in Example 10-1, this latter assumption implies

TABLE 10-4

Cycling Assumption

(Example 10-1)

End of Year	Alternatives	
	Keep Existing Asset	Purchase New Asset
0	—	—
1	$22,450	$31,321
2	•	•
3	•	•
4	•	•
5	22,450	31,321
6	31,321	31,321
7	31,321	31,321
•	•	•
•	•	•
•	•	•
∞	$31,321	$31,321

the cost comparison shown in Table 10-5. This table shows that *for an infinite service life* both assumptions lead to a comparison of the same numerical values ($22,450 and $31,321) and consequently the same choice of an alternative. However, when the service life is finite, the cycling assumption used can make a difference in the choice of an alternative. This text takes the point of view that the first assumption is more plausible than this latter assumption and is the one used in future discus-

TABLE 10-5

Another Cycling Assumption

End of Year	Alternatives	
	Keep Existing Asset	Purchase New Asset
0	—	—
1	$22,450	$31,321
2	22,450	31,321
•	•	•
•	•	•
•	•	•
∞	$22,450	$31,321

sions in this chapter. At this point, the discussions in Chapter 9 of the assumptions regarding the cycling of cost data should be remembered. That is, once a comparison of alternatives indicates a particular choice of asset, there is no requirement that the chosen asset be kept until the end of its cycle. Theoretically, at least, it is possible to replace the asset at any point in time that an economic evaluation indicates a replacement is desirable.

Another point should be understood when making replacement comparisons. There is no requirement that past estimates or values associated with the existing asset be maintained in the *before-tax evaluations* of replacement alternatives. There are some exceptions (for example, tax depreciation) to this point when after-tax comparisons (discussed later) are made. The before-tax evaluation of replacement alternatives should be based on what is *presently* considered to be correct estimates and values. That is, the original estimates and values used for the existing asset can be revised for the evaluation of the alternative of keeping the existing asset. Further, any differences between original estimates made for the existing asset and actual values are *sunk costs*. These sunk costs are a result of *past errors* in estimating and should not be used in the comparison of replacement alternatives. For example, the difference between the book value of the existing asset and the present realizable salvage value is a sunk cost. Using the data in Example 10-1, the book value, based on the book depreciation schedule, after seven years is

$$B_7 = 90,000 - \frac{7}{12}(90,000 - 6,000)$$

$$= \$41,000$$

and the sunk cost is

$$\text{sunk cost} = 41,000 - 30,000$$

$$= \$11,000$$

Since this sunk cost is a result of past estimates, it is not included in a *before-tax* comparison of replacement alternatives. However, it *may* have an effect in an after-tax comparison of the replacement alternatives.

It should be noted that a great deal of the data given in Tables 10-1 and 10-2 is not used in Example 10-1. This is because Example 10-1 uses a before-tax approach and only the equivalent annual amounts of the assets are necessary. It is true that this approach simplifies the calculations and, for this reason, it is often used. However, a before-tax approach can lead to incorrect decisions due to the neglect of specific tax effects. A before-tax approach is presented in this chapter because of its wide use. Also, it serves as a foundation upon which to present after-tax replacement studies.

Finite Service Life In Example 10-1 an infinite service life is used. If a finite service life is used, it is necessary to estimate the salvage value of the *new asset* at the end of a period of use. The length of this use period is dependent upon the period of time from the end of a cycle of an asset to the service life. It should be noted that the concept of a least common multiple (LCM) of the lives of the alternatives introduced in Chapter 9 is not applicable for replacement studies. This is because of the assumption that the new asset replaces the existing asset and consequently an LCM cannot be defined for the alternatives.

Example 10-2 _____

Repeat Example 10-1 for finite service lives of (a) ten years and (b) fifteen years. Assume that the salvage value of the new asset, after five years of use, is $20,000.

For Part a, the cost data cycles are shown in Table 10-6. In order to make a before-tax comparison of the cost data in Table 10-6, the equivalent annual cost for the two alternatives must be calculated. The equivalent annual cost of the new asset is calculated in Example 10-1 and is $31,321. The calculation of the equivalent annual cost of the existing asset can be accomplished in two ways. The first way is to

TABLE 10-6

Cost Data Cycles for Example 10-2

(Part a)

End of Year	Existing Asset		New Asset	
0	K=$30,000		K=$60,000	
1		$7,000		$4,000
2		7,000		4,000
3		7,000		4,000
4		7,000		4,000
5	L=$5,000; K=$60,000	7,000		4,000
6		4,000		4,000
7		4,000		4,000
8		4,000		4,000
9		4,000		4,000
10	L=$20,000	4,000	L=$6,000	4,000

discount all values back to the present (remember salvage values are negative) and then spread this result over the ten-year period using an appropriate A/P factor. The second way is to use Eq. (3-18) for each cycle and then combine these results using the appropriate interest factors. Using this second way, the equivalent annual cost of the first five years (cycle) is

$$(30,000 - 5,000) \, (A/P \; 44.5,5) + 5,000 \, (0.445) + 7,000 = \$22,450$$

which could have been obtained from the solution to Example 10-1. The equivalent annual cost for the second five years is

$$(60,000 - 20,000) \, (A/P \; 44.5,5) + 20,000 \, (0.445) + 4,000 = \$34,060$$

The equivalent annual costs for these two cycles and for one cycle of the new asset are shown in Table 10-7. Combining the equivalent annual costs of the two cycles, the equivalent annual cost for the alternative of keeping the existing asset (E'_d) is

$$E'_d = [22,450 \, (P/A \; 44.5,5)$$
$$+ \; 34,060 \, (P/A \; 44.5,5) \, (P/F \; 44.5,5)] \, (A/P \; 44.5,10)$$

$$= [52,657] \, (0.4565)$$

$$= \$24,038$$

TABLE 10-7

Equivalent Annual Cost Cycles For Example 10-2

(Part a)

End of Year	Alternatives	
	Keep Existing Asset	*Purchase New Asset*
0	—	—
1	$22,450	$31,321
2	22,450	31,321
3	22,450	31,321
4	22,450	31,321
5	22,450	31,321
6	34,060	31,321
7	34,060	31,321
8	34,060	31,321
9	34,060	31,321
10	34,060	31,321

TABLE 10-8

Cost Data Cycles for Example 10-2

(Part b)

End of Year	Existing Asset		New Asset	
0	$K=\$30,000$		$K=\$60,000$	
1		$7,000		$4,000
2		7,000		4,000
3		7,000		4,000
4		7,000		4,000
5	$L=\$5,000; K=\$60,000$	7,000		4,000
6		4,000		4,000
7		4,000		4,000
8		4,000		4,000
9		4,000		4,000
10		4,000	$L=\$6,000; K=\$60,000$	4,000
11		4,000		4,000
12		4,000		4,000
13		4,000		4,000
14		4,000		4,000
15	$L=\$6,000$	4,000	$L=\$20,000$	4,000

Comparing this result ($24,038) with the equivalent annual cost of the new asset alternative ($31,321) indicates that keeping the existing asset is the better choice.

For Part b, the cost data cycles are shown in Table 10-8. The equivalent annual costs for the two alternatives are calculated using the procedure mentioned in Part a. The equivalent annual cost for the first five years for the alternative of keeping the existing asset has been calculated previously and is $22,450. The equivalent annual cost for years six through fifteen has also been calculated in Example 10-1 and is $31,321. Combining these values, the equivalent annual cost of the alternative of keeping the existing asset, E'_d, is

$$E'_d = [22,450\,(P/A\ 44.5,5)$$
$$+ 31,321\,(P/A\ 44.5,10)\,(P/F\ 44.5)]\,(A/P\ 44.5,15)$$

$$= [53,327]\,(0.4468)$$

$$= \$23,827$$

In a similar manner, the equivalent annual cost for the first ten years for the alternative of purchasing a new asset is $31,321 (calculated previously). The equivalent annual cost for years 10 through 15 is $34,060 which is calculated in Part a. Combining these values, the equivalent annual cost of the alternative of purchasing a new asset, E'_n, is

$$E'_n = [31,321\,(P/A\ 44.5,10)$$
$$+\ 34,060\,(P/A\ 44.5)\,(P/F\ 44.5,10)]\,(A/P\ 44.5,15)$$

$$= [70,234]\,(0.4468)$$

$$= \$31,381$$

A comparison of the two equivalent annual costs indicates that keeping the existing asset is the better choice.

THE OVERHAUL ALTERNATIVE

In replacement analysis, there often occurs a third alternative in addition to the two basic alternatives of keeping the existing asset or replacing it with a new asset. This third alternative is to overhaul the existing asset. It is an especially viable alternative when production-type equipment is involved in a replacement study. If the overhaul alternative is feasible, the approach, for a before-tax comparison, is to determine the equivalent annual cost for the overhaul and compare this cost with the equivalent annual costs for the alternatives of keeping the existing asset and purchasing a new asset. The same cycling assumption, mentioned previously, is applicable to the overhaul alternative. That is, at the end of the overhaul cost cycle, the cost data for the new asset begins to cycle out to the service life.

Example 10-3

In Examples 10-1 and 10-2 it is possible to overhaul the existing asset at a cost of $18,000, and this overhaul decreases annual operation and maintenance costs to $5,000. Further, this overhaul will increase the life of the existing asset to eight years and the total salvage (existing and overhaul portions) is estimated to be $4,000 at that time. Determine a before-tax cost comparison for the three alternatives in Examples 10-1 and 10-2.

The equivalent annual cost for the overhaul of the existing asset is

$$E'_o = (30,000\ +\ 18,000\ -\ 4,000)\,(A/P\ 44.5,8)$$
$$+\ (4,000)\,(0.445)\ +\ 5,000$$

$$= \$27,447$$

Since in Example 10-1 the service life is infinity, the cost cycles shown in Table 10-9 are implied. A comparison of the values in Table 10-9 indicates that a choice of an alternative is not as clear as in the case of only two alternatives (keeping the existing asset versus purchasing a new asset). Since the equivalent annual cost of the new asset is larger than both alternatives of keeping the existing asset and the overhaul, the new asset can immediately be eliminated as a possible choice. However, the choice between the remaining two alternatives is not clear without further analysis. This is because in years one through five the equivalent annual cost of the existing asset alternative is less than the overhaul alternative but larger in years six through eight. From year eight to infinity, the equivalent annual costs are the same for these two alternatives. The analysis taken, in this text, for this situation is to compare the equivalent annual costs over a period of time beginning with year one and ending at the point where the equivalent annual costs become the same for the alternatives. This period of time is the first eight years in this example. The equivalent annual cost over this eight-year period for the alternative of keeping the existing asset equals

$$E'_o = [22,450\,(P/A\ 44.5,5)$$
$$+31,321\,(P/A\ 44.5,3)\ (P/F\ 44.5,5)]\ (A/P\ 44.5,8)$$

TABLE 10-9

Equivalent Annual Cost Cycles for Example 10-3

(Infinite Service Life)

End of Year	Alternatives		
	Keep Existing Asset	Purchase New Asset	Overhaul Existing Asset
0	—	—	—
1	$22,450	$31,321	$27,447
2	22,450	31,321	27,447
3	22,450	31,321	27,447
4	22,450	31,321	27,447
5	22,450	31,321	27,447
6	31,321	31,321	27,447
7	31,321	31,321	27,447
8	31,321	31,321	27,447
9	31,321	31,321	31,321
·	·	·	·
·	·	·	·
·	·	·	·
∞	31,321	31,321	31,321

TABLE 10-10

Equivalent Annual Cost Cycles for Example 10-3

(A Finite Service Life of 10 Years)

End of Year	Alternatives		
	Keep Existing Asset	Purchase New Asset	Overhaul Existing Asset
0	—	—	—
1	$22,450	$31,321	$27,447
2	22,450	31,321	27,447
3	22,450	31,321	27,447
4	22,450	31,321	27,447
5	22,450	31,321	27,447
6	34,060	31,321	27,447
7	34,060	31,321	27,447
8	34,060	31,321	27,447
9	34,060	31,321	38,880
10	34,060	31,321	38,880

which gives a value of $23,441. Since this value ($23,441) is less than the overhaul alternative ($27,447), the choice is to keep the existing asset. It is noted that this type of additional analysis is only required in situations where $E_d < E'_o < E'_n$. This situation is discussed in greater detail after this example.

In Example 10-2 two finite service lives are specified. The first service life is ten years. For this case, it is necessary to estimate the salvage value of the new asset after two years of use, since it is assumed that the new asset replaces the overhaul at the end of the cost data for the overhaul (eight years). Consequently, for a ten-year service life, the equivalent annual costs are needed for years nine and ten. Assuming the salvage value is $40,000, the equivalent annual cost for years nine and ten is

$$(50,000 - 40,000) \, (A/P \, 44.5,2) + 40,000 \, (0.445) + 4,000$$

which gives a value of $38,880. The equivalent annual cost cycles are shown in Table 10-10 and are the same as those in Table 10-7 with the addition of the overhaul alternative. Combining the equivalent annual cost cycles, the equivalent annual cost for the overhaul alternative is

$$E'_o = [27,447 \, (P/A \, 44.5,8)$$
$$+ (38,880) \, (P/A \, 44.5,2) \, (P/F \, 44.5,8)] \, (A/P \, 44.5,10)$$

$$= [60,830] \, (0.4565)$$

$$= \$27,769$$

A comparison of this value ($27,538) with the values obtained in Example 10-2 ($24,038 and $31,321) indicates that keeping the existing asset is the best alternative.

For the second part of Example 10-2, where a finite service life of fifteen years is specified, it is necessary to estimate the salvage value of the new asset after seven years of use. Assuming this salvage value is $18,000, the equivalent annual cost for seven years of use of the new asset is

$$(60,000 - 18,000) \, (A/P \ 44.5,7) + 18,000 \, (0.445) + 4,000$$

which gives a value of $32,237. The equivalent annual cost cycles are shown in Table 10-11. Many of the values shown in Table 10-11 are determined in Examples 10-1 and 10-2. The combined equivalent annual cost cycles for the alternatives of keeping the existing asset and purchasing a new asset are, respectively, $23,827 and $31,381 (determined in Example 10-2). The combined equivalent annual cost cycles for the overhaul alternative gives

$$
\begin{aligned}
E'_d &= [27,447 \, (P/A \ 44.5,8) \\
&\quad + 32,237 \, (P/A \ 44.5,7) \, (P/F \ 44.5,8)] \, (A/P \ 44.5,15) \\
&= [61,956] \, (0.4468) \\
&= \$27,682
\end{aligned}
$$

A comparison of these three values indicates that keeping the existing asset is the best alternative.

Some Comments In the case of an infinite service life, the choice of an alternative is very direct when keeping the existing asset and purchasing a new asset are the only alternatives. It is only necessary to determine the equivalent annual costs for the two alternatives over their respective lives in order to choose an alternative. This is because of the cycling assumption previously discussed and shown in Table 10-4. However, when an overhaul alternative is included with the alternatives of keeping the existing asset and purchasing a new asset, there is a special situation where an additional computation is necessary before a choice of an alternative is possible. This special situation is discussed in the first part of Example 10-3 and shown in Table 10-9. It occurs when all of the following three conditions are satisfied

$$E'_d < E'_o < E_n \tag{10-1}$$

$$\text{service life} = \text{infinity} \tag{10-2}$$

$$n_d < n_o < n_n \tag{10-3}$$

TABLE 10-11

Equivalent Annual Cost Cycles for Example 10-3

(A Finite Service Life of 15 Years)

End of Year	Alternatives		
	Keep Existing Asset	Purchase New Asset	Overhaul Existing Asset
0	—	—	—
1	$22,450	$31,321	$27,447
2	22,450	31,321	27,447
3	22,450	31,321	27,447
4	22,450	31,321	27,447
5	22,450	31,321	27,447
6	31,321	31,321	27,447
7	31,321	31,321	27,447
8	31,321	31,321	27,447
9	31,321	31,321	32,237
10	31,321	31,321	32,237
11	31,321	34,060	32,237
12	31,321	34,060	32,237
13	31,321	34,060	32,237
14	31,321	34,060	32,237
15	31,321	34,060	32,237

where n_d, n_o, and n_n are the lives, respectively, of the existing asset, the overhaul, and the new asset. Eq. (10-3) is by far the usual case with the possible exception of

$$n_d = n_o < n_n \tag{10-4}$$

In general, it is not realistic in replacement studies to consider the case of n_n being less than either n_d or n_o or the case of n_o being less than either n_d or n_n. If Eq. (10-4) is the case and both Eqs. (10-1) and (10-2) are satisfied, a direct solution is possible. That is, the choice is E'_d. However, if Eq. (10-1) through (10-3) are satisfied, it is necessary to use the relationship

$$[E'_d (P/A \ k'_b, n_d) \\ + E'_n (P/A \ k'_b, (n_o - n_d)) (P/F \ k'_b, n_d)] (A/P \ k'_b, n_o) \tag{10-5}$$

to determine a value for a comparison with E'_o and E'_n. The use of Eq. (10-5) has been shown in Example 10-3 in obtaining the value of $23,441.

THE REVENUE APPROACH

Minimum annual revenue requirements provide an after-tax *approach* to replacement analysis. It is true that this approach requires more computational effort than the conventional approach. However, it is felt that this computational effort is offset by the ability to obtain the specific yearly costs through a minimum annual revenue requirement approach; thus providing, as in cost comparisons, the ability to evaluate the short-term effects as well as the long-term effects.

The basic approach in using revenue requirements for replacement analysis is the same as the conventional approach. That is, an alternative is chosen on the basis of least cost. Also, the same cycling assumption made in the conventional approach is applicable to the revenue approach. The steps necessary for a revenue approach to replacement analysis are explained in the following examples and discussions.

Example 10-4

Using a minimum annual revenue requirement approach, repeat Example 10-1.

Initially, the solution to this example does not recognize the possible tax effects on the gains and losses resulting from the disposal of assets. Possible tax effects are considered later in this chapter. The first step is to generate the original revenue requirements for the existing asset on the basis of its originally estimated data (Table 10-1). These values are shown in Table 10-12 and are determined using the procedures presented in Chapter 6. In actuality, it is not necessary to determine all the values presented in Table 10-12. However, at this point, it is felt that a table showing all the original data for the existing asset provides greater meaning to future discussions. The next step is to generate the revenue requirements (yearly costs) for the existing asset using current estimates. These values are given in Table 10-13 and are explained by the following sample calculations.

The book depreciation (capital recovery) is based on the *present* realizable salvage value, the estimated remaining life of the existing asset, and the estimated salvage value. For this example, assuming straight-line depreciation, the book depreciation is

$$D_b = \frac{30,000 - 5,000}{5}$$

$$= \$5,000 \text{ per year}$$

As mentioned previously in the discussion of the conventional approach to replacement analysis, there is no requirement that the values used in

TABLE 10-12

Original Revenue Requirements for the Existing Asset

(Example 10-4)

End of Year	Book Depreciation D_b	Tax Depreciation D	Book Value B	Equity Return F_e	Debt Interest I	Tax t	Operation and Maintenance C	Minimum Annual Revenue Requirement R
0	—	—	$90,000	—	—	—	—	—
1	$7,000	$30,000	83,000	$13,500	$5,400	$-10,292	$3,000	$18,608
2	7,000	24,000	76,000	12,450	4,980	-4,929	3,000	22,501
3	7,000	18,000	69,000	11,400	4,560	433	3,000	26,393
4	7,000	12,000	62,000	10,350	4,140	5,796	3,000	30,286
5	7,000	6,000	55,000	9,300	3,720	11,158	3,000	34,178
6	7,000	—	48,000	8,250	3,300	16,520	3,000	38,070
7	7,000	—	41,000	7,200	2,880	15,383	3,000	35,463
8	7,000	—	34,000	6,150	2,460	14,245	3,000	32,855
9	7,000	—	27,000	5,100	2,040	13,108	3,000	30,248
10	7,000	—	20,000	4,050	1,620	11,970	3,000	27,640
11	7,000	—	13,000	3,000	1,200	10,833	3,000	25,033
12	7,000	—	6,000	1,950	780	9,696	3,000	22,426

TABLE 10-13

Revenue Requirements for Existing Asset

(Example 10-4)

End of Year	Book Depreciation D_b	Tax Depreciation D	Book Value B	Equity Return F_e	Debt Interest I	Tax Debt Interest I_t	Taxes t	Operation and Maintenance C	Minimum Annual Revenue Requirement R
0	—	—	$30,000	—	—	—	—	—	—
1	$5,000	$0	25,000	$5,400	$2,100	$2,460	$10,876	$7,000	$30,376
2	5,000	0	20,000	4,500	1,750	2,040	9,977	7,000	28,227
3	5,000	0	15,000	3,600	1,400	1,620	9,078	7,000	26,078
4	5,000	0	10,000	2,700	1,050	1,200	8,179	7,000	23,929
5	5,000	0	5,000	1,800	700	780	7,280	7,000	21,780

determining the book depreciation amounts be related to past estimates of book depreciation, life, or salvage value.

The yearly tax depreciation amounts, D, and the tax debt interest, I_t, are obtained from Table 10-12 and are the remaining amounts based on the original data for the existing asset. What is being implied is that, *from a tax standpoint*, these tax deductions do not change if the use of the existing asset is continued. The tax depreciation is established when the existing asset is initially purchased and does not change. In this example, the existing asset is fully depreciated for tax purposes at the end of five years (see Table 10-2). Consequently, there are no remaining tax depreciation amounts. Hence, the entries from the tax depreciation amounts in Table 10-13 are all zero. The interest for tax purposes, I_t, is a result of debt capital available at the purchase time (seven years ago in this example) of the existing asset. Thus, the interest on this debt capital does not change.

The book depreciation value at the end of the year j, B_j, is determined using the equation

$$B_j = B_o - \sum_{x=1}^{j} D_{bx} \qquad (10\text{-}6)$$

For this example,

$$B_0 = \$30,000$$

$$B_1 = 30,000 - 5,000$$

$$= \$25,000$$

$$B_2 = 30,000 - 10,000$$

$$= \$20,000$$

The required return equity return for year j, F_{ej}, is determined using the relationship

$$F_{ej} = (1 - c)(k_e) B_{j-1} \qquad (10\text{-}7)$$

where k_e is *new* required rate of return on equity. For this example, Eq. (10-7) gives

$$F_{e1} = (1 - 0.40)(0.30)(30,000)$$

$$= \$5,400$$

$$F_{e2} = (1 - 0.40)(0.30)(25,000)$$

$$= \$4,500$$

The debt interest for the year j, I_j, is determined using the equation

$$I_j = (c)(k_d)B_{j-1} \qquad (10\text{-}8)$$

where k_d is the *new* debt interest rate. For this example, Eq. (10-8) gives

$$I_1 = (0.40)(0.175)(30{,}000)$$
$$= \$2{,}100$$
$$I_2 = (0.40)(0.175)(25{,}000)$$
$$= \$1{,}750$$

For replacement studies, the equation for taxes given in Chapter 6 must be modified to

$$t_j = \frac{T}{1-T}(D_{bj} + F_{ej} + I_j - I_{tj} - D_j) \qquad (10\text{-}9)$$

The difference between Eq. (10-9) and Eq. (6-12) are the I_j and I_{tj} terms. These terms do not appear in Eq. (6-12) because they are equal when *new projects* are being considered such as in Chapters 6 and 9. However, in replacement analysis, these terms are not equal because the interest for tax purposes, I_{tj}, is based, as previously mentioned, on the debt capital available at the original purchase time of the existing asset. For this example, the taxes for the first two years, using Eq. (10-9), are

$$t_1 = \frac{0.52}{1-0.52}(5{,}000 + 5{,}400 + 2{,}100 - 2{,}460 - 0)$$
$$= \$10{,}876$$
$$t_2 = \frac{0.52}{1-0.52}(5{,}000 + 4{,}500 + 1{,}750 - 2{,}040 - 0)$$
$$= \$9{,}977$$

The value zero is included in these two calculations to point out that the tax depreciation is considered. In general, the tax depreciation is not necessarily zero.

The yearly revenue requirements are determined using the equation

$$R_j = D_{bj} + F_{ej} + I_j + t_j + C_j \qquad (10\text{-}10)$$

For example, the revenue requirements for the first two years, using Eq. (10-10), are

$$R_1 = 5,000 + 5,400 + 2,100 + 10,876 + 7,000$$

$$= \$30,376$$

$$R_2 = 5,000 + 4,500 + 1,750 + 9,977 + 7,000$$

$$= \$28,227$$

The next step is to determine the minimum annual revenue requirements for the new asset using the procedures given in Chapter 6. For this example, these values are given in Table 10-14.

The next step is to determine the equivalent annual revenue requirements for the existing and new assets using Eq. (6-12). These values, for this example, are

$$E_d = [30,376 \ (P/F \ 25,1) + 28,227 \ (P/F \ 25,2)$$
$$+ \ldots + 21,780 \ (P/F \ 25,5)] \ (A/P \ 25,5)$$

$$= [72,656] \ (0.3718)$$

$$= \$27,014$$

TABLE 10-14

Revenue Requirements for New Asset

(Example 10-4)

End of Year	Book Depreciation D_b	Tax Depreciation D	Book Value B	Equity Return F_e	Debt Interest I	Tax t	Operation and Maintenance C	Minimum Annual Revenue Requirement R
0	—	—	$60,000	—	—	—	—	—
1	$5,400	$20,000	54,600	$10,800	$4,200	$-4,117	$4,000	$20,283
2	5,400	16,000	49,200	9,828	3,822	− 836	4,000	22,214
3	5,400	12,000	43,800	8,856	3,444	2,444	4,000	24,144
4	5,400	8,000	38,400	7,884	3,066	5,724	4,000	26,074
5	5,400	4,000	33,000	6,912	2,688	9,004	4,000	28,004
6	5,400	—	27,600	5,940	2,310	12,285	4,000	29,935
7	5,400	—	22,200	4,968	1,932	11,232	4,000	27,532
8	5,400	—	16,800	3,996	1,554	10,179	4,000	25,129
9	5,400	—	11,400	3,024	1,176	9,126	4,000	22,726
10	5,400	—	6,000	2,052	798	8,073	4,000	20,323

$$E_n = [20{,}283\,(P/F\ 25{,}1) + 22{,}214\,(P/F\ 25{,}2)$$
$$+ \ldots + 20{,}323\,(P/F\ 25{,}10)]\,(A/P\ 25{,}10)$$
$$= [85{,}731]\,(0.2801)$$
$$= \$24{,}013$$

Finally, a comparison is made of both the yearly revenue requirements (short-term effects) and the equivalent annual revenue requirements (long-term effects). With the cycling assumption, the basis for this comparison is shown in Table 10-15. This comparison indicates that purchasing the new asset is probably the better alternative. If this is the decision, it should be noted that this decision is different from the deci-

TABLE 10-15

Comparison of Replacement Alternatives for an Infinite Service Life

(Example 10-4)

End of Year	Existing Asset		New Asset	
	Annual Cost	Equivalent Cost	Annual Cost	Equivalent Cost
0	—	—	—	—
1	$30,376	$27,014	$20,283	$24,013
2	28,227	27,014	22,214	24,013
•	•	•	•	•
•	•	•	•	•
•	•	•	•	•
5	21,780	27,014	28,004	24,013
6	20,283	24,013	29,935	24,013
•	•	•	•	•
•	•	•	•	•
•	•	•	•	•
10	28,004	24,013	20,323	24,013
11	29,935	24,013	20,283	24,013
•	•	•	•	•
•	•	•	•	•
•	•	•	•	•
15	$20,323	$24,013	$28,004	$24,013
•	•	•	•	•
•	•	•	•	•
•	•	•	•	•
∞	•	•	•	•

sion indicated in Example 10-1. This difference in decision is due largely to the explicit consideration of taxes in this example.

Finite Service Life In Example 10-4 an infinite service life is specified. If a finite service life is specified, the basic procedure discussed in the conventional approach is applicable to the revenue requirement approach. That is, a salvage value for the new asset must be estimated at the end of some period of use. This value is then used as the book depreciation salvage value to determine the revenue requirements for the new asset's period of use. This revenue requirements become the revenue requirements for an asset from the end of a cycle to the service life. The following example discusses the case of a finite service life in greater detail.

Example 10-5

Repeat Example 10-4 with the condition that the service life is (a) ten years and (b) fifteen years. Assume for this example that the salvage value of the new asset after five years of use is $33,000 and that there are no tax effects on the gains and losses resulting from the disposal of the assets.

For Part a, it is necessary to determine the annual revenue requirements for both alternatives over the ten-year service. Determining these revenue requirements for this example is a relatively simple matter because they have already been determined in previous examples and because of the "convenient" estimate of a salvage value ($33,000) for the new asset after five years of use. The revenue requirements for the alternative of buying a new asset are the same as those given in Table 10-14 since the life of the new asset and the service life are the same. For the alternative of keeping the existing asset, the revenue requirements for the first five years are the same as those given in Table 10-13. For years six through ten, the annual revenue requirements are the same as the annual revenue requirements for years one through five in Table 10-14. This is because of the assumption that the new asset replaces the existing asset at the end of its life and the estimate of a $33,000 salvage value for the new asset after five years of use. The $33,000 salvage value is exactly equal to the book value of the new asset after five years (see Table 10-14). Consequently, the revenue requirements are the same. If some salvage value other than $33,000 is estimated, it is necessary to recalculate the revenue requirements for the new asset's period of use (five years in this example). A comparison of the annual revenue requirements is given in Table 10-16. The equivalent annual cost for the alternative of buying a new asset ($24,013) is determined in Example 10-4. The

TABLE 10-16

Comparison of Replacement Alternatives for a Ten-Year Service Life

(Example 10-5)

End of Year	Existing Asset		New Asset	
	Annual Cost	Equivalent Cost	Annual Cost	Equivalent Cost
0	—	—	—	—
1	$30,376	$26,103	$20,283	$24,013
2	28,227	26,103	22,214	24,013
3	26,078	26,103	24,144	24,013
4	23,929	26,103	26,074	24,013
5	21,780	26,103	28,004	24,013
6	20,283	26,103	29,935	24,013
7	22,214	26,103	27,532	24,013
8	24,144	26,103	25,129	24,013
9	26,074	26,103	22,726	24,013
10	28,004	26,103	20,323	24,013

equivalent annual cost for the alternative of keeping the existing asset is obtained from

$$E_d = [30,376 \ (P/F \ 25,1) + 28,227 \ (P/F \ 25,2)$$
$$+ \ldots + 20,283 \ (P/F \ 25,6) + \ldots$$
$$+ 28,004 \ (P/F \ 25,10)] \ (A/P \ 25,10)$$

$$= [93,190] \ (0.2801)$$

$$= \$26,103$$

A comparison of the values in Table 10-16 indicates that the most probable choice of an alternative is to purchase a new asset.

Part b of this example specifies a finite service life of fifteen years. For this service life most of the annual revenue requirements have been determined in previous examples. These revenue requirements and their equivalent annual amounts are given in Table 10-17. For the alternative of keeping the existing asset, the first five years of revenue requirements are the same as those given in Table 10-13 and the revenue requirements for years six through fifteen are the same as those given in Table 10-14. For the alternative of buying a new asset, the annual revenue requirements for the first ten years are the same as those given in Table 10-14. For years eleven through fifteen, the revenue require-

TABLE 10-17

Cost Comparison of Replacement Alternatives
for a Service Life of Fifteen Years

(Example 10-5)

End of Year	Existing Asset Annual Cost	Existing Asset Equivalent Cost	New Asset Annual Cost	New Asset Equivalent Cost
0	—	—	—	—
1	$30,376	$26,104	$20,283	$23,956
2	28,227	26,104	22,214	23,956
3	26,078	26,104	24,144	23,956
4	23,929	26,104	26,074	23,956
5	21,780	26,104	28,004	23,956
6	20,283	26,104	29,935	23,956
7	22,214	26,104	27,532	23,956
8	24,144	26,104	25,129	23,956
9	26,074	26,104	22,726	23,956
10	28,004	26,104	20,323	23,956
11	29,935	26,104	20,283	23,956
12	27,532	26,104	22,214	23,956
13	25,129	26,104	24,144	23,956
14	22,726	26,104	26,074	23,956
15	20,323	26,104	28,004	23,956

ments are the same as years one through five in Table 10-14 due to the convenient salvage value ($33,000). The equivalent annual costs given in Table 10-17 for the two alternatives are calculated in the following manner:

$$E_d = [30,376 \, (P/F \ 25,1) + 28,227 \, (P/F \ 25,2)$$
$$+ \ldots + 20,283 \, (P/F \ 25,6)$$
$$+ \ldots + 20,323 \, (P/F \ 25,15)] \, (A/P \ 25,15)$$

$$= [100,749] \, (0.2591)$$

$$= \$26,104$$

$$E_n = [20,283 \, (P/F \ 25,1) + 22,214 \, (P/F \ 25,2)$$
$$+ \ldots + 29,935 \, (P/F \ 25,6)$$
$$+ \ldots + 28,004 \, (P/F \ 25,15)] \, (A/P \ 25,15)$$

$$= [92,460] \, (0.2591)$$

$$= \$23,956$$

A comparison of the values in Table 10-17 indicates that the most probable choice is the alternative of buying a new asset.

Tax Effects on the Disposal of Assets

The previous examples in this chapter do not consider any tax effects on the gains and losses that result from the implied disposal of assets at the end of their cost cycle. This is the usual approach because most replacement studies involve like-kind exchanges and/or the assets are a part of some multiple asset depreciation account (see Chapter 4). Tax effects are therefore not applicable. However, if tax effects on gains and losses are considered applicable, they are included in replacement studies in basically the same way as they are in cost comparisons (Chapter 9). That is, Eq. (9-16) is used to change the tax effect into a revenue requirement effect. This revenue requirement effect is then combined with the annual revenue requirement in the year the tax effect is expected to be experienced. There is one exception to this procedure. The exception is the treatment of the tax effect that may result from a difference between the *present reliable salvage value* and the *present tax salvage value* of the existing asset. Any tax effect resulting from this difference is combined with the present realizable salvage value. This combined value becomes the basis for determining the book depreciation for the remaining life of the existing asset. The basis for this treatment of the tax effect resulting from any difference between the present and tax salvage values is that the existing asset can return to the company, at the present time, the combined salvage and tax effect. However, if the company chooses to continue with the existing asset, the company is, in effect, investing the combined salvage and tax effect in the alternative of keeping the existing asset. Consequently, this combined value must be recovered, minus the book salvage value, over the remaining life of the existing asset.

Example 10-6

In this example Part a of Example 10-5 is repeated, and only the tax effects on the disposal of the assets are taken into account. In this example it is assumed that the present realizable salvage value of the existing asset is $30,000 and the salvage value of the existing asset after five years of service (estimated remaining life) is still $5,000. At other points in time, however, it is assumed that the realizable salvage values for both the existing and new assets are equal to the book value, given by the book depreciation schedule, at the same points in time. This assumption is, of course, not required but it does facilitate the discussion in this example. It is also assumed in this example that the assets are Section 1245 Property (see Chapter 4).

The present tax salvage value is zero. Therefore, a gain of

$$\text{gain} = 30,000 - 0$$

$$= \$30,000$$

is realized if the existing asset is sold at its present realizable salvage value of \$30,000. The zero tax salvage is included in this calculation to show the role of the tax salvage value in determining the tax effect, since it is possible to have a tax salvage that is not zero. Since the \$30,000 value is a gain, this can mean an additional tax of

$$30,000\,(0.52) = \$15,600$$

for Section 1245 Property. Consequently, the combined effect of the present realizable salvage value and the additional taxes is

$$30,000 - 15,600 = \$14,400$$

This combined effect (\$14,400) is the net value that the existing asset can return at the present time to the company. Therefore, this net value is the amount of money the company is initially "investing" if the existing asset is continued. In this example the tax effect is subtracted since a gain results if the existing asset is sold, and this gain implies additional taxes. If the asset is sold and there is a loss, this means a decrease in taxes. Consequently, the tax effect is added to the present net realizable salvage value.

Using the net value (\$14,400), the book depreciation (capital recovery) for the existing asset over its remaining life is

$$D_b = \frac{14,400 - 5,000}{5}$$

$$= \$1,880 \text{ per year}$$

The annual revenue requirements are determined for the existing asset using this book depreciation (\$1,880) and the procedures given in Example 10-4. These revenue requirements are given in Table 10-18. The revenue requirement for the fifth year in Table 10-18 is adjusted for the tax effect on the disposal of the existing asset. Using the data in Table 10-18, the revenue requirement for the fifth year without the tax effect is

$$R_5 = 1,880 + 1,238 + 482 + 3,055 + 7,000$$

$$= \$13,655$$

The realizable salvage value in the fifth year is given as \$5,000 and the

TABLE 10-18

Existing Asset with Tax Effects

(Example 10-6)

End of Year	Book Depre- ciation D_b	Tax Depre- ciation D	Book Value B	Equity Return F_e	Debt Interest I	Tax Debt Interest I_t	Taxes t	Operation and Mainte- nance C	Minimum Annual Revenue Require- ment R
0	—	—	$14,400	—	—	—	—	—	—
1	$1,880	0	12,520	$2,592	$1,008	$2,460	$3,272	$7,000	$15,752
2	1,880	0	10,640	2,254	876	2,040	3,217	7,000	15,227
3	1,880	0	8,760	1,915	745	1,620	3,163	7,000	14,703
4	1,880	0	6,880	1,577	613	1,200	3,109	7,000	14,179
5	1,880	0	5,000	1,238	482	780	3,055	7,000	19,072[a]

[a] Includes a tax effect of $\dfrac{(5,000 - 0)\,(0.52)}{1 - 0.52} = \$5,417.$

tax salvage value at the same time is zero. The revenue requirement for the fifth year adjusted for the tax effect is

$$R_5 = 13,655 + \frac{5,000\,(0.52)}{1 - 0.52}$$

$$= \$19,072$$

Now the revenue requirements given in Table 10-18 are the revenue requirements for the first five years for the alternative of keeping the existing asset. The revenue requirements for years six through ten are the same as those given in Table 10-14 except the revenue requirement for year ten must be adjusted for the tax effect. The tax salvage value at the end of five years for the *new* asset is zero (see Table 10-14), and the net realizable salvage value at the end of five years is $33,000 (see Table 10-14) since it is assumed in this example that realizable salvage value equals the book value. This difference in tax and realizable salvage value means an increase in taxes. Therefore, the revenue requirement for the tenth year for the alternative of keeping the existing asset is

$$R_{10} = 28,004 + \frac{(33,000 - 0)\,(0.52)}{1 - 0.52}$$

$$= \$63,754$$

where the value $28,004 is obtained from Table 10-14.

The revenue requirements for the alternative of buying a new asset are the same as those given in Table 10-14 except the revenue requirement for the tenth year must be adjusted for the tax effect. For the tenth year, the tax salvage and realizable salvage values for the new asset are, respectively, zero and $6,000 (see Table 10-14). Since the difference is a gain, the revenue requirement for the tenth year for the alternative of buying a new asset is

$$R_{10} = 20,323 + \frac{(6,000)(0.52)}{1 - 0.52}$$

$$= \$26,823$$

The final cost comparison with tax effects is shown in Table 10-19 where the equivalent costs for the two alternatives are calculated in the following manner.

$$E_d = [15,752 \, (P/F \; 25,1) + 15,227 \, (P/F \; 25,2)$$
$$+ \ldots + 63,754 \, (P/F \; 25,10)] \, (A/P \; 25,10)$$

$$= [66,304] \, (0.2801)$$

$$= \$18,570$$

$$E_n = [20,283 \, (P/F \; 25,1) + 22,214 \, (P/F \; 25,2)$$
$$+ \ldots + (26,823) \, (P/F \; 25,10)] \, (A/P \; 25,10)$$

$$= [86,429] \, (0.2801)$$

$$= \$24,209$$

The costs in Table 10-19 indicate that keeping the existing asset is the best alternative.

Investment Tax Credits and Penalties   The previous examples do not consider the possibilities of investment tax credits or penalties. In replacement studies, it is very likely that the investment tax credit is applicable to a new asset but not applicable to the present realizable salvage value of the existing asset, since any applicable investment tax credit is taken at the time of an existing asset's original purchase. Also, it is possible to have an investment tax penalty because of the early disposal of the existing asset. That is, the disposal of an asset before the end of its tax depreciation life may result in an investment tax penalty if the proportion of the investment tax credit indicated by the tax depreciation life is taken at the time of its original purchase.

The procedures for including the investment tax credit in the revenue requirements for a new asset involved in a replacement study

TABLE 10-19

Revenue Requirements with Tax Effects

(Example 10-6)

| End of Year | Existing Asset | | New Asset | |
	Annual Cost	Equivalent Cost	Annual Cost	Equivalent Cost
0	—	—	—	—
1	$15,752	$18,570	$20,283	$24,209
2	15,227	18,570	22,214	24,209
3	14,703	18,570	24,144	24,209
4	14,179	18,570	26,074	24,209
5	19,072	18,570	28,004	24,209
6	20,283	18,570	29,935	24,209
7	22,214	18,570	27,532	24,209
8	24,144	18,570	25,129	24,209
9	26,074	18,570	22,726	24,209
10	63,754	18,570	26,823	24,209

are the same as the procedures presented in Chapters 6 and 9. For example, if the investment tax credit is included in the replacement comparison shown in Table 10-19, the first year revenue requirements for the new asset should be decreased by the amount

$$\frac{2}{3}\left[\frac{(0.10)\,(60,000)}{1-0.52}\right] = \$8,333$$

Only two-thirds of the full investment tax credit is taken in this calculation because the tax depreciation life in this example is five years. Consequently, the revenue requirement for the alternative of keeping the existing asset in year six and the revenue requirement for the alternative of purchasing a new asset in year one are changed to

$$R = 20,283 - 8,333$$
$$= \$11,950$$

The remaining revenue requirements for the two alternatives in Table 10-19 do not change.

The replacement comparison in Table 10-19 does not involve any investment tax penalties since there are no early disposals of assets. However, if there are investment tax penalties, they are included in a replacement comparison by dividing the investment tax penalty by the term $(1 - T)$ and then adding this result to the revenue requirement for the year in which the penalty occurs. There is one exception to this procedure for investment tax penalties. This exception occurs if the disposal of an existing asset *at the present time* results in an investment tax penalty. For this exception, the investment tax penalty is only experienced if the new asset is purchased. Therefore, the investment tax penalty, divided by term $(1 - T)$, is added to the first year revenue requirement of the *new asset*.

ANOTHER APPROACH TO THE OVERHAUL ALTERNATIVE

The conventional approach to the overhaul alternative in replacement studies was discussed previously in this chapter. This section discusses the use of revenue requirements for an overhaul alternative. In order to use revenue requirements for an overhaul alternative, certain modifications must be made to the previous definition of the minimum annual revenue requirements. These modifications are due largely to the fact that in an overhaul alternative there are two related but, in some ways, separate investments. The first investment is the present realizable salvage value of the existing asset. The second investment is the initial cost of the overhaul or at least a part of the initial cost. It is sometimes possible to expense a part of the initial cost of an overhaul. The minimum annual revenue requirements for an overhaul alternative are given by

$$R_j = D_{bj} + D'_{bj} + F_{ej} + F_{dj} + F'_{ej} + F'_{dj} + C_j + C'_j + t_j \qquad (10\text{-}11)$$

The various variables in Eq. (10-11) and the procedures for calculating their values are defined and discussed in the following example.

Example 10-7 _____

In this example the minimum annual revenue requirements are determined for the overhaul alternative described in Example 10-3 with certain modifications. One modification is that of the $18,000 required for the overhaul; $4,000 can be expensed. The remaining part of the overhaul ($14,000) is to be depreciated for tax purposes on the basis of SYD depreciation over a five-year period. The total salvage value ($4,000) given in Example 10-3 is assumed to be divided into two parts for book depreciation (capital recovery) and tax depreciation purposes. For the existing asset, the salvage value is $2,000 and for the overhaul part the salvage value is $2,000. Also, it is assumed in this example that there are no tax effects on the gains and losses resulting from the disposal of the existing asset. The minimum annual revenue requirements for the overhaul are shown in Table 10-20 and explained in the following discussion.

The tax depreciation for the existing asset, D, and the tax debt interest, I_t, are obtained from Table 10-12 and are the remaining amounts based on the original data for the existing asset. The reasons for needing this data are explained in Example 10-4.

The tax depreciation amounts for the depreciable portion of the overhaul, D', are obtained using SYD depreciation. For example,

TABLE 10-20

Revenue Requirements for the Overhaul Alternative

(Example 10-7)

End of Year	Tax Depreciation Existing D	Tax Depreciation Overhaul D'	Tax Interest Existing I_t	Book Depreciation Overhaul D'_b	Book Value Overhaul B'	Debt Interest Overhaul F'_d	Equity Return Overhaul F'_e	Book Depreciation Existing D_b	Book Value Existing B
0	—	—	—	—	$14,000	—	—	—	$30,000
1	$0	$4,000	$2,460	$1,500	12,500	$980	$2,520	$3,500	26,500
2	0	3,200	2,040	1,500	11,000	875	2,250	3,500	23,000
3	0	2,400	1,620	1,500	9,500	770	1,980	3,500	19,500
4	0	1,600	1,200	1,500	8,000	665	1,710	3,500	16,000
5	0	800	780	1,500	6,500	560	1,440	3,500	12,500
6	0	—	—	1,500	5,000	455	1,170	3,500	9,000
7	0	—	—	1,500	3,500	350	900	3,500	5,500
8	0	—	—	1,500	2,000	245	630	3,500	2,000

End of Year	Debt Interest Existing F_d	Equity Return Existing F_e	Maintenance and Operation C	Overhaul Cost Expensed C'	t	R
0	—	—	—	—	—	—
1	$2,100	$5,400	$5,000	$4,000	$9,273	$34,273
2	1,855	4,770	5,000	—	9,354	29,104
3	1,610	4,140	5,000	—	9,436	27,936
4	1,365	3,510	5,000	—	9,517	26,767
5	1,120	2,880	5,000	—	9,598	25,598
6	875	2,250	5,000	—	10,069	24,819
7	630	1,620	5,000	—	8,829	22,329
8	385	990	5,000	—	7,589	19,839

$$D'_1 = \frac{5}{15}(14{,}000 - 2{,}000)$$

$$= \$4{,}000$$

$$D'_2 = \frac{4}{15}(14{,}000 - 2{,}000)$$

$$= \$3{,}200$$

In this example the book depreciation (capital recovery) for the overhaul portion is calculated assuming straight-line depreciation

$$D'_b = \frac{14{,}000 - 2{,}000}{8}$$

$$= \$1{,}500 \text{ per year}$$

where the $2,000 is the part of the total salvage value ($4,000) that is attributed to the overhaul and eight years is the life of the overhaul.

The book value of the overhaul at the end of year j, B', is determined using the relationship

$$B'_j = B'_0 - \sum_{x=1}^{j} D'_{bx} \qquad (10\text{-}12)$$

For example, the book values for years one and two are

$$B'_0 = \$14{,}000$$

$$B'_1 = 14{,}000 - 1{,}500 = \$12{,}500$$

$$B'_2 = 14{,}000 - 2\,(1{,}500) = \$11{,}000$$

The debt interest for the overhaul, F'_{dj}, for the year j is determined using the relationship

$$F'_{dj} = (c)k_d\,(B'_{j-1}) \qquad (10\text{-}13)$$

where c is the debt ratio and k_d is the *new* debt interest rate. For this example, Eq. (10-13) gives

$$F'_{d1} = (0.40)\,(0.175)\,(14{,}000)$$

$$= \$980$$

$$F'_{d2} = (0.40)\,(0.175)\,(12{,}500)$$

$$= \$875$$

The required equity return on the overhaul for the year j, F'_{ej}, is determined using the relationship

$$F'_{ej} = (1 - c)k_e (B'_{j-1}) \qquad (10\text{-}14)$$

where k_e is the *new* required rate of return on equity. For this example, Eq. (10-14) gives

$$F'_{e\,1} = (1 - 0.4) (0.30) (14{,}000)$$

$$= \$2{,}520$$

$$F'_{e\,2} = (1 - 0.4) (0.30) (12{,}500)$$

$$= \$2{,}250$$

The book depreciation (capital recovery) for the existing asset is calculated in this example assuming straight-line depreciation

$$D_b = \frac{30{,}000 - 2{,}000}{8}$$

$$= \$3{,}500 \text{ per year}$$

The \$30,000 amount is the present realizable salvage value, and the \$2,000 is the part of the salvage value that is attributed to the existing asset.

The book value of the existing asset at the end of year j, B_j, is determined using the relationship

$$B_j = B_0 - \sum_{x=1}^{j} D_{bx} \qquad (10\text{-}15)$$

For example, the book value for years one and two are

$$B_0 = \$30{,}000$$

$$B_1 = 30{,}000 - 3{,}500$$

$$= \$26{,}500$$

$$B_2 = 30{,}000 - 2\,(3{,}500)$$

$$= \$23{,}000$$

The debt interest for the existing asset, F_{dj}, for the year j is determined using the relationship

$$F_{dj} = (c)k_d (B_{j-1}) \qquad (10\text{-}16)$$

For this example, Eq. (10-16) gives for the first two years

$$F_{d1} = (0.40)\,(0.175)\,(30,000)$$
$$= \$2,100$$
$$F_{d2} = (0.40)\,(0.175)\,(26,500)$$
$$= \$1,855$$

The required equity return on the existing asset, F_{ej}, for the year j is determined using the relationship

$$F_{ej} = (1 - c)\,(k_e)\,(B_{j-1}) \tag{10-17}$$

For this example, Eq. (10-17) gives

$$F_{e1} = (1 - 0.40)\,(0.30)\,(30,000)$$
$$= \$5,400$$
$$F_{e2} = (1 - 0.40)\,(0.30)\,(26,500)$$
$$= \$4,770$$

The annual maintenance and operation costs, C, are given in the statement of the problem. The portion of the overhaul cost that can be expensed, C', is also given in the statement of the problem. This expensed portion of the overhaul cost only occurs in the first year, from the standpoint of the revenue requirements.

An expression for the taxes for year j, t_j, can be obtained by substituting Eq. (10-11) for G in the equation

$$t_j = (G_j - C_j - C'_j - D_j - D'_j - I_{tj} - F'_d)T \tag{10-18}$$

which, after rearranging and cancelling like-terms, gives

$$t_j = \frac{T}{1-T}\,(D_{bj} + D'_{bj} + F'_{ej} + F_{ej} + F_{dj} - D_j - D'_j - I_{tj}) \tag{10-19}$$

For example, Eq. (10-19) gives for the first two years

$$t_1 = \frac{0.52}{1-0.52}\,(3,500 + 1,500 + 2,520 + 5,400 + 2,100$$
$$- 0 - 4,000 - 2,460)$$
$$= \$9,273$$

$$t_2 = \frac{0.52}{1-0.52}\,(3,500 + 1,500 + 2,250 + 4,770 + 1,855$$
$$- 0 - 3,200 - 2,040)$$
$$= \$9,354$$

The revenue requirement for the year j, R_j, is calculated using Eq. (10-11). For, example, the revenue requirements for the first two years are

$$R_1 = 3{,}500 + 1{,}500 + 5{,}400 + 2{,}100 + 2{,}520 + 980$$
$$+ 5{,}000 + 4{,}000 + 9{,}273$$
$$= \$34{,}273$$
$$R_2 = 3{,}500 + 1{,}500 + 4{,}770 + 1{,}855 + 2{,}250 + 875$$
$$+ 5{,}000 + 0 + 9{,}354$$
$$= \$29{,}104$$

The equivalent annual amount of the revenue requirements in Table 10-20 is

$$E_o = [34{,}273 \, (P/F \, 25{,}1) + 29{,}104 \, (P/F \, 25{,}2)$$
$$+ \ldots + 19{,}839 \, (P/F \, 25{,}8)] \, (A/P \, 25{,}8)$$
$$= [94{,}216] \, (0.3004)$$
$$= \$28{,}302$$

In order to fully define the overhaul alternative, it is necessary to know the service life. Example 10-3, the basis of this example, specifies an infinite service life. Consequently, the cost data shown in Table 10-21 is the complete data for the overhaul alternative. It should be noted that the overhaul alternate uses the same assumption that was used previously for the existing asset. That is, the new asset replaces the overhauled asset at the end of its life. Consequently, the data in Table 10-21 beginning in year nine is data from Table 10-15 for the new asset.

If an overhaul alternative is a viable alternative in a replacement study, then its cost data is compared with the cost data for the alternatives of keeping the existing asset, without overhaul, and purchasing a new asset. For example, if the overhaul alternative in this example is a possible alternative in Example 10-4, the data in Table 10-21 is compared with the data in Table 10-15.

Some Comments　In Example 10-7, the service life is infinite. If the service life is finite, the same approach used for the existing asset in Example 10-5 is used for the overhaul alternative in determining the costs after the life of the overhaul. That is, the revenue requirements are determined for the period of time from the end of the overhaul's life to the service life, based on the assumption that the new asset replaces the overhaul.

TABLE 10-21

The Costs for an Overhaul Alternative
with an Infinite Service Life

(Example 10-7)

End of Year	Overhaul	
	Annual Cost	Equivalent Cost
0	—	—
1	$34,273	$28,302
2	29,104	28,302
3	27,936	28,302
4	26,767	28,302
5	25,598	28,302
6	24,819	28,302
7	22,329	28,302
8	19,839	28,302
9	20,283	24,013
10	22,214	24,013
•	•	•
•	•	•
•	•	•
18	20,323	24,013
•	•	•
•	•	•
•	•	•
∞	•	•

In Example 10-7 no tax effects on the gains and losses are included. If tax effects are included, they are included using the procedures discussed in Example 10-6. Also no investment tax credits or penalties are considered in Example 10-7. It is very possible for the depreciable portion of an overhaul's cost to qualify for the investment tax credit. If this is the case, the investment tax credit, divided by the term $(1 - T)$, is subtracted from the overhaul's first year revenue requirement. Any investment tax credit for the new asset is treated in the same manner as previously discussed. If there is an investment tax penalty resulting from the early disposal of the existing asset, the tax penalty is treated in the same manner as previously discussed. However, it should be realized that there is *only one investment tax penalty* even when there is an overhaul alternative.

ECONOMIC LIFE OF AN ASSET

In all of the previous examples, the annual cost of operation and mainte-nance is a constant. However, when the annual cost of operation and maintenance increases yearly for an asset, it is possible to define an economic life for the asset. The economic life is the number of years of use that minimizes an asset's equivalent annual cost. Theoretically, at the end of an asset's economic life, it is replaced with another asset having the same cost data as the initial asset. This replacement is repeated over and over again. In this way, the costs over a period of time are minimized. Also, in comparing assets on the basis of costs, the cost used in the comparison should be based on each asset's respective economic life.

The economic life occurs, with yearly increasing operation and maintenance costs, because the total equivalent annual cost consists of an increasing and a decreasing cost component. That is, the equivalent annual amounts of the yearly operations and maintenance costs increase as the years of use increase. At the same time, the equivalent annual cost of the capital recovery and return decreases as the number of years of use increases. The economic life can be determined using either a con-ventional or revenue requirement approach. These two approaches are presented in the following examples.

Example 10-8

In this example, a conventional approach is used to determine the economic life of an asset having the cost data in Table 10-22. Some of the data in Table 10-22 is not needed here, but is used in a later example that presents the revenue requirement approach to determining the economic life. In this way, a comparison of the two approaches is possible.

Basically, the conventional approach involves the determination of the asset's equivalent annual costs for various use periods. These equivalent annual costs are calculated using the equation

$$E'_u = (K - L_u)(A/P\ k'_b, u) + L_u(k'_b)$$

$$+ (A/P\ k'_b, u)\left[\sum_{j=1}^{u} C_j(P/F\ k'_b, j)\right] \quad (10\text{-}20)$$

where

E'_u = the equivalent annual cost for a period of u years

C_j = operation and maintenance cost for the year j

L_u = salvage value at the end of u years

TABLE 10-22

Cost Data

(Example 10-8)

Initial cost	$30,000
Tax depreciation	SYD
Life, years	5
Salvage value	$ 2,000
Tax rate	50%
Debt ratio	50%
Required return on equity	20%
Debt interest rate	10%

End of Year	Salvage Value	Operation and Maintenance
1	$15,000	$ 4,000
2	10,000	5,000
3	7,000	6,000
4	4,000	8,000
5	2,000	11,000
6	1,000	15,000
7	500	20,000

The remaining nomenclature in Eq. (10-20) has been defined previously.

The before-tax MARR value, k'_b, is determined using Eq. (9-1) and for this example is

$$k'_b = (0.5)\,(10) + \frac{(1-0.5)\,(20)}{1-0.5}$$

$$= 25\%$$

With this value (25%) and Eq. (10-20), the equivalent annual costs for the various periods of use given in Table 10-23 can be determined. For example,

$$E_1 = (30,000 - 15,000)\,(A/P\ 25,1) + 15,000\,(0.25)$$
$$+ (A/P\ 25,1)\,[4,000\,(P/F\ 25,1)]$$

$$= \$26,500$$

$$E_4 = (30,000 - 4,000)\,(A/P\ 25,4) + 4,000\,(0.25)$$
$$+ (A/P\ 25,4)\,[4,000\,(P/F\ 25,1) + 5,000\,(P/F\ 25,2)$$
$$+ 6,000\,(P/F\ 25,3) + 8,000\,(P/F\ 25,4)]$$

$$= \$17,399$$

TABLE 10-23

Equivalent Annual Costs for Various Periods of Use

(Example 10-8)

Period of Use	Equivalent Annual Cost E'_u
1	$26,500
2	20,832
3	18,385
4	17,399
5	16,991
6	16,948
7	17,199

$$
\begin{aligned}
E_6 = {} & (30,000 - 1,000)\,(A/P\ 25,6) + 1,000\,(0.25) \\
& + (A/P\ 25,6)\,[4,000\,(P/F\ 25,1) + 5,000\,(P/F\ 25,2) \\
& + 6,000\,(P/F\ 25,3) + 8,000\,(P/F\ 25,4) \\
& + 11,000\,(P/F\ 25,5) + 15,000\,(P/F\ 25,6)] \\
= {} & \$16,948
\end{aligned}
$$

A comparison of the equivalent annual costs in Table 10-23 indicates that the smallest value occurs after six years of use. Consequently, the economic life is six years. This implies that after six years of use the asset is replaced with another asset having the same cost data given in Table 10-22.

The economic life is sometimes approximated on the basis of a zero return ($k'_b = 0$). When this is done, the terminology is changed from equivalent annual costs to *average annual costs*. The average annual costs for u years, A_u, are determined using the equation

$$
A_u = \frac{P - L_u}{u} + \frac{\sum_{j=1}^{u} C_j}{u} \tag{10-21}
$$

For example, some selected average annual costs, using the data in Table 10-22 and Eq. (10-21), are

$$
\begin{aligned}
A_1 &= \frac{30,000 - 15,000}{1} + \frac{4,000}{1} \\
&= \$19,000
\end{aligned}
$$

$$A_4 = \frac{30,000 - 4,000}{4} + \frac{23,000}{4}$$

$$= \$12,250$$

$$A_6 = \frac{30,000 - 1,000}{6} + \frac{49,000}{6}$$

$$= \$13,000$$

The remaining average annual costs are given in Table 10-24. A comparison of the average annual costs in Table 10-24 indicates that the economic life is four years which is less than the economic life indicated by the equivalent annual costs (five years). This result can be generalized. That is, for the same cost data, the economic life indicated by the average annual costs is always less than the economic life indicated by the equivalent annual costs. However, the difference between these two economic lives is small; usually, only a difference of one or two years. As a result, because of their computational advantage, average annual costs are often used as a beginning point to narrow the range in which the equivalent annual costs must be calculated to determined the economic life of an asset.

Economic Life in Cost Comparisons   In addition to the use of the economic life to determine the time at which a particular asset should be replaced, the economic life is an important consideration in the comparison of assets. That is, all cost comparisons should be based on a comparison of the equivalent annual costs associated with the economic life of the assets.

TABLE 10-24

Average Annual Costs for Various Periods of Use

(Example 10-8)

Period of Use	Average Annual Cost A_u
1	$19,000
2	14,500
3	12,666
4	12,250
5	12,400
6	13,000
7	14,071

Example 10-9

In this example, the use of the economic life and associated equivalent annual costs in cost comprisons is explained.

Two assets, X and Y, have increasing operation and maintenance costs. The equivalent annual costs for various periods of use are determined using Eq. (10-20) and the results shown in Table 10-25 are obtained. Using the results given in Table 10-25, make a cost comparison of the two assets for the following service lives:

a. Infinite.
b. Four years.
c. Fifteen years.
d. Ten years.

Table 10-25 indicates that the economic lives for assets X and Y are four and six years respectively. Therefore, for an infinite service life, the comparison is between the equivalent annual costs for the economic lives. In this example, these equivalent annual costs are $16,000 and $18,000. A comparison of these equivalent annual costs indicates that asset X should be chosen since it has the smaller cost. This comparison implies the assumption that the cost data cycles for each alternative, and therefore the alternatives are replaced at the end of their respective economic lives.

For Part b where the service life is four years, a comparison of the equivalent annual costs for four years of service is made; namely, a comparison of $16,000 and $18,700 for this example. This comparison indicates asset X should be chosen.

TABLE 10-25

Equivalent Annual Costs for Assets X and Y

(Example 10-9)

Period of Use	Equivalent Annual Costs	
	Asset X	Asset Y
1	$19,000	$24,000
2	17,000	21,000
3	16,500	19,000
4	16,000	18,700
5	16,400	18,500
6	17,300	18,000
7	—	18,300
8	—	18,900

For Part c of this example, the service life is greater than the LCM of the economic lives of the alternatives (twelve years). Using the assumption mentioned in Chapter 9 for this case, the cost comparison is numerically the same as an infinite service life ($16,000 and $18,000 in this example).

For Part d, the equivalent annual costs that are to be compared are not as readily apparent as in the first three parts of this example. This is because the specified service life implies partial cycles of the cost data. That is, it is necessary to determine the equivalent annual cost for years nine and ten, E_A, for asset A and the equivalent annual cost for years seven through ten, E_B, for asset B. This situation is shown in Table 10-26. In order to determine values for E_A and E_B in Table 10-26 it is necessary to estimate the costs and salvage values for the partial cycles of each alternative. As mentioned in Chapter 9, the approach taken in this text is to estimate these costs and salvage values on the basis that the original cost data for each alternative cycles. Consequently, for this example, E_A is $17,000 and E_B is $18,700. These values for E_A and E_B are obtained from Table 10-25 and are based on a period of use indicated by the length of their partial cycles. That is, the partial cycle for asset X is two years (years nine and ten). Consequently, for asset X, the equivalent annual cost indicated in Table 10-25 for two years of use is $17,000. Similarly, the partial cycle for asset Y is four years (years seven through ten) and the equivalent annual cost indicated in Table 10-25 for four years of use is $18,700. With these values for E_A and E_B, the equivalent annual

TABLE 10-26

Annual Costs for Partial Cycles

(Example 10-9)

End of Year	Annual Costs	
	Asset X	Asset Y
0	—	—
1	$16,000	$18,000
2	16,000	18,000
3	16,000	18,000
4	16,000	18,000
5	16,000	18,000
6	16,000	18,000
7	16,000	E_B
8	16,000	E_B
9	E_A	E_B
10	E_A	E_B

costs shown in Table 10-27 form the basis of a cost comparison. The remaining step is to convert the costs in Table 10-27 to an equivalent annual amount for each alternative. For example, if the MARR value is 15%, the equivalent annual costs over the service life are

$$E'_X = [16,000 \ (P/A \ 15,8)$$
$$+ \ 17,000 \ (P/A \ 15,2) \ (P/F \ 15,8)] \ (A/P \ 15,10)$$
$$= [80,832] \ (0.1993)$$
$$= \$16,110$$
$$E'_Y = [18,000 \ (P/A \ 15,6)$$
$$+ \ 18,700 \ (P/A \ 15,4) \ (P/F \ 15,6)] \ (A/P \ 15,10)$$
$$= [91,201] \ (0.1993)$$
$$= \$18,176$$

which indicates that asset X should be chosen.

REVENUE REQUIREMENTS AND THE ECONOMIC LIFE

It is possible to use minimum annual revenue requirements to determine the economic life of an asset. However, if revenue requirements are

TABLE 10-27

Annual Costs for Partial Cycles

(Example 10-9)

End of Year	Annual Costs	
	Asset X	Asset Y
0	—	—
1	$16,000	$18,000
2	16,000	18,000
3	16,000	18,000
4	16,000	18,000
5	16,000	18,000
6	16,000	18,000
7	16,000	18,700
8	16,000	18,700
9	17,000	18,700
10	17,000	18,700

used, it is necessary to make some modifications to the procedures given in Chapter 6 for determining revenue requirements. These modifications are discussed in the following example.

Example 10-10

In this example, the economic life is determined for the asset described in Table 10-22 using minimum annual revenue requirements.

In Table 10-22, the book depreciation is not specified. It is not needed because the salvage values at the end of each year are given (estimated). These salvage values become the basis for determining the yearly book depreciation (capital recovery). Using the salvage value given in Table 10-22, the book depreciation amounts for the first three years are

$$D_{b\,1} = 30,000 - 15,000$$
$$= \$15,000$$
$$D_{b\,2} = 15,000 - 10,000$$
$$= \$5,000$$
$$D_{b\,3} = 10,000 - 7,000$$
$$= \$3,000$$

The remaining book depreciation values are given in Table 10-28. The book values given in Table 10-28 are the salvage values.

The tax depreciation amounts in Table 10-28 are calculated using SYD depreciation, a life of five years, and a salvage value of $2,000.

After determining the yearly book depreciation amounts, tax depreciation, and book values, the procedures given in Chapter 6 are used to determine all the other values given in Table 10-28 except for the equivalent annual cost, E. The equivalent annual cost is calculated for a period of usage. That is,

$$E_u = \left[\sum_{j=1}^{u} R_j \, (P/F \, k_b, j) \right] (A/P \, k_b, u) \qquad (10\text{-}22)$$

where k_b is determined using Eq. (5-5) and for this example is

$$k_b = (0.5)\,(10) + (1 - 0.50)\,(20)$$
$$= 15\%$$

For some selected periods of usage, Eq. (10-22) gives

$$E_{u\,1} = [32{,}167\,(P/F\ 15{,}1)]\,(A/P\ 15{,}1)$$

$$= \$32{,}167$$

$$E_{u\,2} = [32{,}167\,(P/F\ 15{,}1) + 11{,}283\,(P/F\ 15{,}2)]\,(A/P\ 15{,}2)$$

$$= \$22{,}453$$

$$E_{u\,5} = [32{,}167\,(P/F\ 15{,}1) + 11{,}283\,(P/F\ 15{,}2)$$
$$+\ 8{,}900\,(P/F\ 15{,}3) + 12{,}017\,(P/F\ 15{,}4)$$
$$+\ 14{,}133\,(P/F\ 15{,}5)]\,(A/P\ 15{,}5)$$

$$= \$16{,}780$$

A comparison of the equivalent annual amounts in Table 10-28 indicates that the smallest cost occurs at the end of five years of service. Consequently, the economic life is five years.

A Comment In theory, the concept of an economic life is sound. However, rarely is it used in practice. This is a result of several considerations: (1) the difficulty in estimating yearly salvage values and increasing operation and maintenance costs; (2) the assumption regarding repetitive cost cycles; and (3) assets are usually replaced on the basis of current costs rather than at the time of original purchase.

TABLE 10-28

Revenue Requirements for Economic Life Determination

(Example 10-10)

End of Year	Book Depreciation D_b	Book Value B	Tax Depreciation D	Equity Return F_e	Debt Interest I	Taxes t	Operation and Maintenance C	Minimum Annual Revenue Requirement R	Equivalent Annual Cost E
0	—	\$30,000	—	—	—	—	—	—	—
1	\$15,000	15,000	\$9,333	\$3,000	\$1,500	\$8,667	\$ 4,000	\$32,167	\$32,167
2	5,000	10,000	7,467	1,500	750	−967	5,000	11,283	22,453
3	3,000	7,000	5,600	1,000	500	−1,600	6,000	8,900	18,551
4	3,000	4,000	3,733	700	350	−33	8,000	12,017	17,244
5	2,000	2,000	1,867	400	200	533	11,000	14,133	16,780
6	1,000	1,000	—	200	100	1,200	15,000	17,500	16,861
7	500	500	—	100	50	600	20,000	21,250	17,259

PROBLEMS

10-1. A company is considering replacing certain equipment that has been in use for seven years. This equipment originally cost $150,000 and had an estimated salvage value of $10,000 at the end of twenty-five years. Operations and maintenance costs have amounted to $15,000 per year. If this existing equipment is continued, it is believed this annual cost of operation and maintenance will be the same. However, it is now estimated that the existing equipment will only last eight more years and have a salvage value of $8,000 at that time. The present realizable salvage value for the existing equipment is $80,000.

Present available equipment that provides equal service indicates that there may be an economic advantage to replacing the existing equipment. There is now equipment available that will reduce the annual cost of operation and maintenance to $5,000 per year. This new equipment initially costs $120,000, lasts fifteen years, and has a salvage value of $10,000.

Assuming the before-tax MARR value is 20%, make a before-tax equivalent annual cost comparison for the following service lives:

(a) Infinity.

(b) Eight years assuming the salvage value of the new equipment is $40,000 after eight years of use.

(c) Twenty years assuming the salvage values of the new equipment after twelve and five years of use are $15,000 and $45,000 respectively.

10-2. What is the sunk cost in Problem 10-1 assuming straight-line depreciation?

10-3. Determine the present realizable salvage value in Part (a) of Problem 10-1 that makes the equivalent annual costs equal. How could such a value be used for decision purposes?

10-4. Repeat Parts (a) and (c) of Problem 10-1 assuming there is an overhaul alternative that costs an additional $25,000, extends the life of the existing asset to ten years with a total salvage of $4,000, and reduces operation and maintenance costs to $8,000 per year. Also assume that the salvage value of the new equipment after ten years of use is $18,000.

10-5. Five years ago, an asset with the data shown below was purchased and put in service. The original estimate of the operation and maintenance costs ($6,000) has been low. The cost of operation and maintenance has amounted to $12,000 per year and is expected to continue at this amount if the asset is not replaced. Therefore, a replacement is being considered for the existing asset. The data for the replacement asset is given below. It is now estimated that the existing asset will last six more years and have a salvage value of $15,000 at that time. The realizable salvage value for the existing asset at the present time is $90,000. Under the following conditions, determine if the existing asset should be replaced:

(a) Infinite service life.

(b) There are no tax effects on the gains and losses resulting from the disposal of assets.

Original Data for Existing Asset

Initial cost	$150,000
Annual cost of operation and maintenance	$ 6,000
Tax depreciation	SYD
Life, years	10
Salvage value	$ 18,000
Book depreciation	SL
Life, years	15
Salvage value	$ 30,000
Debt ratio	40%
Required debt return	10%
Required equity return	20%
Investment tax rate	10%
Tax rate	52%

Data for Replacement Asset

Initial cost	$200,000
Annual cost of operation and maintenance	$ 5,000
Tax depreciation	SYD SL
Life, years	15
Salvage value	$ 20,000
Book depreciation	SL SYD
Life, years	7
Salvage value	$ 4,000
Debt ratio	40%
Required debt return	17.5%
Required equity return	30%
Investment tax rate	10%
Tax rate	52%

10-6. Repeat Problem 10-5 but assume that the service lives are (a) six years, (b) fifteen years, and (c) twenty-five years. Assume that the realizable salvage at any point in time for the new assets is equal to its book value at the same point in time.

10-7. Repeat Problem 10-5 only assume that tax effects on the gains and losses resulting from the disposal of assets are recognized. Also, assume that the assets are Section 1245 Property and that the realizable salvage values are equal to the book values at the same points in time except for the present realizable salvage value ($90,000).

10-8. It has been decided that it is possible to overhaul the existing asset in Problem 10-5. Using the data given below, determine the revenue requirements for the overhaul alternative and include these results in the comparison of alternatives in Problem 10-5.

Overhaul Data	
Total cost of overhaul	$40,000
Repair portion	$10,000
Depreciable portion	$30,000
Tax depreciation for overhaul	SYD
Life, years	7
Salvage value	$ 2,000
Book depreciation	SL
Life, years	10
Salvage value	$ 2,000
Total book salvage of overhaul and existing asset	$ 8,000
Annual operation and maintenance	$ 8,000
Investment tax credit	10%

10-9. If the initial cost of an asset is $50,000 and has the additional data given in the following table, determine the economic life if (a) MARR = 0% and (b) MARR = 15%.

Years of Use	Salvage Value	Operation and Maintenance
1	$34,000	$ 5,000
2	26,000	6,000
3	20,000	7,000
4	16,000	8,000
5	14,000	9,000
6	12,000	10,000
7	10,000	12,000
8	8,000	14,000
9	6,000	18,000
10	4,000	20,000

10-10. Using the data in Problem 10-9 and the additional data given below, determine the economic life of the asset using a revenue requirement approach.

Debt ratio	50%
Required return on equity	20%
Debt interest rate	10%
Tax rate	50%
Tax depreciation	SYD
Life, years	7
Salvage	$5,200

10-11. Repeat Problem 10-10 assuming the investment tax credit is applicable.

10-12. For two assets A and B, the equivalent annual costs for various periods of use have been determined with the results shown below. If MARR = 15%, determine the following:

(a) A cost comparison if the service life is infinite.
(b) A cost comparison if the service life is five years.
(c) A cost comparison if the service life is thirty years.
(d) A cost comparison if the service life is fifteen years.

ASSET A		ASSET B	
Years of Use	Equivalent Annual Cost	Years of Use	Equivalent Annual Cost
0	—	0	—
1	$50,000	1	$45,000
2	40,000	2	38,000
3	35,000	3	33,000
4	33,000	4	30,000
5	31,000	5	28,000
6	28,000	6	26,000
7	25,000	7	26,500
8	24,000	8	25,000
9	25,500	9	24,000
10	26,500	10	23,500
		11	22,000
		12	20,000
		13	21,500
		14	22,000
		15	23,000

APPENDIX

DISCRETE INTEREST FACTORS

TABLE A.1. ½% *Interest Factors for Annual Compounding Interest*

	Single Payment		Equal Payment Series				Uniform gradient-series factor
	Compound-amount factor	Present-worth factor	Compound-amount factor	Sinking-fund factor	Present-worth factor	Capital-recovery factor	
n	To find F Given P F/P i,n	To find P Given F P/F i,n	To find F Given A F/A i,n	To find A Given F A/F i,n	To find P Given A P/A i,n	To find A Given P A/P i,n	To find A Given G A/G i,n
1	1.005	0.9950	1.000	1.0000	0.9950	1.0050	0.0000
2	1.010	0.9901	2.005	0.4988	1.9851	0.5038	0.4988
3	1.015	0.9852	3.015	0.3317	2.9703	0.3367	0.9967
4	1.020	0.9803	4.030	0.2481	3.9505	0.2531	1.4938
5	1.025	0.9754	5.050	0.1980	4.9259	0.2030	1.9900
6	1.030	0.9705	6.076	0.1646	5.8964	0.1696	2.4855
7	1.036	0.9657	7.106	0.1407	6.8621	0.1457	2.9801
8	1.041	0.9609	8.141	0.1228	7.8230	0.1278	3.4738
9	1.046	0.9561	9.182	0.1089	8.7791	0.1139	3.9668
10	1.051	0.9514	10.228	0.0978	9.7304	0.1028	4.4589
11	1.056	0.9466	11.279	0.0887	10.6770	0.0937	4.9501
12	1.062	0.9419	12.336	0.0811	11.6189	0.0861	5.4406
13	1.067	0.9372	13.397	0.0747	12.5562	0.0797	5.9302
14	1.072	0.9326	14.464	0.0691	13.4887	0.0741	6.4190
15	1.078	0.9279	15.537	0.0644	14.4166	0.0694	6.9069
16	1.083	0.9233	16.614	0.0602	15.3399	0.0652	7.3940
17	1.088	0.9187	17.697	0.0565	16.2586	0.0615	7.8803
18	1.094	0.9141	18.786	0.0532	17.1728	0.0582	8.3658
19	1.099	0.9096	19.880	0.0503	18.0824	0.0553	8.8504
20	1.105	0.9051	20.979	0.0477	18.9874	0.0527	9.3342
21	1.110	0.9006	22.084	0.0453	19.8880	0.0503	9.8172
22	1.116	0.8961	23.194	0.0431	20.7841	0.0481	10.2993
23	1.122	0.8916	24.310	0.0411	21.6757	0.0461	10.7806
24	1.127	0.8872	25.432	0.0393	22.5629	0.0443	11.2611
25	1.133	0.8828	26.559	0.0377	23.4456	0.0427	11.7407
26	1.138	0.8784	27.692	0.0361	24.3240	0.0411	12.2195
27	1.144	0.8740	28.830	0.0347	25.1980	0.0397	12.6975
28	1.150	0.8697	29.975	0.0334	26.0677	0.0384	13.1747
29	1.156	0.8653	31.124	0.0321	26.9330	0.0371	13.6510
30	1.161	0.8610	32.280	0.0310	27.7941	0.0360	14.1265
31	1.167	0.8568	33.441	0.0299	28.6508	0.0349	14.6012
32	1.173	0.8525	34.609	0.0289	29.5033	0.0339	15.0750
33	1.179	0.8483	35.782	0.0280	30.3515	0.0330	15.5480
34	1.185	0.8440	36.961	0.0271	31.1956	0.0321	16.0202
35	1.191	0.8398	38.145	0.0262	32.0354	0.0312	16.4915
40	1.221	0.8191	44.159	0.0227	36.1722	0.0277	18.8358
45	1.252	0.7990	50.324	0.0199	40.2072	0.0249	21.1595
50	1.283	0.7793	56.645	0.0177	44.1428	0.0227	23.4624
55	1.316	0.7601	63.126	0.0159	47.9815	0.0209	25.7447
60	1.349	0.7414	69.770	0.0143	51.7256	0.0193	28.0064
65	1.383	0.7231	76.582	0.0131	55.3775	0.0181	30.2475
70	1.418	0.7053	83.566	0.0120	58.9394	0.0170	32.4680
75	1.454	0.6879	90.727	0.0110	62.4137	0.0160	34.6679
80	1.490	0.6710	98.068	0.0102	65.8023	0.0152	36.8474
85	1.528	0.6545	105.594	0.0095	69.1075	0.0145	39.0065
90	1.567	0.6384	113.311	0.0088	72.3313	0.0138	41.1451
95	1.606	0.6226	121.222	0.0083	75.4757	0.0133	43.2633
100	1.647	0.6073	129.334	0.0077	78.5427	0.0127	45.3613

TABLE A.2. ¾% *Interest Factors for Annual Compounding Interest*

	Single Payment		Equal Payment Series				Uniform gradient-series factor
	Compound-amount factor	Present-worth factor	Compound-amount factor	Sinking-fund factor	Present-worth factor	Capital-recovery factor	
n	To find F Given P F/P i, n	To find P Given F P/F i, n	To find F Given A F/A i, n	To find A Given F A/F i, n	To find P Given A P/A i, n	To find A Given P A/P i, n	To find A Given G A/G i, n
1	1.008	0.9926	1.000	1.0000	0.9926	1.0075	0.0000
2	1.015	0.9852	2.008	0.4981	1.9777	0.5056	0.4981
3	1.023	0.9778	3.023	0.3309	2.9556	0.3384	0.9950
4	1.030	0.9706	4.045	0.2472	3.9261	0.2547	1.4907
5	1.038	0.9633	5.076	0.1970	4.8894	0.2045	1.9851
6	1.046	0.9562	6.114	0.1636	5.8456	0.1711	2.4782
7	1.054	0.9491	7.159	0.1397	6.7946	0.1472	2.9701
8	1.062	0.9420	8.213	0.1218	7.7366	0.1293	3.4608
9	1.070	0.9350	9.275	0.1078	8.6716	0.1153	3.9502
10	1.078	0.9280	10.344	0.0967	9.5996	0.1042	4.4384
11	1.086	0.9211	11.422	0.0876	10.5207	0.0951	4.9253
12	1.094	0.9142	12.508	0.0800	11.4349	0.0875	5.4110
13	1.102	0.9074	13.601	0.0735	12.3424	0.0810	5.8954
14	1.110	0.9007	14.703	0.0680	13.2430	0.0755	6.3786
15	1.119	0.8940	15.814	0.0632	14.1370	0.0707	6.8606
16	1.127	0.8873	16.932	0.0591	15.0243	0.0666	7.3413
17	1.135	0.8807	18.059	0.0554	15.9050	0.0629	7.8207
18	1.144	0.8742	19.195	0.0521	16.7792	0.0596	8.2989
19	1.153	0.8677	20.339	0.0492	17.6468	0.0567	8.7759
20	1.161	0.8612	21.491	0.0465	18.5080	0.0540	9.2517
21	1.170	0.8548	22.652	0.0442	19.3628	0.0517	9.7261
22	1.179	0.8484	23.822	0.0420	20.2112	0.0495	10.1994
23	1.188	0.8421	25.001	0.0400	21.0533	0.0475	10.6714
24	1.196	0.8358	26.188	0.0382	21.8892	0.0457	11.1422
25	1.205	0.8296	27.385	0.0365	22.7188	0.0440	11.6117
26	1.214	0.8234	28.590	0.0350	23.5422	0.0425	12.0800
27	1.224	0.8173	29.805	0.0336	24.3595	0.0411	12.5470
28	1.233	0.8112	31.028	0.0322	25.1707	0.0397	13.0128
29	1.242	0.8052	32.261	0.0310	25.9759	0.0385	13.4774
30	1.251	0.7992	33.503	0.0299	26.7751	0.0374	13.9407
31	1.261	0.7932	34.754	0.0288	27.5683	0.0363	14.4028
32	1.270	0.7873	36.015	0.0278	28.3557	0.0353	14.8636
33	1.280	0.7815	37.285	0.0268	29.1371	0.0343	15.3232
34	1.289	0.7757	38.565	0.0259	29.9128	0.0334	15.7816
35	1.299	0.7699	39.854	0.0251	30.6827	0.0326	16.2387
40	1.348	0.7417	46.446	0.0215	34.4469	0.0290	18.5058
45	1.400	0.7145	53.290	0.0188	38.0732	0.0263	20.7421
50	1.453	0.6883	60.394	0.0166	41.5665	0.0241	22.9476
55	1.508	0.6630	67.769	0.0148	44.9316	0.0223	25.1223
60	1.566	0.6387	75.424	0.0133	48.1734	0.0208	27.2665
65	1.625	0.6153	83.371	0.0120	51.2963	0.0195	29.3801
70	1.687	0.5927	91.620	0.0109	54.3046	0.0184	31.4634
75	1.751	0.5710	100.183	0.0100	57.2027	0.0175	33.5163
80	1.818	0.5501	109.073	0.0092	59.9945	0.0167	35.5391
85	1.887	0.5299	118.300	0.0085	62.6838	0.0160	37.5318
90	1.959	0.5105	127.879	0.0078	65.2746	0.0153	39.4946
95	2.034	0.4917	137.823	0.0073	67.7704	0.0148	41.4277
100	2.111	0.4737	148.145	0.0068	70.1746	0.0143	43.3311

Reprinted, by permission, from H. J. Thuesen et al., *Engineering Economy*, pp. 537-577. Copyright © 1977 by Prentice-Hall Inc.

TABLE A.3. *1% Interest Factors for Annual Compounding Interest*

	Single Payment		Equal Payment Series				Uniform gradient-series factor
	Compound-amount factor	Present-worth factor	Compound-amount factor	Sinking-fund factor	Present-worth factor	Capital-recovery factor	
n	To find F Given P F/P i,n	To find P Given F P/F i,n	To find F Given A F/A i,n	To find A Given F A/F i,n	To find P Given A P/A i,n	To find A Given P A/P i,n	To find A Given G A/G i,n
1	1.010	0.9901	1.000	1.0000	0.9901	1.0100	0.0000
2	1.020	0.9803	2.010	0.4975	1.9704	0.5075	0.4975
3	1.030	0.9706	3.030	0.3300	2.9410	0.3400	0.9934
4	1.041	0.9610	4.060	0.2463	3.9020	0.2563	1.4876
5	1.051	0.9515	5.101	0.1960	4.8534	0.2060	1.9801
6	1.062	0.9421	6.152	0.1626	5.7955	0.1726	2.4710
7	1.072	0.9327	7.214	0.1386	6.7282	0.1486	2.9602
8	1.083	0.9235	8.286	0.1207	7.6517	0.1307	3.4478
9	1.094	0.9143	9.369	0.1068	8.5660	0.1168	3.9337
10	1.105	0.9053	10.462	0.0956	9.4713	0.1056	4.4179
11	1.116	0.8963	11.567	0.0865	10.3676	0.0965	4.9005
12	1.127	0.8875	12.683	0.0789	11.2551	0.0889	5.3815
13	1.138	0.8787	13.809	0.0724	12.1338	0.0824	5.8607
14	1.149	0.8700	14.947	0.0669	13.0037	0.0769	6.3384
15	1.161	0.8614	16.097	0.0621	13.8651	0.0721	6 8143
16	1.173	0.8528	17.258	0.0580	14.7179	0.0680	7.2887
17	1.184	0.8444	18.430	0.0543	15.5623	0.0643	7.7613
18	1.196	0.8360	19.615	0.0510	16.3983	0.0610	8.2323
19	1.208	0.8277	20.811	0.0481	17.2260	0.0581	8.7017
20	1.220	0.8196	22.019	0.0454	18.0456	0.0554	9.1694
21	1.232	0.8114	23.239	0.0430	18.8570	0.0530	9.6354
22	1.245	0.8034	24.472	0.0409	19.6604	0.0509	10.0998
23	1.257	0.7955	25.716	0.0389	20.4558	0.0489	10.5626
24	1.270	0.7876	26.973	0.0371	21.2434	0.0471	11.0237
25	1.282	0.7798	28.243	0.0354	22.0232	0.0454	11.4831
26	1.295	0.7721	29.526	0.0339	22.7952	0.0439	11.9409
27	1.308	0.7644	30.821	0.0325	23.5596	0.0425	12.3971
28	1.321	0.7568	32.129	0.0311	24.3165	0.0411	12.8516
29	1.335	0.7494	33.450	0.0299	25.0658	0.0399	13.3045
30	1.348	0.7419	34.785	0.0288	25.8077	0.0388	13.7557
31	1.361	0.7346	36.133	0.0277	26.5423	0.0377	14.2052
32	1.375	0.7273	37.494	0.0267	27.2696	0.0367	14.6532
33	1.389	0.7201	38.869	0.0257	27.9897	0.0357	15.0995
34	1.403	0.7130	40.258	0.0248	28.7027	0.0348	15.5441
35	1.417	0.7059	41.660	0.0240	29.4086	0.0340	15.9871
40	1.489	0.6717	48.886	0.0205	32.8347	0.0305	18.1776
45	1.565	0.6391	56.481	0.0177	36.0945	0.0277	20.3273
50	1.645	0.6080	64.463	0.0155	39.1961	0.0255	22.4363
55	1.729	0.5785	72.852	0.0137	42.1472	0.0237	24.5049
60	1.817	0.5505	81.670	0.0123	44.9550	0.0223	26.5333
65	1.909	0.5237	90.937	0.0110	47.6266	0.0210	28.5217
70	2.007	0.4983	100.676	0.0099	50.1685	0.0199	30.4703
75	2.109	0.4741	110.913	0.0090	52.5871	0.0190	32.3793
80	2.217	0.4511	121.672	0.0082	54.8882	0.0182	34.2492
85	2.330	0.4292	132.979	0.0075	57.0777	0.0175	36.0801
90	2.449	0.4084	144.863	0.0069	59.1609	0.0169	37.8725
95	2.574	0.3886	157.354	0.0064	61.1430	0.0164	39.6265
100	2.705	0.3697	170.481	0.0059	63.0289	0.0159	41.3426

Reprinted, by permission, from H. J. Thuesen et al., *Engineering Economy*, pp. 537-577. Copyright © 1977 by Prentice-Hall Inc.

TABLE A.4. *1¼% Interest Factors for Annual Compounding Interest*

	Single Payment		Equal Payment Series				Uniform gradient-series factor
	Compound-amount factor	Present-worth factor	Compound-amount factor	Sinking-fund factor	Present-worth factor	Capital-recovery factor	
n	To find F Given P $F/P\ i, n$	To find P Given F $P/F\ i, n$	To find F Given A $F/A\ i, n$	To find A Given F $A/F\ i, n$	To find P Given A $P/A\ i, n$	To find A Given P $A/P\ i, n$	To find A Given G $A/G\ i, n$
1	1.013	0.9877	1.000	1.0001	0.9877	1.0126	0.0000
2	1.025	0.9755	2.013	0.4970	1.9631	0.5095	0.4932
3	1.038	0.9635	3.038	0.3293	2.9265	0.3418	0.9895
4	1.051	0.9516	4.076	0.2454	3.8780	0.2579	1.4830
5	1.064	0.9398	5.127	0.1951	4.8177	0.2076	1.9729
6	1.077	0.9282	6.191	0.1616	5.7459	0.1741	2.4618
7	1.091	0.9168	7.268	0.1376	6.6627	0.1501	2.9491
8	1.105	0.9055	8.359	0.1197	7.5680	0.1322	3.4330
9	1.118	0.8943	9.463	0.1057	8.4623	0.1182	3.9158
10	1.132	0.8832	10.582	0.0946	9.3454	0.1071	4.3960
11	1.147	0.8723	11.714	0.0854	10.2177	0.0979	4.8744
12	1.161	0.8616	12.860	0.0778	11.0792	0.0903	5.3506
13	1.175	0.8509	14.021	0.0714	11.9300	0.0839	5.8248
14	1.190	0.8404	15.196	0.0659	12.7704	0.0784	6.2968
15	1.205	0.8300	16.386	0.0611	13.6004	0.0736	6.7669
16	1.220	0.8198	17.591	0.0569	14.4201	0.0694	7.2350
17	1.235	0.8097	18.811	0.0532	15.2298	0.0657	7.7009
18	1.251	0.7997	20.046	0.0499	16.0293	0.0624	8.1645
19	1.266	0.7898	21.296	0.0470	16.8191	0.0595	8.6264
20	1.282	0.7801	22.563	0.0444	17.5991	0.0569	9.0861
21	1.298	0.7704	23.845	0.0420	18.3695	0.0545	9.5439
22	1.314	0.7609	25.143	0.0398	19.1303	0.0523	9.9993
23	1.331	0.7515	26.457	0.0378	19.8818	0.0503	10.4528
24	1.347	0.7423	27.788	0.0360	20.6240	0.0485	10.9044
25	1.364	0.7331	29.135	0.0344	21.3570	0.0469	11.3539
26	1.381	0.7240	30.499	0.0328	22.0810	0.0453	11.8012
27	1.399	0.7151	31.880	0.0314	22.7960	0.0439	12.2465
28	1.416	0.7063	33.279	0.0301	23.5022	0.0426	12.6898
29	1.434	0.6976	34.695	0.0289	24.1998	0.0414	13.1311
30	1.452	0.6889	36.128	0.0277	24.8886	0.0402	13.5703
31	1.470	0.6804	37.580	0.0267	25.5690	0.0392	14.0074
32	1.488	0.6720	39.050	0.0257	26.2410	0.0382	14.4425
33	1.507	0.6637	40.538	0.0247	26.9047	0.0372	14.8756
34	1.526	0.6555	42.045	0.0238	27.5601	0.0363	15.3066
35	1.545	0.6475	43.570	0.0230	28.2075	0.0355	15.7357
40	1.644	0.6085	51.489	0.0195	31.3266	0.0320	17.8503
45	1.749	0.5718	59.915	0.0167	34.2578	0.0292	19.9144
50	1.861	0.5374	68.880	0.0146	37.0125	0.0271	21.9284
55	1.980	0.5050	78.421	0.0128	39.6013	0.0253	23.8925
60	2.107	0.4746	88.573	0.0113	42.0342	0.0238	25.8072
65	2.242	0.4460	99.375	0.0101	44.3206	0.0226	27.6730
70	2.386	0.4192	110.870	0.0091	46.4693	0.0216	29.4902
75	2.539	0.3939	123.101	0.0082	48.4886	0.0207	31.2594
80	2.702	0.3702	136.116	0.0074	50.3862	0.0199	32.9812
85	2.875	0.3479	149.965	0.0067	52.1696	0.0192	34.6560
90	3.059	0.3270	164.701	0.0061	53.8456	0.0186	36.2844
95	3.255	0.3073	180.382	0.0056	55.4207	0.0181	37.8671
100	3.463	0.2888	197.067	0.0051	56.9009	0.0176	39.4048

Reprinted, by permission, from H. J. Thuesen et al., *Engineering Economy*, pp. 537-577. Copyright © 1977 by Prentice-Hall Inc.

TABLE A.5. 1½% Interest Factors for Annual Compounding Interest

	Single Payment		Equal Payment Series				Uniform gradient-series factor
	Compound-amount factor	Present-worth factor	Compound-amount factor	Sinking-fund factor	Present-worth factor	Capital-recovery factor	
	To find F Given P	To find P Given F	To find F Given A	To find A Given F	To find P Given A	To find A Given P	To find A Given G
n	F/P i,n	P/F i,n	F/A i,n	A/F i,n	P/A i,n	A/P i,n	A/G i,n
1	1.015	0.9852	1.000	1.0000	0.9852	1.0150	0.0000
2	1.030	0.9707	2.015	0.4963	1.9559	0.5113	0.4963
3	1.046	0.9563	3.045	0.3284	2.9122	0.3434	0.9901
4	1.061	0.9422	4.091	0.2445	3.8544	0.2595	1.4814
5	1.077	0.9283	5.152	0.1941	4.7827	0.2091	1.9702
6	1.093	0.9146	6.230	0.1605	5.6972	0.1755	2.4566
7	1.110	0.9010	7.323	0.1366	6.5982	0.1516	2.9405
8	1.127	0.8877	8.433	0.1186	7.4859	0.1336	3.4219
9	1.143	0.8746	9.559	0.1046	8.3605	0.1196	3.9008
10	1.161	0.8617	10.703	0.0934	9.2222	0.1084	4.3772
11	1.178	0.8489	11.863	0.0843	10.0711	0.0993	4.8512
12	1.196	0.8364	13.041	0.0767	10.9075	0.0917	5.3227
13	1.214	0.8240	14.237	0.0703	11.7315	0.0853	5.7917
14	1.232	0.8119	15.450	0.0647	12.5434	0.0797	6.2582
15	1.250	0.7999	16.682	0.0600	13.3432	0.0750	6.7223
16	1.269	0.7880	17.932	0.0558	14.1313	0.0708	7.1839
17	1.288	0.7764	19.201	0.0521	14.9077	0.0671	7.6431
18	1.307	0.7649	20.489	0.0488	15.6726	0.0638	8.0997
19	1.327	0.7536	21.797	0.0459	16.4262	0.0609	8.5539
20	1.347	0.7425	23.124	0.0433	17.1686	0.0583	9.0057
21	1.367	0.7315	24.471	0.0409	17.9001	0.0559	9.4550
22	1.388	0.7207	25.838	0.0387	18.6208	0.0537	9.9018
23	1.408	0.7100	27.225	0.0367	19.3309	0.0517	10.3462
24	1.430	0.6996	28.634	0.0349	20.0304	0.0499	10.7881
25	1.451	0.6892	30.063	0.0333	20.7196	0.0483	11.2276
26	1.473	0.6790	31.514	0.0317	21.3986	0.0467	11.6646
27	1.495	0.6690	32.987	0.0303	22.0676	0.0453	12.0992
28	1.517	0.6591	34.481	0.0290	22.7267	0.0440	12.5313
29	1.540	0.6494	35.999	0.0278	23.3761	0.0428	12.9610
30	1.563	0.6398	37.539	0.0266	24.0158	0.0416	13.3883
31	1.587	0.6303	39.102	0.0256	24.6462	0.0406	13.8131
32	1.610	0.6210	40.688	0.0246	25.2671	0.0396	14.2355
33	1.634	0.6118	42.299	0.0237	25.8790	0.0387	14.6555
34	1.659	0.6028	43.933	0.0228	26.4817	0.0378	15.0731
35	1.684	0.5939	45.592	0.0219	27.0756	0.0369	15.4882
40	1.814	0.5513	54.268	0.0184	29.9159	0.0334	17.5277
45	1.954	0.5117	63.614	0.0157	32.5523	0.0307	19.5074
50	2.105	0.4750	73.683	0.0136	34.9997	0.0286	21.4277
55	2.268	0.4409	84.530	0.0118	37.2715	0.0268	23.2894
60	2.443	0.4093	96.215	0.0104	39.3803	0.0254	25.0930
65	2.632	0.3799	108.803	0.0092	41.3378	0.0242	26.8392
70	2.835	0.3527	122.364	0.0082	43.1549	0.0232	28.5290
75	3.055	0.3274	136.973	0.0073	44.8416	0.0223	30.1631
80	3.291	0.3039	152.711	0.0066	46.4073	0.0216	31.7423
85	3.545	0.2821	169.665	0.0059	47.8607	0.0209	33.2676
90	3.819	0.2619	187.930	0.0053	49.2099	0.0203	34.7399
95	4.114	0.2431	207.606	0.0048	50.4622	0.0198	36.1602
100	4.432	0.2256	228.803	0.0044	51.6247	0.0194	37.5295

Reprinted, by permission, from H. J. Thuesen et al., *Engineering Economy*, pp. 537-577. Copyright © 1977 by Prentice-Hall Inc.

TABLE A.6. 2% *Interest Factors for Annual Compounding Interest*

	Single Payment		Equal Payment Series				Uniform gradient-series factor
	Compound-amount factor	Present-worth factor	Compound-amount factor	Sinking-fund factor	Present-worth factor	Capital-recovery factor	
n	To find F Given P F/P i, n	To find P Given F P/F i, n	To find F Given A F/A i, n	To find A Given F A/F i, n	To find P Given A P/A i, n	To find A Given P A/P i, n	To find A Given G A/G i, n
1	1.020	0.9804	1.000	1.0000	0.9804	1.0200	0.0000
2	1.040	0.9612	2.020	0.4951	1.9416	0.5151	0.4951
3	1.061	0.9423	3.060	0.3268	2.8839	0.3468	0.9868
4	1.082	0.9239	4.122	0.2426	3.8077	0.2626	1.4753
5	1.104	0.9057	5.204	0.1922	4.7135	0.2122	1.9604
6	1.126	0.8880	6.308	0.1585	5.6014	0.1785	2.4423
7	1.149	0.8706	7.434	0.1345	6.4720	0.1545	2.9208
8	1.172	0.8535	8.583	0.1165	7.3255	0.1365	3.3961
9	1.195	0.8368	9.755	0.1025	8.1622	0.1225	3.8681
10	1.219	0.8204	10.950	0.0913	8.9826	0.1113	4.3367
11	1.243	0.8043	12.169	0.0822	9.7869	0.1022	4.8021
12	1.268	0.7885	13.412	0.0746	10.5754	0.0946	5.2643
13	1.294	0.7730	14.680	0.0681	11.3484	0.0881	5.7231
14	1.319	0.7579	15.974	0.0626	12.1063	0.0826	6.1786
15	1.346	0.7430	17.293	0.0578	12.8493	0.0778	6.6309
16	1.373	0.7285	18.639	0.0537	13.5777	0.0737	7.0799
17	1.400	0.7142	20.012	0.0500	14.2919	0.0700	7.5256
18	1.428	0.7002	21.412	0.0467	14.9920	0.0667	7.9681
19	1.457	0.6864	22.841	0.0438	15.6785	0.0638	8.4073
20	1.486	0.6730	24.297	0.0412	16.3514	0.0612	8.8433
21	1.516	0.6598	25.783	0.0388	17.0112	0.0588	9.2760
22	1.546	0.6468	27.299	0.0366	17.6581	0.0566	9.7055
23	1.577	0.6342	28.845	0.0347	18.2922	0.0547	10.1317
24	1.608	0.6217	30.422	0.0329	18.9139	0.0529	10.5547
25	1.641	0.6095	32.030	0.0312	19.5235	0.0512	10.9745
26	1.673	0.5976	33.671	0.0297	20.1210	0.0497	11.3910
27	1.707	0.5859	35.344	0.0283	20.7069	0.0483	11.8043
28	1.741	0.5744	37.051	0.0270	21.2813	0.0470	12.2145
29	1.776	0.5631	38.792	0.0258	21.8444	0.0458	12.6214
30	1.811	0.5521	40.568	0.0247	22.3965	0.0447	13.0251
31	1.848	0.5413	42.379	0.0236	22.9377	0.0436	13.4257
32	1.885	0.5306	44.227	0.0226	23.4683	0.0426	13.8230
33	1.922	0.5202	46.112	0.0217	23.9886	0.0417	14.2172
34	1.961	0.5100	48.034	0.0208	24.4986	0.0408	14.6083
35	2.000	0.5000	49.994	0.0200	24.9986	0.0400	14.9961
40	2.208	0.4529	60.402	0.0166	27.3555	0.0366	16.8885
45	2.438	0.4102	71.893	0.0139	29.4902	0.0339	18.7034
50	2.692	0.3715	84.579	0.0118	31.4236	0.0318	20.4420
55	2.972	0.3365	98.587	0.0102	33.1748	0.0302	22.1057
60	3.281	0.3048	114.052	0.0088	34.7609	0.0288	23.6961
65	3.623	0.2761	131.126	0.0076	36.1975	0.0276	25.2147
70	4.000	0.2500	149.978	0.0067	37.4986	0.0267	26.6632
75	4.416	0.2265	170.792	0.0059	38.6771	0.0259	28.0434
80	4.875	0.2051	193.772	0.0052	39.7445	0.0252	29.3572
85	5.383	0.1858	219.144	0.0046	40.7113	0.0246	30.6064
90	5.943	0.1683	247.157	0.0041	41.5869	0.0241	31.7929
95	6.562	0.1524	278.085	0.0036	42.3800	0.0236	32.9189
100	7.245	0.1380	312.232	0.0032	43.0984	0.0232	33.9863

TABLE A.7. *3% Interest Factors for Annual Compounding Interest*

	Single Payment		Equal Payment Series				Uniform gradient-series factor
	Compound-amount factor	Present-worth factor	Compound-amount factor	Sinking-fund factor	Present-worth factor	Capital-recovery factor	
n	To find F Given P F/P i, n	To find P Given F P/F i, n	To find F Given A F/A i, n	To find A Given F A/F i, n	To find P Given A P/A i, n	To find A Given P A/P i, n	To find A Given G A/G i, n
1	1.030	0.9709	1.000	1.0000	0.9709	1.0300	0.0000
2	1.061	0.9426	2.030	0.4926	1.9135	0.5226	0.4926
3	1.093	0.9152	3.091	0.3235	2.8286	0.3535	0.9803
4	1.126	0.8885	4.184	0.2390	3.7171	0.2690	1.4631
5	1.159	0.8626	5.309	0.1884	4.5797	0.2184	1.9409
6	1.194	0.8375	6.468	0.1546	5.4172	0.1846	2.4138
7	1.230	0.8131	7.662	0.1305	6.2303	0.1605	2.8819
8	1.267	0.7894	8.892	0.1125	7.0197	0.1425	3.3450
9	1.305	0.7664	10.159	0.0984	7.7861	0.1284	3.8032
10	1.344	0.7441	11.464	0.0872	8.5302	0.1172	4.2565
11	1.384	0.7224	12.808	0.0781	9.2526	0.1081	4.7049
12	1.426	0.7014	14.192	0.0705	9.9540	0.1005	5.1485
13	1.469	0.6810	15.618	0.0640	10.6350	0.0940	5.5872
14	1.513	0.6611	17.086	0.0585	11.2961	0.0885	6.0211
15	1.558	0.6419	18.599	0.0538	11.9379	0.0838	6.4501
16	1.605	0.6232	20.157	0.0496	12.5611	0.0796	6.8742
17	1.653	0.6050	21.762	0.0460	13.1661	0.0760	7.2936
18	1.702	0.5874	23.414	0.0427	13.7535	0.0727	7.7081
19	1.754	0.5703	25.117	0.0398	14.3238	0.0698	8.1179
20	1.806	0.5537	26.870	0.0372	14.8775	0.0672	8.5229
21	1.860	0.5376	28.676	0.0349	15.4150	0.0649	8.9231
22	1.916	0.5219	30.537	0.0328	15.9369	0.0628	9.3186
23	1.974	0.5067	32.453	0.0308	16.4436	0.0608	9.7094
24	2.033	0.4919	34.426	0.0291	16.9356	0.0591	10.0954
25	2.094	0.4776	36.459	0.0274	17.4132	0.0574	10.4768
26	2.157	0.4637	38.553	0.0259	17.8769	0.0559	10.8535
27	2.221	0.4502	40.710	0.0246	18.3270	0.0546	11.2256
28	2.288	0.4371	42.931	0.0233	18.7641	0.0533	11.5930
29	2.357	0.4244	45.219	0.0221	19.1885	0.0521	11.9558
30	2.427	0.4120	47.575	0.0210	19.6005	0.0510	12.3141
31	2.500	0.4000	50.003	0.0200	20.0004	0.0500	12.6678
32	2.575	0.3883	52.503	0.0191	20.3888	0.0491	13.0169
33	2.652	0.3770	55.078	0.0182	20.7658	0.0482	13.3616
34	2.732	0.3661	57.730	0.0173	21.1318	0.0473	13.7018
35	2.814	0.3554	60.462	0.0165	21.4872	0.0465	14.0375
40	3.262	0.3066	75.401	0.0133	23.1148	0.0433	15.6502
▶45	3.782	0.2644	92.720	0.0108	24.5187	0.0408	17.1556
50	4.384	0.2281	112.797	0.0089	25.7298	0.0389	18.5575
55	5.082	0.1968	136.072	0.0074	26.7744	0.0374	19.8600
60	5.892	0.1697	163.053	0.0061	27.6756	0.0361	21.0674
65	6.830	0.1464	194.333	0.0052	28.4529	0.0352	22.1841
70	7.918	0.1263	230.594	0.0043	29.1234	0.0343	23.2145
75	9.179	0.1090	272.631	0.0037	29.7018	0.0337	24.1634
80	10.641	0.0940	321.363	0.0031	30.2008	0.0331	25.0354
85	12.336	0.0811	377.857	0.0027	30.6312	0.0327	25.8349
90	14.300	0.0699	443.349	0.0023	31.0024	0.0323	26.5667
95	16.578	0.0603	519.272	0.0019	31.3227	0.0319	27.2351
100	19.219	0.0520	607.288	0.0017	31.5989	0.0317	27.8445

TABLE A.8. 4% Interest Factors for Annual Compounding Interest

	Single Payment		Equal Payment Series				Uniform gradient-series factor
	Compound-amount factor	Present-worth factor	Compound-amount factor	Sinking-fund factor	Present-worth factor	Capital-recovery factor	
n	To find F Given P F/P i, n	To find P Given F P/F i, n	To find F Given A F/A i, n	To find A Given F A/F i, n	To find P Given A P/A i, n	To find A Given P A/P i, n	To find A Given G A/G i, n
1	1.040	0.9615	1.000	1.0000	0.9615	1.0400	0.0000
2	1.082	0.9246	2.040	0.4902	1.8861	0.5302	0.4902
3	1.125	0.8890	3.122	0.3204	2.7751	0.3604	0.9739
4	1.170	0.8548	4.246	0.2355	3.6299	0.2755	1.4510
5	1.217	0.8219	5.416	0.1846	4.4518	0.2246	1.9216
6	1.265	0.7903	6.633	0.1508	5.2421	0.1908	2.3857
7	1.316	0.7599	7.898	0.1266	6.0021	0.1666	2.8433
8	1.369	0.7307	9.214	0.1085	6.7328	0.1485	3.2944
9	1.423	0.7026	10.583	0.0945	7.4353	0.1345	3.7391
10	1.480	0.6756	12.006	0.0833	8.1109	0.1233	4.1773
11	1.539	0.6496	13.486	0.0742	8.7605	0.1142	4.6090
12	1.601	0.6246	15.026	0.0666	9.3851	0.1066	5.0344
13	1.665	0.6006	16.627	0.0602	9.9857	0.1002	5.4533
14	1.732	0.5775	18.292	0.0547	10.5631	0.0947	5.8659
15	1.801	0.5553	20.024	0.0500	11.1184	0.0900	6.2721
16	1.873	0.5339	21.825	0.0458	11.6523	0.0858	6.6720
17	1.948	0.5134	23.698	0.0422	12.1657	0.0822	7.0656
18	2.026	0.4936	25.645	0.0390	12.6593	0.0790	7.4530
19	2.107	0.4747	27.671	0.0361	13.1339	0.0761	7.8342
20	2.191	0.4564	29.778	0.0336	13.5903	0.0736	8.2091
21	2.279	0.4388	31.969	0.0313	14.0292	0.0713	8.5780
22	2.370	0.4220	34.248	0.0292	14.4511	0.0692	8.9407
23	2.465	0.4057	36.618	0.0273	14.8569	0.0673	9.2973
24	2.563	0.3901	39.083	0.0256	15.2470	0.0656	9.6479
25	2.666	0.3751	41.646	0.0240	15.6221	0.0640	9.9925
26	2.772	0.3607	44.312	0.0226	15.9828	0.0626	10.3312
27	2.883	0.3468	47.084	0.0212	16.3296	0.0612	10.6640
28	2.999	0.3335	49.968	0.0200	16.6631	0.0600	10.9909
29	3.119	0.3207	52.966	0.0189	16.9837	0.0589	11.3121
30	3.243	0.3083	56.085	0.0178	17.2920	0.0578	11.6274
31	3.373	0.2965	59.328	0.0169	17.5885	0.0569	11.9371
32	3.508	0.2851	62.701	0.0160	17.8736	0.0560	12.2411
33	3.648	0.2741	66.210	0.0151	18.1477	0.0551	12.5396
34	3.794	0.2636	69.858	0.0143	18.4112	0.0543	12.8325
35	3.946	0.2534	73.652	0.0136	18.6646	0.0536	13.1199
40	4.801	0.2083	95.026	0.0105	19.7928	0.0505	14.4765
45	5.841	0.1712	121.029	0.0083	20.7200	0.0483	15.7047
50	7.107	0.1407	152.667	0.0066	21.4822	0.0466	16.8123
55	8.646	0.1157	191.159	0.0052	22.1086	0.0452	17.8070
60	10.520	0.0951	237.991	0.0042	22.6235	0.0442	18.6972
65	12.799	0.0781	294.968	0.0034	23.0467	0.0434	19.4909
70	15.572	0.0642	364.290	0.0028	23.3945	0.0428	20.1961
75	18.945	0.0528	448.631	0.0022	23.6804	0.0422	20.8206
80	23.050	0.0434	551.245	0.0018	23.9154	0.0418	21.3719
85	28.044	0.0357	676.090	0.0015	24.1085	0.0415	21.8569
90	34.119	0.0293	817.983	0.0012	24.2673	0.0412	22.2826
95	41.511	0.0241	1012.785	0.0010	24.3978	0.0410	22.6550
100	50.505	0.0198	1237.624	0.0008	24.5050	0.0408	22.9800

Reprinted, by permission, from H. J. Thuesen et al., *Engineering Economy*, pp. 537-577. Copyright © 1977 by Prentice-Hall Inc.

TABLE A.9. 5% *Interest Factors for Annual Compounding Interest*

	Single Payment		Equal Payment Series				Uniform gradient-series factor
	Compound-amount factor	Present-worth factor	Compound-amount factor	Sinking-fund factor	Present-worth factor	Capital-recovery factor	
n	To find *F* Given *P* F/P i, n	To find *P* Given *F* P/F i, n	To find *F* Given *A* F/A i, n	To find *A* Given *F* A/F i, n	To find *P* Given *A* P/A i, n	To find *A* Given *P* A/P i, n	To find *A* Given *G* A/G i, n
1	1.050	0.9524	1.000	1.0000	0.9524	1.0500	0.0000
2	1.103	0.9070	2.050	0.4878	1.8594	0.5378	0.4878
3	1.158	0.8638	3.153	0.3172	2.7233	0.3672	0.9675
4	1.216	0.8227	4.310	0.2320	3.5460	0.2820	1.4391
5	1.276	0.7835	5.526	0.1810	4.3295	0.2310	1.9025
6	1.340	0.7462	6.802	0.1470	5.0757	0.1970	2.3579
7	1.407	0.7107	8.142	0.1228	5.7864	0.1728	2.8052
8	1.477	0.6768	9.549	0.1047	6.4632	0.1547	3.2445
9	1.551	0.6446	11.027	0.0907	7.1078	0.1407	3.6758
10	1.629	0.6139	12.587	0.0795	7.7217	0.1295	4.0991
11	1.710	0.5847	14.207	0.0704	8.3064	0.1204	4.5145
12	1.796	0.5568	15.917	0.0628	8.8633	0.1128	4.9219
13	1.886	0.5303	17.713	0.0565	9.3936	0.1065	5.3215
14	1.980	0.5051	19.599	0.0510	9.8987	0.1010	5.7133
15	2.079	0.4810	21.579	0.0464	10.3797	0.0964	6.0973
16	2.183	0.4581	23.658	0.0423	10.8378	0.0923	6.4736
17	2.292	0.4363	25.840	0.0387	11.2741	0.0887	6.8423
18	2.407	0.4155	28.132	0.0356	11.6896	0.0856	7.2034
19	2.527	0.3957	30.539	0.0328	12.0853	0.0828	7.5569
20	2.653	0.3769	33.066	0.0303	12.4622	0.0803	7.9030
21	2.786	0.3590	35.719	0.0280	12.8212	0.0780	8.2416
22	2.925	0.3419	38.505	0.0260	13.1630	0.0760	8.5730
23	3.072	0.3256	41.430	0.0241	13.4886	0.0741	8.8971
24	3.225	0.3101	44.502	0.0225	13.7987	0.0725	9.2140
25	3.386	0.2953	47.727	0.0210	14.0940	0.0710	9.5238
26	3.556	0.2813	51.113	0.0196	14.3752	0.0696	9.8266
27	3.733	0.2679	54.669	0.0183	14.6430	0.0683	10.1224
28	3.920	0.2551	58.403	0.0171	14.8981	0.0671	10.4114
29	4.116	0.2430	62.323	0.0161	15.1411	0.0661	10.6936
30	4.322	0.2314	66.439	0.0151	15.3725	0.0651	10.9691
31	4.538	0.2204	70.761	0.0141	15.5928	0.0641	11.2381
32	4.765	0.2099	75.299	0.0133	15.8027	0.0633	11.5005
33	5.003	0.1999	80.064	0.0125	16.0026	0.0625	11.7566
34	5.253	0.1904	85.067	0.0118	16.1929	0.0618	12.0063
35	5.516	0.1813	90.320	0.0111	16.3742	0.0611	12.2498
40	7.040	0.1421	120.800	0.0083	17.1591	0.0583	13.3775
45	8.985	0.1113	159.700	0.0063	17.7741	0.0563	14.3644
50	11.467	0.0872	209.348	0.0048	18.2559	0.0548	15.2233
55	14.636	0.0683	272.713	0.0037	18.6335	0.0537	15.9665
60	18.679	0.0535	353.584	0.0028	18.9293	0.0528	16.6062
65	23.840	0.0420	456.798	0.0022	19.1611	0.0522	17.1541
70	30.426	0.0329	588.529	0.0017	19.3427	0.0517	17.6212
75	38.833	0.0258	756.654	0.0013	19.4850	0.0513	18.0176
80	49.561	0.0202	971.229	0.0010	19.5965	0.0510	18.3526
85	63.254	0.0158	1245.087	0.0008	19.6838	0.0508	18.6346
90	80.730	0.0124	1594.607	0.0006	19.7523	0.0506	18.8712
95	103.035	0.0097	2040.694	0.0005	19.8059	0.0505	19.0689
100	131.501	0.0076	2610.025	0.0004	19.8479	0.0504	19.2337

Reprinted, by permission, from H. J. Thuesen et al., *Engineering Economy*, pp. 537-577. Copyright © 1977 by Prentice-Hall Inc.

TABLE A.10. *6% Interest Factors for Annual Compounding Interest*

	Single Payment		Equal Payment Series				Uniform gradient-series factor
	Compound-amount factor	Present-worth factor	Compound-amount factor	Sinking-fund factor	Present-worth factor	Capital-recovery factor	
n	To find *F* Given *P* *F/P i, n*	To find *P* Given *F* *P/F i, n*	To find *F* Given *A* *F/A i, n*	To find *A* Given *F* *A/F i, n*	To find *P* Given *A* *P/A i, n*	To find *A* Given *P* *A/P i, n*	To find *A* Given *G* *A/G i, n*
1	1.060	0.9434	1.000	1.0000	0.9434	1.0600	0.0000
2	1.124	0.8900	2.060	0.4854	1.8334	0.5454	0.4854
3	1.191	0.8396	3.184	0.3141	2.6730	0.3741	0.9612
4	1.262	0.7921	4.375	0.2286	3.4651	0.2886	1.4272
5	1.338	0.7473	5.637	0.1774	4.2124	0.2374	1.8836
6	1.419	0.7050	6.975	0.1434	4.9173	0.2034	2.3304
7	1.504	0.6651	8.394	0.1191	5.5824	0.1791	2.7676
8	1.594	0.6274	9.897	0.1010	6.2098	0.1610	3.1952
9	1.689	0.5919	11.491	0.0870	6.8017	0.1470	3.6133
10	1.791	0.5584	13.181	0.0759	7.3601	0.1359	4.0220
11	1.898	0.5268	14.972	0.0668	7.8869	0.1268	4.4213
12	2.012	0.4970	16.870	0.0593	8.3839	0.1193	4.8113
13	2.133	0.4688	18.882	0.0530	8.8527	0.1130	5.1920
14	2.261	0.4423	21.015	0.0476	9.2950	0.1076	5.5635
15	2.397	0.4173	23.276	0.0430	9.7123	0.1030	5.9260
16	2.540	0.3937	25.673	0.0390	10.1059	0.0990	6.2794
17	2.693	0.3714	28.213	0.0355	10.4773	0.0955	6.6240
18	2.854	0.3504	30.906	0.0324	10.8276	0.0924	6.9597
19	3.026	0.3305	33.760	0.0296	11.1581	0.0896	7.2867
20	3.207	0.3118	36.786	0.0272	11.4699	0.0872	7.6052
21	3.400	0.2942	39.993	0.0250	11.7641	0.0850	7.9151
22	3.604	0.2775	43.392	0.0231	12.0416	0.0831	8.2166
23	3.820	0.2618	46.996	0.0213	12.3034	0.0813	8.5099
24	4.049	0.2470	50.816	0.0197	12.5504	0.0797	8.7951
25	4.292	0.2330	54.865	0.0182	12.7834	0.0782	9.0722
26	4.549	0.2198	59.156	0.0169	13.0032	0.0769	9.3415
27	4.822	0.2074	63.706	0.0157	13.2105	0.0757	9.6030
28	5.112	0.1956	68.528	0.0146	13.4062	0.0746	9.8568
29	5.418	0.1846	73.640	0.0136	13.5907	0.0736	10.1032
30	5.744	0.1741	79.058	0.0127	13.7648	0.0727	10.3422
31	6.088	0.1643	84.802	0.0118	13.9291	0.0718	10.5740
32	6.453	0.1550	90.890	0.0110	14.0841	0.0710	10.7988
33	6.841	0.1462	97.343	0.0103	14.2302	0.0703	11.0166
34	7.251	0.1379	104.184	0.0096	14.3682	0.0696	11.2276
35	7.686	0.1301	111.435	0.0090	14.4983	0.0690	11.4319
40	10.286	0.0972	154.762	0.0065	15.0463	0.0665	12.3590
45	13.765	0.0727	212.744	0.0047	15.4558	0.0647	13.1413
50	18.420	0.0543	290.336	0.0035	15.7619	0.0635	13.7964
55	24.650	0.0406	394.172	0.0025	15.9906	0.0625	14.3411
60	32.988	0.0303	533.128	0.0019	16.1614	0.0619	14.7910
65	44.145	0.0227	719.083	0.0014	16.2891	0.0614	15.1601
70	59.076	0.0169	967.932	0.0010	16.3846	0.0610	15.4614
75	79.057	0.0127	1300.949	0.0008	16.4559	0.0608	15.7058
80	105.796	0.0095	1746.600	0.0006	16.5091	0.0606	15.9033
85	141.579	0.0071	2342.982	0.0004	16.5490	0.0604	16.0620
90	189.465	0.0053	3141.075	0.0003	16.5787	0.0603	16.1891
95	253.546	0.0040	4209.104	0.0002	16.6009	0.0602	16.2905
100	339.302	0.0030	5638.368	0.0002	16.6176	0.0602	16.3711

TABLE A.11. *7% Interest Factors for Annual Compounding Interest*

	Single Payment		Equal Payment Series				Uniform gradient-series factor
	Compound-amount factor	Present-worth factor	Compound-amount factor	Sinking-fund factor	Present-worth factor	Capital-recovery factor	
n	To find F Given P F/P i, n	To find P Given F P/F i, n	To find F Given A F/A i, n	To find A Given F A/F i, n	To find P Given A P/A i, n	To find A Given P A/P i, n	To find A Given G A/G i, n
1	1.070	0.9346	1.000	1.0000	0.9346	1.0700	0.0000
2	1.145	0.8734	2.070	0.4831	1.8080	0.5531	0.4831
3	1.225	0.8163	3.215	0.3111	2.6243	0.3811	0.9549
4	1.311	0.7629	4.440	0.2252	3.3872	0.2952	1.4155
5	1.403	0.7130	5.751	0.1739	4.1002	0.2439	1.8650
6	1.501	0.6664	7.163	0.1398	4.7665	0.2098	2.3032
7	1.606	0.6228	8.654	0.1156	5.3893	0.1856	2.7304
8	1.718	0.5820	10.260	0.0975	5.9713	0.1675	3.1466
9	1.838	0.5439	11.978	0.0835	6.5152	0.1535	3.5517
10	1.967	0.5084	13.816	0.0724	7.0236	0.1424	3.9461
11	2.105	0.4751	15.784	0.0634	7.4987	0.1334	4.3296
12	2.252	0.4440	17.888	0.0559	7.9427	0.1259	4.7025
13	2.410	0.4150	20.141	0.0497	8.3577	0.1197	5.0649
14	2.579	0.3878	22.550	0.0444	8.7455	0.1144	5.4167
15	2.759	0.3625	25.129	0.0398	9.1079	0.1098	5.7583
16	2.952	0.3387	27.888	0.0359	9.4467	0.1059	6.0897
17	3.159	0.3166	30.840	0.0324	9.7632	0.1024	6.4110
18	3.380	0.2959	33.999	0.0294	10.0591	0.0994	6.7225
19	3.617	0.2765	37.379	0.0268	10.3356	0.0968	7.0242
20	3.870	0.2584	40.996	0.0244	10.5940	0.0944	7.3163
21	4.141	0.2415	44.865	0.0223	10.8355	0.0923	7.5990
22	4.430	0.2257	49.006	0.0204	11.0613	0.0904	7.8725
23	4.741	0.2110	53.436	0.0187	11.2722	0.0887	8.1369
24	5.072	0.1972	58.177	0.0172	11.4693	0.0872	8.3923
25	5.427	0.1843	63.249	0.0158	11.6536	0.0858	8.6391
26	5.807	0.1722	68.676	0.0146	11.8258	0.0846	8.8773
27	6.214	0.1609	74.484	0.0134	11.9867	0.0834	9.1072
28	6.649	0.1504	80.698	0.0124	12.1371	0.0824	9.3290
29	7.114	0.1406	87.347	0.0115	12.2777	0.0815	9.5427
30	7.612	0.1314	94.461	0.0106	12.4091	0.0806	9.7487
31	8.145	0.1228	102.073	0.0098	12.5318	0.0798	9.9471
32	8.715	0.1148	110.218	0.0091	12.6466	0.0791	10.1381
33	9.325	0.1072	118.933	0.0084	12.7538	0.0784	10.3219
34	9.978	0.1002	128.259	0.0078	12.8540	0.0778	10.4987
35	10.677	0.0937	138.237	0.0072	12.9477	0.0772	10.6687
40	14.974	0.0668	199.635	0.0050	13.3317	0.0750	11.4234
45	21.002	0.0476	285.749	0.0035	13.6055	0.0735	12.0360
50	29.457	0.0340	406.529	0.0025	13.8008	0 0725	12.5287
55	41.315	0.0242	575.929	0.0017	13.9391	0.0717	12.9215
60	57.946	0.0173	813.520	0.0012	14.0392	0.0712	13.2321
65	81.273	0.0123	1146.755	0.0009	14.1099	0.0709	13.4760
70	113.989	0.0088	1614.134	0.0006	14.1604	0.0706	13.6662
75	159.876	0.0063	2269.657	0.0005	14.1964	0.0705	13.8137
80	224.234	0.0045	3189.063	0.0003	14.2220	0.0703	13.9274
85	314.500	0.0032	4478.576	0.0002	14.2403	0.0702	14.0146
90	441.103	0.0023	6287.185	0.0002	14.2533	0.0702	14.0812
95	618.670	0.0016	8823.854	0.0001	14.2626	0.0701	14.1319
100	867.716	0.0012	12381.662	0.0001	14.2693	0.0701	14.1703

Reprinted, by permission, from H. J. Thuesen et al., *Engineering Economy*, pp. 537-577. Copyright © 1977 by Prentice-Hall Inc.

TABLE A.12. 8% Interest Factors for Annual Compounding Interest

	Single Payment		Equal Payment Series				Uniform gradient-series factor
	Compound-amount factor	Present-worth factor	Compound-amount factor	Sinking-fund factor	Present-worth factor	Capital-recovery factor	
n	To find F Given P F/P i,n	To find P Given F P/F i,n	To find F Given A F/A i,n	To find A Given F A/F i,n	To find P Given A P/A i,n	To find A Given P A/P i,n	To find A Given G A/G i,n
1	1.080	0.9259	1.000	1.0000	0.9259	1.0800	0.0000
2	1.166	0.8573	2.080	0.4808	1.7833	0.5608	0.4808
3	1.260	0.7938	3.246	0.3080	2.5771	0.3880	0.9488
4	1.360	0.7350	4.506	0.2219	3.3121	0.3019	1.4040
5	1.469	0.6806	5.867	0.1705	3.9927	0.2505	1.8465
6	1.587	0.6302	7.336	0.1363	4.6229	0.2163	2.2764
7	1.714	0.5835	8.923	0.1121	5.2064	0.1921	2.6937
8	1.851	0.5403	10.637	0.0940	5.7466	0.1740	2.0985
9	1.999	0.5003	12.488	0.0801	6.2469	0.1601	3.4910
10	2.159	0.4632	14.487	0.0690	6.7101	0.1490	3.8713
11	2.332	0.4289	16.645	0.0601	7.1390	0.1401	4.2395
12	2.518	0.3971	18.977	0.0527	7.5361	0.1327	4.5958
13	2.720	0.3677	21.495	0.0465	7.9038	0.1265	4.9402
14	2.937	0.3405	24.215	0.0413	8.2442	0.1213	5.2731
15	3.172	0.3153	27.152	0.0368	8.5595	0.1168	5.5945
16	3.426	0.2919	30.324	0.0330	8.8514	0.1130	5.9046
17	3.700	0.2703	33.750	0.0296	9.1216	0.1096	6.2038
18	3.996	0.2503	37.450	0.0267	9.3719	0.1067	6.4920
19	4.316	0.2317	41.446	0.0241	9.6036	0.1041	6.7697
20	4.661	0.2146	45.762	0.0219	9.8182	0.1019	7.0370
21	5.034	0.1987	50.423	0.0198	10.0168	0.0998	7.2940
22	5.437	0.1840	55.457	0.0180	10.2008	0.0980	7.5412
23	5.871	0.1703	60.893	0.0164	10.3711	0.0964	7.7786
24	6.341	0.1577	66.765	0.0150	10.5288	0.0950	8.0066
25	6.848	0.1460	73.106	0.0137	10.6748	0.0937	8.2254
26	7.396	0.1352	79.954	0.0125	10.8100	0.0925	8.4352
27	7.988	0.1252	87.351	0.0115	10.9352	0.0915	8.6363
28	8.627	0.1159	95.339	0.0105	11.0511	0.0905	8.8289
29	9.317	0.1073	103.966	0.0096	11.1584	0.0896	9.0133
30	10.063	0.0994	113.283	0.0088	11.2578	0.0888	9.1897
31	10.868	0.0920	123.346	0.0081	11.3498	0.0881	9.3584
32	11.737	0.0852	134.214	0.0075	11.4350	0.0875	9.5197
33	12.676	0.0789	145.951	0.0069	11.5139	0.0869	9.6737
34	13.690	0.0731	158.627	0.0063	11.5869	0.0863	9.8208
35	14.785	0.0676	172.317	0.0058	11.6546	0.0858	9.9611
40	21.725	0.0460	259.057	0.0039	11.9246	0.0839	10.5699
45	31.920	0.0313	386.506	0.0026	12.1084	0.0826	11.0447
50	46.902	0.0213	573.770	0.0018	12.2335	0.0818	11.4107
55	68.914	0.0145	848.923	0.0012	12.3186	0.0812	11.6902
60	101.257	0.0099	1253.213	0.0008	12.3766	0.0808	11.9015
65	148.780	0.0067	1847.248	0.0006	12.4160	0.0806	12.0602
70	218.606	0.0046	2720.080	0.0004	12.4428	0.0804	12.1783
75	321.205	0.0031	4002.557	0.0003	12.4611	0.0803	12.2658
80	471.955	0.0021	5886.935	0.0002	12.4735	0.0802	12.3301
85	693.456	0.0015	8655.706	0.0001	12.4820	0.0801	12.3773
90	1018.915	0.0010	12723.939	0.0001	12.4877	0.0801	12.4116
95	1497.121	0.0007	18701.507	0.0001	12.4917	0.0801	12.4365
100	2199.761	0.0005	27484.516	0.0001	12.4943	0.0800	12.4545

Reprinted, by permission, from H. J. Thuesen et al., *Engineering Economy*, pp. 537-577. Copyright © 1977 by Prentice-Hall Inc.

TABLE A.13. *9% Interest Factors for Annual Compounding Interest*

	Single Payment		Equal Payment Series				Uniform gradient-series factor
	Compound-amount factor	Present-worth factor	Compound-amount factor	Sinking-fund factor	Present-worth factor	Capital-recovery factor	
n	To find F Given P F/P i,n	To find P Given F P/F i,n	To find F Given A F/A i,n	To find A Given F A/F i,n	To find P Given A P/A i,n	To find A Given P A/P i,n	To find A Given G A/G i,n
1	1.090	0.9174	1.000	1.0000	0.9174	1.0900	0.0000
2	1.188	0.8417	2.090	0.4785	1.7591	0.5685	0.4785
3	1.295	0.7722	3.278	0.3051	2.5313	0.3951	0.9426
4	1.412	0.7084	4.573	0.2187	3.2397	0.3087	1.3925
5	1.539	0.6499	5.985	0.1671	3.8897	0.2571	1.8282
6	1.677	0.5963	7.523	0.1329	4.4859	0.2229	2.2498
7	1.828	0.5470	9.200	0.1087	5.0330	0.1987	2.6574
8	1.993	0.5019	11.028	0.0907	5.5348	0.1807	3.0512
9	2.172	0.4604	13.021	0.0768	5.9953	0.1668	3.4312
10	2.367	0.4224	15.193	0.0658	6.4177	0.1558	3.7978
11	2.580	0.3875	17.560	0.0570	6.8052	0.1470	4.1510
12	2.813	0.3555	20.141	0.0497	7.1607	0.1397	4.4910
13	3.066	0.3262	22.953	0.0436	7.4869	0.1336	4.8182
14	3.342	0.2993	26.019	0.0384	7.7862	0.1284	5.1326
15	3.642	0.2745	29.361	0.0341	8.0607	0.1241	5.4346
16	3.970	0.2519	33.003	0.0303	8.3126	0.1203	5.7245
17	4.328	0.2311	36.974	0.0271	8.5436	0.1171	6.0024
18	4.717	0.2120	41.301	0.0242	8.7556	0.1142	6.2687
19	5.142	0.1945	46.018	0.0217	8.9501	0.1117	6.5236
20	5.604	0.1784	51.160	0.0196	9.1286	0.1096	6.7675
21	6.109	0.1637	56.765	0.0176	9.2923	0.1076	7.0006
22	6.659	0.1502	62.873	0.0159	9.4424	0.1059	7.2232
23	7.258	0.1378	69.532	0.0144	9.5802	0.1044	7.4358
24	7.911	0.1264	76.790	0.0130	9.7066	0.1030	7.6384
25	8.623	0.1160	84.701	0.0118	9.8226	0.1018	7.8316
26	9.399	0.1064	93.324	0.0107	9.9290	0.1007	8.0156
27	10.245	0.0976	102.723	0.0097	10.0266	0.0997	8.1906
28	11.167	0.0896	112.968	0.0089	10.1161	0.0989	8.3572
29	12.172	0.0822	124.135	0.0081	10.1983	0.0981	8.5154
30	13.268	0.0754	136.308	0.0073	10.2737	0.0973	8.6657
31	14.462	0.0692	149.575	0.0067	10.3428	0.0967	8.8083
32	15.763	0.0634	164.037	0.0061	10.4063	0.0961	8.9436
33	17.182	0.0582	179.800	0.0056	10.4645	0.0956	9.0718
34	18.728	0.0534	196.982	0.0051	10.5178	0.0951	9.1933
35	20.414	0.0490	215.711	0.0046	10.5668	0.0946	9.3083
40	31.409	0.0318	337.882	0.0030	10.7574	0.0930	9.7957
45	48.327	0.0207	525.859	0.0019	10.8812	0.0919	10.1603
50	74.358	0.0135	815.084	0.0012	10.9617	0.0912	10.4295
55	114.408	0.0088	1260.092	0.0008	11.0140	0.0908	10.6261
60	176.031	0.0057	1944.792	0.0005	11.0480	0.0905	10.7683
65	270.846	0.0037	2998.288	0.0003	11.0701	0.0903	10.8702
70	416.730	0.0024	4619.223	0.0002	11.0845	0.0902	10.9427
75	641.191	0.0016	7113.232	0.0002	11.0938	0.0902	10.9940
80	986.552	0.0010	10950.574	0.0001	11.0999	0.0901	11.0299
85	1517.932	0.0007	16854.800	0.0001	11.1038	0.0901	11.0551
90	2335.527	0.0004	25939.184	0.0001	11.1064	0.0900	11.0726
95	3593.497	0.0003	39916.635	0.0000	11.1080	0.0900	11.0847
100	5529.041	0.0002	61422.675	0.0000	11.1091	0.0900	11.0930

TABLE A.14. *10% Interest Factors for Annual Compounding Interest*

	Single Payment		Equal Payment Series				Uniform gradient-series factor
	Compound-amount factor	Present-worth factor	Compound-amount factor	Sinking-fund factor	Present-worth factor	Capital-recovery factor	
n	To find F Given P F/P i, n	To find P Given F P/F i, n	To find F Given A F/A i, n	To find A Given F A/F i, n	To find P Given A P/A i, n	To find A Given P A/P i, n	To find A Given G A/G i, n
1	1.100	0.9091	1.000	1.0000	0.9091	1.1000	0.0000
2	1.210	0.8265	2.100	0.4762	1.7355	0.5762	0.4762
3	1.331	0.7513	3.310	0.3021	2.4869	0.4021	0.9366
4	1.464	0.6830	4.641	0.2155	3.1699	0.3155	1.3812
5	1.611	0.6209	6.105	0.1638	3.7908	0.2638	1.8101
6	1.772	0.5645	7.716	0.1296	4.3553	0.2296	2.2236
7	1.949	0.5132	9.487	0.1054	4.8684	0.2054	2.6216
8	2.144	0.4665	11.436	0.0875	5.3349	0.1875	3.0045
9	2.358	0.4241	13.579	0.0737	5.7590	0.1737	3.3724
10	2.594	0.3856	15.937	0.0628	6.1446	0.1628	3.7255
11	2.853	0.3505	18.531	0.0540	6.4951	0.1540	4.0641
12	3.138	0.3186	21.384	0.0468	6.8137	0.1468	4.3884
13	3.452	0.2897	24.523	0.0408	7.1034	0.1408	4.6988
14	3.798	0.2633	27.975	0.0358	7.3667	0.1358	4.9955
15	4.177	0.2394	31.772	0.0315	7.6061	0.1315	5.2789
16	4.595	0.2176	35.950	0.0278	7.8237	0.1278	5.5493
17	5.054	0.1979	40.545	0.0247	8.0216	0.1247	5.8071
18	5.560	0.1799	45.599	0.0219	8.2014	0.1219	6.0526
19	6.116	0.1635	51.159	0.0196	8.3649	0.1196	6.2861
20	6.728	0.1487	57.275	0.0175	8.5136	0.1175	6.5081
21	7.400	0.1351	64.003	0.0156	8.6487	0.1156	6.7189
22	8.140	0.1229	71.403	0.0140	8.7716	0.1140	6.9189
23	8.954	0.1117	79.543	0.0126	8.8832	0.1126	7.1085
24	9.850	0.1015	88.497	0.0113	8.9848	0.1113	7.2881
25	10.835	0.0923	98.347	0.0102	9.0771	0.1102	7.4580
26	11.918	0.0839	109.182	0.0092	9.1610	0.1092	7.6187
27	13.110	0.0763	121.100	0.0083	9.2372	0.1083	7.7704
28	14.421	0.0694	134.210	0.0075	9.3066	0.1075	7.9137
29	15.863	0.0630	148.631	0.0067	9.3696	0.1067	8.0489
30	17.449	0.0573	164.494	0.0061	9.4269	0.1061	8.1762
31	19.194	0.0521	181.943	0.0055	9.4790	0.1055	8.2962
32	21.114	0.0474	201.138	0.0050	9.5264	0.1050	8.4091
33	23.225	0.0431	222.252	0.0045	9.5694	0.1045	8.5152
34	25.548	0.0392	245.477	0.0041	9.6086	0.1041	8.6149
35	28.102	0.0356	271.024	0.0037	9.6442	0.1037	8.7086
40	45.259	0.0221	442.593	0.0023	9.7791	0.1023	9.0962
45	72.890	0.0137	718.905	0.0014	9.8628	0.1014	9.3741
50	117.391	0.0085	1163.909	0.0009	9.9148	0.1009	9.5704
55	189.059	0.0053	1880.591	0.0005	9.9471	0.1005	9.7075
60	304.482	0.0033	3034.816	0.0003	9.9672	0.1003	9.8023
65	490.371	0.0020	4893.707	0.0002	9.9796	0.1002	9.8672
70	789.747	0.0013	7887.470	0.0001	9.9873	0.1001	9.9113
75	1271.895	0.0008	12708.954	0.0001	9.9921	0.1001	9.9410
80	2048.400	0.0005	20474.002	0.0001	9.9951	0.1001	9.9609
85	3298.969	0.0003	32979.690	0.0000	9.9970	0.1000	9.9742
90	5313.023	0.0002	53120.226	0.0000	9.9981	0.1000	9.9831
95	8556.676	0.0001	85556.760	0.0000	9.9988	0.1000	9.9889
100	13780.612	0.0001	137796.123	0.0000	9.9993	0.1000	9.9928

Reprinted, by permission, from H. J. Thuesen et al., *Engineering Economy,* pp. 537-577. Copyright © 1977 by Prentice-Hall Inc.

TABLE A.15. *12% Interest Factors for Annual Compounding Interest*

	Single Payment		Equal Payment Series				Uniform gradient-series factor
	Compound-amount factor	Present-worth factor	Compound-amount factor	Sinking-fund factor	Present-worth factor	Capital-recovery factor	
n	To find F Given P F/P i,n	To find P Given F P/F i,n	To find F Given A F/A i,n	To find A Given F A/F i,n	To find P Given A P/A i,n	To find A Given P A/P i,n	To find A Given G A/G i,n
1	1.120	0.8929	1.000	1.0000	0.8929	1.1200	0.0000
2	1.254	0.7972	2.120	0.4717	1.6901	0.5917	0.4717
3	1.405	0.7118	3.374	0.2964	2.4018	0.4164	0.9246
4	1.574	0.6355	4.779	0.2092	3.0374	0.3292	1.3589
5	1.762	0.5674	6.353	0.1574	3.6048	0.2774	1.7746
6	1.974	0.5066	8.115	0.1232	4.1114	0.2432	2.1721
7	2.211	0.4524	10.089	0.0991	4.5638	0.2191	2.5515
8	2.476	0.4039	12.300	0.0813	4.9676	0.2013	2.9132
9	2.773	0.3606	14.776	0.0677	5.3283	0.1877	3.2574
10	3.106	0.3220	17.549	0.0570	5.6502	0.1770	3.5847
11	3.479	0.2875	20.655	0.0484	5.9377	0.1684	3.8953
12	3.896	0.2567	24.133	0.0414	6.1944	0.1614	4.1897
13	4.364	0.2292	28.029	0.0357	6.4236	0.1557	4.4683
14	4.887	0.2046	32.393	0.0309	6.6282	0.1509	4.7317
15	5.474	0.1827	37.280	0.0268	6.8109	0.1468	4.9803
16	6.130	0.1631	42.753	0.0234	6.9740	0.1434	5.2147
17	6.866	0.1457	48.884	0.0205	7.1196	0.1405	5.4353
18	7.690	0.1300	55.750	0.0179	7.2497	0.1379	5.6427
19	8.613	0.1161	63.440	0.0158	7.3658	0.1358	5.8375
20	9.646	0.1037	72.052	0.0139	7.4695	0.1339	6.0202
21	10.804	0.0926	81.699	0.0123	7.5620	0.1323	6.1913
22	12.100	0.0827	92.503	0.0108	7.6447	0.1308	6.3514
23	13.552	0.0738	104.603	0.0096	7.7184	0.1296	6.5010
24	15.179	0.0659	118.155	0.0085	7.7843	0.1285	6.6407
25	17.000	0.0588	133.334	0.0075	7.8431	0.1275	6.7708
26	19.040	0.0525	150.334	0.0067	7.8957	0.1267	6.8921
27	21.325	0.0469	169.374	0.0059	7.9426	0.1259	7.0049
28	23.884	0.0419	190.699	0.0053	7.9844	0.1253	7.1098
29	26.750	0.0374	214.583	0.0047	8.0218	0.1247	7.2071
30	29.960	0.0334	241.333	0.0042	8.0552	0.1242	7.2974
31	33.555	0.0298	271.293	0.0037	8.0850	0.1237	7.3811
32	37.582	0.0266	304.848	0.0033	8.1116	0.1233	7.4586
33	42.092	0.0238	342.429	0.0029	8.1354	0.1229	7.5303
34	47.143	0.0212	384.521	0.0026	8.1566	0.1226	7.5965
35	52.800	0.0189	431.664	0.0023	8.1755	0.1223	7.6577
40	93.051	0.0108	767.091	0.0013	8.2438	0.1213	7.8988
45	163.988	0.0061	1358.230	0.0007	8.2825	0.1207	8.0572
50	289.002	0.0035	2400.018	0.0004	8.3045	0.1204	8.1597

Reprinted, by permission, from H. J. Thuesen et al., *Engineering Economy*, pp. 537-577. Copyright © 1977 by Prentice-Hall Inc.

TABLE A.16. *15% Interest Factors for Annual Compounding Interest*

	Single Payment		Equal Payment Series				Uniform gradient-series factor
	Compound-amount factor	Present-worth factor	Compound-amount factor	Sinking-fund factor	Present-worth factor	Capital-recovery factor	
n	To find F Given P F/P i,n	To find P Given F P/F i,n	To find F Given A F/A i,n	To find A Given F A/F i,n	To find P Given A P/A i,n	To find A Given P A/P i,n	To find A Given G A/G i,n
1	1.150	0.8696	1.000	1.0000	0.8696	1.1500	0.0000
2	1.323	0.7562	2.150	0.4651	1.6257	0.6151	0.4651
3	1.521	0.6575	3.473	0.2880	2.2832	0.4380	0.9071
4	1.749	0.5718	4.993	0.2003	2.8550	0.3503	1.3263
5	2.011	0.4972	6.742	0.1483	3.3522	0.2983	1.7228
6	2.313	0.4323	8.754	0.1142	3.7845	0.2642	2.0972
7	2.660	0.3759	11.067	0.0904	4.1604	0.2404	2.4499
8	3.059	0.3269	13.727	0.0729	4.4873	0.2229	2.7813
9	3.518	0.2843	16.786	0.0596	4.7716	0.2096	3.0922
10	4.046	0.2472	20.304	0.0493	5.0188	0.1993	3.3832
11	4.652	0.2150	24.349	0.0411	5.2337	0.1911	3.6550
12	5.350	0.1869	29.002	0.0345	5.4206	0.1845	3.9082
13	6.153	0.1625	34.352	0.0291	5.5832	0.1791	4.1438
14	7.076	0.1413	40.505	0.0247	5.7245	0.1747	4.3624
15	8.137	0.1229	47.580	0.0210	5.8474	0.1710	4.5650
16	9.358	0.1069	55.717	0.0180	5.9542	0.1680	4.7523
17	10.761	0.0929	65.075	0.0154	6.0472	0.1654	4.9251
18	12.375	0.0808	75.836	0.0132	6.1280	0.1632	5.0843
19	14.232	0.0703	88.212	0.0113	6.1982	0.1613	5.2307
20	16.367	0.0611	102.444	0.0098	6.2593	0.1598	5.3651
21	18.822	0.0531	118.810	0.0084	6.3125	0.1584	5.4883
22	21.645	0.0462	137.632	0.0073	6.3587	0.1573	5.6010
23	24.891	0.0402	159.276	0.0063	6.3988	0.1563	5.7040
24	28.625	0.0349	184.168	0.0054	6.4338	0.1554	5.7979
25	32.919	0.0304	212.793	0.0047	6.4642	0.1547	5.8834
26	37.857	0.0264	245.712	0.0041	6.4906	0.1541	5.9612
27	43.535	0.0230	283.569	0.0035	6.5135	0.1535	6.0319
28	50.066	0.0200	327.104	0.0031	6.5335	0.1531	6.0960
29	57.575	0.0174	377.170	0.0027	6.5509	0.1527	6.1541
30	66.212	0.0151	434.745	0.0023	6.5660	0.1523	6.2066
31	76.144	0.0131	500.957	0.0020	6.5791	0.1520	6.2541
32	87.565	0.0114	577.100	0.0017	6.5905	0.1517	6.2970
33	100.700	0.0099	664.666	0.0015	6.6005	0.1515	6.3357
34	115.805	0.0086	765.365	0.0013	6.6091	0.1513	6.3705
35	133.176	0.0075	881.170	0.0011	6.6166	0.1511	6.4019
40	267.864	0.0037	1779.090	0.0006	6.6418	0.1506	6.5168
45	538.769	0.0019	3585.128	0.0003	6.6543	0.1503	6.5830
50	1083.657	0.0009	7217.716	0.0002	6.6605	0.1501	6.6205

Reprinted, by permission, from H. J. Thuesen et al., *Engineering Economy*, pp. 537-577. Copyright © 1977 by Prentice-Hall Inc.

TABLE A.17. *20% Interest Factors for Annual Compounding Interest*

	Single Payment		Equal Payment Series				Uniform gradient-series factor
	Compound-amount factor	Present-worth factor	Compound-amount factor	Sinking-fund factor	Present-worth factor	Capital-recovery factor	
n	To find F Given P F/P i,n	To find P Given F P/F i,n	To find F Given A F/A i,n	To find A Given F A/F i,n	To find P Given A P/A i,n	To find A Given P A/P i,n	To find A Given G A/G i,n
1	1.200	0.8333	1.000	1.0000	0.8333	1.2000	0.0000
2	1.440	0.6945	2.200	0.4546	1.5278	0.6546	0.4546
3	1.728	0.5787	3.640	0.2747	2.1065	0.4747	0.8791
4	2.074	0.4823	5.368	0.1863	2.5887	0.3863	1.2742
5	2.488	0.4019	7.442	0.1344	2.9906	0.3344	1.6405
6	2.986	0.3349	9.930	0.1007	3.3255	0.3007	1.9788
7	3.583	0.2791	12.916	0.0774	3.6046	0.2774	2.2902
8	4.300	0.2326	16.499	0.0606	3.8372	0.2606	2.5756
9	5.160	0.1938	20.799	0.0481	4.0310	0.2481	2.8364
10	6.192	0.1615	25.959	0.0385	4.1925	0.2385	3.0739
11	7.430	0.1346	32.150	0.0311	4.3271	0.2311	3.2893
12	8.916	0.1122	39.581	0.0253	4.4392	0.2253	3.4841
13	10.699	0.0935	48.497	0.0206	4.5327	0.2206	3.6597
14	12.839	0.0779	59.196	0.0169	4.6106	0.2169	3.8175
15	15.407	0.0649	72.035	0.0139	4.6755	0.2139	3.9589
16	18.488	0.0541	87.442	0.0114	4.7296	0.2114	4.0851
17	22.186	0.0451	105.931	0.0095	4.7746	0.2095	4.1976
18	26.623	0.0376	128.117	0.0078	4.8122	0.2078	4.2975
19	31.948	0.0313	154.740	0.0065	4.8435	0.2065	4.3861
20	38.338	0.0261	186.688	0.0054	4.8696	0.2054	4.4644
21	46.005	0.0217	225.026	0.0045	4.8913	0.2045	4.5334
22	55.206	0.0181	271.031	0.0037	4.9094	0.2037	4.5942
23	66.247	0.0151	326.237	0.0031	4.9245	0.2031	4.6475
24	79.497	0.0126	392.484	0.0026	4.9371	0.2026	4.6943
25	95.396	0.0105	471.981	0.0021	4.9476	0.2021	4.7352
26	114.475	0.0087	567.377	0.0018	4.9563	0.2018	4.7709
27	137.371	0.0073	681.853	0.0015	4.9636	0.2015	4.8020
28	164.845	0.0061	819.223	0.0012	4.9697	0.2012	4.8291
29	197.814	0.0051	984.068	0.0010	4.9747	0.2010	4.8527
30	237.376	0.0042	1181.882	0.0009	4.9789	0.2009	4.8731
31	284.852	0.0035	1419.258	0.0007	4.9825	0.2007	4.8908
32	341.822	0.0029	1704.109	0.0006	4.9854	0.2006	4.9061
33	410.186	0.0024	2045.931	0.0005	4.9878	0.2005	4.9194
34	492.224	0.0020	2456.118	0.0004	4.9899	0.2004	4.9308
35	590.668	0.0017	2948.341	0.0003	4.9915	0.2003	4.9407
40	1469.772	0.0007	7343.858	0.0002	4.9966	0.2001	4.9728
45	3657.262	0.0003	18281.310	0.0001	4.9986	0.2001	4.9877
50	9100.438	0.0001	45497.191	0.0000	4.9995	0.2000	4.9945

TABLE A.18. *25% Interest Factors for Annual Compounding Interest*

	Single Payment		Equal Payment Series				Uniform gradient-series factor
	Compound-amount factor	Present-worth factor	Compound-amount factor	Sinking-fund factor	Present-worth factor	Capital-recovery factor	
n	To find F Given P F/P i, n	To find P Given F P/F i, n	To find F Given A F/A i, n	To find A Given F A/F i, n	To find P Given A P/A i, n	To find A Given P A/P i, n	To find A Given G A/G i, n
1	1.250	0.8000	1.000	1.0000	0.8000	1.2500	0.0000
2	1.563	0.6400	2.250	0.4445	1.4400	0.6945	0.4445
3	1.953	0.5120	3.813	0.2623	1.9520	0.5123	0.8525
4	2.441	0.4096	5.766	0.1735	2.3616	0.4235	1.2249
5	3.052	0.3277	8.207	0.1219	2.6893	0.3719	1.5631
6	3.815	0.2622	11.259	0.0888	2.9514	0.3388	1.8683
7	4.768	0.2097	15.073	0.0664	3.1611	0.3164	2.1424
8	5.960	0.1678	19.842	0.0504	3.3289	0.3004	2.3873
9	7.451	0.1342	25.802	0.0388	3.4631	0.2888	2.6048
10	9.313	0.1074	33.253	0.0301	3.5705	0.2801	2.7971
11	11.642	0.0859	42.566	0.0235	3.6564	0.2735	2.9663
12	14.552	0.0687	54.208	0.0185	3.7251	0.2685	3.1145
13	18.190	0.0550	68.760	0.0146	3.7801	0.2646	3.2438
14	22.737	0.0440	86.949	0.0115	3.8241	0.2615	3.3560
15	28.422	0.0352	109.687	0.0091	3.8593	0.2591	3.4530
16	35.527	0.0282	138.109	0.0073	3.8874	0.2573	3.5366
17	44.409	0.0225	173.636	0.0058	3.9099	0.2558	3.6084
18	55.511	0.0180	218.045	0.0046	3.9280	0.2546	3.6698
19	69.389	0.0144	273.556	0.0037	3.9424	0.2537	3.7222
20	86.736	0.0115	342.945	0.0029	3.9539	0.2529	3.7667
21	108.420	0.0092	429.681	0.0023	3.9631	0.2523	3.8045
22	135.525	0.0074	538.101	0.0019	3.9705	0.2519	3.8365
23	169.407	0.0059	673.626	0.0015	3.9764	0.2515	3.8634
24	211.758	0.0047	843.033	0.0012	3.9811	0.2512	3.8861
25	264.698	0.0038	1054.791	0.0010	3.9849	0.2510	3.9052
26	330.872	0.0030	1319.489	0.0008	3.9879	0.2508	3.9212
27	413.590	0.0024	1650.361	0.0006	3.9903	0.2506	3.9346
28	516.988	0.0019	2063.952	0.0005	3.9923	0.2505	3.9457
29	646.235	0.0016	2580.939	0.0004	3.9938	0.2504	3.9551
30	807.794	0.0012	3227.174	0.0003	3.9951	0.2503	3.9628
31	1009.742	0.0010	4034.968	0.0003	3.9960	0.2503	3.9693
32	1262.177	0.0008	5044.710	0.0002	3.9968	0.2502	3.9746
33	1577.722	0.0006	6306.887	0.0002	3.9975	0.2502	3.9791
34	1972.152	0.0005	7884.609	0.0001	3.9980	0.2501	3.9828
35	2465.190	0.0004	9856.761	0.0001	3.9984	0.2501	3.9858

Reprinted, by permission, from H. J. Thuesen et al., *Engineering Economy*, pp. 537-577. Copyright © 1977 by Prentice-Hall Inc.

TABLE A.19. *30% Interest Factors for Annual Compounding Interest*

	Single Payment		Equal Payment Series				Uniform gradient-series factor
	Compound-amount factor	Present-worth factor	Compound-amount factor	Sinking-fund factor	Present-worth factor	Capital-recovery factor	
n	To find F Given P F/P i, n	To find P Given F P/F i, n	To find F Given A F/A i, n	To find A Given F A/F i, n	To find P Given A P/A i, n	To find A Given P A/P i, n	To find A Given G A/G i, n
1	1.300	0.7692	1.000	1.0000	0.7692	1.3000	0.0000
2	1.690	0.5917	2.300	0.4348	1.3610	0.7348	0.4348
3	2.197	0.4552	3.990	0.2506	1.8161	0.5506	0.8271
4	2.856	0.3501	6.187	0.1616	2.1663	0.4616	1.1783
5	3.713	0.2693	9.043	0.1106	2.4356	0.4106	1.4903
6	4.827	0.2072	12.756	0.0784	2.6428	0.3784	1.7655
7	6.275	0.1594	17.583	0.0569	2.8021	0.3569	2.0063
8	8.157	0.1226	23.858	0.0419	2.9247	0.3419	2.2156
9	10.605	0.0943	32.015	0.0312	3.0190	0.3312	2.3963
10	13.786	0.0725	42.620	0.0235	3.0915	0.3235	2.5512
11	17.922	0.0558	56.405	0.0177	3.1473	0.3177	2.6833
12	23.298	0.0429	74.327	0.0135	3.1903	0.3135	2.7952
13	30.288	0.0330	97.625	0.0103	3.2233	0.3103	2.8895
14	39.374	0.0254	127.913	0.0078	3.2487	0.3078	2.9685
15	51.186	0.0195	167.286	0.0060	3.2682	0.3060	3.0345
16	66.542	0.0150	218.472	0.0046	3.2832	0.3046	3.0892
17	86.504	0.0116	285.014	0.0035	3.2948	0.3035	3.1345
18	112.455	0.0089	371.518	0.0027	3.3037	0.3027	3.1718
19	146.192	0.0069	483.973	0.0021	3.3105	0.3021	3.2025
20	190.050	0.0053	630.165	0.0016	3.3158	0.3016	3.2276
21	247.065	0.0041	820.215	0.0012	3.3199	0.3012	3.2480
22	321.184	0.0031	1067.280	0.0009	3.3230	0.3009	3.2646
23	417.539	0.0024	1388.464	0.0007	3.3254	0.3007	3.2781
24	542.801	0.0019	1806.003	0.0006	3.3272	0.3006	3.2890
25	705.641	0.0014	2348.803	0.0004	3.3286	0.3004	3.2979
26	917.333	0.0011	3054.444	0.0003	3.3297	0.3003	3.3050
27	1192.533	0.0008	3971.778	0.0003	3.3305	0.3003	3.3107
28	1550.293	0.0007	5164.311	0.0002	3.3312	0.3002	3.3153
29	2015.381	0.0005	6714.604	0.0002	3.3317	0.3002	3.3189
30	2619.996	0.0004	8729.985	0.0001	3.3321	0.3001	3.3219
31	3405.994	0.0003	11349.981	0.0001	3.3324	0.3001	3.3242
32	4427.793	0.0002	14755.975	0.0001	3.3326	0.3001	3.3261
33	5756.130	0.0002	19183.768	0.0001	3.3328	0.3001	3.3276
34	7482.970	0.0001	24939.899	0.0001	3.3329	0.3001	3.3288
35	9727.860	0.0001	32422.868	0.0000	3.3330	0.3000	3.3297

Reprinted, by permission, from H. J. Thuesen et al., *Engineering Economy*, pp. 537-577. Copyright © 1977 by Prentice-Hall Inc.

TABLE A.20. *40% Interest Factors for Annual Compounding Interest*

	Single Payment		Equal Payment Series				Uniform gradient-series factor
	Compound-amount factor	Present-worth factor	Compound-amount factor	Sinking-fund factor	Present-worth factor	Capital-recovery factor	
n	To find F Given P $F/P\ i, n$	To find P Given F $P/F\ i, n$	To find F Given A $F/A\ i, n$	To find A Given F $A/F\ i, n$	To find P Given A $P/A\ i, n$	To find A Given P $A/P\ i, n$	To find A Given G $A/G\ i, n$
1	1.400	0.7143	1.000	1.0001	0.7143	1.4001	0.0000
2	1.960	0.5103	2.400	0.4167	1.2245	0.8167	0.4167
3	2.744	0.3645	4.360	0.2294	1.5890	0.6294	0.7799
4	3.842	0.2604	7.104	0.1408	1.8493	0.5408	1.0924
5	5.378	0.1860	10.946	0.0914	2.0352	0.4914	1.3580
6	7.530	0.1329	16.324	0.0613	2.1680	0.4613	1.5811
7	10.541	0.0949	23.853	0.0420	2.2629	0.4420	1.7664
8	14.758	0.0678	34.395	0.0291	2.3306	0.4291	1.9186
9	20.661	0.0485	49.153	0.0204	2.3790	0.4204	2.0423
10	28.925	0.0346	69.814	0.0144	2.4136	0.4144	2.1420
11	40.496	0.0247	98.739	0.0102	2.4383	0.4102	2.2215
12	56.694	0.0177	139.234	0.0072	2.4560	0.4072	2.2846
13	79.371	0.0126	195.928	0.0052	2.4686	0.4052	2.3342
14	111.120	0.0090	275.299	0.0037	2.4775	0.4037	2.3729
15	155.568	0.0065	386.419	0.0026	2.4840	0.4026	2.4030
16	217.794	0.0046	541.986	0.0019	2.4886	0.4019	2.4262
17	304.912	0.0033	759.780	0.0014	2.4918	0.4014	2.4441
18	426.877	0.0024	1064.691	0.0010	2.4942	0.4010	2.4578
19	597.627	0.0017	1491.567	0.0007	2.4959	0.4007	2.4682
20	836.678	0.0012	2089.195	0.0005	2.4971	0.4005	2.4761
21	1171.348	0.0009	2925.871	0.0004	2.4979	0.4004	2.4821
22	1639.887	0.0007	4097.218	0.0003	2.4985	0.4003	2.4866
23	2295.842	0.0005	5737.105	0.0002	2.4990	0.4002	2.4900
24	3214.178	0.0004	8032.945	0.0002	2.4993	0.4002	2.4926
25	4499.847	0.0003	11247.110	0.0001	2.4995	0.4001	2.4945
26	6299.785	0.0002	15746.960	0.0001	2.4997	0.4001	2.4959
27	8819.695	0.0002	22046.730	0.0001	2.4998	0.4001	2.4970
28	12347.570	0.0001	30866.430	0.0001	2.4998	0.4001	2.4978
29	17286.590	0.0001	43213.990	0.0001	2.4999	0.4001	2.4984
30	24201.230	0.0001	60500.580	0.0001	2.4999	0.4001	2.4988

Reprinted, by permission, from H. J. Thuesen et al., *Engineering Economy*, pp. 537-577. Copyright © 1977 by Prentice-Hall Inc.

TABLE A.21. *50% Interest Factors for Annual Compounding Interest*

	Single Payment		Equal Payment Series				Uniform gradient-series factor
	Compound-amount factor	Present-worth factor	Compound-amount factor	Sinking-fund factor	Present-worth factor	Capital-recovery factor	
n	To find F Given P F/P i, n	To find P Given F P/F i, n	To find F Given A F/A i, n	To find A Given F A/F i, n	To find P Given A P/A i, n	To find A Given P A/P i, n	To find A Given G A/G i, n
1	1.500	0.6667	1.000	1.0000	0.6667	1.5000	0.0001
2	2.250	0.4445	2.500	0.4000	1.1112	0.9001	0.4001
3	3.375	0.2963	4.750	0.2106	1.4075	0.7106	0.7369
4	5.063	0.1976	8.125	0.1231	1.6050	0.6231	1.0154
5	7.594	0.1317	13.188	0.0759	1.7367	0.5759	1.2418
6	11.391	0.0878	20.781	0.0482	1.8245	0.5482	1.4226
7	17.086	0.0586	32.172	0.0311	1.8830	0.5311	1.5649
8	25.629	0.0391	49.258	0.0204	1.9220	0.5204	1.6752
9	38.443	0.0261	74.887	0.0134	1.9480	0.5134	1.7597
10	57.665	0.0174	113.330	0.0089	1.9654	0.5089	1.8236
11	86.498	0.0116	170.995	0.0059	1.9769	0.5059	1.8714
12	129.746	0.0078	257.493	0.0039	1.9846	0.5039	1.9068
13	194.620	0.0052	387.239	0.0026	1.9898	0.5026	1.9329
14	291.929	0.0035	581.858	0.0018	1.9932	0.5018	1.9519
15	437.894	0.0023	873.788	0.0012	1.9955	0.5012	1.9657
16	656.841	0.0016	1311.681	0.0008	1.9970	0.5008	1.9757
17	985.261	0.0011	1968.522	0.0006	1.9980	0.5006	1.9828
18	1477.891	0.0007	2953.783	0.0004	1.9987	0.5004	1.9879
19	2216.837	0.0005	4431.671	0.0003	1.9991	0.5003	1.9915
20	3325.256	0.0004	6648.511	0.0002	1.9994	0.5002	1.9940
21	4987.882	0.0003	9973.765	0.0002	1.9996	0.5002	1.9958
22	7481.824	0.0002	14961.640	0.0001	1.9998	0.5001	1.9971
23	11222.730	0.0001	22443.470	0.0001	1.9999	0.5001	1.9980
24	16834.100	0.0001	33666.210	0.0001	1.9999	0.5001	1.9986
25	25251.160	0.0001	50500.330	0.0001	2.0000	0.5001	1.9991

Reprinted, by permission, from H. J. Thuesen et al., *Engineering Economy*, pp. 537-577. Copyright © 1977 by Prentice-Hall Inc.

APPENDIX

B

CONVERSION OF NOMINAL RATES TO EFFECTIVE RATES

TABLE B.1. *Effective Interest Rates Corresponding to Nominal Rate r*

	Compounding Frequency					
r	Semi-annually $\left(1+\frac{r}{2}\right)^2 -1$	Quarterly $\left(1+\frac{r}{4}\right)^4 -1$	Monthly $\left(1+\frac{r}{12}\right)^{12} -1$	Weekly $\left(1+\frac{r}{52}\right)^{52} -1$	Daily $\left(1+\frac{r}{365}\right)^{365} -1$	Continu-ously $\left(1+\frac{r}{\infty}\right)^{\infty} -1$
.01	.010025	.010038	.010046	.010049	.010050	.010050
.02	.020100	.020151	.020184	.020197	.020200	.020201
.03	.030225	.030339	.030416	.030444	.030451	.030455
.04	.040400	.040604	.040741	.040793	.040805	.040811
.05	.050625	.050945	.051161	.051244	.051261	.051271
.06	.060900	.061364	.061678	.061797	.061799	.061837
.07	.071225	.071859	.072290	.072455	.072469	.072508
.08	.081600	.082432	.082999	.083217	.083246	.083287
.09	.092025	.093083	.093807	.094085	.094132	.094174
.10	.102500	.103813	.104713	.105060	.105126	.105171
.11	.113025	.114621	.115718	.116144	.116231	.116278
.12	.123600	.125509	.126825	.127336	.127447	.127497
.13	.134225	.136476	.138032	.138644	.138775	.138828
.14	.144900	.147523	.149341	.150057	.150217	.150274
.15	.155625	.158650	.160755	.161582	.161773	.161834
.16	.166400	.169859	.172270	.173221	.173446	.173511
.17	.177225	.181148	.183891	.184974	.185235	.185305
.18	.188100	.192517	.195618	.196843	.197142	.197217
.19	.199025	.203971	.207451	.208828	.209169	.209250
.20	.210000	.215506	.219390	.220931	.221316	.221403
.21	.221025	.227124	.231439	.233153	.233584	.233678
.22	.232100	.238825	.243596	.245494	.245976	.246077
.23	.243225	.250609	.255863	.257957	.258492	.258600
.24	.254400	.262477	.268242	.270542	.271133	.271249
.25	.265625	.274429	.280731	.283250	.283901	.284025
.26	.276900	.286466	.293333	.296090	.296796	.296930
.27	.288225	.298588	.306050	.309049	.309821	.309964
.28	.299600	.310796	.318880	.322135	.322976	.323130
.29	.311025	.323089	.331826	.335350	.336264	.336428
.30	.322500	.335469	.344889	.348693	.349684	.349859
.31	.334025	.347936	.358068	.362168	.363238	.363425
.32	.345600	.360489	.371366	.375775	.376928	.377128
.33	.357225	.373130	.384784	.389515	.390756	.390968
.34	.368900	.385859	.398321	.403389	.404722	.404948
.35	.380625	.398676	.411979	.417399	.418827	.419068

APPENDIX

C

CONTINUOUS INTEREST FACTORS

TABLE C.1. *1% Interest Factors for Continuous Compounding Interest*

	Single Payment		Equal Payment Series				Uniform gradient-series factor
	Compound-amount factor	Present-worth factor	Compound-amount factor	Sinking-fund factor	Present-worth factor	Capital-recovery factor	
n	To find F Given P F/P r, n	To find P Given F P/F r, n	To find F Given A F/A r, n	To find A Given F A/F r, n	To find P Given A P/A r, n	To find A Given P A/P r, n	To find A Given G A/G r, n
1	1.010	0.9901	1.000	1.0000	0.9901	1.0101	0.0000
2	1.020	0.9802	2.010	0.4975	1.9703	0.5076	0.4975
3	1.030	0.9705	3.030	0.3300	2.9407	0.3401	0.9933
4	1.041	0.9608	4.061	0.2463	3.9015	0.2563	1.4875
5	1.051	0.9512	5.102	0.1960	4.8527	0.2061	1.9800
6	1.062	0.9418	6.153	0.1625	5.7945	0.1726	2.4708
7	1.073	0.9324	7.215	0.1386	6.7269	0.1487	2.9600
8	1.083	0.9231	8.287	0.1207	7.6500	0.1307	3.4475
9	1.094	0.9139	9.370	0.1067	8.5639	0.1168	3.9334
10	1.105	0.9048	10.465	0.0956	9.4688	0.1056	4.4175
11	1.116	0.8958	11.570	0.0864	10.3646	0.0965	4.9000
12	1.128	0.8869	12.686	0.0788	11.2515	0.0889	5.3809
13	1.139	0.8781	13.814	0.0724	12.1296	0.0825	5.8600
14	1.150	0.8694	14.952	0.0669	12.9990	0.0769	6.3376
15	1.162	0.8607	16.103	0.0621	13.8597	0.0722	6.8134
16	1.174	0.8522	17.264	0.0579	14.7118	0.0680	7.2876
17	1.185	0.8437	18.438	0.0542	15.5555	0.0643	7.7601
18	1.197	0.8353	19.623	0.0510	16.3908	0.0610	8.2310
19	1.209	0.8270	20.821	0.0480	17.2177	0.0581	8.7002
20	1.221	0.8187	22.030	0.0454	18.0365	0.0555	9.1677
21	1.234	0.8106	23.251	0.0430	18.8470	0.0531	9.6336
22	1.246	0.8025	24.485	0.0409	19.6496	0.0509	10.0978
23	1.259	0.7945	25.731	0.0389	20.4441	0.0489	10.5604
24	1.271	0.7866	26.990	0.0371	21.2307	0.0471	11.0213
25	1.284	0.7788	28.261	0.0354	22.0095	0.0454	11.4806
26	1.297	0.7711	29.545	0.0339	22.7806	0.0439	11.9381
27	1.310	0.7634	30.842	0.0324	23.5439	0.0425	12.3941
28	1.323	0.7558	32.152	0.0311	24.2997	0.0412	12.8484
29	1.336	0.7483	33.475	0.0299	25.0480	0.0399	13.3010
30	1.350	0.7408	34.811	0.0287	25.7888	0.0388	13.7520
31	1.363	0.7335	36.161	0.0277	26.5223	0.0377	14.2013
32	1.377	0.7262	37.525	0.0267	27.2484	0.0367	14.6490
33	1.391	0.7189	38.902	0.0257	27.9673	0.0358	15.0950
34	1.405	0.7118	40.293	0.0248	28.6791	0.0349	15.5394
35	1.419	0.7047	41.698	0.0240	29.3838	0.0340	15.9821
40	1.492	0.6703	48.937	0.0204	32.8034	0.0305	18.1711
45	1.568	0.6376	56.548	0.0177	36.0563	0.0277	20.3190
50	1.649	0.6065	64.548	0.0155	39.1505	0.0256	22.4261
55	1.733	0.5770	72.959	0.0137	42.0939	0.0238	24.4926
60	1.822	0.5488	81.802	0.0122	44.8936	0.0223	26.5187
65	1.916	0.5221	91.097	0.0110	47.5569	0.0210	28.5045
70	2.014	0.4966	100.869	0.0099	50.0902	0.0200	30.4505
75	2.117	0.4724	111.142	0.0090	52.5000	0.0191	32.3567
80	2.226	0.4493	121.942	0.0082	54.7922	0.0183	34.2235
85	2.340	0.4274	133.296	0.0075	56.9727	0.0176	36.0513
90	2.460	0.4066	145.232	0.0069	59.0468	0.0169	37.8402
95	2.586	0.3868	157.779	0.0063	61.0198	0.0164	39.5907
100	2.718	0.3679	170.970	0.0059	62.8965	0.0159	41.3032

Reprinted, by permission, from H. J. Thuesen et al., *Engineering Economy*, pp. 537–577. Copyright © 1977 by Prentice-Hall Inc.

TABLE C.2. 2% Interest Factors for Continuous Compounding Interest

	Single Payment		Equal Payment Series				Uniform gradient-series factor
	Compound-amount factor	Present-worth factor	Compound-amount factor	Sinking-fund factor	Present-worth factor	Capital-recovery factor	
n	To find F Given P F/P r, n	To find P Given F P/F r, n	To find F Given A F/A r, n	To find A Given F A/F r, n	To find P Given A P/A r, n	To find A Given P A/P r, n	To find A Given G A/G r, n
1	1.020	0.9802	1.000	1.0000	0.9802	1.0202	0.0000
2	1.041	0.9608	2.020	0.4950	1.9410	0.5152	0.4950
3	1.062	0.9418	3.061	0.3267	2.8828	0.3469	0.9867
4	1.083	0.9231	4.123	0.2426	3.8059	0.2628	1.4750
5	1.105	0.9048	5.206	0.1921	4.7107	0.2123	1.9600
6	1.128	0.8869	6.311	0.1585	5.5976	0.1787	2.4417
7	1.150	0.8694	7.439	0.1344	6.4670	0.1546	2.9200
8	1.174	0.8522	8.589	0.1164	7.3191	0.1366	3.3951
9	1.197	0.8353	9.763	0.1024	8.1544	0.1226	3.8667
10	1.221	0.8187	10.960	0.0913	8.9731	0.1115	4.3351
11	1.246	0.8025	12.181	0.0821	9.7757	0.1023	4.8002
12	1.271	0.7866	13.427	0.0745	10.5623	0.0947	5.2619
13	1.297	0.7711	14.699	0.0680	11.3333	0.0882	5.7203
14	1.323	0.7558	15.995	0.0625	12.0891	0.0827	6.1754
15	1.350	0.7408	17.319	0.0578	12.8299	0.0780	6.6272
16	1.377	0.7262	18.668	0.0536	13.5561	0.0738	7.0757
17	1.405	0.7118	20.046	0.0499	14.2679	0.0701	7.5209
18	1.433	0.6977	21.451	0.0466	14.9655	0.0668	7.9628
19	1.462	0.6839	22.884	0.0437	15.6494	0.0639	8.4015
20	1.492	0.6703	24.346	0.0411	16.3197	0.0613	8.8368
21	1.522	0.6571	25.838	0.0387	16.9768	0.0589	9.2688
22	1.553	0.6440	27.360	0.0366	17.6208	0.0568	9.6976
23	1.584	0.6313	28.913	0.0346	18.2521	0.0548	10.1231
24	1.616	0.6188	30.497	0.0328	18.8709	0.0530	10.5453
25	1.649	0.6065	32.113	0.0312	19.4774	0.0514	10.9643
26	1.682	0.5945	33.762	0.0296	20.0719	0.0498	11.3801
27	1.716	0.5828	35.444	0.0282	20.6547	0.0484	11.7925
28	1.751	0.5712	37.160	0.0269	21.2259	0.0471	12.2018
29	1.786	0.5599	38.910	0.0257	21.7858	0.0459	12.6078
30	1.822	0.5488	40.696	0.0246	22.3346	0.0448	13.0106
31	1.859	0.5380	42.518	0.0235	22.8725	0.0437	13.4102
32	1.896	0.5273	44.377	0.0225	23.3998	0.0427	13.8065
33	1.935	0.5169	46.274	0.0216	23.9167	0.0418	14.1997
34	1.974	0.5066	48.209	0.0208	24.4233	0.0410	14.5897
35	2.014	0.4966	50.182	0.0199	24.9199	0.0401	14.9765
40	2.226	0.4493	60.666	0.0165	27.2591	0.0367	16.8630
45	2.460	0.4066	72.253	0.0139	29.3758	0.0341	18.6714
50	2.718	0.3679	85.058	0.0118	31.2910	0.0320	20.4028
55	3.004	0.3329	99.210	0.0101	33.0240	0.0303	22.0588
60	3.320	0.3012	114.850	0.0087	34.5921	0.0289	23.6409
65	3.669	0.2725	132.135	0.0076	36.0109	0.0278	25.1507
70	4.055	0.2466	151.238	0.0066	37.2947	0.0268	26.5899
75	4.482	0.2231	172.349	0.0058	38.4564	0.0260	27.9604
80	4.953	0.2019	195.682	0.0051	39.5075	0.0253	29.2640
85	5.474	0.1827	221.468	0.0045	40.4585	0.0247	30.5028
90	6.050	0.1653	249.966	0.0040	41.3191	0.0242	31.6786
95	6.686	0.1496	281.461	0.0036	42.0978	0.0238	32.7937
100	7.389	0.1353	316.269	0.0032	42.8024	0.0234	33.8499

Reprinted, by permission, from H. J. Thuesen et al., *Engineering Economy*, pp. 537-577. Copyright © 1977 by Prentice-Hall Inc.

TABLE C.3. *3% Interest Factors for Continuous Compounding Interest*

	Single Payment		Equal Payment Series				Uniform gradient-series factor
	Compound-amount factor	Present-worth factor	Compound-amount factor	Sinking-fund factor	Present-worth factor	Capital-recovery factor	
n	To find *F* Given *P* F/P r, n	To find *P* Given *F* P/F r, n	To find *F* Given *A* F/A r, n	To find *A* Given *F* A/F r, n	To find *P* Given *A* P/A r, n	To find *A* Given *P* A/P r, n	To find *A* Given *G* A/G r, n
1	1.030	0.9705	1.000	1.0000	0.9705	1.0305	0.0000
2	1.062	0.9418	2.030	0.4925	1.9122	0.5230	0.4925
3	1.094	0.9139	3.092	0.3234	2.8262	0.3538	0.9800
4	1.128	0.8869	4.186	0.2389	3.7131	0.2693	1.4625
5	1.162	0.8607	5.314	0.1882	4.5738	0.2186	1.9400
6	1.197	0.8353	6.476	0.1544	5.4090	0.1849	2.4126
7	1.234	0.8106	7.673	0.1303	6.2196	0.1608	2.8801
8	1.271	0.7866	8.907	0.1123	7.0063	0.1427	3.3427
9	1.310	0.7634	10.178	0.0983	7.7696	0.1287	3.8003
10	1.350	0.7408	11.488	0.0871	8.5105	0.1175	4.2529
11	1.391	0.7189	12.838	0.0779	9 2294	0.1084	4.7006
12	1.433	0.6977	14.229	0.0703	9.9271	0.1007	5.1433
13	1.477	0.6771	15.662	0.0639	10.6041	0.0943	5.5811
14	1.522	0.6571	17.139	0.0584	11.2612	0.0888	6.0139
15	1.568	0.6376	18.661	0.0536	11.8988	0.0841	6.4419
16	1.616	0.6188	20.229	0.0494	12.5176	0.0799	6.8650
17	1.665	0.6005	21.845	0.0458	13.1181	0.0762	7.2831
18	1.716	0.5828	23.511	0.0425	13.7008	0.0730	7.6964
19	1.768	0.5655	25.227	0.0397	14.2663	0.0701	8.1049
20	1.822	0.5488	26.995	0.0371	14.8152	0 0675	8.5085
21	1.878	0.5326	28.817	0.0347	15.3477	0.0652	8.9072
22	1.935	0.5169	30.695	0.0326	15.8646	0.0630	9.3012
23	1.994	0.5016	32.629	0.0307	16.3662	0.0611	9.6904
24	2.054	0.4868	34.623	0.0289	16.8529	0.0593	10.0748
25	2.117	0.4724	36.678	0.0273	17.3253	0 0577	10.4545
26	2.181	0.4584	38.795	0.0258	17.7837	0.0562	10.8294
27	2.248	0.4449	40.976	0.0244	18.2286	0.0549	11.1996
28	2.316	0.4317	43.224	0.0231	18.6603	0.0536	11.5652
29	2.387	0.4190	45.540	0.0220	19.0792	0.0524	11.9261
30	2.460	0.4066	47.927	0.0209	19.4858	0.0513	12.2823
31	2.535	0.3946	50.387	0.0199	19.8803	0.0503	12.6339
32	2.612	0.3829	52.921	0.0189	20.2632	0.0494	12.9810
33	2.691	0.3716	55.533	0.0180	20.6348	0.0485	13.3235
34	2.773	0.3606	58.224	0.0172	20.9954	0.0476	13.6614
35	2.858	0.3499	60.998	0.0164	21.3453	0.0469	13.9948
40	3.320	0.3012	76.183	0.0131	22.9459	0.0436	15.5953
45	3.857	0.2593	93.826	0.0107	24.3235	0.0411	17.0874
50	4.482	0.2231	114.324	0.0088	25.5092	0.0392	18.4750
55	5.207	0.1921	138.140	0.0072	26.5297	0.0377	19.7623
60	6.050	0.1653	165.809	0.0060	27.4081	0.0365	20.9538
65	7.029	0.1423	197.957	0.0051	28.1642	0.0355	22.0540
70	8.166	0.1225	235.307	0.0043	28.8149	0.0347	23.0677
75	9.488	0.1054	278.702	0.0036	29.3750	0.0341	23.9996
80	11.023	0.0907	329.119	0.0030	29.8570	0.0335	24.8543
85	12.807	0.0781	387.696	0.0026	30.2720	0.0330	25.6368
90	14.880	0.0672	455.753	0.0022	30.6291	0.0327	26.3516
95	17.288	0.0579	534.823	0.0019	30.9365	0.0323	27.0033
100	20.086	0.0498	626.690	0.0016	31.2010	0.0321	27.5963

Reprinted, by permission, from H. J. Thuesen et al., *Engineering Economy*, pp. 537-577. Copyright © 1977 by Prentice-Hall Inc.

TABLE C.4. 4% Interest Factors for Continuous Compounding Interest

	Single Payment		Equal Payment Series				Uniform gradient-series factor
	Compound-amount factor	Present-worth factor	Compound-amount factor	Sinking-fund factor	Present-worth factor	Capital-recovery factor	
n	To find F Given P F/P r,n	To find P Given F P/F r,n	To find F Given A F/A r,n	To find A Given F A/F r,n	To find P Given A P/A r,n	To find A Given P A/P r,n	To find A Given G A/G r,n
1	1.041	0.9608	1.000	1.0000	0.9608	1.0408	0.0000
2	1.083	0.9231	2.041	0.4900	1.8839	0.5308	0.4900
3	1.128	0.8869	3.124	0.3201	2.7708	0.3609	0.9734
4	1.174	0.8522	4.252	0.2352	3.6230	0.2760	1.4500
5	1.221	0.8187	5.425	0.1843	4.4417	0.2251	1.9201
6	1.271	0.7866	6.647	0.1505	5.2283	0.1913	2.3835
7	1.323	0.7558	7.918	0.1263	5.9841	0.1671	2.8402
8	1.377	0.7262	9.241	0.1082	6.7103	0.1490	3.2904
9	1.433	0.6977	10.618	0.0942	7.4079	0.1350	3.7339
10	1.492	0.6703	12.051	0.0830	8.0783	0.1238	4.1709
11	1.553	0.6440	13.543	0.0738	8.7223	0.1147	4.6013
12	1.616	0.6188	15.096	0.0663	9.3411	0.1071	5.0252
13	1.682	0.5945	16.712	0.0598	9.9356	0.1007	5.4425
14	1.751	0.5712	18.394	0.0544	10.5068	0.0952	5.8534
15	1.822	0.5488	20.145	0.0497	11.0556	0.0905	6.2578
16	1.896	0.5273	21.967	0.0455	11.5829	0.0863	6.6558
17	1.974	0.5066	23.863	0.0419	12.0895	0.0827	7.0474
18	2.054	0.4868	25.837	0.0387	12.5763	0.0795	7.4326
19	2.138	0.4677	27.892	0.0359	13.0440	0.0767	7.8114
20	2.226	0.4493	30.030	0.0333	13.4933	0.0741	8.1840
21	2.316	0.4317	32.255	0.0310	13.9250	0.0718	8.5503
22	2.411	0.4148	34.572	0.0289	14.3398	0.0697	8.9105
23	2.509	0.3985	36.983	0.0270	14.7383	0.0679	9.2644
24	2.612	0.3829	39.492	0.0253	15.1212	0.0661	9.6122
25	2.718	0.3679	42.104	0.0238	15.4891	0.0646	9.9539
26	2.829	0.3535	44.822	0.0223	15.8425	0.0631	10.2896
27	2.945	0.3396	47.651	0.0210	16.1821	0.0618	10.6193
28	3.065	0.3263	50.596	0.0198	16.5084	0.0606	10.9431
29	3.190	0.3135	53.661	0.0186	16.8219	0.0595	11.2609
30	3.320	0.3012	56.851	0.0176	17.1231	0.0584	11.5730
31	3.456	0.2894	60.171	0.0166	17.4125	0.0574	11.8792
32	3.597	0.2780	63.626	0.0157	17.6905	0.0565	12.1797
33	3.743	0.2671	67.223	0.0149	17.9576	0.0557	12.4746
34	3.896	0.2567	70.966	0.0141	18.2143	0.0549	12.7638
35	4.055	0.2466	74.863	0.0134	18.4609	0.0542	13.0475
40	4.953	0.2019	96.862	0.0103	19.5562	0.0511	14.3845
45	6.050	0.1653	123.733	0.0081	20.4530	0.0489	15.5918
50	7.389	0.1353	156.553	0.0064	21.1872	0.0472	16.6775
55	9.025	0.1108	196.640	0.0051	21.7883	0.0459	17.6498
60	11.023	0.0907	245.601	0.0041	22.2805	0.0449	18.5172
65	13.464	0.0743	305.403	0.0033	22.6834	0.0441	19.2882
70	16.445	0.0608	378.445	0.0027	23.0133	0.0435	19.9710
75	20.086	0.0498	467.659	0.0021	23.2834	0.0430	20.5737
80	24.533	0.0408	576.625	0.0017	23.5045	0.0426	21.1038
85	29.964	0.0334	709.717	0.0014	23.6856	0.0422	21.5687
90	36.598	0.0273	872.275	0.0012	23.8338	0.0420	21.9751
95	44.701	0.0224	1070.825	0.0009	23.9552	0.0418	22.3295
100	54.598	0.0183	1313.333	0.0008	24.0545	0.0416	22.6376

TABLE C.5. 5% Interest Factors for Continuous Compounding Interest

	Single Payment		Equal Payment Series				Uniform gradient-series factor
	Compound-amount factor	Present-worth factor	Compound-amount factor	Sinking-fund factor	Present-worth factor	Capital-recovery factor	
n	To find F Given P F/P r, n	To find P Given F P/F r, n	To find F Given A F/A r, n	To find A Given F A/F r, n	To find P Given A P/A r, n	To find A Given P A/P r, n	To find A Given G A/G r, n
1	1.051	0.9512	1.000	1.0000	0.9512	1.0513	0.0000
2	1.105	0.9048	2.051	0.4875	1.8561	0.5388	0.4875
3	1.162	0.8607	3.156	0.3168	2.7168	0.3681	0.9667
4	1.221	0.8187	4.318	0.2316	3.5355	0.2829	1.4376
5	1.284	0.7788	5.540	0.1805	4.3143	0.2318	1.9001
6	1.350	0.7408	6.824	0.1466	5.0551	0.1978	2.3544
7	1.419	0.7047	8.174	0.1224	5.7598	0.1736	2.8004
8	1.492	0.6703	9.593	0.1043	6.4301	0.1555	3.2382
9	1.568	0.6376	11.084	0.0902	7.0678	0.1415	3.6678
10	1.649	0.6065	12.653	0.0790	7.6743	0.1303	4.0892
11	1.733	0.5770	14.301	0.0699	8.2513	0.1212	4.5025
12	1.822	0.5488	16.035	0.0624	8.8001	0.1136	4.9077
13	1.916	0.5221	17.857	0.0560	9.3221	0.1073	5.3049
14	2.014	0.4966	19.772	0.0506	9.8187	0.1019	5.6941
15	2.117	0.4724	21.786	0.0459	10.2911	0.0972	6.0753
16	2.226	0.4493	23.903	0.0418	10.7404	0.0931	6.4487
17	2.340	0.4274	26.129	0.0383	11.1678	0.0896	6.8143
18	2.460	0.4066	28.468	0.0351	11.5744	0.0864	7.1721
19	2.586	0.3868	30.928	0.0323	11.9611	0.0836	7.5222
20	2.718	0.3679	33.514	0.0298	12.3290	0.0811	7.8646
21	2.858	0.3499	36.232	0.0276	12.6789	0.0789	8.1996
22	3.004	0.3329	39.090	0.0256	13.0118	0.0769	8.5270
23	3.158	0.3166	42.094	0.0238	13.3284	0.0750	8.8471
24	3.320	0.3012	45.252	0.0221	13.6296	0.0734	9.1599
25	3.490	0.2865	48.572	0.0206	13.9161	0.0719	9.4654
26	3.669	0.2725	52.062	0.0192	14.1887	0.0705	9.7638
27	3.857	0.2593	55.732	0.0180	14.4479	0.0692	10.0551
28	4.055	0.2466	59.589	0.0168	14.6945	0.0681	10.3395
29	4.263	0.2346	63.644	0.0157	14.9291	0.0670	10.6170
30	4.482	0.2231	67.907	0.0147	15.1522	0.0660	10.8877
31	4.711	0.2123	72.389	0.0138	15.3645	0.0651	11.1517
32	4.953	0.2019	77.101	0.0130	15.5664	0.0643	11.4091
33	5.207	0.1921	82.054	0.0122	15.7584	0.0635	11.6601
34	5.474	0.1827	87.261	0.0115	15.9411	0.0627	11.9046
35	5.755	0.1738	92.735	0.0108	16.1149	0.0621	12.1429
40	7.389	0.1353	124.613	0.0080	16.8646	0.0593	13.2435
45	9.488	0.1054	165.546	0.0061	17.4485	0.0573	14.2024
50	12.183	0.0821	218.105	0.0046	17.9032	0.0559	15.0329
55	15.643	0.0639	285.592	0.0035	18.2573	0.0548	15.7480
60	20.086	0.0498	372.247	0.0027	18.5331	0.0540	16.3604
65	25.790	0.0388	483.515	0.0021	18.7479	0.0533	16.8822
70	33.115	0.0302	626.385	0.0016	18.9152	0.0529	17.3245
75	42.521	0.0235	809.834	0.0012	19.0455	0.0525	17.6979
80	54.598	0.0183	1045.387	0.0010	19.1469	0.0522	18.0116
85	70.105	0.0143	1347.843	0.0008	19.2260	0.0520	18.2742
90	90.017	0.0111	1736.205	0.0006	19.2875	0.0519	18.4931
95	115.584	0.0087	2234.871	0.0005	19.3354	0.0517	18.6751
100	148.413	0.0067	2875.171	0.0004	19.3728	0.0516	18.8258

Reprinted, by permission, from H. J. Thuesen et al., *Engineering Economy*, pp. 537-577. Copyright © 1977 by Prentice-Hall Inc.

TABLE C.6. 6% Interest Factors for Continuous Compounding Interest

	Single Payment		Equal Payment Series				Uniform gradient-series factor
	Compound-amount factor	Present-worth factor	Compound-amount factor	Sinking-fund factor	Present-worth factor	Capital-recovery factor	
n	To find F Given P $F/P \quad r,n$	To find P Given F $P/F \quad r,n$	To find F Given A $F/A \quad r,n$	To find A Given F $A/F \quad r,n$	To find P Given A $P/A \quad r,n$	To find A Given P $A/P \quad r,n$	To find A Given G $A/G \quad r,n$
1	1.062	0.9418	1.000	1.0000	0.9418	1.0618	0.0000
2	1.128	0.8869	2.062	0.4850	1.8287	0.5469	0.4850
3	1.197	0.8353	3.189	0.3136	2.6640	0.3754	0.9600
4	1.271	0.7866	4.387	0.2280	3.4506	0.2898	1.4251
5	1.350	0.7408	5.658	0.1768	4.1914	0.2386	1.8802
6	1.433	0.6977	7.008	0.1427	4.8891	0.2045	2.3254
7	1.522	0.6571	8.441	0.1185	5.5461	0.1803	2.7607
8	1.616	0.6188	9.963	0.1004	6.1649	0.1622	3.1862
9	1.716	0.5828	11.579	0.0864	6.7477	0.1482	3.6020
10	1.822	0.5488	13.295	0.0752	7.2965	0.1371	4.0080
11	1.935	0.5169	15.117	0.0662	7.8133	0.1280	4.4044
12	2.054	0.4868	17.052	0.0587	8.3001	0.1205	4.7912
13	2.181	0.4584	19.106	0.0523	8.7585	0.1142	5.1685
14	2.316	0.4317	21.288	0.0470	9.1902	0.1088	5.5363
15	2.460	0.4066	23.604	0.0424	9.5968	0.1042	5.8949
16	2.612	0.3829	26.064	0.0384	9.9797	0.1002	6.2442
17	2.773	0.3606	28.676	0.0349	10.3403	0.0967	6.5845
18	2.945	0.3396	31.449	0.0318	10.6799	0.0936	6.9157
19	3.127	0.3198	34.393	0.0291	10.9997	0.0909	7.2379
20	3.320	0.3012	37.520	0.0267	11.3009	0.0885	7.5514
21	3.525	0.2837	40.840	0.0245	11.5845	0.0863	7.8562
22	3.743	0.2671	44.366	0.0225	11.8517	0.0844	8.1525
23	3.975	0.2516	48.109	0.0208	12.1032	0.0826	8.4403
24	4.221	0.2369	52.084	0.0192	12.3402	0.0810	8.7199
25	4.482	0.2231	56.305	0.0178	12.5633	0.0796	8.9913
26	4.759	0.2101	60.786	0.0165	12.7734	0.0783	9.2546
27	5.053	0.1979	65.545	0.0153	12.9713	0.0771	9.5101
28	5.366	0.1864	70.598	0.0142	13.1577	0.0760	9.7578
29	5.697	0.1755	75.964	0.0132	13.3332	0.0750	9.9980
30	6.050	0.1653	81.661	0.0123	13.4985	0.0741	10.2307
31	6.424	0.1557	87.711	0.0114	13.6542	0.0732	10.4561
32	6.821	0.1466	94.135	0.0106	13.8008	0.0725	10.6743
33	7.243	0.1381	100.956	0.0099	13.9389	0.0718	10.8855
34	7.691	0.1300	108.198	0.0093	14.0689	0.0711	11.0899
35	8.166	0.1225	115.889	0.0086	14.1914	0.0705	11.2876
40	11.023	0.0907	162.091	0.0062	14.7046	0.0680	12.1809
45	14.880	0.0672	224.458	0.0045	15.0849	0.0663	12.9295
50	20.086	0.0498	308.645	0.0032	15.3665	0.0651	13.5519
55	27.113	0.0369	422.285	0.0024	15.5752	0.0642	14.0654
60	36.598	0.0273	575.683	0.0017	15.7298	0.0636	14.4862
65	49.402	0.0203	782.748	0.0013	15.8443	0.0631	14.8288
70	66.686	0.0150	1062.257	0.0010	15.9292	0.0628	15.1060
75	90.017	0.0111	1439.555	0.0007	15.9920	0.0625	15.3291
80	121.510	0.0082	1948.854	0.0005	16.0386	0.0624	15.5078
85	164.022	0.0061	2636.336	0.0004	16.0731	0.0622	15.6503
90	221.406	0.0045	3564.339	0.0003	16.0986	0.0621	15.7633
95	298.867	0.0034	4817.012	0.0002	16.1176	0.0621	15.8527
100	403.429	0.0025	6507.944	0.0002	16.1316	0.0620	15.9232

TABLE C.7. *7% Interest Factors for Continuous Compounding Interest*

	Single Payment		Equal Payment Series				Uniform gradient-series factor
	Compound-amount factor	Present-worth factor	Compound-amount factor	Sinking-fund factor	Present-worth factor	Capital-recovery factor	
n	To find F Given P F/P r, n	To find P Given F P/F r, n	To find F Given A F/A r, n	To find A Given F A/F r, n	To find P Given A P/A r, n	To find A Given P A/P r, n	To find A Given G A/G r, n
1	1.073	0.9324	1.000	1.0000	0.9324	1.0725	0.0000
2	1.150	0.8694	2.073	0.4825	1.8018	0.5550	0.4825
3	1.234	0.8106	3.223	0.3103	2.6123	0.3828	0.9534
4	1.323	0.7558	4.456	0.2244	3.3681	0.2969	1.4126
5	1.419	0.7047	5.780	0.1730	4.0728	0.2455	1.8603
6	1.522	0.6571	7.199	0.1389	4.7299	0.2114	2.2965
7	1.632	0.6126	8.721	0.1147	5.3425	0.1872	2.7211
8	1.751	0.5712	10.353	0.0966	5.9137	0.1691	3.1344
9	1.878	0.5326	12.104	0.0826	6.4463	0.1551	3.5364
10	2.014	0.4966	13.981	0.0715	6.9429	0.1440	3.9272
11	2.160	0.4630	15.995	0.0625	7.4059	0.1350	4.3069
12	2.316	0.4317	18.155	0.0551	7.8376	0.1276	4.6756
13	2.484	0.4025	20.471	0.0489	8.2401	0.1214	5.0334
14	2.664	0.3753	22.955	0.0436	8.6154	0.1161	5.3804
15	2.858	0.3499	25.620	0.0390	8.9654	0.1161	5.7168
16	3.065	0.3263	28.478	0.0351	9.2917	0.1076	6.0428
17	3.287	0.3042	31.542	0.0317	9.5959	0.1042	6.3585
18	3.525	0.2837	34.829	0.0287	9.8795	0.1012	6.6640
19	3.781	0.2645	38.355	0.0261	10.1440	0.0986	6.9596
20	4.055	0.2466	42.136	0.0237	10.3906	0.0963	7.2453
21	4.349	0.2299	46.191	0.0217	10.6205	0.0942	7.5215
22	4.665	0.2144	50.540	0.0198	10.8349	0.0923	7.7882
23	5.003	0.1999	55.205	0.0181	11.0348	0.0906	8.0456
24	5.366	0.1864	60.208	0.0166	11.2212	0.0891	8.2940
25	5.755	0.1738	65.573	0.0153	11.3949	0.0878	8.5335
26	6.172	0.1620	71.328	0.0140	11.5570	0.0865	8.7643
27	6.619	0.1511	77.500	0.0129	11.7080	0.0854	8.9867
28	7.099	0.1409	84.119	0.0119	11.8489	0.0844	9.2009
29	7.614	0.1313	91.218	0.0110	11.9802	0.0835	9.4070
30	8.166	0.1225	98.833	0.0101	12.1027	0.0826	9.6052
31	8.758	0.1142	106.999	0.0094	12.2169	0.0819	9.7958
32	9.393	0.1065	115.757	0.0086	12.3233	0.0812	9.9790
33	10.047	0.0993	125.150	0.0080	12.4226	0.0805	10.1550
34	10.805	0.0926	135.225	0.0074	12.5151	0.0799	10.3239
35	11.588	0.0863	146.030	0.0069	12.6014	0.0794	10.4860
40	16.445	0.0608	213.006	0.0047	12.9529	0.0772	11.2017
45	23.336	0.0429	308.049	0.0033	13.2006	0.0758	11.7769
50	33.115	0.0302	442.922	0.0023	13.3751	0.0748	12.2347
55	46.993	0.0213	634.316	0.0016	13.4981	0.0741	12.5957
60	66.686	0.0150	905.916	0.0011	13.5847	0.0736	12.8781
65	94.632	0.0106	1291.336	0.0008	13.6458	0.0733	13.0974
70	134.290	0.0075	1838.272	0.0006	13.6889	0.0731	13.2664
75	190.566	0.0053	2614.412	0.0004	13.7192	0.0729	13.3959
80	270.426	0.0037	3715.807	0.0003	13.7406	0.0728	13.4946
85	383.753	0.0026	5278.761	0.0002	13.7556	0.0727	13.5695
90	544.572	0.0019	7496.698	0.0001	13.7662	0.0727	13.6260
95	772.784	0.0013	10644.100	0.0001	13.7737	0.0726	13.6685
100	1096.633	0.0009	15110.476	0.0001	13.7790	0.0726	13.7003

Reprinted, by permission, from H. J. Thuesen et al., *Engineering Economy*, pp. 537-577. Copyright © 1977 by Prentice-Hall Inc.

TABLE C.8. *8% Interest Factors for Continuous Compounding Interest*

	Single Payment		Equal Payment Series				Uniform gradient-series factor
	Compound-amount factor	Present-worth factor	Compound-amount factor	Sinking-fund factor	Present-worth factor	Capital-recovery factor	
n	To find F Given P F/P r, n	To find P Given F P/F r, n	To find F Given A F/A r, n	To find A Given F A/F r, n	To find P Given A P/A r, n	To find A Given P A/P r, n	To find A Given G A/G r, n
1	1.083	0.9231	1.000	1.0000	0.9231	1.0833	0.0000
2	1.174	0.8522	2.083	0.4800	1.7753	0.5633	0.4800
3	1.271	0.7866	3.257	0.3071	2.5619	0.3903	0.9467
4	1.377	0.7262	4.528	0.2209	3.2880	0.3041	1.4002
5	1.492	0.6703	5.905	0.1694	3.9584	0.2526	1.8405
6	1.616	0.6188	7.397	0.1352	4.5772	0.2185	2.2676
7	1.751	0.5712	9.013	0.1110	5.1484	0.1942	2.6817
8	1.896	0.5273	10.764	0.0929	5.6757	0.1762	3.0829
9	2.054	0.4868	12.660	0.0790	6.1624	0.1623	3.4713
10	2.226	0.4493	14.715	0.0680	6.6117	0.1513	3.8470
11	2.411	0.4148	16.940	0.0590	7.0265	0.1423	4.2102
12	2.612	0.3829	19.351	0.0517	7.4094	0.1350	4.5611
13	2.829	0.3535	21.963	0.0455	7.7629	0.1288	4.8998
14	3.065	0.3263	24.792	0.0403	8.0891	0.1236	5.2265
15	3.320	0.3012	27.857	0.0359	8.3903	0.1192	5.5415
16	3.597	0.2780	31.177	0.0321	8.6684	0.1154	5.8449
17	3.896	0.2567	34.774	0.0288	8.9250	0.1121	6.1369
18	4.221	0.2369	38.670	0.0259	9.1620	0.1092	6.4178
19	4.572	0.2187	42.891	0.0233	9.3807	0.1066	6.6879
20	4.953	0.2019	47.463	0.0211	9.5826	0.1044	6.9473
21	5.366	0.1864	52.416	0.0191	9.7689	0.1024	7.1963
22	5.812	0.1721	57.781	0.0173	9.9410	0.1006	7.4352
23	6.297	0.1588	63.594	0.0157	10.0998	0.0990	7.6642
24	6.821	0.1466	69.890	0.0143	10.2464	0.0976	7.8836
25	7.389	0.1353	76.711	0.0130	10.3818	0.0963	8.0937
26	8.004	0.1249	84.100	0.0119	10.5067	0.0952	8.2948
27	8.671	0.1153	92.105	0.0109	10.6220	0.0942	8.4870
28	9.393	0.1065	100.776	0.0099	10.7285	0.0932	8.6707
29	10.176	0.0983	110.169	0.0091	10.8267	0.0924	8.8461
30	11.023	0.0907	120.345	0.0083	10.9175	0.0916	9.0136
31	11.941	0.0838	131.368	0.0076	11.0012	0.0909	9.1734
32	12.936	0.0773	143.309	0.0070	11.0785	0.0903	9.3257
33	14.013	0.0714	156.245	0.0064	11.1499	0.0897	9.4708
34	15.180	0.0659	170.258	0.0059	11.2157	0.0892	9.6090
35	16.445	0.0608	185.439	0.0054	11.2765	0.0887	9.7405
40	24.533	0.0408	282.547	0.0035	11.5173	0.0868	10.3069
45	36.598	0.0273	427.416	0.0023	11.6786	0.0856	10.7426
50	54.598	0.0183	643.535	0.0016	11.7868	0.0849	11.0738
55	81.451	0.0123	965.947	0.0010	11.8593	0.0843	11.3230
60	121.510	0.0082	1446.928	0.0007	11.9079	0.0840	11.5088
65	181.272	0.0055	2164.469	0.0005	11.9404	0.0838	11.6461
70	270.426	0.0037	3234.913	0.0003	11.9623	0.0836	11.7469
75	403.429	0.0025	4831.828	0.0002	11.9769	0.0835	11.8203
80	601.845	0.0017	7214.146	0.0002	11.9867	0.0834	11.8735
85	897.847	0.0011	10768.146	0.0001	11.9933	0.0834	11.9119
90	1339.431	0.0008	16070.091	0.0001	11.9977	0.0834	11.9394
95	1998.196	0.0005	23979.664	0.0001	12.0007	0.0833	11.9591
100	2980.958	0.0004	35779.360	0.0000	12.0026	0.0833	11.9731

Reprinted, by permission, from H. J. Thuesen et al., *Engineering Economy*, pp. 537-577. Copyright © 1977 by Prentice-Hall Inc.

TABLE C.9.   9% Interest Factors for Continuous Compounding Interest

	Single Payment		Equal Payment Series				Uniform gradient-series factor
	Compound-amount factor	Present-worth factor	Compound-amount factor	Sinking-fund factor	Present-worth factor	Capital-recovery factor	
n	To find F Given P F/P r, n	To find P Given F P/F r, n	To find F Given A F/A r, n	To find A Given F A/F r, n	To find P Given A P/A r, n	To find A Given P A/P r, n	To find A Given G A/G r, n
1	1.094	0.9139	1.000	1.0000	0.9139	1.0942	0.0000
2	1.197	0.8353	2.094	0.4775	1.7492	0.5717	0.4775
3	1.310	0.7634	3.291	0.3038	2.5126	0.3980	0.9401
4	1.433	0.6977	4.601	0.2173	3.2103	0.3115	1.3878
5	1.568	0.6376	6.035	0.1657	3.8479	0.2599	1.8206
6	1.716	0.5828	7.603	0.1315	4.4306	0.2257	2.2388
7	1.878	0.5326	9.319	0.1073	4.9632	0.2015	2.6424
8	2.054	0.4868	11.197	0.0893	5.4500	0.1835	3.0316
9	2.248	0.4449	13.251	0.0755	5.8948	0.1697	3.4065
10	2.460	0.4066	15.499	0.0645	6.3014	0.1587	3.7674
11	2.691	0.3716	17.959	0.0557	6.6730	0.1499	4.1145
12	2.945	0.3396	20.650	0.0484	7.0126	0.1426	4.4479
13	3.222	0.3104	23.594	0.0424	7.3230	0.1366	4.7680
14	3.525	0.2837	26.816	0.0373	7.6066	0.1315	5.0750
15	3.857	0.2593	30.342	0.0330	7.8658	0.1271	5.3691
16	4.221	0.2369	34.199	0.0293	8.1028	0.1234	5.6507
17	4.618	0.2165	38.420	0.0260	8.3193	0.1202	5.9201
18	5.053	0.1979	43.038	0.0232	8.5172	0.1174	6.1776
19	5.529	0.1809	48.091	0.0208	8.6981	0.1150	6.4234
20	6.050	0.1653	53.620	0.0187	8.8634	0.1128	6.6579
21	6.619	0.1511	59.670	0.0168	9.0144	0.1109	6.8815
22	7.243	0.1381	66.289	0.0151	9.1525	0.1093	7.0945
23	7.925	0.1262	73.532	0.0136	9.2787	0.1078	7.2972
24	8.671	0.1153	81.457	0.0123	9.3940	0.1065	7.4900
25	9.488	0.1054	90.128	0.0111	9.4994	0.1053	7.6732
26	10.381	0.0963	99.616	0.0100	9.5958	0.1042	7.8471
27	11.359	0.0880	109.997	0.0091	9.6838	0.1033	8.0122
28	12.429	0.0805	121.356	0.0083	9.7643	0.1024	8.1686
29	13.599	0.0735	133.784	0.0075	9.8378	0.1017	8.3169
30	14.880	0.0672	147.383	0.0068	9.9050	0.1010	8.4572
31	16.281	0.0614	162.263	0.0062	9.9664	0.1003	8.5900
32	17.814	0.0561	178.544	0.0056	10.0225	0.0998	8.7155
33	19.492	0.0513	196.358	0.0051	10.0739	0.0993	8.8341
34	21.328	0.0469	215.850	0.0046	10.1207	0.0988	8.9460
35	23.336	0.0429	237.178	0.0042	10.1636	0.0984	9.0516
40	36.598	0.0273	378.004	0.0027	10.3285	0.0968	9.4950
45	57.397	0.0174	598.863	0.0017	10.4336	0.0959	9.8207
50	90.017	0.0111	945.238	0.0011	10.5007	0.0952	10.0569
55	141.175	0.0071	1488.463	0.0007	10.5434	0.0949	10.2263
60	221.406	0.0045	2340.410	0.0004	10.5707	0.0946	10.3464
65	347.234	0.0029	3676.528	0.0003	10.5880	0.0945	10.4309
70	544.572	0.0019	5771.978	0.0002	10.5991	0.0944	10.4898
75	854.059	0.0012	9058.298	0.0001	10.6062	0.0943	10.5307
80	1339.431	0.0008	14212.274	0.0001	10.6107	0.0943	10.5588
85	2100.646	0.0005	22295.318	0.0001	10.6136	0.0942	10.5781
90	3294.468	0.0003	34972.053	0.0000	10.6154	0.0942	10.5913
95	5166.754	0.0002	54853.132	0.0000	10.6166	0.0942	10.6002
100	8103.084	0.0001	86032.870	0.0000	10.6173	0.0942	10.6063

Reprinted, by permission, from H. J. Thuesen et al., *Engineering Economy*, pp. 537-577. Copyright © 1977 by Prentice-Hall Inc.

TABLE C.10. *10% Interest Factors for Continuous Compounding Interest*

	Single Payment		Equal Payment Series				Uniform gradient-series factor
	Compound-amount factor	Present-worth factor	Compound-amount factor	Sinking-fund factor	Present-worth factor	Capital-recovery factor	
n	To find *F* Given *P* $F/P \quad r, n$	To find *P* Given *F* $P/F \quad r, n$	To find *F* Given *A* $F/A \quad r, n$	To find *A* Given *F* $A/F \quad r, n$	To find *P* Given *A* $P/A \quad r, n$	To find *A* Given *P* $A/P \quad r, n$	To find *A* Given *G* $A/G \quad r, n$
1	1.105	0.9048	1.000	1.0000	0.9048	1.1052	0.0000
2	1.221	0.8187	2.105	0.4750	1.7236	0.5802	0.4750
3	1.350	0.7408	3.327	0.3006	2.4644	0.4058	0.9335
4	1.492	0.6703	4.676	0.2138	3.1347	0.3190	1.3754
5	1.649	0.6065	6.168	0.1621	3.7412	0.2673	1.8009
6	1.822	0.5488	7.817	0.1279	4.2901	0.2331	2.2101
7	2.014	0.4966	9.639	0.1038	4.7866	0.2089	2.6033
8	2.226	0.4493	11.653	0.0858	5.2360	0.1910	2.9806
9	2.460	0.4066	13.878	0.0721	5.6425	0.1772	3.3423
10	2.718	0.3679	16.338	0.0612	6.0104	0.1664	3.6886
11	3.004	0.3329	19.056	0.0525	6.3433	0.1577	4.0198
12	3.320	0.3012	22.060	0.0453	6.6445	0.1505	4.3362
13	3.669	0.2725	25.381	0.0394	6.9170	0.1446	4.6381
14	4.055	0.2466	29.050	0.0344	7.1636	0.1396	4.9260
15	4.482	0.2231	33.105	0.0302	7.3867	0.1354	5.2001
16	4.953	0.2019	37.587	0.0266	7.5886	0.1318	5.4608
17	5.474	0.1827	42.540	0.0235	7.7713	0.1287	5.7086
18	6.050	0.1653	48.014	0.0208	7.9366	0.1260	5.9437
19	6.686	0.1496	54.063	0.0185	8.0862	0.1237	6.1667
20	7.389	0.1353	60.749	0.0165	8.2215	0.1216	6.3780
21	8.166	0.1225	68.138	0.0147	8.3440	0.1199	6.5779
22	9.025	0.1108	76.305	0.0131	8.4548	0.1183	6.7669
23	9.974	0.1003	85.330	0.0117	8.5550	0.1169	6.9454
24	11.023	0.0907	95.304	0.0105	8.6458	0.1157	7.1139
25	12.183	0.0821	106.327	0.0094	8.7279	0.1146	7.2727
26	13.464	0.0743	118.509	0.0084	8.8021	0.1136	7.4223
27	14.880	0.0672	131.973	0.0076	8.8693	0.1128	7.5631
28	16.445	0.0608	146.853	0.0068	8.9301	0.1120	7.6954
29	18.174	0.0550	163.297	0.0061	8.9852	0.1113	7.8198
30	20.086	0.0498	181.472	0.0055	9.0349	0.1107	7.9365
31	22.198	0.0451	201.557	0.0050	9.0800	0.1101	8.0459
32	24.533	0.0408	223.755	0.0045	9.1208	0.1097	8.1485
33	27.113	0.0369	248.288	0.0040	9.1576	0.1092	8.2446
34	29.964	0.0334	275.400	0.0036	9.1910	0.1088	8.3345
35	33.115	0.0302	305.364	0.0033	9.2212	0.1085	8.4185
40	54.598	0.0183	509.629	0.0020	9.3342	0.1071	8.7620
45	90.017	0.0111	846.404	0.0012	9.4027	0.1064	9.0028
50	148.413	0.0067	1401.653	0.0007	9.4443	0.1059	9.1692
55	244.692	0.0041	2317.104	0.0004	9.4695	0.1056	9.2826
60	403.429	0.0025	3826.427	0.0003	9.4848	0.1054	9.3592
65	665.142	0.0015	6314.879	0.0002	9.4940	0.1053	9.4105
70	1096.633	0.0009	10417.644	0.0001	9.4997	0.1053	9.4445
75	1808.042	0.0006	17181.959	0.0001	9.5031	0.1052	9.4668
80	2980.958	0.0004	28334.430	0.0001	9.5052	0.1052	9.4815
85	4914.769	0.0002	46721.745	0.0000	9.5064	0.1052	9.4910
90	8103.084	0.0001	77037.303	0.0000	9.5072	0.1052	9.4972
95	13359.727	0.0001	127019.209	0.0000	9.5076	0.1052	9.5012
100	22026.466	0.0001	209425.440	0.0000	9.5079	0.1052	9.5038

TABLE C.11. *12% Interest Factors for Continuous Compounding Interest*

	Single Payment		Equal Payment Series				Uniform gradient-series factor
	Compound-amount factor	Present-worth factor	Compound-amount factor	Sinking-fund factor	Present-worth factor	Capital-recovery factor	
n	To find F Given P F/P r, n	To find P Given F P/F r, n	To find F Given A F/A r, n	To find A Given F A/F r, n	To find P Given A P/A r, n	To find A Given P A/P r, n	To find A Given G A/G r, n
1	1.128	0.8869	1.000	1.0000	0.8869	1.1275	0.0000
2	1.271	0.7866	2.128	0.4700	1.6736	0.5975	0.4700
3	1.433	0.6977	3.399	0.2942	2.3712	0.4217	0.9202
4	1.616	0.6188	4.832	0.2070	2.9900	0.3345	1.3506
5	1.822	0.5488	6.448	0.1551	3.5388	0.2826	1.7615
6	2.054	0.4868	8.270	0.1209	4.0256	0.2484	2.1531
7	2.316	0.4317	10.325	0.0969	4.4573	0.2244	2.5257
8	2.612	0.3829	12.641	0.0791	4.8402	0.2066	2.8796
9	2.945	0.3396	15.253	0.0656	5.1798	0.1931	3.2153
10	3.320	0.3012	18.197	0.0550	5.4810	0.1825	3.5332
11	3.743	0.2671	21.518	0.0465	5.7481	0.1740	3.8337
12	4.221	0.2369	25.261	0.0396	5.9850	0.1671	4.1174
13	4.759	0.2101	29.482	0.0339	6.1952	0.1614	4.3848
14	5.366	0.1864	34.241	0.0292	6.3815	0.1567	4.6364
15	6.050	0.1653	39.606	0.0253	6.5468	0.1528	4.8728
16	6.821	0.1466	45.656	0.0219	6.6935	0.1494	5.0947
17	7.691	0.1300	52.477	0.0191	6.8235	0.1466	5.3025
18	8.671	0.1153	60.167	0.0166	6.9388	0.1441	5.4969
19	9.777	0.1023	68.838	0.0145	7.0411	0.1420	5.6785
20	11.023	0.0907	78.615	0.0127	7.1318	0.1402	5.8480
21	12.429	0.0805	89.638	0.0112	7.2123	0.1387	6.0058
22	14.013	0.0714	102.067	0.0098	7.2836	0.1373	6.1528
23	15.800	0.0633	116.080	0.0086	7.3469	0.1361	6.2893
24	17.814	0.0561	131.880	0.0076	7.4031	0.1351	6.4160
25	20.086	0.0498	149.694	0.0067	7.4528	0.1342	6.5334
26	22.646	0.0442	169.780	0.0059	7.4970	0.1334	6.6422
27	25.534	0.0392	192.426	0.0052	7.5362	0.1327	6.7428
28	28.789	0.0347	217.960	0.0046	7.5709	0.1321	6.8358
29	32.460	0.0308	246.749	0.0041	7.6017	0.1316	6.9215
30	36.598	0.0273	279.209	0.0036	7.6290	0.1311	7.0006
31	41.264	0.0242	315.807	0.0032	7.6533	0.1307	7.0734
32	46.525	0.0215	357.071	0.0028	7.6748	0.1303	7.1404
33	52.457	0.0191	403.597	0.0025	7.6938	0.1300	7.2020
34	59.145	0.0169	456.054	0.0022	7.7107	0.1297	7.2586
35	66.686	0.0150	515.200	0.0020	7.7257	0.1294	7.3105
40	121.510	0.0082	945.203	0.0011	7.7788	0.1286	7.5114
45	221.406	0.0045	1728.720	0.0006	7.8079	0.1281	7.6392
50	403.429	0.0025	3156.382	0.0003	7.8239	0.1278	7.7191

Reprinted, by permission, from H. J. Thuesen et al., *Engineering Economy*, pp. 537–577. Copyright © 1977 by Prentice-Hall Inc.

TABLE C.12. *15% Interest Factors for Continuous Compounding Interest*

	Single Payment		Equal Payment Series				Uniform gradient-series factor
	Compound-amount factor	Present-worth factor	Compound-amount factor	Sinking-fund factor	Present-worth factor	Capital-recovery factor	
n	To find F Given P F/P r, n	To find P Given F P/F r, n	To find F Given A F/A r, n	To find A Given F A/F r, n	To find P Given A P/A r, n	To find A Given P A/P r, n	To find A Given G A/G r, n
1	1.162	0.8607	1.000	1.0000	0.8607	1.1618	0.0000
2	1.350	0.7408	2.162	0.4626	1.6015	0.6244	0.4626
3	1.568	0.6376	3.512	0.2848	2.2392	0.4466	0.9004
4	1.822	0.5488	5.080	0.1969	2.7880	0.3587	1.3137
5	2.117	0.4724	6.902	0.1449	3.2603	0.3067	1.7029
6	2.460	0.4066	9.019	0.1109	3.6669	0.2727	2.0685
7	2.858	0.3499	11.479	0.0871	4.0168	0.2490	2.4110
8	3.320	0.3012	14.336	0.0698	4.3180	0.2316	2.7311
9	3.857	0.2593	17.657	0.0566	4.5773	0.2185	3.0295
10	4.482	0.2231	21.514	0.0465	4.8004	0.2083	3.3070
11	5.207	0.1921	25.996	0.0385	4.9925	0.2003	3.5645
12	6.050	0.1653	31.203	0.0321	5.1578	0.1939	3.8028
13	7.029	0.1423	37.252	0.0269	5.3000	0.1887	4.0228
14	8.166	0.1225	44.281	0.0226	5.4225	0.1844	4.2255
15	9.488	0.1054	52.447	0.0191	5.5279	0.1809	4.4119
16	11.023	0.0907	61.935	0.0162	5.6186	0.1780	4.5829
17	12.807	0.0781	72.958	0.0137	5.6967	0.1756	4.7394
18	14.880	0.0672	85.765	0.0117	5.7639	0.1735	4.8823
19	17.288	0.0579	100.645	0.0099	5.8217	0.1718	5.0127
20	20.086	0.0498	117.933	0.0085	5.8715	0.1703	5.1313
21	23.336	0.0429	138.018	0.0073	5.9144	0.1691	5.2390
22	27.113	0.0369	161.354	0.0062	5.9513	0.1680	5.3367
23	31.500	0.0318	188.467	0.0053	5.9830	0.1672	5.4251
24	36.598	0.0273	219.967	0.0046	6.0103	0.1664	5.5050
25	42.521	0.0235	256.566	0.0039	6.0339	0.1657	5.5771
26	49.402	0.0203	299.087	0.0034	6.0541	0.1652	5.6420
27	57.397	0.0174	348.489	0.0029	6.0715	0.1647	5.7004
28	66.686	0.0150	405.886	0.0025	6.0865	0.1643	5.7529
29	77.478	0.0129	472.573	0.0021	6.0994	0.1640	5.8000
30	90.017	0.0111	550.051	0.0018	6.1105	0.1637	5.8422
31	104.585	0.0096	640.068	0.0016	6.1201	0.1634	5.8799
32	121.510	0.0082	744.653	0.0014	6.1283	0.1632	5.9136
33	141.175	0.0071	866.164	0.0012	6.1354	0.1630	5.9438
34	164.022	0.0061	1007.339	0.0010	6.1415	0.1628	5.9706
35	190.566	0.0053	1171.361	0.0009	6.1467	0.1627	5.9945
40	403.429	0.0025	2486.673	0.0004	6.1639	0.1622	6.0798
45	854.059	0.0012	5271.188	0.0002	6.1719	0.1620	6.1264
50	1808.042	0.0006	11166.008	0.0001	6.1758	0.1619	6.1515

TABLE C.13.   *20% Interest Factors for Continuous Compounding Interest*

	Single Payment		Equal Payment Series				Uniform gradient-series factor
	Compound-amount factor	Present-worth factor	Compound-amount factor	Sinking-fund factor	Present-worth factor	Capital-recovery factor	
n	To find *F* Given *P* F/P *r, n*	To find *P* Given *F* P/F *r, n*	To find *F* Given *A* F/A *r, n*	To find *A* Given *F* A/F *r, n*	To find *P* Given *A* P/A *r, n*	To find *A* Given *P* A/P *r, n*	To find *A* Given *G* A/G *r, n*
1	1.221	0.8187	1.000	1.0000	0.8187	1.2214	0.0000
2	1.492	0.6703	2.221	0.4502	1.4891	0.6716	0.4502
3	1.822	0.5488	3.713	0.2693	2.0379	0.4907	0.8676
4	2.226	0.4493	5.535	0.1807	2.4872	0.4021	1.2528
5	2.718	0.3679	7.761	0.1289	2.8551	0.3503	1.6068
6	3.320	0.3012	10.479	0.0954	3.1563	0.3168	1.9306
7	4.055	0.2466	13.799	0.0725	3.4029	0.2939	2.2255
8	4.953	0.2019	17.854	0.0560	3.6048	0.2774	2.4929
9	6.050	0.1653	22.808	0.0439	3.7701	0.2653	2.7344
10	7.389	0.1353	28.857	0.0347	3.9054	0.2561	2.9515
11	9.025	0.1108	36.246	0.0276	4.0162	0.2490	3.1460
12	11.023	0.0907	45.271	0.0221	4.1069	0.2435	3.3194
13	13.464	0.0743	56.294	0.0178	4.1812	0.2392	3.4736
14	16.445	0.0608	69.758	0.0143	4.2420	0.2357	3.6102
15	20.086	0,0498	86.203	0.0116	4.2918	0.2330	3.7307
16	24.533	0.0408	106.288	0.0094	4.3326	0.2308	3.8368
17	29.964	0.0334	130.821	0.0077	4.3659	0.2291	3.9297
18	36.598	0.0273	160.785	0.0062	4.3933	0.2276	4.0110
19	44.701	0.0224	197.383	0.0051	4.4156	0.2265	4.0819
20	54.598	0.0183	242.084	0.0041	4.4339	0.2255	4.1435
21	66.686	0.0150	296.683	0.0034	4.4489	0.2248	4.1970
22	81.451	0.0123	363.369	0.0028	4.4612	0.2242	4.2432
23	99.484	0.0101	444.820	0.0023	4.4713	0.2237	4.2831
24	121.510	0.0082	544.304	0.0018	4.4795	0.2232	4.3175
25	148.413	0.0067	665.814	0.0015	4.4862	0.2229	4.3471
26	181.272	0.0055	814.228	0.0012	4.4917	0.2226	4.3724
27	221.406	0 0045	995.500	0.0010	4.4963	0.2224	4.3942
28	270.426	0.0037	1216.906	0.0008	4.5000	0.2222	4.4127
29	330.300	0.0030	1487.333	0.0007	4.5030	0.2221	4.4286
30	403.429	0.0025	1817.632	0.0006	4.5055	0.2220	4.4421
31	492.749	0.0020	2221.061	0.0005	4.5075	0.2219	4.4536
32	601.845	0.0017	2713.810	0.0004	4.5092	0.2218	4.4634
33	735.095	0.0014	3315.655	0.0003	4.5105	0.2217	4.4717
34	897.847	0.0011	4050.750	0.0003	4.5116	0.2217	4.4788
35	1096.633	0.0009	4948.598	0.0002	4.5125	0.2216	4.4847
40	2980.958	0.0004	13459.444	0.0001	4.5152	0.2215	4.5032
45	8103.084	0.0001	36594.322	0.0000	4.5161	0.2214	4.5111
50	22026.466	0.0001	99481.443	0.0000	4.5165	0.2214	4.5144

TABLE C.14. *25% Interest Factors for Continuous Compounding Interest*

	Single Payment		Equal Payment Series				Uniform gradient-series factor
	Compound-amount factor	Present-worth factor	Compound-amount factor	Sinking-fund factor	Present-worth factor	Capital-recovery factor	
n	To find *F* Given *P* F/P r, n	To find *P* Given *F* P/F r, n	To find *F* Given *A* F/A r, n	To find *A* Given *F* A/F r, n	To find *P* Given *A* P/A r, n	To find *A* Given *P* A/P r, n	To find *A* Given *G* A/G r, n
1	1.284	0.7788	1.000	1.0000	0.7788	1.2840	0.0000
2	1.649	0.6065	2.284	0.4378	1.3853	0.7219	0.4378
3	2.117	0.4724	3.933	0.2543	1.8577	0.5383	0.8351
4	2.718	0.3679	6.050	0.1653	2.2256	0.4493	1.1929
5	3.490	0.2865	8.768	0.1141	2.5121	0.3981	1.5131
6	4.482	0.2231	12.258	0.0816	2.7352	0.3656	1.7975
7	5.755	0.1738	16.740	0.0597	2.9090	0.3438	2.0486
8	7.389	0.1353	22.495	0.0445	3.0443	0.3285	2.2687
9	9.488	0.1054	29.884	0.0335	3.1497	0.3175	2.4605
10	12.183	0.0821	39.371	0.0254	3.2318	0.3094	2.6266
11	15.643	0.0639	51.554	0.0194	3.2957	0.3034	2.7696
12	20.086	0.0498	67.197	0.0149	3.3455	0.2989	2.8921
13	25.790	0.0388	87.282	0.0115	3.3843	0.2955	2.9964
14	33.115	0.0302	113.072	0.0089	3.4145	0.2929	3.0849
15	42.521	0.0235	146.188	0.0069	3.4380	0.2909	3.1596
16	54.598	0.0183	188.709	0.0053	3.4563	0.2893	3.2223
17	70.105	0.0143	243.307	0.0041	3.4706	0.2881	3.2748
18	90.017	0.0111	313.413	0.0032	3.4817	0.2872	3.3186
19	115.584	0.0087	403.430	0.0025	3.4904	0.2865	3.3550
20	148.413	0.0067	519.014	0.0019	3.4971	0.2860	3.3851
21	190.566	0.0053	667.427	0.0015	3.5023	0.2855	3.4100
22	244.692	0.0041	857.993	0.0012	3.5064	0.2852	3.4305
23	314.191	0.0032	1102.685	0.0009	3.5096	0.2849	3.4474
24	403.429	0.0025	1416.876	0.0007	3.5121	0.2847	3.4612
25	518.013	0.0019	1820.305	0.0006	3.5140	0.2846	3.4725
26	665.142	0.0015	2338.318	0.0004	3.5155	0.2845	3.4817
27	854.059	0.0012	3003.459	0.0003	3.5167	0.2844	3.4892
28	1096.633	0.0009	3857.518	0.0003	3.5176	0.2843	3.4953
29	1408.105	0.0007	4954.151	0.0002	3.5183	0.2842	3.5002
30	1808.042	0.0006	6362.256	0.0002	3.5189	0.2842	3.5042
31	2321.572	0.0004	8170.298	0.0001	3.5193	0.2842	3.5075
32	2980.958	0.0004	10491.871	0.0001	3.5196	0.2841	3.5101
33	3827.626	0.0003	13472.829	0.0001	3.5199	0.2841	3.5122
34	4914.769	0.0002	17300.455	0.0001	3.5201	0.2841	3.5139
35	6310.688	0.0002	22215.223	0.0001	3.5203	0.2841	3.5153

TABLE C.15. *30% Interest Factors for Continuous Compounding Interest*

	Single Payment		Equal Payment Series				Uniform gradient-series factor
	Compound-amount factor	Present-worth factor	Compound-amount factor	Sinking-fund factor	Present-worth factor	Capital-recovery factor	
n	To find F Given P F/P r, n	To find P Given F P/F r, n	To find F Given A F/A r, n	To find A Given F A/F r, n	To find P Given A P/A r, n	To find A Given P A/P r, n	To find A Given G A/G r, n
1	1.350	0.7408	1.000	1.0000	0.7408	1.3499	0.0000
2	1.822	0.5488	2.350	0.4256	1.2896	0.7754	0.4256
3	2.460	0.4066	4.172	0.2397	1.6962	0.5896	0.8030
4	3.320	0.3012	6.632	0.1508	1.9974	0.5007	1.1343
5	4.482	0.2231	9.952	0.1005	2.2205	0.4504	1.4222
6	6.050	0.1653	14.433	0.0693	2.3858	0.4192	1.6701
7	8.166	0.1225	20.483	0.0488	2.5083	0.3987	1.8815
8	11.023	0.0907	28.649	0.0349	2.5990	0.3848	2.0602
9	14.880	0.0672	39.672	0.0252	2.6662	0.3751	2.2099
10	20.086	0.0498	54.552	0.0183	2.7160	0.3682	2.3343
11	27.113	0.0369	74.638	0.0134	2.7529	0.3633	2.4371
12	36.598	0.0273	101.750	0.0098	2.7802	0.3597	2.5212
13	49.402	0.0203	138.349	0.0072	2.8004	0.3571	2.5897
14	66.686	0.0150	187.751	0.0053	2.8154	0.3552	2.6452
15	90.017	0.0111	254.437	0.0039	2.8266	0.3538	2.6898
16	121.510	0.0082	344.454	0.0029	2.8348	0.3528	2.7255
17	164.022	0.0061	465.965	0.0022	2.8409	0.3520	2.7540
18	221.406	0.0045	629.987	0.0016	2.8454	0.3515	2.7766
19	298.867	0.0034	851.393	0.0012	2.8487	0.3510	2.7945
20	403.429	0.0025	1150.261	0.0009	2.8512	0.3507	2.8086
21	544.572	0.0018	1553.689	0.0007	2.8531	0.3505	2.8197
22	735.095	0.0014	2098.261	0.0005	2.8544	0.3503	2.8283
23	992.275	0.0010	2833.356	0.0004	2.8554	0.3502	2.8351
24	1339.431	0.0008	3825.631	0.0003	2.8562	0.3501	2.8404
25	1808.042	0.0006	5165.062	0.0002	2.8567	0.3501	2.8445
26	2440.602	0.0004	6973.104	0.0002	2.8571	0.3500	2.8476
27	3294.468	0.0003	9413.706	0.0001	2.8574	0.3500	2.8501
28	4447.067	0.0002	12708.174	0.0001	2.8577	0.3499	2.8520
29	6002.912	0.0002	17155.241	0.0001	2.8578	0.3499	2.8535
30	8103.084	0.0001	23158.153	0.0001	2.8580	0.3499	2.8546
31	10938.019	0.0001	31261.237	0.0000	2.8580	0.3499	2.8555
32	14764.782	0.0001	42199.257	0.0000	2.8581	0.3499	2.8561
33	19930.370	0.0001	56964.038	0.0000	2.8582	0.3499	2.8566
34	26903.186	0.0001	76894.409	0.0000	2.8582	0.3499	2.8570
35	36315.503	0.0000	103797.595	0.0000	2.8582	0.3499	2.8573

Reprinted, by permission, from H. J. Thuesen et al., *Engineering Economy*, pp. 537-577.
Copyright © 1977 by Prentice-Hall Inc.

APPENDIX

D

FUNDS FLOW FACTORS

TABLE D.1. *Funds Flow Conversion Factors*

r	$\dfrac{e^r - 1}{r}$ $(A/\bar{A}\ r)$
1	1.005020
2	1.010065
3	1.015150
4	1.020270
5	1.025422
6	1.030608
7	1.035831
8	1.041088
9	1.046381
10	1.051709
11	1.057073
12	1.062474
13	1.067910
14	1.073384
15	1.078894
16	1.084443
17	1.090028
18	1.095652
19	1.101313
20	1.107014
21	1.112752
22	1.118530
23	1.124347
24	1.130204
25	1.136101
26	1.142038
27	1.148016
28	1.154035
29	1.160094
30	1.166196
31	1.172339
32	1.178524
33	1.184751
34	1.191022
35	1.197335
36	1.203692
37	1.210093
38	1.216538
39	1.223027
40	1.229561

APPENDIX

E

COMPUTER PROGRAM FOR INTERNAL RATE OF RETURN

A computer program for determining the internal rate of return is provided in this appendix. The input data consists of the yearly cash flows and number of years. This program uses a beginning of the year conversion.

```
        $JOB
        C
        C
        C
        C       INTERNAL RATE OF RETURN
     1          DIMENSION PV(50),CF(50)
     2          READ(5,10) N,(CF(I),I=1,N)
     3       10 FORMAT(I5,/,(F15.2))
     4          WRITE(6,20) (I,CF(I),I=1,N)
     5       20 FORMAT(1H1,4X,'PERIOD',6X,'    CASH FLOW ',//,(/,4X,I6,6X,F15.2))
     6          WRITE(6,30)
     7       30 FORMAT(////,1X,'ITERATION',6X,' RATE OF RETURN',//)
     8          ERROR=CF(1)*.00001
     9          ITER=1
    10          RATE=1.
    11          IFLAG=1
    12          PV(1)=CF(1)
    13          IF(PV(1)) 1,2,2
    14        1 DO 40 J=2,N
    15          PV(J)=PV(J-1)*(1.0+RATE)+CF(J)
    16          IF(PV(J)+ERROR) 40,40,50
    17       40 CONTINUE
    18          WRITE(6,60) ITER,RATE
    19       60 FORMAT(/,1X,I9,6X,F16.5)
    20          ITER=ITER+1
    21          IF(PV(N)-ERROR) 35,55,55
    22       35 IFLAG=0
    23          M=N
    24       11 ARATE=PV(1)
    25          MK=M-1
    26          ML=MK-1
    27          IF(ML) 45,15,45
    28       45 DO 17 I=2,MK
    29       17 ARATE=ARATE*(1.+RATE)+PV(I)
    30       15 RATE=RATE-PV(M)/ARATE
    31          GO TO 1
    32       50 IF(IFLAG) 55,19,46
    33       46 M=J
    34          GO TO 11
    35        2 J=1
    36       19 WRITE(6,21)
    37       21 FORMAT(///,2X,'NO SINGLE FEASIBLE SOLUTION EXISTS.')
    38       55 WRITE(6,18)
    39       18 FORMAT(1H1)
    40          STOP
    41          END

        $ENTRY
```

Reprinted, by permission from G. T. Stevens, Jr., *Economic and Financial Analysis of Capital Investments*, p. 351. Copyright © 1979 by John Wiley and Sons, Inc.

APPENDIX

F

COMPUTER PROGRAM FOR MINIMUM ANNUAL REVENUE REQUIREMENTS

A computer program is provided for determining the minimum annual revenue requirements. Three depreciation models are possible: (1) straight-line, (2) SYD, and (3) DDB with a switch over to straight-line.

```
        $JOB
        C
        C
        C
        C
        C
        C          MINIMUM ANNUAL REVENUE REQUIREMENT BY FLOW THROUGH METHOD
   1               REAL INITC,INVTCR,NB,NT,INC
   2               DIMENSION DEPB(50),DEPS(50),DEPT(50),DTX(50),TXC(50),AMTXC(50),
                  1CAPINV(50),FD(50),FE(50),TAX(50),COST(50),RN(50),CAPINT(50)
                  2,SDEPT(50)
        C          INPUT DATA ENTERED AS FOLLOW;
        C          "INITC" REPRESENTS INITIAL INVESTMENT COST.
   3               READ(5,5000) INITC
        C          "SALV" REPRESENTS THE SALVAGE VALUE AT THE END OF THE USEFUL LIFE.
   4               READ(5,5000) SALV
        C          "TXSALV" REPRESENTS THE ESTIMATED SALVAGE VALUE FOR TAX PURPOSE.
   5               READ(5,5000) TXSALV
        C          "NB" REPRESENTS THE USEFUL LIFE FOR BOOK PURPOSE.
   6               READ(5,5000) NB
        C          "NT" REPRESENTS THE USEFUL LIFE FOR TAX PURPOSE.
   7               READ(5,5000) NT
        C          "RE" REPRESENTS THE RATE OF RETURN ON EQUITY.
   8               READ(5,5000) RE
        C          "RD" REPRESENTS THE RATE OF RETURN ON DEBT.
   9               READ(5,5000) RD
        C          "DR" REPRESENTS THE RATIO OF DEBT PORTION.
  10               READ(5,5000) DR
        C          "T" REPRESENTS THE TAX RATE.
  11               READ(5,5000) T
        C          "CAPIRA" REPRESENTS THE CAPITAL INTEREST RATE.
  12               READ(5,5000) CAPIRA
        C          "INVTCR" REPRESENTS THE INVESTMENT TAX CREDIT RATE.
  13               READ(5,5000) INVTCR
        C          "BDEP" REPRESENTS THE BOOK DEPRECIATION METHOD.
  14               READ(5,5000) BDEP
        C          "TDEP" REPRESENTS THE TAX DEPRECIATION METHOD.
  15               READ(5,5000) TDEP
  16               IF(NB.GE.NT) GO TO 31
  17               N=NT
  18               K=NB
  19               GO TO 32
  20            31 N=NB
  21               K=NT
  22            32 READ(5,5000) (COST(I),I=1,N)
  23               CAP=INITC
  24               CALL SLDEP(DEPS,INITC,SALV,NB,NT)
        C          CHOOSE APPROPRIATE DEPRECIATION METHOD FOR BOOK AND TAX PURPOSES
        C          FROM THE SUBROUTINES.
        C          SUBROUTINE "SLDEP" REPRESENTS THE STRAIGHT LINE DEPRECIATION
        C          METHOD.( BDEP OR TDEP AS 1.)
        C          SUBROUTINE "SYDEP" REPRESENTS THE SUM-OF-THE -YEARS-DIGITS METHOD.
        C          ( BDEP OR TDEP AS 2.)
        C          SUBROUTINE "DDBDEP" REPRESENTS THE DOUBLE DECLINING BALANCE
        C          DEPRECIATION METHOD.( BDEP OR TDEP AS 3.)
        C          "DEPB" REPRESENTS BOOK DEPRECIATION AMOUNT FOR A PARTICULAR YEAR
        C          "DEPS" REPRESENTS THE STRAIGHT LINE DEPRECIATION AMOUNT FOR A
        C          PARTICULAR YEAR.
        C          "DEPT" REPRESENTS TAX DEPRECIATION AMOUNT FOR A PARTICULAR
        C          YEAR.
        C          "CAP" REPRESENTS CAPITALIZED INVESTMENT COST FOR NORMALIZING
```

```
        C      METHOD
        C      THIS "CAP" ALSO REPRESENTS INITIAL INVESTMENT COST FOR
        C      FLOW THROUGH METHOD.
25             IBDEP=BDEP
26             ITDEP=TDEP
27             GO TO (111,222,333),IBDEP
28       111 CALL SLDEP(DEPB,CAP,SALV,NB,NT)
29             GO TO 1234
30       222 CALL SYDDEP(DEPB,CAP,SALV,NB,NT)
31             GO TO 1234
32       333 CALL DDBDEP(DEPB,CAP,SALV,NB,NT)
33      1234 GO TO (1111,2222,3333),ITDEP
34      1111 CALL SLDEP(DEPT,INITC,TXSALV,NB,NT)
35             GO TO 4321
36      2222 CALL SYDDEP(DEPT,INITC,TXSALV,NB,NT)
37             GO TO 4321
38      3333 CALL DDBDEP(DEPT,INITC,TXSALV,NB,NT)
39      4321 TXC(1)=INITC*INVTCR
40             DO 200 I=2,N
41             TXC(I)=0.
42       200 CAPINT(I)=0.
43             CAPINT(1)=INITC*CAPIRA
44             DO 500 I=1,N
45             AMTXC(I)=TXC(1)/NB
46             IF(I.EQ.1) GO TO 300
47             XCAP=CAPINV(I-1)
48             GO TO 400
49       300 XCAP=CAP
50       400 CONTINUE
51             DTX(I)=(DEPT(I)-DEPS(I))*T
52             CAPINV(I)=XCAP-DEPB(I)
53             FD(I)=XCAP*DR*RD
54             FE(I)=XCAP*(1.-DR)*RE
55             TAX(I)=(T/(1.-T))*(FE(I)+DEPB(I)-DEPT(I))-TXC(I)/(1.-T)
56             RN(I)=DEPB(I)+FD(I)+FE(I)+CAPINT(I)+TAX(I)+COST(I)
57       500 CONTINUE
58             IF(NT.GT.NB) GO TO 663
59             GO TO 670
60       663 SDEPT(1)=DEPT(1)
61             DO 655 I=2,K
62             SDEPT(I)=DEPT(I)+SDEPT(I-1)
63             TXBV=INITC-SDEPT(I)
64       655 CONTINUE
65             TAX(K)=(T/(1.-T))*(FE(K)+DEPB(K)-DEPT(K))-TXC(K)/(1.-T)+(SALV-TXBV
              1)*(T/(1.-T))
66             RN(K)=DEPB(K)+FD(K)+FE(K)+CAPINT(K)+TAX(K)+COST(K)
67             M=NB+1
68             DO 665 I=M,N
69             CAPINV(I)=0.0
70             FD(I)=0.0
71             FE(I)=0.0
72             TAX(I)=0.0
73             RN(I)=0.0
74       665 CONTINUE
75       670 WRITE(6,6000)
76             DO 700 I=1,N
77             WRITE(6,6100) I,DEPB(I),DEPS(I),DEPT(I),TXC(I)
78       700 CONTINUE
79             WRITE(6,6200) CAP
80             DO 800 I=1,N
81             WRITE(6,6100) I,CAPINV(I),CAPINT(I),FD(I),FE(I)
```

```
82      800 CONTINUE
83          WRITE(6,6201)
84          DO 801 I=1,N
85          WRITE(6,6100) I,TAX(I),COST(I),RN(I)
86      801 CONTINUE
87     5000 FORMAT(F10.0)
88     6100 FORMAT(I5,5F12.2)
89     6200 FORMAT(/,1X,'YEAR      CAP INV      CAP INT  RET ON DEBT    RET ON EQT
           1Y',/,5X,F12.2)
90     6201 FORMAT(33X,'ANNUAL COST OR',/,1X,'YEAR        TAX        OPRT.COST
           1MIN ANN REV')
91     6000 FORMAT(1H1,' YEAR',' BOOK DEP ',' S.L DEP ',' TAX DEP ',
           1' TAX CREDIT')
92          WRITE(6,3900)
93     3900 FORMAT(/,5X,'MIN. ANNUAL REV. REQMT BY FLOW THROUGH METHOD')
94          WRITE(6,4000) INITC,SALV,NB,NT,RE,RD,DR,T,CAPIRA,INVTCR,TXSALV
95     4000 FORMAT(///,1X,'INPUT DATA;',//,1X,'INITIAL INVESTMENT COST=',F10.2
           1,5X,'SALVAGE VALUE=',F10.2,/,1X,'NO. OF USEFUL LIFE FOR BOOK PURPO
           1SE=',F5.0,/,1X,'NO. OF USEFUL LIFE FOR TAX PURPOSE=',F5.0,/,1X,
           2'RATE OF RETURN ON EQUITY=',F5.3,3X,'RATE OF RETURN ON DEBT=',
           3F5.3,/,1X,'DEBT RATIO=',F5.3,5X,'TAX RATE=',F5.3,5X,/,1X,
           4'CAPITAL INTEREST RATE=',F5.3,5X,'INVESTMENT TAX CREDIT RATE='
           5,F5.3,5X,/,1X,'TAX SALVAGE VALUE=',F10.2)
96          GO TO (555,666,777),IBDEP
97      555 WRITE(6,8000)
98     8000 FORMAT(/,1X,'BOOK DEP. METHOD ; STRAIGHT LINE DEP.')
99          GO TO 8301
100     666 WRITE(6,8100)
101    8100 FORMAT(/,1X,'BOOK DEP. METHOD ; SUM OF THE YEARS DIGITS DEP.')
102         GO TO 8301
103     777 WRITE(6,8200)
104    8200 FORMAT(/,1X,'BOOK DEP. METHOD ; DOUBLE DECLINING BALANCE DEP.')
105    8301 GO TO(999,805,705),ITDEP
106     999 WRITE(6,8400)
107    8400 FORMAT(/,1X,'TAX DEP. METHOD ; STRAIGHT LINE DEP.')
108         GO TO 8402
109     805 WRITE(6,8500)
110    8500 FORMAT(/,1X,'TAX DEP. METHOD ; SUM OF THE YEARS DIGITS DEP.')
111         GO TO 8402
112     705 WRITE(6,8600)
113    8600 FORMAT(/,1X,'TAX DEP. METHOD ; DOUBLE DECLINING BALANCE DEP.')
114    8402 WRITE(6,4500) (COST(I),I=1,N)
115    4500 FORMAT(/,2X,'COST DATA;',/,(2X,5(F13.1),/))
116         STOP
117         END

118         SUBROUTINE DDBDEP(DEP,INC,SALV,NX,NY)
119         REAL INC,NX,NY
120         DIMENSION DEP(50),BV(50),RBVSL(50),SDEP(50)
121         IF(NX.GE.NY) GO TO 1561
122         N=NY
123         K=NX
124         GO TO 116
125    1561 N=NX
126         K=NY
127     116 D=2./NY
128         BV(1)=INC*(1.-D)**1.
129         DEP(1)=INC-BV(1)
130         RBVSL(1)=(INC-SALV)/NY
131         SDEP(1)=DEP(1)
132         P=INC-SALV
```

Reprinted, by permission from G. T. Stevens, Jr., *Economic and Financial Analysis of Capital Investments*, pp. 355-360. Copyright © 1979 by John Wiley and Sons, Inc.

```
133              M=0
134              DO 200 I=2,N
135              IF(NY.GT.NX) K=N
136              IF(I.LE.K) GO TO 220
137              GO TO 210
138          220 AI=I
139              IF(M.EQ.1) GO TO 205
140              BV(I)=INC*(1.-D)**AI
141              ADEP=BV(I-1)
142              DEP(I)=ADEP-BV(I)
143              IF(I.EQ.K) GO TO 900
144              RBVSL(I)=(BV(I)-SALV)/(NY-AI)
145              IF(DEP(I).LE.RBVSL(I-1)) GO TO 600
146              IF(M.EQ.0) DEP(I)=ADEP-BV(I)
147              GO TO 250
148          205 IF(M.EQ.1) DEP(I)=RBVSL(II)
149              GO TO 250
150          600 IF(M.EQ.1) GO TO 205
151              M=1
152              II=I-1
153              GO TO 205
154          900 SDEP(I)=DEP(I)+SDEP(I-1)
155              IF(SDEP(I).LT.P) DEP(I)=P-(INC-SDEP(I))
156              DEP(I)=INC-SDEP(I-1)-SALV
157              GO TO 200
158          210 DEP(I)=0.
159              GO TO 200
160          250 SDEP(I)=DEP(I)+SDEP(I-1)
161              IF(SDEP(I).LT.P) GO TO 200
162              DEP(I)=P-SDEP(I-1)
163              JI=I+1
164              DO 255 L=JI,N
165          255 DEP(L)=0.
166              GO TO 70
167          200 CONTINUE
168           70 RETURN
169              END

170              SUBROUTINE SLDEP(DEP,INC,SALV,NX,NY)
171              REAL INC,NX,NY
172              DIMENSION DEP(50)
173              IF(NX.GE.NY) GO TO 1564
174              N=NY
175              K=NX
176              GO TO 115
177         1564 N=NX
178              K=NY
179          115 DO 200 I=1,N
180              IF(I.GT.NX) GO TO 210
181              DEP(I)=(INC-SALV)/NX
182              GO TO 200
183          210 DEP(I)=0.0
184          200 CONTINUE
185              RETURN
186              END
```

Reprinted, by permission from G. T. Stevens, Jr., *Economic and Financial Analysis of Capital Investments*, pp. 355-360. Copyright © 1979 by John Wiley and Sons, Inc.

```
187          SUBROUTINE SYDDEP(DEP,INC,SALV,NX,NY)
188          REAL INC,NX,NY
189          DIMENSION DEP(50)
190          IF(NX.GE.NY) GO TO 1562
191          N=NY
192          K=NX
193          GO TO 117
194     1562 N=NX
195          K=NY
196          DO 200 I=1,N
197          IF(I.LE.K) GO TO 220
198          GO TO 210
199      220 DEP(I)=2.*(NY-I+1.)/NY/(NY+1.)*(INC-SALV)
200          GO TO 200
201      210 DEP(I)=0.
202      200 CONTINUE
203          GO TO 230
204      117 DO 201 I=1,N
205          DEP(I)=2.*(NY-I+1.)/NY/(NY+1.)*(INC-SALV)
206      201 CONTINUE
207      230 RETURN
208          END

        $ENTRY
```

INDEX